AF678737

APPLIED BEHAVIOURAL ECONOMICS

VOLUME II

APPLIED BEHAVIOURAL ECONOMICS

VOLUME II

EDITED BY

SHLOMO MAITAL

NEW YORK UNIVERSITY PRESS
Washington Square, New York

First published in the U.S.A. in 1988 by
NEW YORK UNIVERSITY PRESS
Washington Square
New York, NY 10003

© Shlomo Maital, 1988

Library of Congress Cataloging-in-Publication Data

Applied behavioural economics/edited by Shlomo Maital.
p. cm.
Bibliography: v. 1, p.
Includes index.
ISBN 0-8147-5437-6 (set) ISBN 0-8147-5439-2 (v. 1).
ISBN 0-8147-5440-6 (v. 2)
1. Economics—Psychological aspects. I. Maital, Shlomo.
HB74.P8A66 1988
330′.01′9—dc19 88-4971
CIP

Printed in Great Britain

All rights reserved

Part Nine
Entrepreneurship

ECONOMIC PERCEPTION AND JUDGMENT IN SMALL AND MEDIUM SIZE MANUFACTURING ENTERPRISES: FINDINGS AND PRELIMINARY HYPOTHESES FROM IN-DEPTH INTERVIEWS IN ARGENTINA, MEXICO AND THE UNITED STATES.

Hugh H. SCHWARTZ
Senior Economist
Inter-American Development Bank

ABSTRACT

In-depth interviews with decision makers in 113 primarily well regarded small-medium size metalworking enterprises in Argentina, Mexico and the United States suggest that such individuals often perceive market, technological and public policy data in a highly imperfect manner, and thus address themselves to problems which are variants, sometimes remote variants, of those actually confronted. This leads to mistaken judgments, and the use of judgmental heuristics to solve problems further biases results. Additional complications result from the fact that enterprise objectives often vary from task to task. If verified, these findings and preliminary hypotheses would have major implications for the analysis of entrepreneurial behavior.

1. INTRODUCTION

This study, based on in-depth interviews with over a hundred enterprises, provides preliminary verification in the economic sphere of hypotheses developed by cognitive psychologists, and indicates the kind of additional behavioral hypotheses which can be obtained by relatively open-ended questioning and direct observation.

Firms in the United States and in two semi-industrialized economies, Argentina and Mexico, were interviewed in an attempt to gauge whether the perception of data or the nature of the judgments vary in economies which differ in their level of industrial development, degree of government interventionism and cultural and educational background. This paper summarizes the findings on economic perception and judgment. Another paper, under revision, elaborates further and also deals more directly with enterprise motivation. The metal fabricating industries selected for this study were characterized at the time covered, by: 1) a relatively stable technology; 2) economies of scale that were not especially great or were derived principally from length of production run; and 3) relatively little market power, all desirable characteristics for an initial effort of this type.

The term, economic perception, refers to the process by which economic agents confronted with technological, market and public policy data "read" those data, assigning quantitative or qualitative values to them. It is these perceived values which are employed in financial and economic calculations. Most economic literature is presented as if information ordinarily is perceived at its face value.

Economic judgment refers to the process of assessing the probable economic consequences of the perceived technological, market and public policy data. It may involve formal financial or economic analysis, or various short cut cognitive processes, such as judgment heuristics; the latter provide simple means for dealing with complex problems, but yield results which are biased from those derived from Bayesian analysis.

The rationale for focusing on economic perception and judgment derives from their critical role in economic decision making and from the mounting evidence on cognitive limitations. Cognitive limitations cause decision makers to construct simplified models to deal with the world, leading to a kind of bounded rationality. Judgment heuristics are proxies for fuller reasoning processes--"guiding principles for transforming information to solve a problem or form a judgment" (Kahneman et al, [2], 447) "which reduce the complex tasks of assessing probabilities and predicting values" (Kahneman et al, [2], 3). The solutions which heuristics lead to are often in the right direction, but can involve serious error. Some of that error is systematic, though even in those cases, the ability to ascertain error seems to vary.

The selection of enterprises to be interviewed was determined largely by suggestions of trade association officials. The sample is biased towards the financially successful, towards those likely to be survivors. The interviews followed a common guideline, but featured many questions which varied from firm to firm. The two initial visits lasted from one to four hours, and a handful of third visits, from half a day to three days.

2. PRELIMINARY FINDINGS AND HYPOTHESES

2.1 Hypotheses Applying to Both Economic Perception and Judgment

2.1.1 The Principle of the Just Noticeable Difference.

Marginalist reasoning has become almost synonymous with microeconomic analysis, but evidence uncovered on both economic perception and judgment suggest the importance of a somewhat conflicting, Principle of the Just Noticeable Difference. The gist of this proposition is that small differences at the margin often are not well perceived. Ordinarily, changes must be somewhat larger in order for economic decision makers to notice them, or, at any rate, to take effective note of them at the time the changes actually occur. In addition, the perception of these differences seems to vary according to institutional circumstances.

2.1.2. The Inclination to Attribute Representative, Near Mean-Like Properties to Small Samples (The Failure to Recognize that Small Samples Do Not Have the Properties of Large Samples)

Cognitive psychologists Tversky and Kahneman have shown that people have a tendency to view small samples as if they were highly representative of the populations from which they were drawn--not recognizing that the registration of data which are high on some scale tends to be followed by data lower on the scale, and vice versa. This reflects what decision theorists have referred to as the Law of Small Numbers and the failure to expect regression toward mean values (Kahneman et al, [2], Ch 2); such a reaction was found in many small and medium size firms. Some of the examples which seem to support the generalization are drawn from dynamic processes rather than static populations but this need not invalidate the gist of the point if the direction of change is unambiguous. For those cases in which the direction of movement is less obvious, what is observed may not be so much the attribution of mean-like qualities to given data points as the manifestation of a tendency towards anchoring, in which the starting point or "anchor" is then adjusted in a manner not really adequate to take account of the statistical implications of the additional information (Kahneman _et al_, [2], Ch. 1).

The assignation of too high a weight to favorable or strongly unfavorable incentives or occurrences tends to be reversed when the incentives result from domestic policies and are _extraordinarily_ favorable, however; entrepreneurs assume that such incentives will decline sharply in the period ahead. They recognize that unusually large new incentives provoke a political reaction against the changes, bringing about their modification or elimination. (Prevailing economic formulation might attempt to explain this by stating that beyond some point, additions to incentives generate more than proportional additions to risk.)

2.2. Preliminary Findings and Hypotheses Concerning Economic Perception

Indication by psychologists that many factors affect perception led to an attempt to pinpoint the principal categories of data which seem to be perceived differently, as well as some of the factors which appear to help explain those differences.

2.2.1. Categories of Data Which Individual Decision Makers Tend to Perceive Differently

Metalworking Technology and Machine Life Characteristics. An effort was made to assess the degree to which firms were aware of recent changes in metalworking technology; attention was given in particular, to the familiarity of metal stampers and tool and die makers with the then relatively new, wire electrical discharge machining (wire EDM) used for cutting dies. Clear judgments were possible in only 28 enterprise interviews, but these included half of the enterprises with metal stamping facilities. Awareness of metalworking technology seemed only fair to good in U.S. enterprises, somewhat weaker among those from Argentina, and weaker still in the Mexican group. Small enterprises were relatively well represented among those most aware of changes in technology, and also among those least aware, with the larger enterprises primarily in the intermediate group. Firms which exported were more aware of technological change than those than did not, as were firms which had been in existence for less than ten years. The biggest distinction was based on the education and professional experience of the leading decision makers in the firms. The engineering/technician group was almost evenly divided between those in the top or middle category of technology awareness, whereas the business administration/business group was evenly spread out over the three categories. This advantage of the engineering/technical group in perceiving technological data may not come as much of a surprise (note recent comparisons of the role of engineers in management in Japan and the United States, e.g.), but it is not the sort of phenomenon taken into account by standard economic formulations.

Relatively less was being done to eliminate the technology gap in the two Latin American countries than in the United States (even by trade associations). This is contrary to what standard economic analysis might predict, but it follows if one takes account of economic perception; in Argentina and Mexico, perception of metalworking technology was sufficiently poorer than in the United States so that entrepreneurs were unaware that the gap between technological standards and current practice was significantly larger in their countries than in the United States. Even such matters as the expected life characteristics of some key components of equipment were not well recognized by a sizeable minority of the metal-metalworking enterprises in Argentina and Mexico.

<u>The Perception of Factor Costs</u>. A tendency to err in perceiving minimum prices for basic inputs was found, even for inputs representing a substantial proportion of total costs and even when the data on costs were relatively easy and inexpensive to obtain. Poor perception of domestic raw material costs was found in approximately two-thirds of the 26 cases judged to be free of doubt on the point. The tendency of enterprises to overestimate minimum costs was found relatively most often in the United States and least often in Argentina. (The error tended to range between 10 and 15 per cent.) Enterprises that perceived minimum prices worst tended to be unaware of their degree of weakness and were inclined to assume that prices lower than the initial ones quoted to them were likely to reflect quality differences or less satisfactory delivery, which was not necessarily the case. Weakness in being able to determine minimum cost prices for inputs was greatest for small firms, undoubtedly due to less specialized access to information.

The tendency to underestimate the price differential between domestic and imported raw materials and intermediate goods plus applicable duties, also seemed to be fairly widespread, with support for this found in 12 of the 19 enterprise for which the evidence seemed unequivocal. More than half of these were from the United States. This was probably due largely to the recency of experience in finding imported inputs to be competitive with those available domestically.

The prices of equipment, more difficult to ascertain because complex judgments are required, were perceived/judged even less accurately than raw material prices, with errors often more than 20 per cent. These conclusions are based on widespread impressions and on firmer evidence for 23 enterprises. Those from the United States were particularly unacustomed to having to look abroad to find the "best buy," and in making this geographically more limited search, were relatively less likely to become aware of minimum costs; only a minority of Argentine and Mexican firms were comparably in error, probably because they were more accustomed to getting foreign quotes. Again, small firms failed to perceive lowest cost equipment most often.

Implicit costs such as time in designing machinery to be constructed in-house, did not appear to be well perceived, but in few cases was the evidence unequivocal; it is difficult to estimate the implicit cost of an owner's time, for example, if designing is in part a hobby, as was claimed in one case involving particularly successful in-house machinery construction.

<u>Money Illusion</u>. Money illusion was exemplified by the error with which metalworking enterprises perceived interest rates. While an even moderately high rate of inflation not accompanied by corresponding increases in the charges for supplier credits led to delays in payments, there was a general tendency among metalworking enterprises in 1976-77 to overestimate real rates of interest on loans from the banking system. At low and even moderate rates of inflation, real interest rates were often assessed to be closer to high nominal rates than was actually the case, though the misperception/misjudgment tended to subside and eventually disappear as the rate of inflation climbed above 100 per cent and remained at or returned regularly to such levels. In Argentina, where nominal interest rates had long included a substantial subsidy, the new real rate of interest tended to be overestimated when rates were increased sharply in 1976 to reach the zero to slightly positive range in real terms. Of 24 Argentine firms which provided unequivocal responses on this point in September 1976, four months after the long and heavy subsidization of interest rates came to an end, 15 substantially overstated the real rate of interest, and 11 still did so as late as March 1977. A number of these firms declined to take out loans in both periods because of misperceived real interest rates. Small and medium size firms erred much more often than large firms. Twice as large a share of firms led by engineer/technicians badly misperceived/misjudged real rates as those led by the business administration/business group.

<u>The Perception of Indirect Effects</u>. Most indirect consequences of changes in market and public policy variables which affect metalworking enterprises were poorly perceived ex ante by metalworking enterprises and trade associations alike. Perhaps the most notable finding was that the present and prospective competition of metalworking components represented by the increased level of imported final goods (a major concern of metalworking trade associations by 1980-82), was unrecognized or substantially discounted by all 32 U.S. firms interviewed in 1976-77.

2.2.2. Factors that Appear to be Related to the Imperfect Perception of Economic Data

The Professional Background of Those Perceiving the Information. Differences in the professional background and experience of the leading individual (or individuals) in the enterprise seemed to be a factor in the accuracy with which certain information was perceived in small and medium size metalworking enterprises. Nearly twice as many of those with engineering or technical backgrounds seemed well aware of the latest, most appropriate technology as those with a business administration or general business background. On the other hand, the former were almost twice as likely as the latter to overestimate the real rate of interest when long subsidized real rates of interest were made positive--though they did no worse in ascertaining market variables such as the minimum prices of raw materials and equipment.

The Importance of Frequency. Many changes in the value of public policy or market variables are not perceived well (or are perceived only with a considerable lag), unless they are repeated, reflecting, in effect, "learning by repetition." This is brought out in the sections on money illusion, and in the findings on devaluation, investment and depreciation allowances, which are not covered in this paper. Economics employs the concept of lagged adjustments, but does not generally attempt to explain the basic rationale for lags, nor distinguish between the time required to accurately discern the value of a variable and any lapse which follows that determination and truly reflects a lag in the judgment and decision making process.

Institutional Causes of Error in Perception. Perception is better under some circumstances than others. Many errors (or lags) in the perception of data are due to a limited ability to discriminate or to ignorance of some essential information, and particular institutions or conventions can contribute to this. Accounting conventions and their counterparts in tax regulations provide a case in point. Historic cost accounting, often only partially modified even after appreciable rates of inflation, leads to financial and economic illusion, and a tendency to overstate profits. Many metalworking enterprises indicated that they recognized that their net return on equity was not what the figures suggested, but conceded that they did not have a good idea of the true rate, and were, of course, less aware of the real rate of return in other firms in the same industry, not to mention the returns which could be obtained in other fields of activity. This obviously impedes decisions about allocating resources to most profitable uses.

2.3. Findings and Preliminary Hypotheses Concerning Economic Judgment

Interview questions probed to see if support could be found for several concepts--particularly the judgment heuristics, representativeness, anchoring and availability. At the same time, the approach was to listen and observe carefully for indication of other judgment heuristics that might be in use.

2.3.1. Demand and Pricing of Output

Demand. Enterprise perception of demand at prices other than those recently charged, seemed quite limited. Despite this, the metalworking firms tended to rely for their estimates of demand, on orders received and information gathered by their salesman, including short to medium term purchasing plans. For the most part, they did not utilize national forecasts of an aggregate character, they did not make their own independent estimates of demand, and, with the exception of tool and diemakers in the United States, they did not have their trade associations prepare estimates of demand. Of 53 unequivocal responses, 40 were as just outlined, 5 somewhat less extreme, with only 8 firms indicating that they prepared some type of demand analyses or utilized those prepared by a trade association. Large firms were overwhelmingly in the latter group, however. Those with a business administration/business background were as disinclined to prepare estimates of demand or ask their trade associations to do so as those with an engineering/technical background. Perhaps because of their generally poor intelligence of demand, enterprises in all three countries prepared themselves for the long run primarily by paying more attention to general production capability than to individual products, upgrading their equipment and personnel. In the majority of cases this meant increasing the range of production capacity, but in others it led to increases in the enterprise's degree of specialization.

More was not done to improve estimates of demand because of an inadequate recognition of the importance for profitability of having better estimates of demand, and because of doubts about the usefulness of formally estimating demand. For many firms, salesmen's assessments of current and future demand seemed to influence enterprise estimates of demand in a manner analogous to the judgment heuristic, representativeness, with likelihood estimates of demand highly sensitive to, but not completely dominated by the assessments. (The use of the representativeness heuristic refers to the estimation of probability by assessing similarity. Kahneman et al, [2], 207. Like perceptual similarity, representativeness "is easier to assess than to characterize. In both cases, no general definition is available, yet there are many situations where people agree which of two stimuli is more similar to a standard, or which of two events is more representative of a given process." Kahneman et al, [2], 33.)

In some cases, it was not that the enterprises were fully convinced that the demand estimates of salesmen were beyond doubt; they simply concluded that they were the only ones at hand and might even be as reliable as more formal estimates of demand. This seems to be a reflection of the use of an availability heuristic. Availability refers to the tendency to regard certain data or situations as being likely because they have occurred frequently in a recent period, or because they are easy to imagine or there is strong recall of them (as, e.g., a recent disaster).

Output Pricing Decisions. The imperfect perceptions of some input prices, combined with limited recordkeeping in many metalworking firms, lead to variations in the degree to which enterprise estimates of costs reflect opportunity costs. This was a general impression, though unequivocal judgments of this for a large portion of input prices were reflected in only 11 responses. Costing estimates are further thrown off, in most cases, by a failure to recognize that average fixed costs vary according to the number of shifts worked. The unitemized and frequently inaccurate nature of cost estimation, was the focus of a monthly meeting of one of the leading chapters of the American Metal Stamping Association. This is a noteworthy error because most initial price quotations are based on those cost estimates plus some markup. Such markup pricing constitutes a sort of judgment heuristic, the biases of which have been analyzed by economists for decades, but whose supposed approximation to profit maximization at certain levels of output, assumes accurate perception of costs. Variation in the degree to which cost estimates reflect opportunity costs becomes accentuated during periods of increased inflation.

2.3.2. Determination of the Composition of Output

The Choice of Product Mix. The firms interviewed tended to favor those products and processes with characteristics which, experience had convinced them, represented their areas of relative strength, but they did not determine product choice by means of careful calculation, most doubted that their prevailing product mix was the most profitable for their enterprise, and, in general, they halted production only of products with extraordinary records of losses.

Of 48 unequivocal responses, only 9 indicated a conviction that they knew which products were among the most profitable for them at the outset and emphasized those products (six of those in Argentina, where profitability calculations were the most difficult and therefore such affirmations most subject to doubt).

Table 1

The Choice of Product Mix

Total number of enterprises interviewed	113
Unequivocal responses regarding product mix	48
Enterprises which believed that they were able to discern the most profitable products and which concentrated on manufacture of those products	9
Enterprises which endeavored to ascertain the most profitable products (and concentrated on their manufacture) but were uncertain whether they were, in fact, the most profitable	4
Enterprises which endeavored to ascertain the most profitable products in the past but had not made as careful an effort in recent years	4
Enterprises interested in high profitability but for whom risk aversion was a major factor in product selection	4
Enterprises which aimed at the most profitable product mix but doubted that they ever came close to achieving it	14
Enterprises which did not engage in extensive search for the most profitable product mix, doubted that their product mix ever was the most profitable and were not attempting to alter it:	
because of their belief that concentration on operational efficiency was more likely to lead to an approximation to profit maximization	4
because of a conclusion that their prevailing product mix and level of operational efficiency resulted in satisfactory profits	5
Enterprises for which factors other than profitability or risk reduction were major considerations in production selection	4

These findings suggest that the guidelines used in determining product mix reflect a search for high profits in relatively familiar product lines or with relatively familiar production processes. This appears to be conceived as a means of achieving high profits subject to relatively low search costs; the search costs are kept low, first, because there is often a financial constraint, and second, because many metalworking managers believe that the identification of new product alternatives that are unambiguously more profitable is unlikely, even with considerable expense in the search process.

The Make or Buy Decision (Internal vs. External Sourcing). The tendency to Make rather than Buy is undergoing change, especially in industries which have gained in terms of comparative advantage. Nonetheless, metalworking enterprises continue to produce more inputs in their own facilities than profit maximization would call for. In some cases they are unaware of the relative unprofitability of certain components or services; more often, as in the decision to continue with underutilized machine tool facilities, they are. Fifty unequivocal responses on the question of whether there was an inclination to Make rather than Buy without a careful calculation to justify it can be categorized, as follows: generally yes: 16; occasionally: 12: rarely: 22. Argentine firms were overwhelmingly in the first category (9-2-0), and U.S. firms primarily in the last (3-5-21). The inclination towards in-house fabrication may reflect what psychologists call reinforcement behavior. After making a decision, the entrepreneur tends to reflect approvingly upon that decision and sometimes seeks out colleagues who came to the same conclusion. Both actions tend to reinforce his decision and make him more likely to make the same determination in the future, even without examining whether the reasons for doing so (e.g., quality, timeliness of delivery) are as good as before. In some cases he makes the same choice because competitors who had decided to Make rather than Buy previously are doing so again (which may be taken as evidence of the profit-oriented nature of the decision).

2.3.3. Price Increases for Inputs and Entrepreneurial Response

Small metalworking enterprises seemed to base their expectations about inflation primarily on the rate for the period immediately preceding, reflecting use of the anchoring judgment heuristic, but only a few of the cases were entirely clear. Similarly, metalworking enterprises which assigned too low a probability to price increases for the inputs they purchase in situations of low and relatively stable inflation (even discounting the likely effectiveness of announced increases), probably were engaged in a kind of anchoring, in this case, reflecting a lagged realization of the implications of the general price rise, due in part to an incomplete perception of inter-industry linkages. More cases of strong response were found for what might be judged as unusual behavior regarding inventory accumulation in the face of expected increases in raw material prices; even when there was no storage space or financing problem which would have prevented or made uneconomic the purchase of larger inventories, decisions against a large increase were made more often than might be expected, in at least 13 of 32 cases, and this was particularly common if the last experience with inventory speculation had been adverse even though most of the prior experiences had been favorable. This latter group at least appears to reflect a confusion of the <u>disutility</u> of the recent experience with the <u>probability</u> of such an event taking place in the future, a phenomenon dealt with by Ward Edwards and his collaborators. Edwards [6], [7].

2.3.4. Process and Equipment Choices

The decision of a firm to purchase new, used, or used and rebuilt equipment, or to construct its own equipment, is sometimes constrained by lack of financing or by government regulations such as those which have prevented the import of used equipment from time to time. Another influence is the lack of technological expertise of some decision makers. Of 39 enterprises which provided responses enabling a clear judgment, a small but clearly discernible minority (all of them in Argentina or Mexico) purchased new equipment primarily because of the manufacturer's guarantee, rather than attempting to assess used equipment. They purchased from individuals who had a vested interest in the sale rather than enter the used equipment market with a technical expert in their own employ (though some other firms offset their limited technological expertise in this way). This would seem to reflect a very great degree of risk aversion.

2.3.5. Capacity Utilization and Production Efficiency

Efforts to Improve Operational Efficiency. Although most metalworking enterprises are continually engaged in some efforts to increase productivity, such efforts vary greatly and the principal stimulus to increased operational efficiency for 9 of the 20 enterprises for which the evidence permitted unequivocal conclusion, was adversity or anticipated adversity, notably in the form of a lower than expected rate of profits, or the onset of higher costs which led to a concern that an inability to pass those costs on to others might lead to reduced profit levels in the period ahead. This supports the search thesis of Cyert and March [9] even though the opportunities for cost control and productivity improvements may be greatest at the time production is initiated and during periods of strong demand, as several firms maintained.

2.3.5. The Acquisition and Processing of Information

Acquisition of Information. Metalworking firms elected not to receive a considerable amount of information, some of which was very nearly thrust upon them. In part, this was because the cost of analyzing the information was judged to be too great relative to the likely benefits--though the cost considered often was the opportunity cost of a key decision maker, rather than the lowest cost feasible for dealing adequately with the data. A great deal of information which seemed to be relatively easy and inexpensive to analyze and apply, also was not obtained. Responses from many enterprises suggest three general lines of hypotheses.

(1) Small and medium size metalworking firms do not collect considerable information that could be obtained (and analyzed) at low cost because it is their judgment that such data tends to be representative of much data which they are already aware of. This is a risky extension of the representativeness judgment heuristic, in particular, the "law of small numbers." Even in those cases in which such representativeness is valid initially, it is less likely to hold over the course of time since data which have not been seen are likely to contain an increasing proportion of sources which are new and thus less "represented" by the sources previously collected. In addition, some of the tendency not to collect the type of information originally obtained to deal with problems similar to those formerly resolved may reflect reinforcement type reasoning. The latter is likely to be an unsatisfactory approach because of the passage of time and an increasing unfamiliarity with the costs which analysis of the data might entail or the benefits which it might yield; thus there will be a greater tendency than before to make mistaken judgments and collect too little information. The use of one or the other of these two approaches to make judgments is exemplified by the frequent decision not to obtain

information on equipment prices before deciding that an equipment purchase is to be made at a given time (presumably on the assumption that new equipment prices would be of the same order as those quoted previously, allowing for an increase of the same order as the rise in the general price level).

(2) Firms make judgments not to collect some information even if they believe that the benefits of having that information may exceed the costs, in those cases in which their entrepreneurial activities already are absorbing more than some given proportion of their time, particularly if they believe that their competitors are not collecting such information. This may be exemplified in Latin America in the construction of dies, especially those for short to intermediate production life;

(3) The more competitive the market structure, or the more aggressive the efforts are to obtain business, the greater the amount of readily available data relevant for decision making that will be collected, and the larger the number of judgments which will involve careful calculations.

The disinclination to obtain extensive amounts of new data also may be explained by the findings of psychologists that highly redundant or correlated sources of information are preferred to non-redundant ones even if the latter contain more information. One explanation offered for this is that new information has to be integrated with existing structures, and the human information processor is more concerned with coherence than with objective informativeness. Another reason advanced is that decision makers need to feel confidence or validity in their decisions and thus search for information that is likely to increase perceived validity.

Information Processing

The decision of entrepreneurs in small and medium size metalworking to receive less information than is available and can be inexpensively analyzed, also is related to the way in which information is processed, which in 1976-77, was essentially as it had been done two decades before. The computer had not yet made many inroads into the processing of information in metalworking enterprises, even in the United States. In those enterprises in which the computer was employed, such assistance was not used in making key operational decisions. This is easiest to rationalize for firms which specialized in short runs and emergency work, but, overall, it suggests that there was considerable suboptimalization. Even so, these small and medium size metalworking enterprises competed successfully with the metalworking sections of much larger enterprises, some of which had begun to utilize the computer for decision making, including decision making in the metalworking area. The apparent success of the smaller firms may be because much metalworking involved so many possible combinations of different kinds of factors that in many of the subsector's enterprises, an able decision maker still was able to best then limited applications of the computer. Perhaps in the larger firm, control--in the form of the management decision maker--was more distant from the elements actually involved in the decision and this led to added communication costs as well as distortions of some information in the process (see, e.g., Nelson, [10], 46-48). That, combined with the varying character of so many decision situations in discontinuous process industries such as metalworking, raises the cost of obtaining more nearly optimizing decisions that the larger enterprises are in a better position to arrange for, while reducing the degree to which they are, in fact, more optimizing. Beyond that, of course, as international trade flows would soon help to reveal, U.S. metalworking firms, small and large, were no longer employing "best practice" to the degree that had formerly been true.

3. CONCLUSIONS AND IMPLICATIONS

3.1. Conclusions

This study of perception, judgment and motivation in a group of primarily well regarded small and medium size metalworking enterprises has led to a series of findings and preliminary hypotheses. First, entrepreneurial decision makers often fail to perceive market, technological and public policy data as well as is presumed by standard economic formulations, at least initially, and, as a consequence, they frequently address themselves to problems which are sometimes distant variants of the ones they actually confront. This is a phenomenon which has not yet been recognized in the literature of economics. Imperfect data perceptions appear to be key factors explaining mistaken judgments. Second, the determination of judgments involves the use of cognitive mechanisms such as judgmental heuristics--a reasonable first approximation approach, but one which yields results that can differ significantly from the subjective probability calculations of most standard economic analysis. Finally, the larger study suggests that the objectives of decision makers differ from, and are more complicated than those which most economists assume (profit maximization) or those which their principal critics maintain (satisficing, revenue maximization); there appear to be differing objectives for many of the individual aspects of industrial activity. Thus, it may not be possible to refer in a meaningful way to the "objective function" of these small and medium size enterprises, particularly if the composition or relative importance of the various tasks shifts; it would be necessary to make many separate calculations, even at the level of a single enterprise, in order to estimate the consequences of particular incentives or disincentives.

Various of the findings have important implications for the way in which models of economic behavior should be formulated, and for the way in which economic analysis might be used, both in the private and public sectors. Some findings, though better explained by reference to psychological variables not customarily employed by economists, are consistent with standard economic analysis. Others are not consistent, but the adverse implications seem limited. A third category of findings is inconsistent, and of much greater importance.

Findings Largely Consistent with Standard Economic Analysis and Its Projections: the limited recognition of indirect and secondary effects; the relative lack of sensitivity in certain inventory adjustments; the especially high risk aversion of technologically unknowledgeable purchasers of equipment; the preference for internal over external funds if the difference in cost is only moderate; the potential of institutional factors for obstructing calculation; and, the treatment of defective production pieces.

Findings Less Consistent with Standard Economic Analysis, but with Adverse Implications for Economic Analysis and Its Projections which are of a Limited Nature: limited search to determine product mix; use of judgment heuristics instead of economic analysis as the primary measure to estimate demand; unsatisfactory recognition of major implicit costs; lagged recognition of gradual devaluations (unless frequent) and of the indirect implications of devaluations on the demand for an enterprise's output; frequent manufacture of specialized machinery by firms not dedicated to machinery manufacture; and, reticence to reduce prices as much as would be consistent with profit maximization/loss minimization.

Findings Inconsistent with Standard Economic Analysis and Its Projections which are of Major Consequence: the limited perception of the minimum prices of major raw material and machinery inputs; the limited recognition of recent technological advances affecting an industry; serious money illusion in perceiving interest rates; the dependence of good perception of data on frequency of exposure and the nature of professional training and business background; the frequent inability to recognize the importance of sample size; the difficulty of discerning small changes, even in major variables; the disinclination to respond very favorably to exceptionally large incentives; the tendency to resort to internal sourcing even when external sourcing is considerably less expensive; the disinclination to operate second or third shifts; the disinclination to emphasize cost cutting until the onset of serious adversity; the disinclination to acquire some information likely to be justified in cost-benefit terms; the frequent incidence of less than profit maximizing motivations, not only as "revealed" by various of the above, but also in terms of expressed enterprise objectives, and particularly, in terms of the objectives sought in carrying out individual tasks--indeed, the very notion that the behavior of successful enterprises (i.e., survivors) may be determined by considerations other than an overall enterprise objective.

3.2 Implications.

3.2.2. The problems created by the imperfect or lagged perception of technological, market and public policy data are likely to extend far beyond the range considered in the interviews undertaken. Consider three examples. First, some of the distinction between short and long run price elasticity of demand may be attributable to lags in the perception of the altered relative price relationships. Second, difficulties in perceiving data which vary from person to person, suggest that many markets may be quite loose, not relatively tight and impersonal, as economic analysis tends to assume. Third, the findings with respect to perception, judgment and motivation are simply inconsistent with the Rational Expectations line of reasoning.

All this supports giving careful consideration of techniques for improving data perception. It is in the interest of producers, consumers and government alike to become aware of, and take account of the errors or lags with which different categories of data are perceived. If producers have two apparently comparable investment choices, but one is based relatively more on data which the firm has reason to believe it perceives quite poorly, then this should be taken into account in its decision making. If government seeks to influence producers or consumers, and it can be determined that the target group perceives differently, alternative incentives with comparable costs to the community, then that has important implications either for the choice of policies or for the need to improve the perception of those public measures which are favored but tend to be less well perceived.

3.2.3. Problems of economic judgment also may be serious for producers, consumers and government. The possible conflict between presumed overall enterprise objectives and the objectives which hold for individual tasks may extend to large corporations, too, particularly inasmuch as often functionaries with their own notions of "what really is needed" are involved in implementing individual tasks--or insofar as critical data inputs are incorrectly perceived or some economic judgments are made with the aid of judgment heuristics. The problem of taking the correct objectives into account in the analysis may be even more difficult in the case of consumers and government. If the objectives of economic agents differ according to the nature of the tasks, then government policies may have to vary somewhat from those now in effect in order to effectively take advantage of what the targeted economic units actually seek. Government should bear in mind, moreover, that some ways of introducing policies aid, while others inhibit their perception.

3.2.5. Analyses of economic behavior which do not take explicit account of the way in which man actually behaves are often likely to lead to incorrect results. Unless we learn more about the nature of perception, judgment and decision making patterns, we will not come to recognize the size of the gap between prevailing and optimizing behavior in different types of activities; in that case, we will not know in which areas the potentially greatest marginal returns to efforts at improving efficiency lie. More attention to the careful formulation of hypotheses about the behavior of microeconomic units would seem to be required. Moreover, in order to obtain the necessary insights about producer behavior, it would seem essential on many points to go directly to the producers--preferably in their own environment, so as to better ascertain how it is they actually behave, as well as how they say they behave or how they behave in a laboratory setting. The same holds true for understanding consumer behavior and the government sector. Perhaps after that is done it will be possible to develop models of economic behavior which yield reasonable results even after unexpected, exogenous shocks to the system.

ACKNOWLEDGMENTS

The views expressed do not reflect those of the Inter-American Development Bank. I am grateful for observations on earlier drafts to Sixto Aquino, Gerardo Bueno, Richard Day, David Felix, Joseph Hadar, Donald Hester, Robert Kilpatrick, Elio Londero, Raymond Magloire, Richard Nelson, Julio H.G. Olivera, William Peirce, Paul Slovic, Simón Teitel, Francisco Thoumi, and two referees of The Journal of Economic Behavior and Organization. My special debt is to the enterprises visited in 1976 and 1977, and the trade associations which facilitated those visits. Jorge Lucángeli and Roberto Hipp prepared preliminary materials for the project. An early draft of this paper was presented to the IDB/ECLA Seminar on Science and Technology in Buenos Aires in November 1978. A more extended version of this paper will be published in a forthcoming issue of The Journal of Economic Behavior and Organization, under the title "Perception, Judgment and Motivation in Manufacturing Enterprises: Findings and Preliminary Hypotheses from In-Depth Interviews."

NOTES

1 See Slovic, Fischhoff and Lichtenstein [1], Kahneman [2], Slovic and Lichtenstein [3], Slovic [4], Edwards [5], [6], and [7] and Carroll and Payne [8].

2 The findings assume that one person had enterprise responsibility for perceiving the type of information sought and for making judgments, or that the decision maker relied on the initial perceptions and judgments of particular individuals whose biases he had come to recognize, and made his final determination of perceptions and judgments accordingly. In the larger organizations visited, account also should be taken of the problems of intra-firm communication analyzed in the literature on organizations.

3 The situation also may reflect use of the availability heuristic; the subjective probability of an event may be perceived to be greater because the adverse character of the event gives it such a strong place in the individual's memory.

REFERENCES

[1] Slovic, Paul, Baruch Fischhoff and Sarah Lichtenstein, 1977, Behavioral decision theory, Annual Review of Psychology, vol 28, 1-39.

[2] Kahneman, D., P. Slovic and A. Tversky, eds., 1982, Judgement under uncertainty: Heuristics and biases (Cambridge University Press, Cambridge, England).

[3] Slovic, Paul and Sarah Lichetenstein, 1971, Comparison of Bayesian and regression approaches to the study of information processing in judgment, Organization Behavior and Human Performance, vol. 6, 649-744.

[4] Slovic, Paul, 1972, Psychological study of human judgment: implications for investment decision making, The Journal of Finance,

vol XXVII, 4, 779-799.
[5] Edwards, Ward, 1961, Behavioral decision theory, Annual Review of Psychology, vol. 12, 473-498.
[6] Edwards, Ward, 1968, Conservation in human information processing, in B. Kleinmuntz, ed., Formal representation of human judgment (John Wiley, New York).
[7] Edwards, Ward, 1978, Technology for Director Dubious: evaluation and decision in public contexts, in Kenneth R. Hammond, ed., Judgement and decision in public policy formation (Westview Press, Boulder, Col.).
[8] Carroll, John S. and John W. Payne, eds, 1976, Cognition and Social Behavior (John Wiley, New York).
[9] Cyert, Richard M. and James G. March, 1963, A behavioral theory of the firm (Prentice-Hall, Inc., Englewood Cliffs, N.J.).
[10] Nelson, Richard, Issues and suggestions for the study of industrial organization in a regime of rapid technical change, 1972, in Victor R. Fuchs, ed., Policy issues and research opportunities in industrial organizations (National Bureau of Economic Research, New York).
[11] Simon, Herbert, 1957, Models of man (John Willy, New York).
[12] Simon, Herbert, 1963, Economics and psychology, in Sigmund Koch, ed., Psychology. A study of a science, vol. 6 (McGraw Hill, New York), 710-711, reprinted in Simon, H.A., 1982, Models of bounded rationality. Behavioral economics and business organization, vol. 2 (The MIT Press, Cambridge, MA).
[13] Leibenstein, Harvey, 1979, A branch of economics is missing: micro-micro theory, Journal of Economic Literature, vol. xvii, 2, 477-502.

INNOVATION, ENTREPRENEURSHIP, EFFICIENCY AND THE STRATEGY-MANAGER FIT IN IRISH AGRICULTURAL CO-OPERATIVES

ELEANOR R.E. O'HIGGINS

Radio Telefis Eireann, Donnybrook, Dublin 4, Ireland*

I Background to the Research

Introduction

The focus of the reported research was the exploration of possible links between the strategic objectives of an executive's role and the characteristics and business attitudes of that executive. Specifically, should executives pursuing a strategy of growth and innovation be different to those whose strategic objective is to maximise on a steady-state situation? Do certain matches of managers with strategies lead to greater success in terms of innovation and return on investment?

There was an investigation of what has been termed the "readaptive process", i.e. the reconciliation of efficiency and innovation amongst the different business activities in a corporate context. Does the behaviour of the Chief Executive and does the way that different strategic roles in the company portfolio of activities are co-ordinated have any impact on readaptation?

The Irish Economic Context

The necessity for innovation and the shortage of it in Irish industry have often been expounded. The gap in per capita income and living standards between Ireland and other industrialised countries is a large one. In 1983, the Irish per capita GDP was 58 percent of the EEC average, better only than Greece (NESC, 1984).

Wealth creation comes about by increasing the value-added per workhour embodied in the goods and services produced in the country. This can be accomplished by two means - 1. Improving productivity; more outputs from the same inputs, thus achieving greater efficiency than competitors; 2. Shifting resources across industrial activities to those that command a higher international price per unit of input, most likely entailing innovation to command the higher price. Natural resource based industries may obviously have an advantage over those.

* Research carried out at Department of Business Administration, University College Dublin, Belfield, Dublin 4.

which require imported inputs. Ireland's major natural resource is its grassland; this makes agribusiness, especially the dairy and beef sectors, a vital industry in national wealth creation.

(i) The dairy sector

The dairy sector is the most important agricultural sector in Ireland but unfortunately, Ireland has not maximised the potential for value added in dairying. The combination of inefficient farming practices and an inefficient food processing sector that is uncompetitive, competing largely on price with a heavy dependency on commodity type products, creates a vicious cycle whereby the two components - primary production and processing - drag each other down. Full income potential from resource - based agribusiness remains unrealised (NESC, 1984).

Of the milk committed to processing, at present over 80 percent is allocated to the manufacture of bulk commodities, such as butter and skim milk powder; 10 percent is utilised as liquid milk and only 10 percent is converted via secondary processing into other higher value added products. The extreme seasonality of Irish milk production for manufacturing relative to EEC competitors is a major constraint. It means that the Irish dairy industry is effectively excluded from the development of certain high value products that have a short shelf life, for example, certain varieties of soft cheeses for which there is a growing European market (IDA, 1984). Seasonality also leads to poor plant utilisation of processing capacity compared to EEC competitors. Incentive schemes designed to induce milk producers to alter their seasonal pattern have met resistance from producers who are discouraged by the high cost of winter feed and from processors who consider that the premium to be paid for winter milk to make fresh products is unjustified given the margins already available anyway on intervention type commodity products through the EEC (CII, 1985). However, world and EEC conditions are now changing in such a way that the intervention option is becoming less viable. An oversupply of dairy commodities on the world market has engendered intense competition, based mainly on price.

A number of factors put the Irish indigenous dairy processing industry at a disadvantage. In general, the industry is underdeveloped compared to key foreign competitors, especially when it comes to marketing and distribution. The industry is served by a relatively inefficient agricultural sector.

(ii) Agricultural co-operation

An important theme of industrial development and the introduction of innovation is the use of existing larger businesses to spawn new enterprises as they are more likely to have the necessary resources, (Drucker, 1985). In this respect, larger Irish farmers' co-operatives are vital to the development of indigenous innovation in the agricultural sector. Farmers' co-operatives are intrinsically identified with dairying in Ireland. Over 90 percent of milk processed in Ireland is converted by farmer-owned co-operative societies (ICOS, 1984). When it comes to food processing, there are so few significantly large indigenous food processing companies, that it has fallen to the larger co-operatives to provide a native food processing industry. Their foundation, built on the natural resources of the country, reinforces this assessment of their vital importance.

Entrepreneurs and Intrapreneurs

In the literature, a special kind of manager has been accorded a central role in economic development - the entrepreneur. Entrepreneurship may be seen as residing in a synthesis of two opposing schools of thought - one which roots entrepreneurship in the economic opportunities available in the society and the other based on the supply of entrepreneurs. (Murray, 1981).

What are the essential qualities of entrepreneurs and how the entrepreneurial process is experienced by the entrepreneur himself has long been a fascinating topic to psychologists, economists, management experts and novelists. Observations and research have yielded a list of features that are now commonly accepted as characterising entrepreneurs: - high drive and energy level, self-confidence, commitment to long-term goals, using money as a performance measure rather than as an end in itself, persistence in problem-solving, setting challenging but realistic goals, taking moderate risks, the ability to learn from failure and not to be discouraged by it, using criticism constructively, taking the initiative, seeking personal responsibility, competing against self-imposed standards, internal locus of control, tolerance of ambiguity and high achievement motivation. (Timmons, Smollen and Dingee, 1977; Jacobs, 1984).

The study of entrepreneurship has tended to concentrate on founder-owners of small firms. Some authors would make a strong distinction between independent and corporate entrepreneurs. (Collins, Moore & Unwalla, 1975). It is conventional wisdom that there is a natural tension between the organisation and the entrepreneur. The entrepreneur may be stultified by the organisation and the organisation may find the entrepreneur disruptive. In a corporate context, this tension is seen to have potential detrimental effects on innovation. Susbauer (1979) contends that the risk/reward balance is tilted in favour of individual rather than corporate entrepreneurship. The data show that when an independent entrepreneur fails, he is quite likely to begin acquiring resources to start up again. On the other hand, failure by an entrepreneur within a large company may spell disaster for his career. Conversely, the fruits of success are more directly perceived and enjoyed by the independent entrepreneur than by the internal company entrepreneur. Collins, Moore and Unwalla (1964) saw the business executive in an established company as diametrically opposed to the independent entrepreneur in every way. They did not conceive of entrepreneurial activity as an ongoing feature of corporate life; they labelled the corporate executive a "successful hierarch".

Nevertheless, nowadays, the term "intrapreneuring" has become an accepted concept, used to signify entrepreneurial activity inside large companies. Some authors, for example, Pinchot (1985), enthuse about the potential benefits that intrapreneurs can bring to a company, in the way of innovations that enable growth and profitability. Pinchot is willing to embrace the concept of intrapreneuring, because certain myths about personalities and motivation of entrepreneurs have been dispelled; i.e. that entrepreneurs are motivated primarily by the acquisition of wealth, and that there is an irreconcilable opposition between the entrepreneur and the organisation man. Rather, any entrepreneur is motivated primarily to satisfy a personal need for achievement by bringing into existence new products and services that are meaningful to himself and the marketplace. The entrepreneur is committed to the action that makes a reality of his ideas. Such conceptions of the entrepreneur, Pinchot contends, are not inimical to the corporation at all. He describes other aspects of the intrapreneur as: goal oriented and self-motivated, but also responds to corporate rewards and recognition; cynical about the system but optimistic about his ability to outwit it; not afraid of being fired so likes moderate risk; pleases self, customers and sponsors; works out problems within the system or bypasses it without leaving; adept at getting others to agree to private vision; somewhat more patient and willing to compromise than the entrepreneur, but still a "doer". Schrage (1965) had made the point that yesterday's models of leadership frequently do not apply today. Traditionally, the entrepreneur was seen as aggressive, independent, and insensitive to his own and other people's feelings, the type of person who could not fit into a corporation. Now, the increasing need to relate to customers and employees, and to develop interpersonal skills as part of business life is inherent in both corporate and individual entrepreneurship.

Strategic Situations of Growth/Innovation versus Steady-State or Decline.

Let us accept the proposition that entrepreneurial activity is feasible within large companies. The idea that some people are suited to be entrepreneurs and others are not implies that certain types of people are more fit to carry out a strategy that is aimed toward the business implementation of innovation than are others. Other people might be highly suited to manage ongoing businesses, something the entrepreneurial type might mismanage altogether. As a general principle, various business models propose that different strategies require people with different profiles to manage and implement them. All of the models, in some way, discriminate between the management of growth versus steady state or declining situations, of novel-innovative versus ongoing businesses. It has been argued that in a corporation with a portfolio of different business units, managers in charge of new growth oriented business units need to be more entrepreneurial than those in charge of static, mature units (Gupta, 1982; Business Week, 1984). The new business unit, perhaps launched for diversification or growth purposes requires risk-taking and innovating while the mature business unit requires cost-cutting and maximisation of productivity. The idea is for the corporation to employ management teams with varying characteristics, suitable to its different types of business. The contrast between the desirable management characteristics for new versus old businesses is spelt out by Susbauer, (1979). The management type for new businesses is defined by an emphasis on young, ambitious, aggressive, competitive entrepreneurs with strong development and growth potential, and high risk tolerance. The management type for old businesses is defined by an emphasis on seasoned, experienced, "hard nosed" operators with low change tolerance who seek high efficiency and instant results, having an immediate rather than a long-term developmental orientation.

Miles and Snow (1978) have described four company "types". - 1. The Prospector whose objective is to locate and exploit new product/market opportunities and who needs to co-ordinate numerous diverse operations and to maintain technological flexibility; 2. The Defender which protects its market position vis-a-vis products and customers maintaining strict organisation control and the highest level of efficiency; 3. The Analyser tries to combine the achievments of both the Prospector and Defender, locating and exploiting new opportunities while protecting traditional product markets, attaining efficiency in stable portions of the domain and flexibility in changing portions in an organisational structure and process context that accommodates both stable and dynamic areas of operation; 4. The Reactor has no strategy at all, merely reacting to immediate situations without any plan or direction.

In Ireland, a shortage of growth opportunities brought about by economic recession and a high level of foreign competition in most industries mean that companies should best be placed in the analyser mode, i.e. they should be both innovative and efficient to perform well in the long term. Lawrence and Dyer (1983) present an economic/behavioural model for firms wherein the reconciliation of efficiency and innovation is called the readaptive process; this process is a dynamic one, consisting of evolutionary changes brought about through continuous interaction between the organisation and its environment. The authors hypothesise that innovation has an inverted U-curve relation to information complexity (Figure 1a: See next page.)

When information complexity is low, there is little stimulus and variety to provoke innovation. When information complexity is too high, information overload may overwhelm and inhibit innovation.

Efficiency, defined in the traditional economic sense as ratio of inputs to ourputs is seen as having a U-curve relationship with resource scarcity (Figure 1b: See next page.).

When resource scarcity is low and "the living is easy" there is no fncentive to strive for efficiency. At very high resource scarcity levels, the firm cannot afford to invest in measures (such as new technology) that improve efficiency.

Each cell of the matrix in Figure 2 represents an environmental niche that the firm may inhabit. (See Figure 2 ff.)

Location on the matrix will determine the environment faced by the firm and should thereby determine its strategic behaviour. Basically, firms should be striving for maximum readaptation by strategies that will achieve intermediate levels of information complexity and resource scarcity.

Figure 1a **Relationship Between Information Complexity and Effective Innovation**

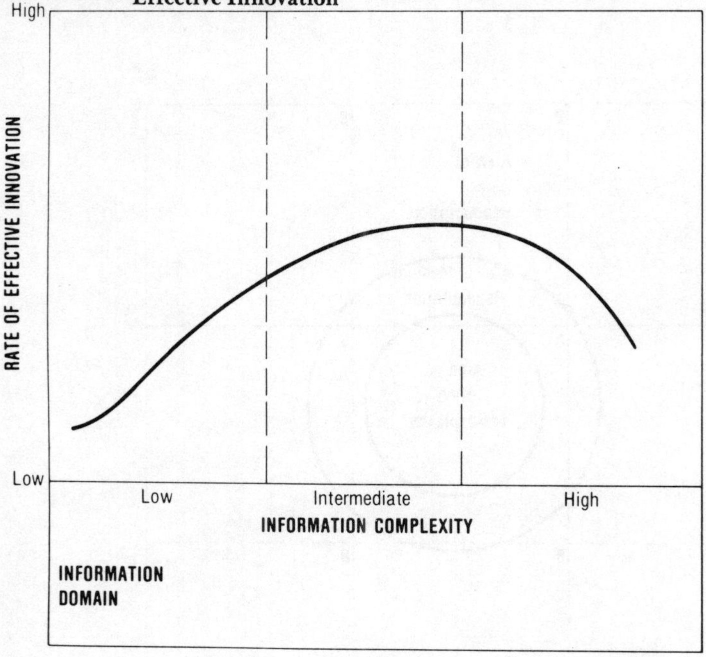

Figure 1b **Relationship Between Resource Scarcity and Efficiency**

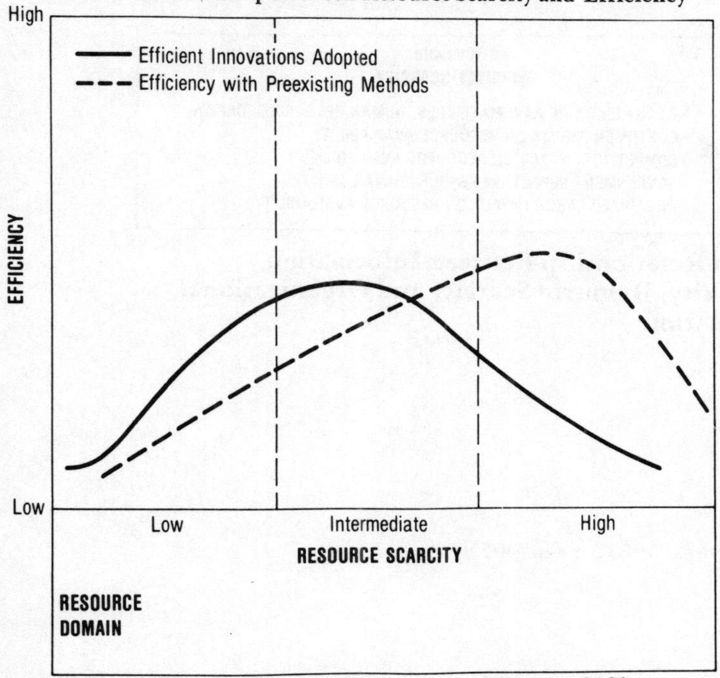

(from Lawrence and Dyer, 1983, pages 302 and 303)

Figure 2

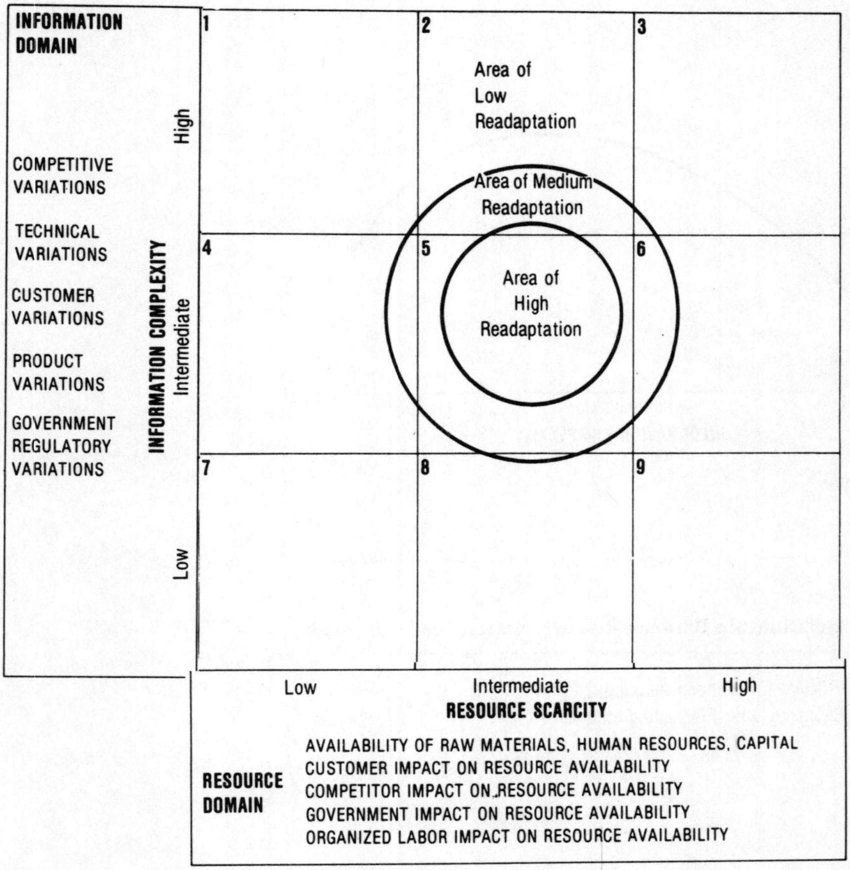

General Relationship Between Information Complexity, Resource Scarcity and Organizational Readaptation

(from Lawrence and Dyer, 1983, page 305)

Figure 3 shows how the Miles and Snow (1978) typology of companies is integrated with the Lawrence and Dyer model of the readaptive process.

<u>Figure 3</u>

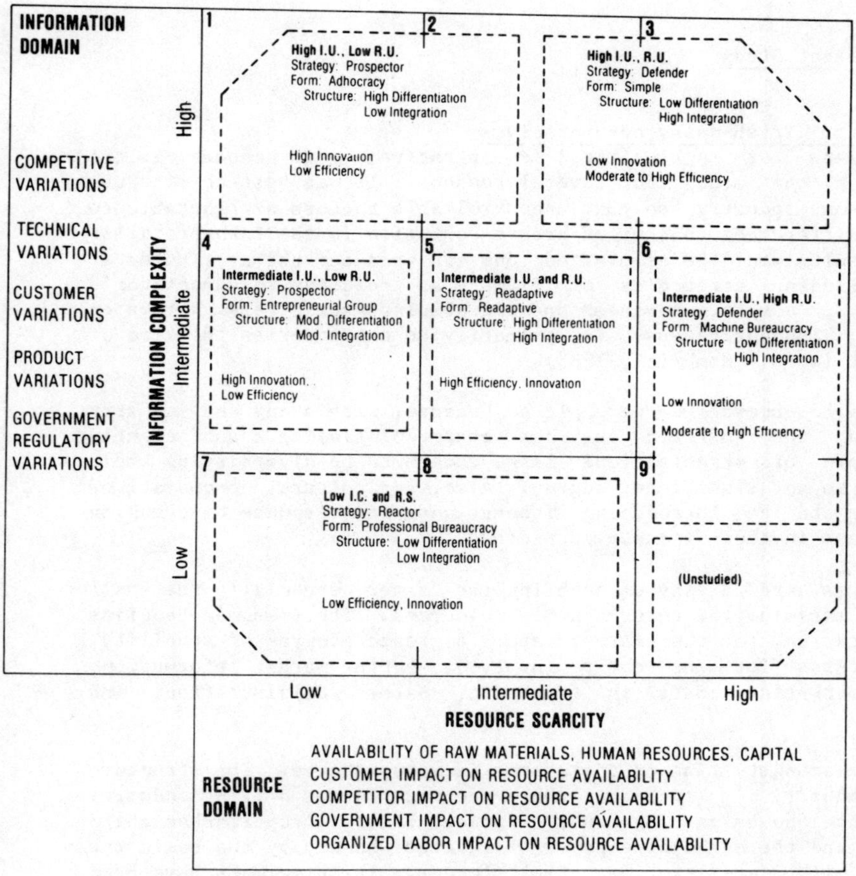

Summary of Findings by Areas

(from Lawrence and Dyer, 1983, page 257)

It is proposed that Prospectors predominate amongst firms moving through the early life cycle stages and pursuing high growth (expressed as movement from Area 4 through Area 1). Analysers move through Area 2 and then Area 5, pursuing a strategy that tries to attain and retain a competitive advantage. Defenders whose strategy is designed to withstand stress move through Area 3 to Area 6. Reactors may be found in the low stress zones where information complexity and resource scarcity do not exist.

II The Present Study

The Subjects: Irish dairy co-operatives

The managers of agricultural co-operatives were chosen as the subjects of the study for several reasons. It was best to site the study in one industry, so that uncontrollable factors attributable to industry differences that might create confusion in the interpretation of the results would be eliminated; one can then see the attributes of firms, including strategies of firms, as relative to competitor's strategies. To rate a business on some absolute scale (e.g. Return on Investment, Innovativeness) is primarily to characterise the kind of industry it is in. (Hambrick, 1983).

Agricultural co-operatives were picked because, within any one industry in Ireland, they offered the best chance of finding a sufficiently large sample of organisations large enough to be diversifying their activities to any significant degree. Also, agricultural co-operatives were known to be introducing innovations in response to changing circumstances in their industry structure.

Co-operatives are a way of enabling the farmer, especially the small farmer to maximise the return on his resources. The presumed benefits of co-operation to the farmer are: a greater degree of stability, better returns for the costs involved, better market information, reduced marketing costs in transport, sales administration, and packaging.

Competition amongst Irish co-operatives is very intense. The structure of the industry is such that there are many forces driving industry competition; the bargaining power of powerful retail supermarket chain customers and the bargaining power of farmers who supply the basic raw material, milk, are two important forces. Irish farmers have been enticed into switching co-operatives for the sake of obtaining higher milk prices. The "one-man, one-vote" form of democracy that exists in co-operatives allows the smallest stakeholder to have as much influence as the largest. The wide distribution of power in the system, with its multiplicity of conflicting interests, makes it difficult to take definitive decisions. There is no incentive for investor-members to invest in their co-operative, since an investor cannot gain control by the size of his shareholding. Unlike private industry, co-operatives do not find any substantial resources to expand by turning to their shareholder/farmers. Co-operative shares are not marketable. They have no scarcity value since there is no legal value to buying or selling them; any co-operative can sell shares to anyone at any time.

Thus, they never trade over their par value. These deterrents to finding equity in the co-operatives is reflected in the capital structures of the largest co-operatives where share capital constitutes only 5 percent of capital employed, and they act as a constraint on investment in innovation (Mohn, Garoyan & Butler, 1984).

Various recommendations to secure the well-being of agricultural co-operatives have been made by people close to the industry. (Russell, 1985; Horan, 1984). The recommendations fall into two groups, one based on improving efficiency, the other on innovation. With respect to efficiency, there must be a reduction in costs, one element being the price paid for milk, the other being labour costs. Rationalisation, the streamlining of operations, the optimum utilisation of processing facilities, more efficient milk assembly, reduction of the summer/winter milk supply ratio and further computerisation are recommended. The innovation-oriented recommendations emphasise the necessity to diversify out of commodity dairy products into higher value-added products either within the dairy industry, or out of the dairy industry into potentially more attractive industries. In any case, most of the measures require a great deal of capital which the co-operatives are finding increasingly difficult to acquire in the face of squeezed profitability and limited equity investment.

It may yet happen that the elusive ideal of achievement of inter-co-operative co-operation will become a reality, out of necessity. The huge resource requirements of innovation and diversification may well lie outside the scope of any single society. Thus, joint ventures between societies, already observed in a few instances may become more numerous. Joint ventures could provide for synergies between co-operatives, and greater efficiency, while resolving some of the futile competition that has been so damaging to the industry.

As for the 10 co-operatives in the study, all of them fall within the top 200 of Ireland's companies based on 1983 turnover and 8 of the 10 are within the top one hundred. Sixty-five percent of milk processed, 64 percent of turnover and 73 percent of assets in the dairy sector are accounted for by the 10 sample co-operatives (ICOS, 1984). It would be fair to surmise that these co-operatives represent the major part of the activities in their sector.

The Chief Executive and 2 senior managers of each of the 10 co-operatives were interviewed. This gave a total of 30 subjects, all male. The 2 senior managers were chosen according to the following requirements: (1) Category A - a manager in charge of an "old" mature business unit, traditional to the co-operative concerned, receiving very little investment and/or being managed frugally to maximise short-term cash flow. The managers picked for this category tended to be in charge of factory processing mainly of commodies, or trading in farm inputs, and had a good deal of contact with farmers. (2) Category B - a manager in charge of a "new" recently introduced product/function, novel to the co-operative concerned, a business receiving a generous level of investment with returns expected in the medum to long-term. The activities under this heading included R&D, new business development/marketing functions and new products/divisions such as cheeses or meats. They were all at the embryonic stage, surrounded by uncertainty but with hope and promise; two of the managers spontaneously used "the jewel in the crown' to describe the role of their enterprise in their co-operatives' portfolios of business units.

Method

The central interview method employed in the study was Repertory Grid, a technique developed by psychologists to attempt to measure how we perceive the world and the interrelationships amongst the various people and objects in our environment (Eden & Jones, 1984). Repertory Grid technique was used in this study to ascertain what hypotheses the subjects apply about managerial characteristics and business success in certain strategic situations, and how they themselves operate on these hypotheses in their own lives. George Kelly (1955) the creator of Repertory Grid, believed that we behave like scientists, deriving hypotheses about the way our social/psychological world works, based on our personal experiences. We construct cognitive maps of the worlds about us, having built up a system of hypotheses and theories. Repertory Grid is a way of drawing the cognitive map of a person or group of people. Repertory Grid resolves the conflict between the tidy structure of questionnaires, which give the respondent little freedom of response, but do enable detailed statistical analysis and alternatively, open-ended interviews which give freedom to the respondent but play havoc with statistical analysis. Repertory Grid, on the one hand elicits data that subjects find personally meaningful. At the same time, the meaningful material produced by the individual is amenable to quantitative analysis and structuring. In the present study, entrepreneurship and management styles in general could be described in terms that the subjects considered personally relevant.

The cognitive maps produced by Repertory Grids have 2 main contents - (i) "elements" are the objects of thought, typically other people in the world around us; (ii) "constructs" are characteristics which we use to describe the elements. Constructs are related to each other in a system whereby elements in the system might be seen as similar or dissimilar to each other. The elements in this study were arrived at thus - Each subject was presented with 12 different strategic situations and asked to think of a manager whom he knew, either personally or by reputation that was a good example of a manager dealing with a strategic situation of that kind. The instructions and strategic situations are given in Figure 4 (See next page).

The actual 12 people chosen as elements to represent each category would have been unique to each individual subject. The focus was on the characteristics that each subject named spontaneously to describe and differentiate between these elements. These characteristics thereby became the constructs of the Grid.

Results

A classification was carried out of the sorts of characteristics that emerged from the subjects during construct elicitation. The maximum frequency possible for any construct was 30, for the 30 subjects involved. It is surmised that the more the number of subjects out of a

Figure 4

You are asked to think of 12 different real-life people who manage or are in charge of a business enterprise. Each person should represent one of the categories listed below because he/she is a good example of that kind of manager:

1. A manager who runs an enterprise in a risky business environment.

2. A manager who runs an enterprise in a relatively safe environment.

3. A manager of a high growth enterprise.

4. A manager of a low growth enterprise.

5. A manager who is introducing changes

6. A manager who is not introducing changes.

7. A manager of a new/recent enterprise.

8. A manager of an old mature enterprise.

9. A manager of an enterprise that is rich in resources.

10. A manager who runs a business in a highly competitive industry.

11. A manager who runs a business in a high growth/dynamic industry.

12. A manager who runs a business in a static or declining industry.

---

group spontaneously deliver a construct the more meaningful that construct can be deemed to be to that group. The list of constructs that emerged and their frequency is given in descending order of frequency:

- Risk taking versus careful, cautious - 30
- Innovative versus conservative, traditional - 29
- Insightful, understands industry, foresees future developments and their strategic implications - 26
- Dynamic, growth-oriented - 26
- Resourceful, enterprising, decisive - 26
- Good judgement, business acumen - 22
- Energetic, committed, hard-working - 21
- Maximises profit, has an eye on the "bottom line" - 17
- Leadership abilities, commands respect from and motivates subordinates - 16
- Planner, sets clear short-term objectives - 16
- Tough, prepared to take unpopular decisions, can be ruthless - 15
- Market, customer-oriented, "the customer is king" - 15
- Methodical versus impulsive - 14

- Strategic planner - set long term plan based on threats, opportunities and own strengths, weaknesses - 13
- Persevering versus gives up easily - 13
- Cost-conscious versus profligate - 13
- Good delegator - delegates well but still maintains effective control - 12
- Competitive, aggressive - 12
- Adaptable, flexible, versus rigid related to tolerance of ambiguity concept - 12
- Implementer, "doer", carries out plans - 10
- Drive, initiative, achievement motivation - 9
- Trustworthy, has integrity, straightforward in business dealngs - 8
- A politician, can size up/deal effectively with power situations - 8
- High profile, charismatic, dynamic, great personal style - 8
- Individualist versus "Corporation Man", has a strong influence on his company rather than being dominated by it - 7
- Full of new ideas, creative thinker - 5
- Self confident - 5
- Intelligent - 4
- Good communicator - 4

It can be seen that characteristics that pertain to entrepreneurship feature very strongly at the top of the list. In particular, we have risk-taking, innovativeness, and growth-orientation. This is remarkable in an economic sector that has not been noted for its entrepreneurial flair in the past, i.e. agribusiness in Ireland, especially in the context of the co-operative structure and financial circumstances. It is of interest that the theme of stress or personal adjustment did not arise as an issue at all.

* * * *

Elements and constructs featuring the self, ideal self and future self were added by the researcher to elements and constructs elicited spontaneously from the subjects themselves, in order to evaluate the subjects' own self-concepts and identification and aspirations. The subjects were expected to rate all the elements with respect to all the constructs on a 5 point scale. The method used for Grid analysis was a Principal Components Analysis Program devised by Slater (1977). Essentially, it factor analyses all the constructs and elements, including the "self-concept" ones so that patterns may be discerned amongst them.

Three group Repertory Grids (called "Consensus Grids") were derived from the 30 Grids completed. One was of the 10 Chief Executives, another of the Group A "old" managers and the third of the Group B "new" managers. The 3 Consensus Grids were analysed in an attempt to discover whether there is any matching of type of manager and type of role he plays in his co-operative. In the Principal Components Analysis, in this study, the first principal component always accounted for, by far, the major part of the variation in all the Grids. Fortunately, constructs denoting self-concept and identification always loaded heavily on the first component so that it may be taken that the other constructs and the elements loading on this component had personal relevance to the subjects. Figures 5a and 5b (on the following 2 pages) show the loadings of all the constructs and elements respectively on the first self-identity component for the 3 Consensus Grids. It is remarkable how closely the lines follow each other. Thus, it is clearly seen how, by-and-large, the same constructs and elements load heavily for all 3 groups. The 3 groups patently share a common system, whereby the composition of their actual and ideal self-concepts in all groups have to do with innovation and growth, exuding an attitude of entrepreneurship. Other constructs important to all the groups were: understanding of the industry, resourcefulness and moderate risk-taking. By-and-large, similarities amongst the 3 groups outweigh any differences. The few differences resided mainly in the fact that managers of "old" activities were most concerned about avoiding failures, managers of "new" activities were more interested in technology, and Chief Executives had the most positive images of themselves. The striking homogeneity amongst the subjects is probably due to strong similarities in their educational and work experience backgrounds in the closely-knit subculture of Irish agribusiness. This homogeneity may itself mitigate against innovation in the industry.

* * * * *

The next question was whether co-operatives that are most readaptive have a different sort of alignment of manager type with strategic role, as compared to co-operatives that are less successful. Readaptation is defined here as the continuous reconciliation of innovation and efficiency. Innovativeness with respect to new products, technology, marketing and general business in each of the co-operatives was measured by means of an Innovativeness Rating Scale filled out by industry experts. Efficiency of each co-operative was measured by the ratio of return on Net Assets averaged over the last 3 years' financial statements. This ratio is a good indicator of how efficiently the assets of a business are being put to use (Figure 6 ff.) Four strategic groups were derived from the 10 co-operatives - 3 co-operatives high in efficiency and innovation, called E+I+, 3 co-operatives low in efficiency and innovation called E-I-, 1 co-operative high in efficiency and low in innovation called E+I-, and 3 co-operatives low in efficiency and high in innovation called E-I+.Three comparisons of consensus Repertory Grids were carried out across the 4 derived groups, one on the Chief Executive, one on the managers of the old activities and one on the managers of the new activities. The comparisons were made in order to ascertain whether different strategic roles were differently played in the various co-operative groupings.

It was found that managers of "old" activities in the high efficiency - high innovation co-operatives were very profit-oriented and identified less with a high growth outlook than their "old" business counterparts in other co-operatives. They were inward looking, primarily motivated toward efficient production. Managers of "new" activities in these E+I+ co-operatives conveyed an impression of innovativeness that is well organised, close to the customer, and profit oriented. It appears that entrepreneurial decisions involving growth, risk, and innovation are made by the Chief Executives in these co-operatives which leaves less room for entrepreneurship at the managerial level, but a high need for competent management. The Chief Executives of these co-operatives are particularly self-confident. While they have a strong internal

Figure 5a

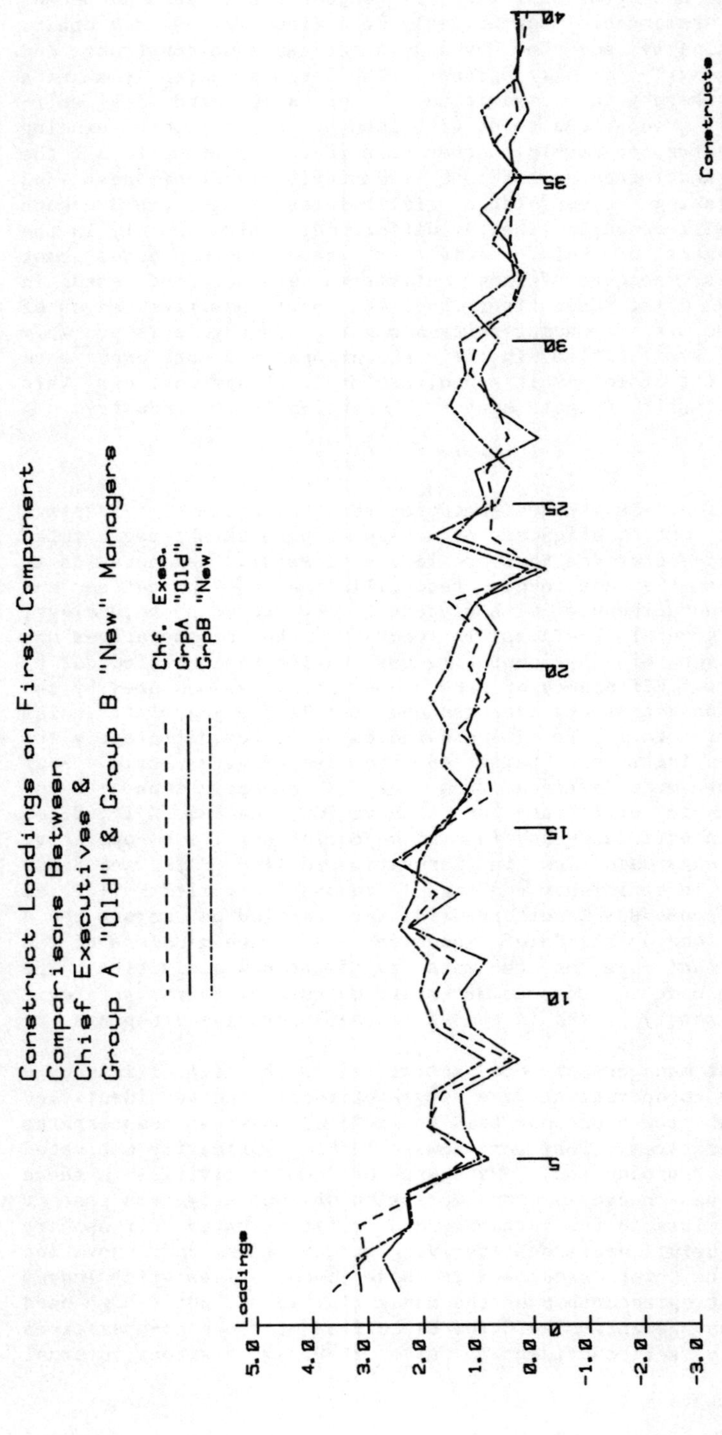
Construct Loadings on First Component
Comparisons Between
Chief Executives &
Group A "Old" & Group B "New" Managers
Chf. Exec.
GrpA "Old"
GrpB "New"
Loadings
Constructs
5.0
4.0
3.0
2.0
1.0
0.0
-1.0
-2.0
-3.0
0
5
10
15
20
25
30
35
40

Figure 5b

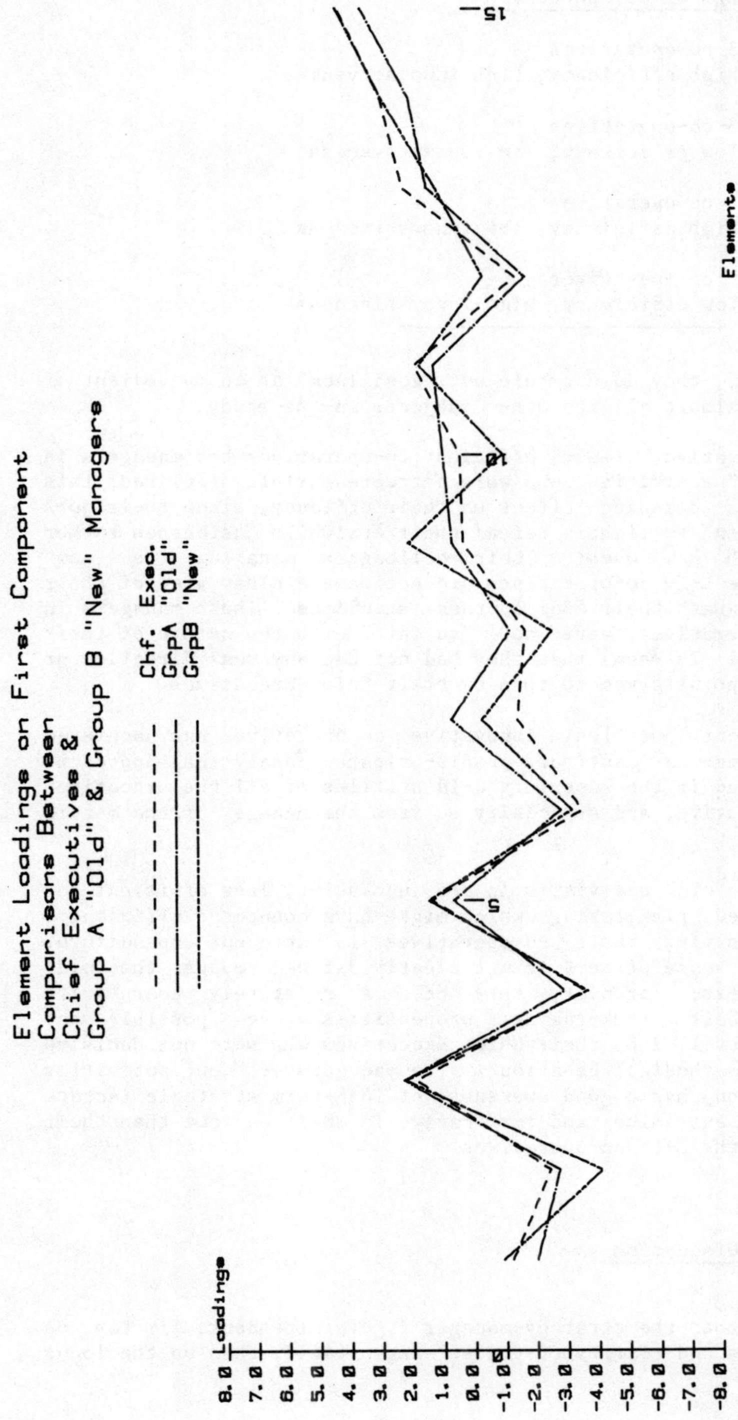
Element Loadings on First Component
Comparisons Between
Chief Executives &
Group A "Old" & Group B "New" Managers
Chf. Exec.
GrpA "Old"
GrpB "New"
Loadings
Elements
8.0
7.0
6.0
5.0
4.0
3.0
2.0
1.0
0.0
-1.0
-2.0
-3.0
-4.0
-5.0
-6.0
-7.0
-8.0
1
5
10
15

Figure 6

Strategic Groupings of Co-operatives

Group E+I+ - 3 co-operatives
- high efficiency, high innovativeness

Group E-I- - 3 co-operatives
- low efficiency, low innovativeness

Group E+I- - 1 co-operative
- high efficiency, low innovativeness

Group E-I+ - 3 co-operatives
- low efficiency, high innovativeness

locus of control, they do not rule out "good luck" as an ingredient of success, unlike almost all the other subjects in the study.

The least innovative, least efficient co-operatives had managers in charge of "old" activities, who were entrepreneurially inclined; this may have had a damaging effect on their effiency, since their jobs should have been to tightly defend their erstwhile businesses rather than to launch new ones. Their colleagues managing the "new" activities in the E-I- co-operatives did not have a clear view of their objectives or what their modi operandi should be. These managers in the E-I- co-operatives were not "au fait" with the nature of their strategic roles. It seems that they had not had any real direction or support on this point given to them by their Chief Executives.

The one efficient but less innovative co-operative has achieved efficiency through a cautious, profit-oriented, analytical approach, which is detected in the Repertory Grid profiles of all the executives in this co-operative, and especially so from the manager of the mature activity.

The managers of "old" activities in the innovative, less efficient co-operatives valued risk-taking which might have countered efficiency, perhaps by involving their co-operatives in imprudent expenditure. Generally, the sense of self is not clearly defined amongst the "old" activity managers; moreover, they hold a relatively poor self-evaluation. Their risk-taking propensities are possibly not sufficiently controlled by their Chief Executives who were not decisive and disdained methodical behaviour. The managers of "new" activities in the E-I+ group had a good awareness of long-term strategic factors and were more expansive and imaginative in their outlook than their counterparts in the E+I+ co-operatives.

Conclusions and Discussion

It is concluded that the strategy-manager fit is dependent, firstly, on the effectiveness and clarity of the strategy itself, then on the locus of entrepreneurial decision-making and on other organisational factors. If a strategy-manager fit is to be pursued, strategic decisions cannot be pushed down; they must be made at corporate level. Only then can the appropriate strategy-manager fit be specified and allocated. There are strong indications that entrepreneurially inclined people should not be in charge of activities that call for cash flow, tight controls, and low growth and/or innovation.

This model of intra-corporate entrepreneurship is different to one proposed by Burgelman (1984) whereby entrepreneurial initiatives are taken at lower levels in the organisation and the role of corporate management is limited to the retroactive rationalisation of those initiatives. Perhaps that was indeed the case in the I-E- co-operatives where the Chief Executive might have left the discretion for innovative activities to the managers of the "new" activities, managers who were themselves not very clear about how entrepreneurship works. On the other hand, the Burgelman model may have actually operated in the E-I+ co-operatives where the Group 3 managers (in charge of new activities) had a strategic entrepreneurial outlook that provided the initiatives for innovation in their co-operatives, initiatives that might have been reinforced at a later stage at corporate level.

It has been suggested that the co-existence of efficiency and innovation cannot be achieved in one fell swoop. It may be more usual to first attain a moderate degree of innovativeness and graft efficiency on to it or to first become highly efficient and then move into innovation. (Murray, 1985). Future scenarios should then see the E-I+ group of co-operatives become more efficient, perhaps as they can get themselves into a position to achieve economies of scale with expanding markets for their new products. By the same token, the E+I- co-operative could begin to explore new territories and become more innovative. The E-I- co-operatives should strike out in one or other direction - efficiency or innovation, depending on the peculiar strengths or weaknesses of each co-operative. Perhaps the very reason for the non-readaptive position of these co-operatives is that they are trying to strike out in too many directions at once and have become immobilised.

(Figure 7: See next page.) If we return to the Lawrence & Dyer model of readaptation, we can speculate that the E+I+ co-operatives fell into Area 5, like Analysers; the E-I- co-operatives fell into Areas 7 and 8, like Reactors; the E-I+ co-operatives fell into Areas 1 and 4, like Prospectors; the E+I- co-operative fell into Area 3 or 6, like Defenders. The E+I+ group possibly reduced information complexity by simplifying objectives from the top, so that managers do not need to deal with information that is not immediately relevant to them. Efficiency diminished resource scarcity in these co-operatives. Basically, the achievement of Area 5 calls for high differentiation and high integration to attain efficiency and innovation. The way to implement this is to differentiate the management and organisation of business subunits according to their strategic aims of efficiency or innovation, and then to co-ordinate/integrate the running of these subunits so that they complement each other. The E+I+ co-operatives seemed to come closest to this ideal.

Figure 7

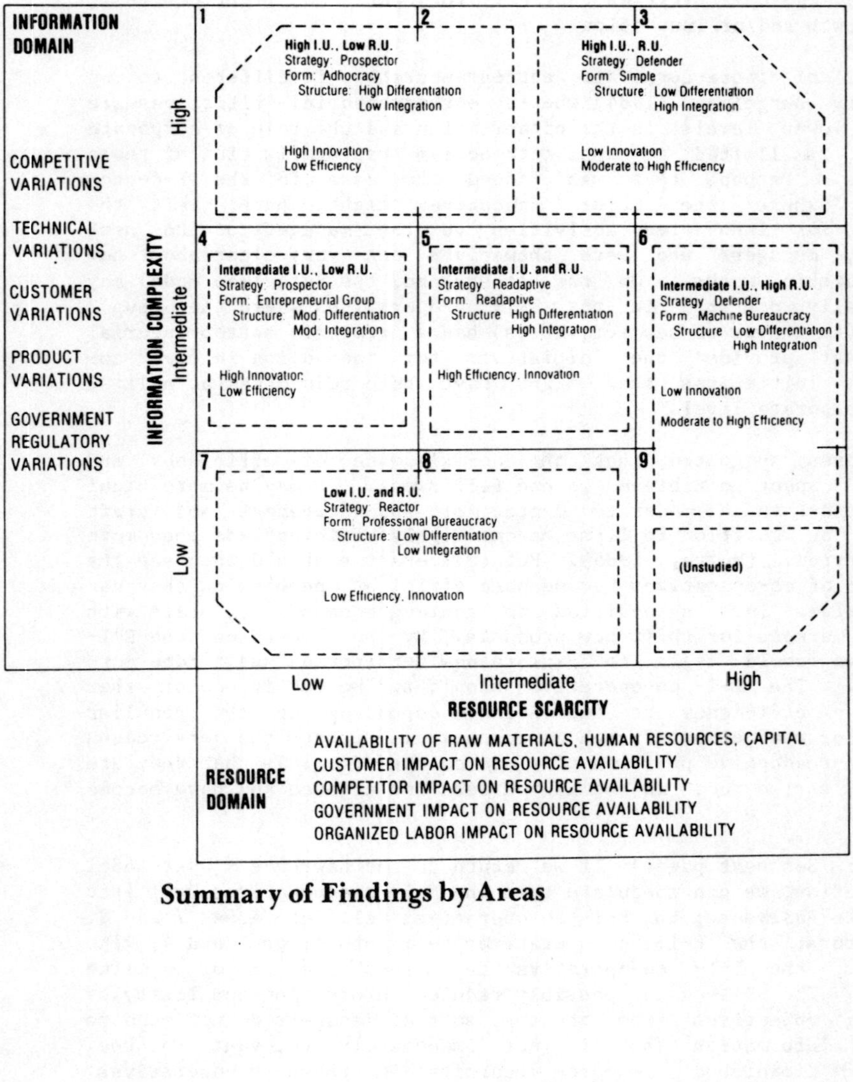

Summary of Findings by Areas

(from Lawrence and Dyer, 1983, page 257)

The study divided into sub-groups, a number of firms in a basically homogeneous industry on the innovativeness and efficiency dimensions. The Lawrence & Dyer model really conceives of a whole industry being allocated to a particular space on the 9 area grid. It is conceivable that all 10 co-operatives would fall into one small space if they were examined in relation to co-operatives in the dairy sector abroad or to other industries, domestic or foreign. A repeat of this study, involving agricultural co-operatives from different countries, or companies in other industries would shed further light on the issues examined.

The concept of innovation is itself multidimensional, involving not only the content and magnitude of the innovation, but also timing,risk and possible contributions to efficiency. The concept of efficiency is also multidimensional, again involving dimensions of content, magnitude and timing and elements of innovation that improve efficiency. The interactions of the various dimensions of innovation and efficiency would surely affect the readaptive process. More knowledge about such interactions might promote the reconciliation of innovation and efficiency.

Perhaps the essence of the philosophy behind this paper is summed up by a quotation from Drucker (1980, P. 41) "The fundamentals pertain to today's enterprise. But all institutions live and perform in two time periods, that of today and that of tomorrow. Tomorrow is being made today, irrevocably in most cases. Managers therefore always have to manage both today - the fundamentals - and tomorrow. In turbulent times, managers cannot assume that tomorrow will be an extension of today. On the contrary, they must manage for change; change alike as an opportunity and a threat".

* * * * *

ACKNOWLEDGEMENT

The author wishes to thank Dr. John A. Murray, University College Dublin for his supervision of the research and his constructive comments on the manuscript.

REFERENCES

Burgelman, RA: Managing the internal corporate venturing process. Sloan Management Review, 1984, 25, 33 - 48.

Business Week: Wanted: a manager to fit each strategy. In BA Weitz and R Wensley (Eds). Strategic Marketing: Planning, Implementation, and Control. Boston: Kent Publishing Company, 1984.

CII (Confederation of Irish Industry, Food Drink and Tobacco Federation): Whether the Food Industry? Response to Government. 1985.

Collins OF, Moore DG, and Unwalla DB: The enterprising man and the business executive. In CM Baumback and JR Mancuso (Eds): Entrepreneurship and Venture Management. Englewood Cliffs, N.J.: Prentice-Hall, Inc, 1975.

Collins OF, Moore DG, and Unwalla DB; The Enterprising Man. East Lansing: MSU Business Studies, 1964.

Drucker PF: Innovation and Entrepreneurship: Practices and Principles. London: Heinemann, 1985.

Drucker PF: Managing in Turbulent Times. London: Heinemann, 1980.

Eden C and Jones S: Using repertory grids for problem construction. Journal of the Operational Research Society, 1984, 35(9), 779 - 790.

Gupta AK and Govindarajan V: An empirical examination of linkages between strategy, managerial characteristics and performance. Proceedings of the National Meeting of the Academy of Management, 1982, New York, 31 - 35.

Hambrick DC: Some tests of the effectiveness and functional attributes of Miles and Snow's strategic types. Academy of Management Journal, 1983, 26, 5 - 26.

Horan M: The Financing of Irish Dairy Co-operatives - Trends and Prospects. University College Dublin: Unpublished M.B.A. dissertation, 1984.

IDA (Industrial Development Authority): A Strategy for the Development of the Agricultural Processing Industry in Ireland. June, 1984.

ICOS (Irish Co-operative Organisation Society): Annual Report, 1984.

Jacobs R: Entrepreneurs as managers. Management Forum, 1984, 10(3) 115 - 112.

Kelly GA: The Psychology of Personal Constructs. New York: Norton, 1955

Lawrence P and Dyer D: Renewing American Industry. New York: Free Press, 1983.

Miles RE and Snow CC: Organisational Strategy, Structure, and Process. New York: McGraw-Hill, 1978.

Mohn PO, Garoyan L and Butler J: Capital Structures of Co-operatives. University College Cork, Bank of Ireland Centre for Co-operative Studies: Working Paper No. 2, May 1984.

Murray JA: Enterprise development and innovation. Irish Business and Administrative Research, 1985, 7(i), 1 - 9

Murray JA: In search of entrepreneurship, Irish Business and Administrative Research, 1981, 3(2), 41-55.

NESC (National Economic and Social Council): A Review of Industrial Policy. Dublin: National Economic and Social Council, 1984.

Pinchot III, G: Intrapreneuring. New York: Harper & Row, 1985.

Russell J: A decade of change for Irish Co-ops. Irish Farmers Monthly, June 1985.

Schrage H: The R&D entrepreneur: Profile of success: Harvard Business Review, Nov-Dec 1965, 43, 56-69.

Slater P: The Measurement of Intrapersonal Space by Grid Technique, Vol. 2: Dimensions of Intrapersonal Space. London: Wiley, 1977.

Susbauer JC: Commentary in DE Schendel and CW Hoger (Eds). Strategic Management - A New View of Business Policy and Planning. Boston: Little Brown & Co, 1979.

Timmons JA, Smollen LE and Dingee ALM: New Venture Creation. Homewood, Ill: Irwin, 1977.

The Entrepreneurial Way With Information

B. Gilad Rutgers
S. Kaish Rutgers
J. Ronen NYU

This is a report on the first phase of a research project funded by The New York University Entrepreneurial Research Center.

Research on entrepreneurship has proliferated in recent years. After a long period of neglect the central importance of entrepreneurship to economic prosperity has become recognized again. It is unfortunate for economic science that little new in the way of useful theory has been developed since Schumpeter's Theory of Economic Development (1934). Perhaps this was due to a general shift in political philosophy away from free markets and toward state interventionism. Perhaps it was due to a focus on big business as the major actor in the economy and a resulting focus on concentration ratios and antitrust. Perhaps it resulted from the methodological choices made by the profession to adapt the physical sciences as the ideal model for scientific investigation, thereby downplaying the volitional considerations of the economic actors in favor of the more easily understood reaction to forces. Whatever the cause, mainstream economics finds itself in the position of not only having no theory of entrepreneurship but worse, having no role for entrepreneurship itself.

Mainstream economics focuses on equilibrium states growing out of market forces among competing entities. Despite disclaimers in the footnotes, the assumption underlying the

---

The first two authors are associated with the Dept. of Business, Rutgers University, Newark. Prof. Ronen is with the Graduate School of Business at New York University. The authors gratefully acknowledge a grant from the Center for Entrepreneurial Studies, New York University, and the invaluable research help of Cynthia Wilcox and Cynthia Homiek.

models is that information is fully and rationally considered, and any information not taken into account is either unavailable or available at such cost as to be impractical to process. As a result, every opportunity for cost reduction, profit enhancement or product development has been exploited. There is no room for entrepreneurship in neoclassical economics because there is no room for information that has not already been acted upon. And yet, of course, there is entrepreneurship. New products, new processes, new firms add daily to the swirl of economic activity in capitalistic economies. To the extent that they succeed and earn more than a normal profit--and they do-- we are left with the syllogism that says neoclassical economics is the science of competitive capitalist economics. Entrepreneurial effort is at the soul of neoclassical, competitive economics. Yet neoclassical economics cannot account for entrepreneurship. What can?

Before attempting to deal with this serious methodological question it seems prudent to sort out two terms: enterprise and entrepreneurship. There is a tendency, particularly among schools of business, to use the word "entrepreneur" when they really are referring to enterprisers, ie. people who undertake to open and manage new businesses. In this usage, there is a failure to distinguish imitative from innovative businesses. Schumpeter was very clear on the distinction, pointing out that imitative businesses clustered around innovations, creating, in fact, the underlying climate for business expansion and contraction. The innovator is the hero of the capitalistic process. The imitator, often realizing more in gain due to sounder managerial practices develops the industry, and plays a major social role. But it is the vision of the entrepreneurial innovator that captures the imagination and about whom we wish to talk today.

Leibenstein (1976) has suggested entrepreneurial opportunity and equilibrium economics may be compatible if we hypothesize the presence of inert areas, i.e. areas of opportunity that emerge and which are not closed out quickly because the search effort involves costs that are greater than the benefit derived. We believe that these inert areas are more appropriate to discussions of opportunities for imitative enterprise than for innovative entrepreneurship. Premised as they are on cost benefit analysis, they only allow modest gaps to form before awareness closes them out. Innovative entrepreneurship as represented by a MacDonalds, an Apple Computer, a David's Cookies involves opportunity for major profit. There must be a reason other than inertia that allows this opportunity to exist unexploited in a competitive economy.

Kirzner (1979) comes a little closer to recognizing the qualities of the innovating entrepreneur when he suggests that they have the ability to observe things that are invisible to the rest of us. They have an alertness, an antennae that permits recognition or gaps in the market that give little outward sign. It is not that the rest of us are inadequate. It is simply that the innovating entrepreneur has somehow acquired a superior perception of economic opportunity. The gap in the offering of economic goods and services needn't be so small that no one takes the trouble to find out about it. It can be an opportunity that has grown substantial because no one has brought sufficient perceptive power to the situation to become aware of it.

This paper is an attempt to gain insight into the question of what makes a successful entrepreneur. It is a preliminary report based on dozens of hours of in-depth interviews with 21 founders of rapidly growing, innovative corporations. The interviews focused on one particular area: the way entrepreneurs handle information.

The narrowing of our focus to information processing is the result of several considerations. The first is the realization following Kirzner that information processing is at the heart of the role of entrepreneurial activity in economic theory. Complementary to the Kirznerian observation is the belief expressed by Etzioni (1986) that rational decision making is the exception rather than the rule. Etzioni feels that rational behavior is only attained at considerable cost in the form of search and mental effort and in the absence of such effort decisions come to be based on habit, impulse or heuristic. A good deal of work in the laboratory by Tversky, Kahneman, Slovic, Fischoff, Lichtenstein, etc. (see eg. Kahneman, Slovic and Tversky, 1982) lends support to the idea that decision making in the population at large is not done in a manner that is consistent with the economists' assumptions of rational processing of complete information.

Research aimed at finding the traits of entrepreneurs is by no means novel. Several studies have attempted to isolate a fundamental personality characteristic common to all successful entrepreneurs.[1] Studies on the entrepreneurial personality typically use standard psychological evaluations ranging from projective instruments (Thematic Apperception Test, Rorschach, etc.) to clinical judgements (as in 150 interviews conducted by Collins, More and Unwalla (1964)[2]. Results have shown the importance of certain personality traits such as high need for achievement and high locus of control. However, the search for a unique entrepreneurial trait that identifies entrepreneurs and differentiates them from successful managers is still elusive. Mintzberg observed in his seminal work on management behavior (1973) that "trait is an intangible concept, difficult to operationalize and to link to... behavior" (p 194). Mintzberg proposes instead research on skill --a "specific behavior that results in effective performance" (ibid). A skill is easier to identify because it is directly related to behavior. It is also easier to develop and influence than a personality trait. We treat information processing as a skill in the Mintzberg sense of the word.

Among the few attempts already conducted to identify informational skill in successful entrepreneurship is Schrage'

---

[1] The problem of research concentrating on successful entrepreneurs is all too familiar to researchers in the field. The main obstacle to more generalized studies is lack of access to appropriate subjects. One possible defense is to lump failing entrepreneurs with non-entrepreneurs and to attribute a systematic difference to successful entrepreneurs alone.

[2] For a recent survey of findings see Robert H. Brockhaus: "The Psychology of the entrepreneur" in Kent et al., 1982 as well as George T. Solomon: "Characteristic of Entrepreneurs" in Keys to the Future of American Business, 1985

(1965) research on R&D entrepreneurs. In his research Schrage found a characteristic of "veridical perception" to be useful in differentiating between successful and unsuccessful entrepreneurs. Schrage defines "veridical" as the act of "recognizing people, things or situations as they truthfully are, rather than attributing to them qualities which are products of one's emotions and imagination" (p. 12) According to Schrage, the lack of veridial perception led to the development of wrong future scenarios and policies based on distorted data.

There is a sense of a tautological argument in these findings. By necessity, a successful entrepreneur has identified reality as is rather than relied on false data. Schrage's findings will be perhaps less trivial if one recognizes that the common mode of information processing (including choices made) by people is one of distortion and biases and not accurate perception/ judgement. (see Tversky, Kahneman and Slovic (1982) and Ungson and Braunstein (1982). The question is then: How do successful entrepreneurs differ from us, the mortals, when it comes to biases, heuristics and distortion of the facts? Do they fail, like us in some respects but succeed in others? What is their way of looking at the world? If we find that entrepreneurs are cognitively different, are immune to the biases that affect most of our information processing abilities and appear to think rationally we would have some empirical justification of Kirzner's position.

THE RESEARCH AGENDA

When we set to interview our entrepreneurs, the interview was deliberately left as little structured as possible. The disadvantages of using an in-depth interview dealing with intro- and retrospective answers are numerous, from lack control to suspected memory/social desirability problems. It is only reasonable, therefore, to use the greatest virtue of such an interview - the wealth of data it may reveal, deliberately and serendipitously - to the fullest extent.

The interview addressed three areas of interest:

1) The discovery of opportunities (informational aspects of ("alertness")

2) The biases in information processing for decision making

3) Information-processing mechanisms in instances of failure.

The first category relates to the Kirznerian concept of alertness to opportunities.[3] Our questions directed the entrepreneur to reminisce about the first days of the venture(s), the ways in which the ideas developed, and ways information was sought regarding opportunities.

The second category dealt with the judgmental process in making decisions. Through a series of questions regarding current projects, the research attempted to identify the existence (or nonexistence) of common biases in making decisions. (The main source for "popular" biases was Kahneman et al., 1982).

----

[3]Some of our findings in this category obtained from the new sample are similar to those reported in Ronen (1983, pp. 143-148). Others are new insights derived from the different emphasis of the current research.

While it is true that "veridical perception" is necessary for successful entrepreneurship, it was hypothesized that some heuristics may be more damaging to entrepreneurial behavior than others. Also, if luck plays a major role in success, entrepreneurs may still survive and prosper despite the existence of "normal" biases in their cognitive processing.

The third category dealt with reaction to failure. Following Gilad and Kaish (1986) we were interested in cognitive mechanisms of dealing with wrong decisions. Specifically, was negative information distorted and/or blocked (a possible reaction due to what psychologists call "cognitive dissonance")? Was it easier for entrepreneurs to admit/recognize failure than for managers, and if so, why?

Lastly, a note regarding the choice of the subjects. Following the distinction between entrepreneurs and enterprisers (the former being innovators, the latter self-employed) we concentrated on successful entrepreneurs, chosen from Venture`s and Inc's listings of the fastest growing new companies. Our entrepreneurs ranged from owners of high-tech companies to fashion-design and publishing companies.

PRELIMINARY RESULTS: ARE THEY LIKE US?

a) The process behind alertness: A few observations.

Alertness is the ability to spot opportunities before others do so. By definition, entrepreneurs possess this skill. How do they discover opportunities? The process is far from clear, and each case is different, to a degree. "Being at the right place, at the right time" is surely an important element. Thus, the majority of our entrepreneurs started their business in areas that were easily accessible to them, either through education, previous jobs, family involvement in the field, or some prior knowledge of the particular business' environment. Thus, a very innovative publishing entrepreneur has first worked as a media representative. A fashion-designer has first opened a clothing store (in itself, an enterprising act but not as innovative as her later fashion venture). A genetic engineering entrepreneur happened to have two biochemists as brothers-in-law, etc. Thus, entrepreneurial acts occurred in areas to which these individuals were alerted. This, however, does not detract from the fact that realizing "this is the right time and place" is a skill possessed by these people and not others in the same circumstances.

The most immediate, and striking, demonstration of the formal label "alertness" in our sample, was the quality of "being on the lookout." The first thing which becomes apparent is the obsession of these entrepreneurs with collecting information. One entrepreneur labeled it "walking and talking". Every one of our entrepreneurs described him/herself as constantly seeking new ideas. The process by which this is done is an incessant search, unsystematic, many times without any clear objective.

The process can easily take an obsessive dimension. One entrepreneur told us that he has not spent more than 7 consecutive days in the same city in the last two years. Traveling, in general, seems to be a very important information-gathering tool, whether this is its main or ancilliary purpose.

The constant search requires a high level of energy. The lay impression of many entrepreneurs as hyperactive, workaholics, etc., can in part be related to their 24 hours-a-day preoccupation with the business, and information which may prove useful to their business. In this search, the entrepreneurs make use of a network of people, from friends to business acquaintences to strangers on the plane. Their reading habits resemble a machine more than a person: They read a very high volume of trade literature, and also books, newspapers, magazines, as long as they believe it may generate ideas for thier business.

This obsession with information-assimilation is not restricted to working hours. They all "take their work home" in the sense of looking for new opportunities in their immediate environment. One entrepreneur uses the consumption habits of his children to identify possible trends. Another used his vacation to close a deal. Yet another, looks for opportunities while shopping for her own clothes, or taking a stroll in and around the city. This is definitely a high-powered search which is not the ordinary search conducted by all of us from time-to-time. The "weakness" of <u>unsystematic</u> search is compensated by the <u>volume</u> of search - the number of hours devoted to it, the number of sources used, etc. Sometime, the lack of clear objective is an advantage - it allows for more flexibility.

It shouldn't be inferred, though, that the search is completely flexible. The areas searched are always those that spark the entrepreneurs' attention by appealing to his/her personal preferences. Several entrepreneurs commented that some excellent opportunities were passed over by them several times, and picked up only after "knocking" on several occasions. Thus one entrepreneur who later became famous for a particular cosmetic product he introduced to the U.S. was asked to take on the product several times by his friend who was selling it in Europe, with little success. The entrepreneur kept turning down the offer until an instance when a question he asked established that the friend was an expert on the product from previous employment. Once the creditibility of the opportunity was recognized, he took on the product and thus made his fame. It is still useful to remember, that despite the "slowness" of identifying opportunities, these entrepreneurs were the fastest and the first to notice them.

The unsystematic search is replaced by a systemaic one once an opportunity is discovered. At this stage the entrepreneur becomes more of an economic man than at any other time. Though the majority of our entrepreneurs took pride in ignoring formal market research, they did claim to acquire quite an expertise by the time they make their move, or as one subject put it: "we research (the deal) to death informally, we do no formal research almost". Yet, it is the intensity of the unsystematic, diffused, perhaps subconscious, continuous search that we believe separates them from the rest of humanity.

The energy required for such a constant mental effort seems to be provided by the fact that for the entrepreneurs, as opposed to nonentrepreneurs or even enterprisers, their business is their <u>passion</u>. This word was used often by all of our interviewers to describe their motivation-level. Passion is more often than not associated with vision and indeed the majority of our sample regarded themselves as having a social vision, as being a trend setter (or spotter) who contributes to society's welfare. The philosophy of "if its good for society, if it serves a real need, it will succeed" seems to be prevalent. The desire to fulfill a vision, to see it becomes true, supersedes the desire to make a profit. As Ronen (1983) observed, money is seen as a reward for excellence, for "veridical perception". To judge by the answers, money is much more important at the early days of the entrepreneurial career, and as success builds up, the entrepreneur seems to develop the vision as a primary driving force, in a kind of Maslow-hierarchial process.

The pursuit of vision rather than money does not mean that the economist's conception of the firm's profit seeking behavior is incorrect. Rather, it may suggest a preference toward long term profit strategy over short term maximization. As long as a vision is the prime objective, the strategy is to tolerate lower than maximum profit, and present sacrifices of profit are judged against a progress toward the future vision. Thus an entrepreneur whose company was losing money for several years was more interested and proud in the growth of the company and the spread of his idea on a national level. The predominance of the vision does not mean, however, that tactical errors are tolerated. (See Section C).

Another implication is that one can expect larger proportions of new ideas from smaller firms than big corporations, based on search time alone. Thus a typical CEO of a big corporation will spend more time solving internal problems and less searching for new opportuniteis (see Mintzberg, 1973, Ch.3) than the entrepreneur. The latter tend to delegate "managerial" jobs to subordinates mostly because of personal dislike of bureaucratic/administrative work. With passion somewhat less typical of an "organization man", search time is much longer with entrepreneurs.

b) Biases and Heuristics in Decision Making.

In their research, Tversky, Kahneman and others have pointed to several anomalies in people's cognitive processes. They have clustered these under three conceptual umbrellas referred to as "representativeness", "availability" and "anchoring". While we cannot do justice to the richness of their work here we can briefly summarize these as follows: Representativeness means that people's judgement in classifying a situation is based on a stereotyped impression of what the class is like, ignoring prior probability, sample size effect, population incidence of categories, etc. By generalization, employing representativeness may impair the ability to discriminate opportunity from background noise. Thus an instance which carries a unique characteristic may be judged and classified by its stereotyped qualities.

Availability is the tendency to see things in the manner most easily recalled or brought to mind. Here people take cues from the environment immediately available and tend to create scenarios of outcomes in ways that mirror these cues. Here a bandwagon effect will be seen. If we are trying to decide on a way to accomplish a task we will think first of those ways that we have read of most recently and/ or frequently.

Anchoring refers to the tendency of people to remain close to the starting point, the initial judgement. This heuristic biases perception of variabiity and causes people to underestimate spread. Also anchoring may inhibit innovation if used to anchor perception in what is, rather than the full range of possibilities. People avoid making radical deviations from their initial judgements and perceptions.

We should note that all three mechanism inhibit departure from the status quo. Availability produces scenarios that are common to those already in the environment. Representativeness assures that stereotyped thinking prevails. Anchoring further inhibits the chance for additional information to produce change from the decisions thereby made. Clearly all three are antithetical to innovation and creative thinking and hence, entrepreneurship.

Our subjects seem largely to avoid stereotyped judgements. An entrepreneur who introduced expensive watches to America at the time when watches were considered "disposable", cheap and functional only, had to judge a watch by its less representative characteristic. To his aid came the fact that in the country where he came from watches served as jewels as well. Yet people around him suggested to him that in the U. S. A. a watch is a watch is a watch. Another stereotyped judgment was that academic research is academic only. The entrepreneur who founded a bio-tech company in our sample told us that at the time he realized the commercial aspect of the particular biological research, the entire field was widely considered abstract and confined to university laboratories. Another entrepreneur describes his latest venture--community newspapers--as a break from the common view of these local media as "unprofitable little newspapers." Another example is the entrepreneur who founded a very successful furniture rental business. His assumption was that people are not going to abuse the furniture and therefore wear and tear will not be a problem. This is clearly the frequent case but not the image of behavior held by most people. When we think of rented furniture, we immediately think of furniture which is in bad shape, maintained poorly, dirty, etc. Yet the entrepreneur, asking himself the same question, judged the situation by the true underlying frequencies, not the stereotyped ones.

Evidence of the lack of anchoring in judgmental processes of entrepreneurs is directly related to the sense of vision so prominent in our sample. While for an entrepriser, for example, a successful jewelry store or magazine or clothing store will remain just that, for our entrepreneurs the success of one step seemed only to open the doors to a larger vision. The development of a larger social vision ("People can be educated to see that this is the way to be", as one entrepreneur put it)[4] is especially interesting when one considers that the majority of

---

[4] For example, an entrepreneur who started with a clothing store went on to the vision of "putting colour on America". An entrepreneur marketed a communication network is now developing a new communication <u>industry</u> which "will change the shopping habits of America." Another has started from customizing computer programs to client needs to developing one of the most successful packaged programs for business reporting. And so on.

our successful respondents did not initially expect the spectacular success of their businesses. The change in their initial judgement was rather quick and led to rapid expansion. We wonder if the successful enterprisers remain confined essentially to their initial business rather than innovate because of cognitive anchoring rather than risk avoidance.

The availability bias too seems to play a minor role in entrepreneurial information processing since entrepreneurs seem able to reinterpret the environmental cues about them and to ignore the conventional wisdom. We were struck at the beginning of our research project by many of the stories of innovation reported in the literature. Fucini and Fucini (1985) relate brief biographies of some of the famous innovators of business history. They describe case after case in which a product which was designed for one purpose but an entrepreneurial insight tells them it will be a success in another. The Burpee seed business was founded as a catalog company to sell livestock and fowl by mail order. To provide customers with the proper feed for their pedigreed animals they also included several varieties of farm seed in the catalog. "Much to Burpee's surprise, the majority of early orders received by the firm were for seeds rather than livestock." (p.7) Joshua Lionel Cowen, founder of the Lionel Toy Train Company built his first engine, not as a toy but as a department store window display. When people wanted to buy the display rather than the merchandise he recognized his prospects. The Eveready flashlight was first marketed as an "electric flowerpot" with the light attached to illuminate a plant. It was only after the light was detached and marketed for its illuminatory merit that the product sold. The first Kellogg Corn Flakes were produced by accident when a food prepared for use in a sanitarium was left out over night and dried out. Will Kellogg saw the possibilities for selling the product. His more affluent but less entrepreneurial (anchored?) brother who owned the sanitarium would have nothing of the venture. Anecdotal as these episodes are, they supplement our own data on the ability of innovators to select, not what is available to them as the obvious path to go, but instead to perceive associations that are not evident to others with similar opportunities but less Kirznerian vision.

c)Who is afraid of failure?

The prominent absence of anchoring from our interviewers' cognitive repertoire is also related to the third category of our research - the reaction to failure.

Failure is an unpleasant experience to most people. The reaction to a wrong decision can take two forms: Correcting the situation (thereby admitting the mistake); ignoring the signs and either committing further (as in the escalating committment paradigm, see Staw (1981) and Fox and Staw (1979) or procastinating, and delaying the change in course. There is evidence (admittedly controversial) that certain cognitive mechanisms blocking the perception of negative evidence operate once an ego-involved decision is made (see Wicklund & Brehm, 1976) prolonging the committment to the errorenous course of action. How do entrepreneurs deal with failure?

The interviews revealed relatively little information avoidance. Except for one entrepreneur who said he avoided consulting anyone at the time of his initial decison to become an entrepreneur, for fear of being ridiculed or discouraged, most of our entreprenenurs seems to welcome criticism. Furthermore, all but that one claimed to have no difficulty in discontinuing a project which they initiated and is performing relatively poor. Even when they went against others' advice (which will create an ego-involvement, see Wicklund & Brehm, 1976) our entrepreneurs seemed to have very little ego-problems in admitting mistakes. All claimed that failures are inevitable but the trick is to be right more times than wrong. Once this attitude is adopted, quick changes in course seem easy enough. In one company the owner created a program in which failures were celebrated in the hope of encouraging employees to recognize and admit wrong decisions.

It is interesting to note a common theme underlying the entrepreneurs' apparent lack of "ego-problems" in admitting failures. For our group, as for other samples (see Solomon, 1985) the self-identification with the business is complete: it is seen as an extension of the self. It is therefore unthinkable that a wrong decision will not be recognized and reversed since it is the business that will be hurt if the mistake is not admitted, and the business _is_ their ego. In contrast, as our interviewers suggested, professional management always report to someone, and admitting mistakes does not make one look good to superiors.

SUMMARY AND CONCLUSIONS

What insights to the entrepreneurial process can we gain from our preliminary results? To begin with, our findings seem to support Kirzner's impression that information and perception are at the heart of entrepreneurship. Entrepreneurs can indeed see opportunities that others miss. However, it appears that these insights are gained as a result of immense search effort. Rather than being people who are struck by inspiration in the form of a lightening bolt while going about their business, our entrepreneurs are in constant search of the high ground where the lightening can more easily find them.

Their relative immunity from cognitive biases allows them to recognize the opportunities they meet, i.e. grants them a measure of veridical thinking. Does this mean that in the entrepreneur we have economic man--information seeking, information processing and rationally making decisions that are maximizing at the margin? Not quite. While the information seeking and processing facets are descriptive, our sample of entrepreneurs prided itself on being immensely intuitive. They showed great faith in their "gut" feelings. Whether it was selecting an investment banker ("I felt comfortable with him") or pricing a product ("I priced it just below the level the buyers were authorized to approve") or introducing a product ("I don't have the time or patience for market research. I know what sells") they were self-reliant and self confident but far from strict practitioners of the marginalists' cost benefit analysis.

Can entrepreneurship be taught? Certainly we can tell would be entrepreneurs where to look, as Drucker (1985) and

Pinchot (1985) do in their recent books. We can teach them how to prepare a business plan and look for financing as the business schools do. But can we teach people how to seek information 24 hours a day from everything and everyone around them? Perhaps we can encourage networking, friendliness, openness in communication; perhaps we can teach people to be more aggressive in their search for opportunities. But we doubt that it is possible to teach <u>obsession</u>.

If Kirznerian entrepreneurial perception is the rare, personal quality we believe it to be policy makers find themselves confronted with a situation whose parameters are well known to economists. The task is to attract people of entrepreneurial perceptiveness into business pursuits rather than the myriad of interesting occupations gifted people can enjoy. This is most likely to occur when cultural norms support business, when mechanisms are in place to encourage easy exchange of ideas among entrepreneurs, when tax policy facilitates mobility of capital from old to new areas, when failure is acknowledged as necessary to eventual success. It is difficult to develop a specific agenda for enhancing entrepreneurship but it is clear that it is the product of the joint effort of the educational establishment, the government, the religious institutions, the media, the philanthropic institutions, the corporate culture. Even if entrepreneurship cannot be taught, a social climate can be created in which it is more to occur and more likely to flourish when it does.

Lastly, if the cost of admitting failure is higher in corporations than in entrepreneurial ventures, one should encourage the Small Business Administration (SBA). As Gray (1985) argues, small business are more efficient in discovering changing circumstances and adjusting resources to new conditions. On the other side of the coin, Corporate America invests larger amounts in market experimentation and takes longer to recognize errors. Thus SBA supported <u>failures</u> are still quicker and more efficient ways to experiment than corporate ventures. In the discovery process which comprises the free market system (Kirzner, 1986) entpreneurs' reaction to failure is one more virtue of entrepreneurship.

BIBLIOGRAPHY

Collins, Orvis F., David G. Moore and Darab B. Unwalla: The Enterprising Man and the Business Executive, MSU Business Topics, Winter, 1964, 20-27.

Drucker, Peter, Innovation and Entrepreneurship, New York: Harper & Row, 1985.

Etzioni, Amitai, "Rationality is anti-entropic," Journal of Economic Psychology, forthcoming.

Fucini, Joseph and Suzy Fucini, Entrepreneurs, Boston: G. K. Hall, 1985.

Gilad, B., S. Kaish and P. D. Loeb, "A Theory of Surprise and Business Failure." Journal of Behavioral Economics, Summer, 1986 (forthcoming).

Gray, Thomas, "Small Business Dynamics, Effective Resource Utilization and Innovation," In Keys to the Future of American Business, George Solomon (ed.) U. S. Small Business Administration, 1985.

Kahneman, D., P. Slovic and A. Tversky, Judgment Under Uncertainty: Heuristics and Biases, Cambridge: Cambridge University Press, 1982.

Kent, Calvin A., Donald L. Sexton and Karl H. Vesper, Encyclopedia of Entrepreneurship, Prentice-Hall, 1982.

Kirzner, Israel M. Perception, Opportunity and Profit, Chicago: Chicago University Press, 1979.

Kirzner, Israel M. Discovery and the Capitalistic Process, Chicago: Chicago University Press, 1986.

Leibenstein, Harvey, Beyond Economic Man, Cambridge, Ma., Harvard University Press, 1976.

Pinchot, Gifford III, Intrapreneuring, New York: Harper & Row, 1985.

Ronen, Joshua, Entrepreneurship, Mass: Lexington Books, 1983.

Schrage, Harry, "The R&D Entrepreneurs: Profile of Success," Harvard Business Review, Nov.-Dec., 1985.

Schumpeter, Joseph A., The Theory of Economic Development, Cambridge: Harvard University Press, 1934.

Staw, B.M., "The Escalation of Committment to a Course of Action", Academy of Management Review, 1981, 6, 577-587.

Ungson, Geraldo R. and Daniel N. Braunstein: Decision Making, Boston: Kent Publishing Co., 1982.

Wicklund, R. A. and J. W. Brehm, Perspectives in Cognitive Dissonance, N.J.: Lawrence, Elbaum Associates, 1976.

Part Ten
Economic Psychology of Hazards and Stress

HYPERTENSION LABELLING AS A STRESSFUL EVENT LEADING TO AN INCREASE IN ABSENTEEISM: A POSSIBLE EXPLANATION FOR AN EMPIRICALLY MEASURED PHENONMEN

Mina Westman* and Amiram Gafni**

* Department of Organizational Behavior
Faculty of Management
Tel Aviv University
Tel Aviv, Israel

** Program of Health Systems Management
Faculty of Management
Tel Aviv University
Tel Aviv, Israel
AND
Department of Clinical Epidemiology and Biostatistics
McMaster University Medical Centre
Hamilton, Ontario Canada

ABSTRACT

What is the impact of being told that one has hypertension? According to evidence from randomized controlled trials, one effect of labelling is an increase in illness related absenteeism among those who were previously unaware of their blood pressure status. This effect exists without objective medical reasons to justify such an immediate increase in absenteeism. In this paper, we present a possible explanation for this phenomenon. We claim that labelling can be seen as a stressful event. A condition of stress results in various outcomes, one of which is absenteeism from work. We also claimed, that three mediating variables, personality dispositions, coping styles, and social support, affect the level and strength of the relationship described. Potential intervening strategies are discussed.

INTRODUCTION

Hypertension, or high blood pressure, is a common medical disorder which the pressure of the blood in the arteries is excessive. The condition causes damage to blood vessels that can lead to stroke, heart attack and kidney failure.

What is the impact of being told that one has hypertension? One of such "labelling" among those who were previously unaware of their blood pressure status is an increase in absenteeism from work. The first published account of hypertension labelling is a study carried out among Canadian steel mill workers (Gibson et al 1972). Workers who were detected and labelled as hypertensive had much higher absenteeism rates than their non-labelled co-workers, regardless of whether the condition was being treated. Since then, several studies have specifically examined hypertension labelling and its effect on absenteeism. These studies are summarized and discussed in detail in Macdonald et al (1984), according to whom, these studies reveal three consistent trends: 1) Absenteeism from work is greater among aware hypertensives than either normotensives or unaware hypertensives; 2) Labelling by itself may be harmful, and; 3) Certain circumstances of care and compliance with treatment appear to present or reverse increased absenteeism.

The progression of hypertension is generally very slow, with no major damage or symptoms appearing until some years after the blood pressure first became elevated. Thus, no objective medical reasons exist to justify such an immediate increase in absenteeism. Alternative psychological and economical explanations are available for this empirically measured phenomenon.

Gafni and Peled (1984) presented a possible economic explanation for this phenomenon, interpreting absenteeism as a demand for days off work. In a two-period life cycle model, it was argued that labelling can be interpreted as information which reduces the perceived probability of surviving. This leads to an increase in the demand for leisure. That is, the empirically measured effect of labelling on illness related absenteeism is explained as a rational response to a decline in the perceived probability of survival. As the subjective probability of living a long life falls, the value of working for a retirement nest egg decreases, and present leisure activities become more attractive.

An alternative and more common explanation is a psychological one. Macdonald et al (1984) summarized six empirical studies which dealt with the effect of labelling on various measures of psychological functioning and well-being. Five of these six studies documented psychological disadvantages resulting from labelling. A possible explanation is that people labelled as sick change their self-perception and adopt a "sick role". For example, attribution theory would explain the labelling effect as mistaken attribution to hypertension of a host of vague and transient symptoms that accompany the arousal caused by being told that one is hypertensive. These symptoms may become permanent and contribute to the adoption of "sick role" behaviour (see for example: Mechanic 1975, 1978).

In this paper we present another possible psychological explanation for the phenomenon described. We claim that labelling can be seen as a stressful event. A condition of stress results in various outcomes, one of which is absenteeism from work. Absenteeism may be the first step in the direction of quitting and is costly to the employer. For all these reasons, absenteeism should be treated seriously. The paper is organized as follows: in the second section, we present the model. The model describes the direct relationships between a stressful event and absenteeism and the effect of mediating variables (resistance resources). In the third section, we discuss the potential intervening strategies available in the event the hypothesis postulated is empirically supported.

THE MODEL

In Figure 1, a relationship between stressful events and their outcomes is presented. We claim that labelling as hypertensive is a stressful event which leads to subjective stress. The condition of stress results in various outcomes one of which is absenteeism.

BEING LABELLED: A STRESSFUL EVENT

Brown and Harris (1978) dealt with the question of how life events become stressful. They observed instances in which seemingly trivial life events such as "child leaves home" or "moving to a new apartment" precipitated episodes of depression. They concluded that life events can bring into focus the unfavourable implications of life problems. It is the new meaning of the old problems that cause distress. Life events, from their perspective, lead to strain by adversely altering the meaning of persistent stress. This seems to

FIGURE 1: RELATIONSHIP BETWEEN STRESSFUL EVENTS AND OUTCOMES

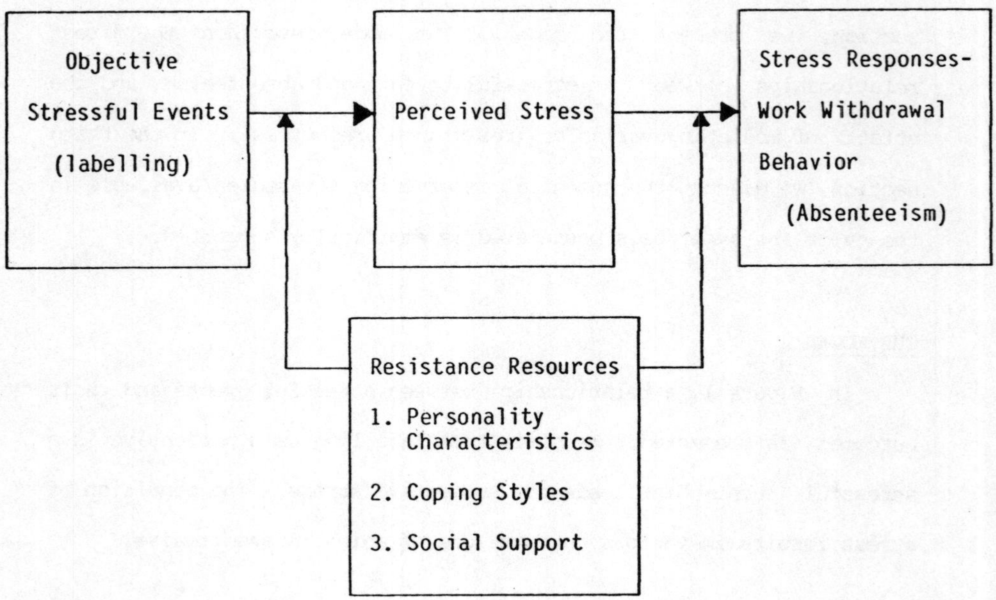

aptly explain the outcome of the discrete life event of being labelled as hypertensive. The act of being labelled is in itself stressful. It is a perceived state involving uncertainty about something important. It might mean a threat to life as high blood pressure may lead to stroke, heart attack, kidney failure. Further it might mean a constraint (e.g., a change in current lifestyle) preventing fulfillment of important needs, values and goals. Such changes may intensify the level of perceived stress. That is, events create stress not only through their direct demand for readjustment but also through their indirect exacerbation of role strains. This might also cause the employee to look back and think about what caused the change in the blood pressure. He might bring into focus all sorts of trivial job-related hassles and stressful events which are now evaluated differently and might be preceived as the causes of the current unhealthy state.

The term "life stress" (or stressful event or life event) is usually used to refer to life changes that cause a need to adapt, resulting in stress (Sarason 1979). Examples include death or illness of family members, divorce, and changes which are viewed as undesirable. Being labelled as hypertensive is an undesirable experience which requires change in two crucial dimensions. First, when people who regard themselves as healthy suddenly discover they have a medical disorder, there is mainly a change in their attitude towards themselves and also in the attitude of others towards them. Secondly, adaptation to the new situation requires changes in lifestyle and habits, such as, diet, et cetera.

Labelling, as a stressful event, may lead to a diminished sense of control over the forces that affect one's life, and an inability to alter the unwanted circumstance. The diminishing of self esteem and control is the final step in the process leading to strain (Pearlin et al,1981).

BEHAVIOURAL CONSEQUENCES OF STRESSFUL EVENTS

Life stress may be interpreted by the individual as work stress. Stressful events in the workplace are associated with dysfuctional behaviours on the job, mainly withdrawal behaviours such as absenteeism and turnover (Gupta & Breechr 1979, Porter & Steers 1974, Margolis et al 1974). Argeris (1974) names absenteeism and turnover as antagonistic adaptive activities to some job stress. He claims that employees are limited in creating adaptive activities. They can resolve the issue by withdrawing from the situation psychologically or physically so that frustration and stress are not too incapacitating.

In a study of employees in five organizations, Gupta & Breechr (1979) found that stress is related to withdrawal. In a study of nurses, Jamal (1974) found that job stress was positively related to absenteeism, tardiness and anticipated turnover. In a longitudinal study, Johnson & Graen (1973) supported the hypothesized relationship between increased role conflict with supervisors and voluntary turnover of secretaries. Schuler (1982) found that stress associated with demand and constraint situations is positively related to turnover and absenteeism.

Another possible explanation to the relationship between stress and absenteeism involves assignment of blame. If an employee believes, as documented by the media, that a relationship exists between stress and hypertension, he might blame the organization for his illness and, thus, avoid it by using certain kinds of withdrawal behaviour such as absenteeism, tardiness, and quitting, if possible. This might be explained as a "compensation neurosis" phenomenon. Namely, the employee feels that the "boss owes him" and should compensate him for the damage caused at work. Thus, he compensates himself by being absent.

Being labelled as hypertensive is a stressful event over which the person feels no control. One of the possible reactions to this state is a feeling of helplessness. Blaming the organization for the illness might cause the employee to choose an indirect and passive way of coping -- withdrawal from the organization. The employee thus finds different justifications to be absent from work. He might even think that occasional absence from work and the avoidance of work-related hassles might result the lowering of his blood pressure. However, if the high blood pressure phenomenon resulted from the job stress, then absenteeism is a direct and active coping strategy to deal with the cause of the disorder. The above explanation naturally applies to those who believe that high job stress caused their hypertension. Those who believe other sources of stress, such as family stress, caused the disorder might behave differently.

RESISTANCE RESOURCES

The objective condition (being labelled as hypertensive) produces a subjective definition of the situation in the mind of the individual. It is the perceived situation that is the primary determinant of the stress response (Billing et al, 1980). An individual's subjective appraisal and responses to the stressful events will vary, depending upon personality and coping skills. We now consider a group of variables which are assumed to intervene in the relationship between the stressful event and subjective stress and between subjective stress and stress responses.

Stress effects are assumed to occur only when the situation is appraised as threatening or demanding and with the individual perception that insufficient resources are available to to cope with the situation. Response is not based solely on the intensity or other inherent quality of the event, but is dependent on personal and contextual factors as well (Cohen, Kamark Mermelstein 1983). Stress cannot be understood solely in terms of antecedent conditions, for people differ on how they perceive and react to the same conditions. These differences include internal resistance resources (personality and coping) and external ones (social support). It is now accepted that the intensity of the stress responses that people exhibit cannot be adequately predicted solely from the intensity of its source. People typically, confront stressful situations with a variety of behaviours, perceptions, and cognitions that are often capable of altering the difficult circumstances or of mediating their impact.

In reviewing reseach on life event, Rabkin and Struening (1976) emphasized that demonstration of the effects of mediating variables such as coping and social support is required to advance the knowledge of the relationship between life events and their outcomes. Chan (1977) points out that differences in reaction to stress are probably the results of three factors: 1) The significance of the event to the individual, which depends on his appraisal of the situation; 2) Personality attributes of the individual such as self esteem and control; 3) The particular coping patterns that the individual adopts to manage the stress. Sarson (1979) found in his experiments that viewing stress only in terms of appraisng the situation leaves out two important variables: personality characteristics and social support. Johnson & Sarason (1979) and Kobasa (1979) found that personality characteristics may lessen the impact of stressful life events.

PERSONALITY CHARACTERISTICS

Recently, researchers have begun to search for mediating variables which can explain individual differences in reaction to stress. An interest has arisen in the study of generalized resistance resources which can be applied to buffer the effects of the varied and unpredictable stressors which individuals encounter (Antonovsky 1979). It was found that personality characteristics may lessen the adverse effects of stressful life events in the generation of life stress (Johnson & Sarason 1979, Kobasa 1979). A general resistance resource for which there is a growing body of empirical research is that of hardiness (Kobasa 1979).

Hardiness is a particular personality resource that moderates the relationship between stress and its outcomes. Hardy persons possess three characteristics which help them to deal with stressful events: 1) commitment -- an ability to feel deeply involved in or committed to the activities of their their lives; 2) challenge -- the anticipation of change as an exciting challenge to future development, and; 3) control -- the belief that they can control or influence the events they experience. These three characteristics should facilitate transformational coping used to solve stress related problems. Kobasa and her associates found in retrospective and prospective studies (1979, 1982) that hardiness serves as a buffer in the stress illness relationships and that hardy persons use transformational coping while less hardy persons tend to use regressive coping.

Control is one of the components of hardiness. People who believe they are primarily responsible for what happens to them are said to possess an internal locus of control. People who believe that their actions have little impact on what happens to them and who attribute outcomes to fate and luck are said to have an external locus of control (Rotter 1966). Internals cope better with stressful events because they use more active coping strategies and try to remove or reduce the source of stress (Anderson 1977).

COPING STYLES

Coping is also considered to be a resistance resource. A coping process starts when a stressor has entered the individual's environment and is interpreted as stressful, that is, a dynamic situation of uncertainty with something of importance at stake (Schuler 1985). Pearlin et al (1981) distinguished between coping behaviours according to their functions: 1) modification of the stressful events; 2) modification of the meaning of the problems in a manner that reduces their threat, and; 3) the management of stress symptoms.

The most adaptive response to stress is a task-oriented coping strategy which directs the individual's attention to the task at hand rather than to an emotional reaction. Some people are able to maintain task-oriented coping because achieving a particular goal or a solution to a problem is in the forefront of their thinking. Others are unable to engage in realistic planning and weighing of alternatives. The anxious person reacts to stress with catastrophizing, thoughts of helplessness and withdrawal behaviours. Anxious, depressive and angry thoughts direct attention away from the most salient aspects of the situation. Not everyone selects the best strategy to cope. The ability to set aside unproductive worries and preoccupations is crucial in functioning well under stressful events.

SOCIAL SUPPORT

Another possible moderating variable is social support. After an extensive review of the literature, Browlby 1973, concluded that indviduals are at their happiest and most effective when they are confident that there are trusted people behind them who will come to their help in case of difficulties. Social support facilitates coping with crisis (Nukolls et al 1972). This study and others suggest that there is a protective effect of close social ties. There is evidence that social support serves both immunizing and therapeutic functions (Sarason 1979). Social support is effective because the presence of interested and caring others reverses the person's assumption that he must deal with the stressful situation alone.

Several studies show that support does modify the impact of stressful circumstances (Gore 1978, LaRocco et al 1980). Cassel (1976) and Henderson (1977) reviewed studies which indicate that the social support provided by primary groups serves to protect the individual from physiological, psychological and behavioural outcomes of exposure to stressful situations. Maddison (1967) found that patients with relatively better outcomes reported that they received more support than did patients with relatively poor outcomes. Westman et al (1985) found that peer support buffers the relationship between job stress and decreased smoking.

Pearlin et al (1981) point out that both coping and social support are resources that people can use to mediate stressful impact of life events. Although they are two distinct phenomena, they have similar functions in the stress process. Each has the capacity to regulate the effects of stress conditions. Individuals faced with stressful life events use one or both of them to avoid, eliminate, and reduce distress and negative outcomes.

An additional perspective is illuminated by Schuler (1985). He claims that coping strategies to reduce the effect of stress can include taking advantage of the main or buffering effects of social support groups, dietary changes, physical exercise, meditation, et cetera. All these techniques are useful for people who were labelled as hypertensives. Some people may not implement the appropriate coping strategy either because they cannot diagnose the situation, cannot implement the most appropriate strategy, or because they lack adequate information.

From the literature reviewed, it appears that the simple

causative model of stressful event-stress-outcomes can be expanded to include these three factors: personality dispositions, coping styles and social support. It is not clear whether these factors exert their effect independent of life event stress or whether their importance is by moderating the effect of high life event stress.

SUMMARY AND CONCLUSIONS

The empirically measured phenomenon of absenteeism attributed to labelling as hypertensive has received different explanations in the literature. In this paper, we suggest that higher rates of absenteeism following the label of hypertensive might be a reaction to the stressfulness of a life situation that might be interpreted as related to work. As we documented, there is considerable empirical evidence relating stressful events to withdrawal behaviour, such as absenteeism. Our contribution has been in showing that the act of being labelled hypertensive is in itself a stressful critical event that might contribute to the outcome of absenteeism. We support this view with evidence from general stress research. Based on the existing literature, we also claim that the three mediating variables, personality dispositions, coping styles, and social support, affect the level and strength of the effects of the relationship described. The existence of these mediating variables creates various successful intervening options discussed later.

The proposed hypothesis does not rule out the other possible explanations described in the literature (the "economic" explanation and the "sick role" explanation). It should, however, be noted that there is an important difference between the two psychological explanations and the economic explanation. In the economic explanation, the increase in absenteeism, is seen as a rational response to the information conveyed. In the psychological explanations, the increase in absenteeism is seen as an irrational response to the information conveyed. The two psychological explanations differ in their conceptualization of the effect of labelling on the individual's behaviour. Only further empirical research can determine which of the possible explanations best predicts the relationship which was empirically found.

The hypothesis presented in this paper calls for empirical life event research, which should (Andrews et al 1979): (a) determine the significance of the event to the individual; (b) measure the multiplied effect of relevant personality attributes; (c) identify the likely effectiveness of coping, and; (d) identify the extent of support utilized. The significance of such research lies in the prediction of withdrawal behaviours and in delineating the relative importance of the moderators for prevention.

If the hypothesis postulated in this paper is supported, there is a enormous potential for different effective intervening strategies. There are several junctions at which the mediating variables (resistance resources) may intervene: prior to an event, between the event and the strain it stimulates, or prior to the stress outcome. Treating behavioural disorders subsequent to being labelled as hypertensive can stem from two main strategies: 1) The preventive strategy: train doctors and nurses how to give the information (how to define it, what connotations to give, what kind of instructions should be given to the patient, et cetera); 2)

Curative strategy: build support groups. Caplan et al (1976) found that people who reported having supportive ties were more adherent to medical regimens in treatment for hypertension. Peled et al (1984) and Peled (1986) found that people who suffer from high blood pressure and participate in support groups may return to their normal blood pressure after an average period of six months. Training in hardiness also appears to be effective. Maddi (1985) reports a decrease in blood pressure after participation in hardiness workshops. Developing coping skills, especially direct action strategies, could also help people labelled as hypertensives to cope successfully with this perceived threatening information. From the organizational perspective, another possible way to reduce the stress stemming from being labelled is to create a special workplace counselling office to deal with problems that might arise.

REFERENCES

Anderson CR. Locus of control, coping behaviours, and performance in a stress setting: A Longitudinal study. Journal of Applied Psychology, 1977, 62, 446-451.

Andrews G, Tennant C, Hewson D and Vaillant G. Life event stress, social support, coping style, and risk of psychological impairment. The Journal of Nervous and Mental Disease, 1978, 166, 307-316.

Antonovsky A. Health Stress and Coping. San Francisco: Jossey-Bass, 1979.

Argeris C. Intervention theory and method: A behavioral science view. Mass: Reading: Addison-Wesley, 1970.

Billings RA, Millburn TM, and Schaolman MLA. A model of crisis perception: A theoretical and empirical analysis: Administrative Science Quarterly, 1980, 25, 300-316.

Browlby J. Separation: Anxiety and Anger. New York: Basic Books, 1973.

Brown GW and Harris T. Social Origins of Depression, New York: Free Press, 1978, 138-149.

Caplan RD, Robinson EAR, French JRP, Caldwell JR, Shinn M. Adhering to Medical Regimens: Pilot Experiments in Patient Education and Social Support, The University of Michigan, Ann Arbor, Michigan 1976.

Cassel J. The contribution of the social environment to host resistance. American Journal of Epidemiology, 1976, 104, 107-123.

Chan KB. Individual differences in reactions to stress and their personality and situational determinants: Some implications for community health. Social Science and Medicine, 1977, 11, 89-103.

Cohen S, Kamark T and Mermelstein R. A global measure of perceived stress. Journal of Health and Social Behavior, 1983, 24, 385-396.

Gafni A and Peled D. The Effect of Labelling on Illness Related Absenteeism: An Economic Explanation for the Case of Hypertension. Journal of Health Economics, 1984, 3, 173-178.

Gibson ES, Mishkel M, Gent M. Absenteeism from Work Among Hypertensives. Newsletter of the Council on Epidemiology of the American Heart Association. American Heart Association, January 1972.

Gore S. The effect of social support in moderating the health consequences of unemployment. Journal of Health and Social Behavior, 1978, 19, 228-244.

Gupta N and Breechr TA. Job stress and employee behaviors. Orgaizational Behavior and Human Performance, 1979, 23, 383-387.

Henderson AS. The social network, support and neurosis. The function of attachment in adult life. British Journal of Psychiatry, 1977, 131, 185-191.

Jamal M. Job stress and job performance controversy: An empirical assessment. Organizational Behavior and Human Performance, 1984, 33, 1-21.

Johnson TW and Graen G. Organizational assimilation and role rejection. Organizational Behavior and Human Performance, 1973, 10, 72-87.

Johnson JH, Sarason IG. Moderator Variables in Life Stress Research in J Sarason and C Spielberger (Eds). Stress and Anxiety, Vol 6. New York: Halstead, 1979.

Kobasa SC. Stressful life events, personality and health: An inquiry into hardiness. Journal of Personality and Social Psychology, 1979, 37, 1-11.

Kobasa SC. The hardy personality: Toward a social psychology of stress and health. In GS Sanders and J Suls (Eds). The social & psychology of health and illness. Hillsdale, New Jersey: Lawrence Endbaum, 1982.

LaRocco JM, House JS, and French JRP (Jr). Social support, occupational stress, and health. Journal of Health and Social Behavior, 1980, 21, 202-218.

Maddi SR and Kobasa SC. The hardy executive. Homewood K: Dow Jones-Irwin, 1984.

Maddison D and Walker WL. Factors affecting the outcome of conjugal bereavement. British Journal of Psychiatry, 1967, 113, 1057-1067.

Macdonald LA, Sackett DS, Haynes RB and Taylor DW. Labelling in hypertension: A review of the behavioral and psychological consequences. Journal of Chronic Disease. Vol 37(12), 1984, 933-942.

Mechanic D. Social psychologic factors affecting the presentation of bodily complaints. New England Journal of Medicine, 286: 1132-1139, 1975.

Mechanic D. Sociology of Medicine. Boston: Little Brown 1978.

Margolis BL, Kroes WH and Quinn RP. Job stress: An unlisted hazard. Journal of Occupational Medicine, 1974, 10, 659-661.

Nuckolls KB, Cassel J, and Kaplan BH. Psychological assets, life crisis and prognosis of pregnancy. American Journal of Epidemiology, 1972, 95, 431-441.

Pearlin LI, Lieberman MA, Mengahan EG, and Mullan JT. The stress process. Journal of Health and Social Behavior, 1981, 22, 337-356.

Peled R, Silverberg DS, Rosenteld JM. A controlled study of the therapy in essential hypertension. Israel Journal of Medical Sciences, 1984, 20:12-16.

Peled R. Pressure and hypertension, Tel Aviv: Sifriat Poalim, 1986.

Porter LW and Steers RM. Organizational, work, and personal factors in employee turnover and absenteeism. Psychological Bulletin, 1973, 80, 151-176.

Rabkin JG and Struening EL. Life events, stress and illness. Science, 1976, 194, 1013-1020.

Rotter JB. Generalized expectancies for internal vs. external control of reinforcement. Psychological Monographs, 1966, 80, 1-28.

Sarason IG. Life stress, self-preoccupation, and social supports. 1979, Report SCS-LS-008.

Sarason IG and Johnson JH. Life stress, organizational stress, and job satisfaction. Psychological Reports, 1979, 44, 75-79.

Schuler RS. An integrative transactional process model of stress in organizations. Journal of Occupational Behavior, 1982, 3, 5-19.

Schuler RS. Integrative transactional process model of coping with stress in organizations. In TA Beehr and RS Bhagat (Eds). Human stress and conditions in organizations: An integrated perspective. New York: Wiley, 1985.

Westman M, Eden D, Shrom A. Job Stress, Cigarette Smoking and Cessation: The Conditioning Effects of Peer Support. Social Science and Medicine, 1985, 20:637-644.

INCORPORATING ANXIETY INDUCED BY ENVIRONMENTAL EPISODES IN LIFE VALUATION*

Mordechai SHECHTER
University of Haifa, Haifa, 31999 Israel

Environmental pollution is recognized as a public bad, constituting a threat of involuntary health-risks. In addition to its potential tangible health effects, it imposes utility losses in the form of uncertainty which in turn generates psychological phenomena such as anxiety. Characteristically there exists little or no information on either the extent of these uncertainties or the timing of their resolution. Moreover, since in the meanwhile a community may be forced to continue to rely on the degraded environmental resource (air, water, etc.), irreversible health effects are an ever-present danger, which, in turn, would tend to, exacerbate those psychological reactions. The paper addresses itself to the question of how to incorporate these psychological phenomena into the benefit-cost calculus, through formal utility theory, in order to arrive at a more comprehensive valuation of health risks, including the loss of life.

1. INTRODUCTION

Anxiety is a psychological state which is characterized by "feelings of uncertainty and helplessness in the face of danger" (May [13]). Without going so far as some who have called the mid-twentieth century the "Age of Anxiety," we can confidently assert that anxiety has in our time become a recurrent and routine feature of the public's response to environmental episodes. Abt [1], in calculating the social costs of cancer in the United States, counted anxiety and depression among the psychological costs of cancer. These costs, he claimed, exceeded the economic costs by more than an order of magnitude. Moreover, because certain cancers have been increasingly associated with exposure to pollution, a growing share of these costs may be attributable to them. Such episodes are often characterized by three features which Fischoff et al. [6] found to be associated with health risks that are perceived to be the least acceptable - namely, that the risks are incurred involuntarily, that they are considered to be uncontrollable, and that they are believed to have a delayed effect.

The case of devastations that are the result of natural disasters and wars is plain; their causes and effects are easily delineated. Similar in their impact are certain non-natural disasters, namely low-probability catastrophic events such as core meltdowns or the eruption and spread of deadly gases. However, because of their special nature,

* This research was partially supported by a grant from Israel's Water Commissioner. The author is solely responsible for the views expressed in this paper.

they tend to heighten feelings of anxiety among public. Otway [14] reports that the attitudes of people who oppose nuclear energy are dominated not by a sense of environmental risk but by anxiety. Under the heading, "Fear as a Form of Pollution," Marshall [12] has written an account of the now famous ruling of the D.C. Federal Court of Appeals, which granted a petition by PANE (People Against Nuclear Energy), a citizens group which demanded that the Nuclear Regulatory Commission be required to consider the psychological stress that might be inflicted upon the community, were the undamaged reactor at the Three Mile Island plant allowed to resume operation. (This was the twin of the reactor that was damaged in the widely publicized accident that took place in March of 1979.)

The impact of many other sorts of environmental episodes, on the other hand, is uncertain and delayed. Consider the case of episodes of groundwater contamination (Shechter, [19]). The deleterious effect of drinking such contaminated water might be delayed for a considerable time. Carcinogens may be slow to act, and persons who have been exposed to them may have to wait for years before finding out whether they have been victimized. Mutagenic disorders often remain latent for a generation or more before they become manifest. In the meantime, fears, uncertainties, and conjectures may become inextricably mingled in the public mind with the realities of the episode. It is also clear that we seldom have the means deal with the psychological responses to environmental episodes, unless it is to eliminate their causes. The problem is exacerbated by the absence of any mechanism to compensate future generations for the involuntary risks that have been imposed upon them by our current actions. Even in an intra-generational context, legal institutions are often unequipped to deal adequately with problems consequent upon a person's exposure to hazardous substances, that he may have ingested a good many years before dying of causes possibly attributable to that event. Nor is the medical profession able in such cases to furnish evidence which would stand up in a court of law, so that the families of the victims might collect compensation.

In this paper we shall begin by briefly discussing the evolution of the concept of anxiety in psychology and economics, although we cannot claim to have exhausted all of the relevant literature, particularly in the field of psychology. We shall next focuse on the determination of value-of-life as reflected in the temporal allocation of wealth (or consumption) in the face of anxiety. The results suggest that a person who is willing to trade wealth for safety would shift wealth from a period of uncertainty to a period of certainty, and that willingness to give up wealth would be more pronounced in anxiety-laden situations. Consequently, the derived value of life would tend to be higher when anxiety is taken into account. Ignoring the factor of anxiety may lead to an underestimation of the true value-of-life, particularly in cost-benefit analyses of environmental regulation.

2. THE CONCEPT OF ANXIETY IN THE PSYCHOLOGICAL LITERATURE[1]

Psychologists have been grappling with the concept of anxiety for the past three decades. Freud considered the role of anxiety in neurosis, but it was not until the 1950s that the investigation of normal anxiety began. Even so, in spite of the more than thirty years of research, there still appears to be no universal agreement concerning the exact scientific meaning of the concept. However, Lewis [9] has proposed that normal anxiety can be defined as "an emotional state, with the subjective experience quality of fear or a closely related emotion" (p.77).

During the same period, the concept of stress has also become a focus of research. This is a logical development if we accept Levitt's [8] argument that "the word stress is used constantly in connection with emotional states; it appears almost as often in discussions of anxiety as does the word 'anxiety' itself" (p. 9). Spielberger [22,23] had earlier pointed out that these two terms have been used interchangeably in the psychological literature, and May [13] proposed that "anxiety is how the individual relates to stress, accepts it, interprets it. Anxiety is how we handle stress" (p. 113).

In order to formalize the relationship between the two concepts, Spielberger [23], Endler [4], and others have offered the interactional model of anxiety. This model, which has been supported by empirical research, consisting both of laboratory experiments and of field studies, treats stress as a situational variable whose perception is influenced by the individual's predisposition to react to stress with increased anxiety. The model proposes that the nature of the threat perceived in a stressful situation interacts with the personal characteristics of the subject to yield anxiety states, as well as to change their intensity. Individuals with different personality traits would necessarily differ in their responses to such situations.

In economic parlance, we would speak of the shape of the individual's utility function as being determined by his personality traits. This would in turn determine the level of a person's anxiety in various stressful situations (e.g., environmental episodes), and would thus affect his economic behavior.

3. THE TREATMENT OF ANXIETY IN ECONOMICS

An early treatment of anxiety in the economic literature is offered by Schelling [17] in his eloquent paper on the value-of- life. He argues that anxiety, which is associated with the awareness of the prospect of dying, and which is considered to be separate from the impact of actual death, is commensurate with the monetized utility loss of death. Anxiety may be conceived of as a purely psychic consumer good, and what the consumer "buys" is a state of mind. But "it counts, and is part of the consumer interest in reducing the risk of death . . . and it is not double counting to bring it into the calculation" (p. 146). A number of examples in kind may be cited. One such example would be that of a person who must sooner or later undergo an operation that entails a moderate risk of being fatal, and who may choose to have the operation earlier, thereby raising the stakes against himself in the gamble. Another is that of a patient who may elect to take a risky diagnostic test in order to detemine the state of his health, even though the test could not lead to an improvement in his health, and might even do him harm. And, finally, consider the case of a group of patients among whom one was mistakenly injected with a substance that would kill him at the end of five years. If the physician did not himself know who among them had received the fatal injection, and if none of the patients were aware of the mistake, then the doctor would probably cause even greater harm by telling them about the error than the harm he had already done in administering the injection.

Zeckhauser [24] seems to have been the first economist who incorporated anxiety as such in the von Nuemann-Morgenstern utility model in the form of the probability of an undesirable event. Weinstein et al. [25] have incorporated a contextial factor, that of the probability of death, within the von Neumann-Morgenstern utility model. Employing what they refer to as an "innocuous" assumption — namely, that the marginal utility of assets is greater in life than in death - they showed that the willingness to pay for a change in the probability of death (i.e., the value-of-life) depends not only on the change in the probability of death, but on the baseline probability as well.

Weinstein and Quinn [26] set out to inquire into the kinds of psychological and contextual concerns that the public would like environmental decision makers to take into account. They have also taken up the issue of how the standard economic models should be modified and extended to reflect these concerns. They suggest that, among other attributes, the three attributes of risk that were analyzed by Fischoff et al. [6] may be accorded normative status in this regard.

Consider the "delayed effect" attribute. Since anxiety is a function of the time it takes for the uncertainty surrounding the probabilities and stakes of the events to be resolved, this attribute may be thought of as deriving from a more fundamental state of mind, consisting in the aversion to "anxiety." Weinstein and Quinn argue that two factors may contribute to the preference for an immediate resolution. The first is that subsequent decisions may be made under conditions of less uncertainty, thereby improving expected outcomes. Spence and Zeckhauser [21] have likewise claimed that a person's knowing the outcome of the lottery, whatever, would improve the decisions of that individual. The second contributing factor is anxiety. This state of mind, in which one does not know what is going to happen (or has already happened), "may be sufficiently unpleasant that other carriers of utility (e.g., health, money) may be sacrificed to reduce it" (Weinstein and Quinn [26], p. 671). Thus Litai [11], who calculated a ratio between different types of risk for a given utility level, found that individuals are willing to accept a 30-fold higher risk if it offers immediate resolution, as compared to a risk with delayed consequences. Weinstein and Quinn, however, did not offer a specification which formally incorporated anxiety.

Viscusi [27] amplified Zeckhauser's earlier contribution and extended its application to employment at hazardous jobs. In Viscusi's proposed framework, anxiety is expressed through its effect on the welfare of individuals awaiting the outcome of a job hazard lottery. Thus, for example, a worker may prefer the cancer hazards posed by job A to those posed by job B if he is informed immediately about the effect of the job on his health, whereas his preference might be reversed if given by $U_a(W) > U_b(W)$, $U'_a > U'_b$, for all W, where $U'_i \equiv \partial U_i/\partial W$, $i=a,b$. As indicated earlier, the relationship between the two marginal utilities is a cornerstone of Weinstein's (1980) model. Following Hirshleifer [7]), Rapaport [15] and others, we further assume that $U_a(0)=U_b(0)=0$, i.e., that both functions begin at the origin. We believe this to be a more general specification than is the alternative one - namely, $U_a(W)-U_b(W)$ = constant, for all W (Cook and Graham, [3]), which implies that the utility difference is independent of wealth levels.

The maximization problem (before anxiety is introduced) is therefore,

$$(1)\ \text{Max } U_0(W_1) + \{(1-p)U_a(W_2) + pU_b(W_2)\}$$

$$\text{s.t. } W_1 + W_2 \leq \bar{W},$$

where W_i is wealth allocated (for consumption) in period i. The value of a statistical life (commonly referred to as the value-of-life) is given by dW/dp (e.g., Rosen [16]; Linnerooth [10]).

Now, let us introduce anxiety into this framework. As elaborated above, anxiety results from a lottery whose outcome may affect one's health (e.g., the consequences of exposure to high pollution levels), and from the fact that a period of time will pass before the uncertainty associated with that outcome is resolved. Here we stipulate that the utility loss stemming from anxiety materializes in the periods preceding the lottery. Specifically, let us postulate that at the beginning of the first period the individual receives a signal telling him that, in consequence of an environmental event, a lottery will be held at the beginning of the second period to determine with probability p whether he will die then, or will live until the end of the second period. This information generates, or heightens, the level of anxiety during the first period.

Anxiety itself therefore appears only in the utility function of the first period. It will be defined as a function of (a) the difference between second-period utilities, $U_a(W)-U_b(W)$ (i.e., utility loss if the worst happens in the second period),[4] and of (b) the probability of this eventuality, p:

$$(2)\quad f\{U_a(W_2) - U_b(W_2),\ p\}$$

where $f_z>0$ $(z=U_a-U_b)$, $f_p>0$, and (following Viscusi) $f_{pp}<0$.

After we incorporate anxiety, the two-period utility function becomes

$$(3)\ U_0\{W_1, f(z,p)\} + \{(1-p)U_a(W_2) + pU_b(W_2)\}.$$

Given our assumptions, it can be shown that $\partial f(\cdot)/\partial W_2>0$. That is, anxiety is a strictly increasing function of wealth allocated to the second period; the higher the stakes at risk, the greater is the associated anxiety level.

The risk-averse individual can do one of two things in the context of our two-period model. He may trade wealth for risk reduction, so giving up wealth in return for a decrease in the probability of death. The value of a statistical life is usually derived from aggregating this willingness to pay for risk reduction. Or he can modify the allocation of wealth between the two periods, in order to reduce the potential impact of anxiety. In the companion paper (Shechter and Heiman [20]) we analyze how anxiety affects the shift in wealth (hence, consumption) between the two periods and then compare the willingness to pay, namely $\partial W_1/\partial p$, when anxiety is present, with the situation in which anxiety is absent.

In this context it is shown, first, that in the presence of anxiety, an individual shifts consumption from the second to the first (certainty) period. Intuitively, one can think of the individual transferring consumption to the first (certain) period from the second period, when his survival is uncertain. As the survival probability decreases (p increases), an optimizing individual who equates utilities at the margin would shift consumption to the first period. An individual who is anxiety prone, or whose level of anxiety is sensitive to the stakes involved (second-period wealth), would be more inclined to shift wealth from the period of uncertainty to the period of certainty. This result supports Tversky and Kahenman's [24] conclusions. If we reverse the order of the two periods - that is, if we make the second the period of certainty, and the first the period of uncertainly - then the individual will transfer wealth from the first to the second period (in Tversky and Kahenman's example - lottery rounds in a Russian roulette game).

Next, we show that when anxiety is present, the willingness of an individual to pay for risk reduction is positive, and is higher when anxiety is present than when it is absent. Consequently, the value-of-life is higher in the former case, too. Thus, consider an individual who is anxious about the risks of radiation. He may be willing to pay more — if it were possible to do so — during "period a" to reduce the exposure-related anxiety, (to be distinguished from what he would have been willing to pay to reduce the risk of dying from it!). Or, alternatively, the inherently anxiety-inclined person may be willing to pay more to reduce anxiety in comparison with a less anxious individual.

5. CONCLUSIONS

This paper takes up a problem that was discussed by Schelling [17] in his seminal paper, and was treated more formally by Weinstein and Quinn [26]. It represents an attempt to suggest a way in which psychological phenomena such as anxiety can be incorporated into a formal utility framework. To an extent it is a response to the challenge of psychologists and economists (e.g., Schoemaker [18]) who have expressed reservations concerning the expected-utility model and, by implication, the derivation from it of normative measures of the value-of-life.

The development, in psychological literature, of the concept of anxiety in its relation to stress, demonstrates that anxiety is a valid attribute of situations in which risky decision must be made. There is ample justification, therefore, for its explicit inclusion in an economic theory of choice. The behavioral responses of individuals tend to support the view that we are concerned in this case with situations which may lead to real utility losses, and which should therefore be included in any cost-benefit calculus of life-saving and health improvement programs.

Our formal results would indicate that, given plausible assumptions, intuition can be supported by theory - although these results require additional elaboration and amplification. They nevertheless show that when psychological considerations are incorporated into the standard model, the usual results obtained concerning value-of-life need to be qualified.

FOOTNOTES

1 This section is based on Endler and Edwards [5].

2 Life insurance is sometimes explained in this connection as the desire to reduce anxiety. Thus, Cook and Graham [3] have shown that even when fair insurance markets exist, risk-averse individuals would not fully insure themselves against accidental death, because life is an irreplaceable commodity. The availability of insurance cannot fully compensate for the loss of life, and anxiety cannot be totally eliminated even in such circumstances.

3 In this section we provide only a sketchy and intuitive explanation of the formal model. A fuller treatment can be found in a companion paper (Shechter and Heiman [20]).

4 This can be thought of as an adaptation of the model of Akerlof and Dickens [2]), who have included in the utility function the undesired outcome, representing the state of being afraid of the outcome of the lottery.

REFERENCES

[1] Abt, C. C. "The Social Costs of Cancer." Social Indicators Research, 2 (1975): 175-190.

[2] Akerlof, G. A., and Dickens, W. T. "The Economic Consequences of Cognitive Dissonance." American Economic Review 72 (1982): 307-319.

[3] Cook, P. J., and Graham, D. A. "The Demand for Insurance and Protection: The Case of the Irreplaceable Commodity." Quarterly Journal of Economics 91 (1977): 141-156.

[4] Endler, N. S. "A Person-Situation Interaction Model of Anxiety." In Stress and Anxiety, vol. 1, edited by C. D. Spielberger and I. G. Sarason. Washington, D. C.: Hemisphere, 1975.

[5] Endler, N. S., and Edwards, J. "Stress and Personality." In Handbook of Stress, edited by L. S. Goldberger and S. Breznitz. New York: Free Press, 1982.

[6] Fischoff, B. et al. "How Safe is Safe Enough? A Psychometric Study of Attitudes towards Technological Risks and Benefits." Policy Sciences 8 (1978): 127-152.
[7] Hirshleifer, J. "An Economic Approach to Risk-Benefit Analysis." In Risk-Benefit Methodology and Application, edited by D. Okrenet. Asilomar, CA. 1975.
[8] Levitt, E. E. The Psychology of Anxiety, 2nd ed. Hillsdale: Erlbaum, 1980
[9] Lewis, A. "The Ambiguous Word 'Anxiety'." International Journal of Psychiatry 9 (1970): 62-79.
[10] Linnerooth, J. "The Value of Human Life: A Review of the Models." Economic Inquiry 17 (1979): 52-74.
[11] Litai, D. A Risk Comparison Methodology for the Assessment of Acceptable Risk. Unpublished Ph.D. dissertation. Massachusetts Institute of Technology, 1980.
[12] Marshall, E. "Fear as a Form of Pollution." Science 215 (1982): 481.
[13] May, R. The Meaning of Anxiety. New York: Norton, 1977.
[14] Otway, H. J. "The Perception of Technological Risks." In Technological Risk, edited by M. Dierkes. Boston: Oelgeschlager, 1980.
[15] Rapaport, E. "Economic Analysis of Life and Death Decision Making." In Applying Cost-Benefit Concepts to Projects Which Alter Human Mortality, edited by J. Hirshleifer et al. U. of California. 1974.
[16] Rosen, S. "Valuing Health Risks." American Economic Review 71 (1981): 241-245.
[17] Schelling, T. C. "The Life You Save May Be Your Own." In Problems in Public Expenditure Analysis, edited by S. B. Chase, Jr. Washington, D.C.: Brookings, 1968.
[18] Schoemaker, P.J. "The Expected Utility Model: Its Variants, Purposes, Evidence, and Limitations." Journal of Economic Literature 20 (1982): 529-563.
[19] Shechter, M. "An Anatomy of a Groundwater Contamination Episode." Journal of Environmental Economics and Management 12 (1985): 72-88.
[20] Shechter, M., and Heiman, A. "Valuing Anxiety Induced by Environmental Episodes." Department of Economics, U. of Haifa. Mimeo, 1986.
[21] Spence, A. M., and Zeckhauser, R. "The Effect of Timing of Consumption Decisions and the Resolution of Lotteries on the Choice of Lotteries." Econometrica 40 (1972): 401-403.
[22] Spielberger, C. D. "Trait-State Anxiety and Motor Behavior." Journal of Motor Behavior 3 (1971): 265-279.
[23] Spielberger, C. D. "The Nature and Measurement of Anxiety." In Cross-Cultural Anxiety, edited by C. D. Spielberger and R. Diaz-Guerrero. Washington, D.C.: Hemisphere, 1976.
[24] Tversky, A., and Kahenman, D. "The Framing of Decisions and the Rationality of Choice." Science 211 (1981): 453-458.
[25] Weinstein, M. C. et al. "The Economic Value of Changing Mortality Probabilities: A Decision-Theoretic Approach." Quarterly Journal of Economics 94 (1980): 373-396.
[26] Weinstein, M. C., and Quinn, R. J. "Psychological Considerations in Valuing Health Risk Reductions." Natural Resources Journal 23 (1983): 659-673.
[27] Viscusi, W. K. Employment Hazards. Cambridge, MS.: Harvard U., 1979.
[28] Zeckhausr, R. "Risk Spreading and Distribution." In Redistribution Through Public Choice, edited by H. Hochman and G. Peterson. New York: Columbia, 1974.

THE JOY OF THINKING ABOUT NUCLEAR ENERGY:

individual differences in search and desire for external information and in beliefs-attitude-intention consistency.

Rik G.M. PIETERS,

Department of Economics,
Erasmus University,
P.O. Box 1738,
3000 DR Rotterdam, and

Bas VERPLANKEN,

Department of Psychology,
University of Leiden,
Hooigracht 15,
2312 KM Leiden.

The effect of an interpersonal difference factor, the need for cognition, on the search and desire for external information about the advantages and disadvantages of using nuclear energy for the generation of electricity was studied. Also, the effect of need for cognition on the belief-attitude, attitude-intention relationship was analyzed. To investigate the robustness of the effects, two groups differing in a number of sociodemographic characteristics were included in the present study. The results indicate that individuals low and high in need for cognition differ to a large extent in their search and desire for external information and that they do not differ in beliefs, attitudes and intentions. Individuals high in need for cognition search and desire more information about the advantages and disadvantages of using nuclear energy than individuals low in need for cognition. The hypothesis that need for cognition moderates the relationship between beliefs, attitudes and intentions was confirmed.

1. INTRODUCTION

In the Netherlands electricity is mainly generated using natural gas, oil and coal. There are also two nuclear power plants in operation. For many years, the future supply of electricity and the alternatives of generating electricity have been an important issue of public debate. Extensively, information about the advantages and disadvantages of the various options of generating electricity has been and is transferred to the public. In this paper we will focus on the use and search for external information about nuclear energy by consumers.

2. EXTERNAL SEARCH

In making a choice between alternatives, an individual examines the relevant information in memory, and in some cases may acquire additional information about alternatives or aspects of the alternatives from the external environment. Bettman [1] indicates that information search generally begins with internal search, with memory examined for relevant information. If the information is insufficient or conflicting, external search for information starts.

Internal search may lead to new knowledge by combining or reorganizing stored knowledge elements. Largely due to the measurement problems involved [1], research on internal search is relatively scarce [2]. Much more research has been performed on external search for information. Here, we will elaborate on this topic.

Engel and Blackwell [3] state that external search represents a motivated and completely voluntary decision to seek new information. Research on external search for information has, implicitly or explicitly, used a cost-benefit framework derived from economics. The cost-benefit framework is based on the notion that in many decision making situations information is a means to an end. Information is used, e.g., to direct an individual to behavioral alternatives that mitigate a certain drive (hunger, thirst, pain) [4]. Sometimes information is gathered because of its potential usefulness in future decision making or because it may allow a better evaluation of the behavioral alternative actually chosen. In these contexts, gathering information is instrumental and leads to certain costs, whether financial costs (money) or behavioral costs (time, mental and physical effort) [5]. The benefits of the information might include an increased satisfaction about the actual choice or feelings such as that one did a thorough job.
Marschak [6] and Stigler [7] suggested that individuals will continue to gather information until the marginal costs of the search exceed the expected benefits. Research supports this suggestion [see, e.g., 8].
Confronted with a choice between specific alternatives or after a decision has been made, individuals differ largely in the amount of external search for information [9]. This has led to research on the determinants of external search. Some authors have provided categorizations of these determinants [see e.g., 1, 2, 8, 10]. A central place in these categoriza- is taken by individual difference factors.

3. INDIVIDUAL DIFFERENCE FACTORS AND EXTERNAL SEARCH

Demographic characteristics have been shown to be related to external search behavior. For instance, Katona and Mueller [11] found that income is positively, though not linearly, related to external search for durables. Newman and Staelin [12] found that education was positively related to external search, with consumers less than high school education searching the least. They also found that women were more likely to search for information about major durables than men.

Decision-specific person variables are also related to external search. After studying the determinants of external search for information about automobiles Punj and Staelin [8] concluded that prior relevant knowledge was the most important factor in search activity; those who had the least need for the external information conducted the least amount of search. Moore and Lehmann [2] reached a similar conclusion. Katona and Mueller [11] found that an individual difference factor labelled as 'fun of shopping' waspositively related to deliberation and external information search prior to the actual purchase of consumer durables. 'Highly circumspect decision making as well as active information seeking were more likely to occur among families who liked to shop around than among those who preferred to arrive at a quick decision' [11, p.66]. Other decision-specific person variables related to external search include product class importance [13, 14] and shopping style [2].

In most global personality variables categorizations of the determinants of external search take a central position. In only a few studies the hypothesized relationships have actually been studied empirically. In some studies the relationship between intelligence and external search has been analyzed. The results of these analyses are not always clear cut and consistent [15]. Green [16] e.g., did not find a relationship between intelligence and information sensitivity. Moore and Lehmann (1980) found that intelligence, as indicated by GMAT-scores, was negatively and significantly related to total search and to the number of attributes searched. Malhotra [15] critiqued this study questioning whether GMAT-scores actually measure intelligence. The relationship between other global personality variables and external search has hardly been studied.

4. NEED FOR COGNITION

Both in internal and in external search for information thinking is involved. Therefore, it can be expected that interpersonal difference factors influencing the amount of thinking will also affect the search for information. Many authors have thought about such determinants of thinking. Freud [17] postulated that under certain conditions individuals could develop a generalized and stable drive to know or to research ('der Wiss- oder Forschertrieb'). Analyzing the factors underlying the amount of thinking, Cattell [18] found an individual difference factor, labelled as 'exploration', that is represented, e.g., in desires to read books, newspapers and magazines, to know more about science and to learn more about mechanical and electrical gadgets. Others have found similar factors (e.g., Dollard and Miller [19]: the drive of being oriented, Guilford [20]: sensitivity to problems, Berlyne [4]: epistemic curiosity).

Cohen, Stotland and Wolfe [21] postulated a global personality characteristic defined as: 'a need to experience an integrated and meaningful world'. Although the characteristic refers to a tendency, it was labelled as the need for cognition. In their research, Cohen et al. focused on the tension reduction benefits of information search. Unfortunately, the assessment instrument to measure individual differences in need for cognition was never described in detail or published. Sparked by Cohen's work, Cacioppo and Petty [22] reconceptualized the need for cognition concept and developed a new assessment instrument. In their conceptualization the focus is more on the intrinsic enjoyment of thinking. Cacioppo and Petty (1982) define need for cognition as 'the tendency of individuals to engage in and enjoy cognitive endeavors'. In a series of studies they constructed and validated a scale containing 34 items. Results of Principal Components Analyses indicate that one dimension underlies the scale. No sex differences in need for cognition were found. The relationship between need for cognition and test anxiety, social desirability and intelligence was found to be weak or non existent [22, study 2 and 3]. The effect of need for cognition has been studied in a number of contexts. E.g., Cacioppo, Petty and Morris [23] found that individuals with a high need for cognition tend to base their attitude more on a careful consideration of the arguments in a persuasive message than individuals low in need for cognition.

Other research shows that need for cognition moderates the belief-attitude-behavior relationship. E.g., Pieters, Petty and Haugtvedt [24] found that the relationship between the expected consequences of participating in an energy saving program and the attitude towards participating was stronger for individuals high in need for cognition than for individuals low in need for cognition. Cacioppo, Petty, Kao and Rodriguez [25] found that individuals who differed in need for cognition also differed in the extent to which their attitudes predicted their voting intentions and subsequent reports of voting behavior. Attitudes towards the Presidential candidates during the 1984 electoral campaign in the U.S. predicted voting intentions and behavior better for individuals who were high than low in need for cognition.

To date, the relationship between need for cognition and external search for information is less well documented. The results of some studies do make such a relationship likely. Ferguson, Chung and Weigold [26] found that high need for cognition subjects tend to have greater exposure to the mass media. Cacioppo et al. [25] found that high need for cognition subjects tend to be more informed about social issues. Ahlering and McClure [27] reported that individuals high in need for cognition were more likely to intend to watch the 1984 Presidential debates than individuals low in need for cognition.

5. HYPOTHESES

In the Netherlands two nuclear power stations are in operation. During the preceding years there has been an extensive and often furious discussion about the advantages and disadvantages of using nuclear energy to generate electricity. The issue has received much media coverage. Research shows that, in general, attitudes towards nuclear power have become stabilized in the Netherlands [28].

The current study was performed to pursue several hypotheses. The main hypothesis concerned the use of and desire for external information about using nuclear energy for the generation of electricity. It was expected that individuals high in need for cognition would read more in the newspapers about nuclear energy than individuals low in need for cognition. It was also expected that individuals high in need for cognition would desire more external information, both about the advantages and the disadvantages of using nuclear energy for the generation of electricity, than individuals low in need for cognition.

A second hypothesis concerned the effect of need for cognition on the link between individuals' beliefs, attitudes and intentions. On the basis of the results of prior research, it was expected that the relationship between beliefs, attitudes and intentions would be stronger for individuals high than low in need for cognition.

6. METHOD

6.1. Subjects

The study was performed in the fall of 1985. Two groups of subjects participated in the study. The two groups differed in a number of socio-demographic characteristics. Group 1 comprised of 87 participants in an adult education plan in the city of The Hague in the Netherlands. All participants had a low educational level (unfinished high school or less). Their age varied between 18 and 67 years (mean age was 33 years). The group comprised of 76 males and 11 females. Group 2 comprised of 253 students enrolled in introductory psychology courses at the University of Leiden in the Netherlands. The age of the subjects varied between 18 and 47 years (mean age was 24). The group comprised of 87 males and 165 females. One person did not indicate his or her sexe. By incorporating these two groups the robustness of the results of the analyses could be investigated. Differences between group 1 and group 2 were not studied, since the emphasis was on differences <u>between</u> subjects <u>within</u> groups. A questionnaire was administered to each group of subjects during regular classroom hours.

6.2. Questionnaire

Recently, Cacioppo, Petty and Kao [29] published an abridged version of the original 34 item need for cognition scale. The 18 items of this scale were translated into Dutch. All items were accompanied by 5-point Likert scales ranging from 'totally disagree' (1) to 'totally agree' (5). The need for cognition scale was included in a questionnaire on 'the use of energy sources for the generation of electricity'. The questionnaire also contained questions on beliefs, attitudes and intentions, on the desire for external information and on reading behavior. The belief, attitude and intention items were selected from a questionnaire that had been used in a nation wide study on attitudes towards energy sources [28]. The five beliefs representing best the main clusters of beliefs that appeared in the mentioned study were included in the questionnaire. Beliefs were measured on 9-point scales ranging from 'this is totally unlikely' (0) to 'this is sure to happen' (8). The attitude was measured on a 9-point bi-polar scale ranging from 'very negative' (0) to 'very positive' (8) (about using nuclear energy for the large scale generation of electricity). Three behavioral intentions were asked: 1. signing a petition against nuclear energy, 2. demonstrating against nuclear energy and 3. supporting nuclear energy in conversations. These three items represented main clusters of behavioral intentions in the afore mentioned study. The three intention items were accompanied by seven-point Likert scales ranging from 'totally disagree' (0) to 'totally agree' (6). Six items on the desire for external information about nuclear energy were formulated: 1. the probability of a disaster with a nuclear power plant, 2. the price of electricity, 3. harmful consequences of nuclear energy for the physical health of citizens and for the natural environment, 4. the positive consequences on the economy, 5. consequences on technological developments, 6. negative consequences on the economy. The desire for information items were accompanied by 6-point scales ranging from 'not at all' (0) to 'very much' (5). Also, subjects were asked how often they read articles about nuclear energy that appeared in the newspapers. This item was accompanied by a 4-

point scale ranging from 'never' (0) to 'always' (3).

7. RESULTS

7.1. Scale construction

The need for cognition scale used here was a translated version of the Cacioppo et al. [29] scale. Prior to testing the hypotheses, the overall validity of the Dutch scale was analyzed. For group 1 a Principal Components Analysis (PCA) was performed on the 18 items in the need for cognition scale. As expected, one component, explaining 24.8% of the common variance, dominated the solution (eigenvalue was 4.46). A second component explained only 10.9% of the variance (eigenvalue was 1.97). These results compare well to the findings in the Cacioppo and Petty [22] study. Two criteria were used to select items to be included in the final need for cognition scale. Items were selected that had a loading on the first component higher than .30, and an item-total correlation significant at the .1% level. On the basis of these two criteria three items were excluded from the scale. These three items were not different from the other items in general content. A PCA performed on the remaining 15 items again revealed a one component structure (eigenvalue 4.59, 30.6% of the common variance explained). Cronbach's alpha of the 15-item scale was .83. In group 2, the 15 items all correlated significantly with the total scale at the .1% level. After reverse coding the items that were worded negatively, the scores on the 15 items were summed. This sum score was divided by 15 to form a need for cognition index ranging from 1, a very low need for cognition, to 5, a very high need for cognition. Scale construction is described more in depth in Pieters, Verplanken en Modde [30].

7.2. Differences between individuals low and high in need for cognition

In order to compare individuals low and high in need for cognition, both group 1 and group 2 were split on the .33 and .67 percentiles of the need for cognition scale. The lower 33% (low need for cognition) and the upper 33% (high need for cognition) were included in the subsequent analyses. Both for group 1 and 2, individuals low and high in need for cognition were compared on their desire for external information and actual reading behavior. (Group 1: $N_{low} = 29$, $N_{high} = 30$; Group 2: $N_{low} = 90$, $N_{high} = 89$.). Differences were analyzed using Student t-tests. The results of the analyses are presented in table 1.
Both in group 1 and in group 2, individuals low and high in need for cognition differ to a large extent in their actual reading behavior and in their desire for external information about aspects of using nuclear energy for the generation of electricity. Although, individuals low and high in need for cognition in group 2, do not differ, statistically significant in three of the six aspects, the differences are in the expected direction.

Next, differences in the overall desire for external information were analyzed. Both for group 1 and group 2 a PCA was performed on the six desire for external information items. For group 1, the first component in the solution explained 61.6% of the variance (eigenvalue was 3.69). For group 2, the first component explained 61.0% of the variance (eigenvalue was 3.66). In both groups Cronbach's alpha for the six desire for information items was .87. The scores on the six items were summed and the resulting sum score was divided by six to form a desire for information index. Differences in the desire for information index were analyzed using t-tests. Both in group 1 and in group 2, individuals low and high in need for cognition differed significantly in the expected direction. The t-value for differences in group 1 was -3.26 (df = 46, significant at the .1% level). The t-value in group 2 was -3.33 (df = 161, significant at the .1% level). Overall, individuals high in need for cognition have a stronger desire for external information about the advantages and the disadvantages of using nuclear energy for the large scale generation of electricity. Individuals low and high in need for cognition did not differ in any of the beliefs and intentions, nor in the attitude. This result is stable; it is obtained both for group 1 and for group 2.

To investigate the moderating effect of need for cognition on the belief-attitude-intention relationship, multiple regression analyses were performed. In the analysis the attitude acted as the criterion and the five beliefs as the predictors. For group 1 and 2 the analyses were performed separately for individuals low and high in need for cognition. Also, the correlation between the attitude and each of the three behavioral intentions was calculated. Differences between individuals low and high in need for cognition were tested for significance after a Fisher's Z_r transformation of the correlations. The results of the analyses are presented in table 2.

For group 1, two of the three differences in the correlations of the attitude with the intentions are in the expected direction. Only, the difference in the correlations was statistically significant. Although neither of the two correlations is significantly different from zero, the correlations are different from each other. Since the greater the positivity of the correlation, the greater the attitude-intention consistency, the significant difference between the correlations indicates that individuals high in need for cognition showed greater attitude-intention consistency than individuals low in need for cognition.

The overall results for group 1 confirm the second hypothesis partially. In group 2 all differences in correlations were in the expected direction; only the difference in the correlation of the beliefs with the attitude was statistically significant. The second hypothesis can be confirmed on this aspect.

8. DISCUSSION

The Dutch version of the 18-item need for cognition scale performed well in the present study. Principal Components Analyses revealed that the scale was dominated by one component. As in prior research no differences in need for cognition between sexes were found. In group 1, the mean values of the need for cognition scale for males and females were respectively 3.23 and 3.52 (t-value = -1.56, df = 82, not significant). In group 2, the mean values were respectively 3.53 for males and 3.46 for females (t-value =1.18, df = 240, not significant).

Strong support was found for the hypothesis that individuals high in need for cognition read more in the newspapers about nuclear energy and desire more external information about all the specific advantages and disadvantages of using nuclear energy than individuals low in need for cognition.

This effect is not due to differences in attitudes between individuals low and high in need for cognition. The analyses showed that individuals differing in need for cognition did not differ in beliefs, attitudes and intentions. Need for cognition is defined as a tendency 'to engage in and enjoy effortful cognitive endeavors' [31, p.151]. The results of the present study indicate that some individuals (those high in need for cognition) think more and enjoy to think more about the specific advantages and disadvantages of using nuclear energy for the generation of electricity, than other individuals (those low in need for cognition). Such behavior can explain part of the knowledge gap [32]. Some individuals, that already have more information than others, seem to acquire and desire more additional specific information, thus widening the gap between the informed and the uninformed in society.

Also, the moderating effect of need for cognition on the relationships between beliefs, attitudes and intentions was found. Individuals in group 2 replicate Pieters, Petty and Haugtvedt (1986) in that the beliefs-attitude correlation is larger for individuals high than low in need for cognition. Individuals in group 1 partially replicate Cacioppo, Petty, Kao and Rodriguez (in press) in that the attitude-intention correlation is larger for individuals high than low in need for cognition. However, the moderating effect of need for cognition is less than expected. It was only found for one of the three attitude-intention relationships. Several factors may explain this. The first factor concerns the reliability and validity of the Dutch version of the need for cognition scale. Although the main results are as hypothesized, it is possible that the translated need for cognition scale is not a valid or reliable indicator of the need for cognition construct.
A second factor concerns the personal relevance of the issue under study and the effects of personal relevance. It is well documented [see, e.g., 31] that the correlations between beliefs, attitudes, intentions and behavior are higher under conditions of high personal relevance than under conditions of low personal relevance. Research shows that the use of nuclear energy for the generation of electricity is an issue of high personal relevance in the Netherlands [28]. In general, the moderate to strong correlations between beliefs, attitudes and intentions in the present study illustrate the personal relevance of the issue. Therefore, it is possible that a ceiling effect was operating on some of the correlations here. Such an effect may have attenuated the effect due to differences in need for cognition.
Further research with the Dutch need for cognition scale should focus on its construct and predictive validity. In such research several issues differing in personal relevance could be included.

Research on external search for information has used a cost-benefit framework derived from economics. According to this viewpoint individuals will continue to gather information until the marginal costs of search exceed the expected marginal benefits. The costs of search comprise financial and behavioral costs. Behavioral costs include time, mental and physical costs. Verhallen and Pieters [5] define perceived cost as the price (outlay) divided by the budget. Identical outlays for two acts are perceived as different costs if the budgets reserved for the two acts are different. A certain outlay can be perceived as a high cost if the budget reserved was small, and as a low cost if the budget reserved was large. Need for cognition can be conceived as one of the prime determinants of the mental budget that individuals reserve for activities. Individuals high in need for cognition will generally reserve more of their cognitive capacity than individuals low in need for cognition. Consequently, it can be hypothesized that a cognitive outlay for search activity will be perceived as a lower cost by individuals high in need for cognition than by individuals low in need for cognition. Individuals high in need for cognition will reach the point that the marginal costs of search exceed the marginal benefits later. From this viewpoint it is not unexpected that the results of studies equating intelligence to external search for information may be inconsistent. It is not solely the wealth of individuals that determines if an outlay is perceived as a high or a low cost. Costs are determined by wealth, outlays _and_ the budget reserved. More research to unravel the relationships between intelligence, need for cognition and search for information seems warranted.

Finally, we note that the results of the present study may have considerable relevance for the design of information and advertising campaigns. Our results suggest that the actual information search and desire for additional information may differ for individuals low and high in need for cognition, even if they do not differ in beliefs, attitudes and intentions concerning a certain issue. Changing the attitudes of high need for cognition individuals may require extensive information and argumentation, whereas changing the attitudes (and behavior) of low need for cognition individuals may require other measures (attractive endorsers, personal selling, etc.). Given the enormous amounts spent annually on information and advertising campaigns, and given the central position of interpersonal difference factors in categorizations of the determinants of external search, it is somewhat odd that only limited research attention is directed to empirically equating interpersonal differences factors to external search for information.
Information and advertising campaigns could be designed more effectively if the determinants of external search were more fully understood. Hopefully, the present study has contributed somewhat to such an understanding.

ACKNOWLEDGEMENTS

We would like to thank Jacqueline Modde and Richard Petty for their insightful comments on an earlier version.

REFERENCES

[1] Bettman, J.R. (1979)
An Information Processing Theory of Consumer Choice. Reading, Mass: Addison-Wesley.

[2] Moore, W.L. and D.R. Lehmann (1980)
Individual differences in search behavior for a nondurable. _Journal of Consumer Research_ _7_, 296-307.

[3] Engel, J. and R. Blackwell (1982)
Consumer Behavior (4th ed.). Hinsdale, Ill.: Dryden Press.

[4] Berlyne, D.E. (1960)
Conflict, Arousal and Curiosity. New York: McGraw-Hill.

[5] Verhallen, Th.M.M. and R.G.M. Pieters (1984)
Attitude theory and behavioral costs. Journal of Economic Psychology 5, 223-249.

[6] Marschak, J. (1954)
Towards an economic theory of organization and information. In: R.M. Thrally et al. (Eds.), Decision Processes. New York: Wiley.

[7] Stigler, G.J. (1961)
The economics of information. Journal of Political Economy 69, 213-225.

[8] Punj, G.N. and R. Staelin (1983)
A model of consumer information search behavior for new automobiles. Journal of Consumer Research 9, 366-380.

[9] Duncan, C.P. and R.W. Olshavski (1982)
External search: the role of consumer beliefs. Journal of Marketing Research 19, 32-43.

[10] Newman, J.W. (1977)
Consumer external search: amount and determinants. In: A.G. Woodside et al. (Eds.), Consumer and Industrial Buyer Behavior. Amsterdam: North Holland Publishing.

[11] Katona, G. and E. Mueller (1954)
A study of purchase decisions. In: L.H. Clark (Ed.), Consumer Behavior: the Dynamics of Consumer Reaction. New York: New York University Press.

[12] Newman, J.W. and R. Staelin (1972)
Prepurchase information seeking for new cars and major household appliances. Journal of Marketing Research 9, 249-257.

[13] Houston, M.J. and M.L. Rothschild (1978)
A paradigm for research on consumer involvement. Working paper. Madison: University of Wisconsin.

[14] Bloch, P.H. (1981)
An exploration into the scaling of consumers' involvement with a product class. In: K.B. Monroe (Ed.), Advances in Consumer Research 8. Ann Arbor: Association for Consumer Research.

[15] Malhotra, N.K. (1983)
On 'individual differences in search behavior for a nondurable'. Journal of Consumer Research 10, 125-131.

[16] Green, P. (1966)
Consumer use of information. In: J.W. Newman (Ed.), On Knowing the Consumer. New York: Wiley.

[17] Freud, S. (1905)
Drei Abhandlungen zur Sexualtheorie. Leipzig und Wien: Deuticke.

[18] Cattell, R.B. (1957)
Personality and Motivation Structure and Measurement. New York: World, Yonkers.

[19] Dollard, J. and N.E. Miller (1950)
Personality and Psychotherapy. New York: McGraw-Hill.

[20] Guilford, J.P. (1956)
The structure of intellect. Psychological Bulletin 53, 267-293.

[21] Cohen, A.R., E. Stotland and D.M. Wolfe (1955)
An experimental investigation of need for cognition. Journal of Abnormal and Social Psychology 51, 291-294.

[22] Cacioppo, J.T. and R.E. Petty (1982)
The need for cognition. Journal of Personality and Social Psychology 42, 116-131.

[23] Cacioppo, J.T., R.E. Petty and K.J. Morris (1983)
Effects of need for cognition on message evaluation, recall, and persuasion. Journal of Personality and Social Psychology 45, 805-818.

[24] Pieters, R.G.M., R.E. Petty and C. Haugtvedt (1986)
The external and moderating effect of need for cognition on attitude-belief and attitude-behavior consistency: A field study. Internal Report, Erasmus University, Rotterdam.

[25] Cacioppo, J.T., R.E. Petty, C.F. Kao and R. Rodriguez (in press)
Central and peripheral routes to persuasion: an individual difference perspective. Journal of Personality and Social Psychology.

[26] Ferguson, M., M. Chung and M. Weigold (1985)
Need for cognition medium dependency components of reliance and exposure. Presented at the International Communication Association Meeting, Honolulu, Hawaii.

[27] Ahlering, R. and K. McClure (1985)
Need for cognition, attitudes, and the 1984 presidential election. Presented at the meeting of the Midwestern Psychological Association, Chicago, Ill.

[28] Midden, C.J.H., D.D.L. Daamen and B. Verplanken (1984)
Personal attitudes towards large scale technologies. In: Linking Economics and Psychology, Proceedings of the 1984 IAREP colloquium. Tilburg: Tilburg University.

[29] Cacioppo, J.T., R.E. Petty and C.F. Kao (1984)
The efficient assessment of need for cognition. Journal of Personality Assessment 48, 306-307.

[30] Pieters, R.G.M., B. Verplanken and J.M. Modde (1986)
'Neiging tot nadenken': effecten op cognities, attitudes, intenties en informatiebehoefte. Under editorial review.

[31] Petty, R.E. and J.T. Cacioppo (1986)
The elaboration likelihood model of persuasion. In: L. Berkowitz (Ed.), Advances in Experimental Social Psychology 19. New York: Academic Press.

[32] Genova, B.K.L. and B.S. Greenberg (1979)
Interests in use and the knowledge gap. Public Opinion Quarterly 43, 79-91.

TABLE 1: Differences in means between individuals low and high in need for cognition: The results for group 1 and group 2

description	group 1 need for cognition		t-value(df)	sign.[1]	group 2 need for cognition		t-value (df)	sign.
	low	high			low	high		
search and desire for external information:								
- reading in the newspapers about nuclear energy	1.12	1.70	-2.48 (47)	**	1.47	1.89	-3.79 (162)	***
- probability of a nuclear disaster	1.68	2.61	-3.00 (46)	**	1.93	2.19	-1.51 (160)	
- price of electricity	1.80	2.65	-2.52 (46)	**	1.53	1.79	-1.64 (159)	
- harmful consequences for citizens and the environment	2.32	2.91	-1.72 (46)	*	2.48	2.72	-1.44 (161)	
- positive consequences on the economy	1.76	2.48	-2.29 (46)	*	1.67	2.05	-2.23 (161)	*
- consequences on technological development	2.12	2.87	-2.25 (46)	*	1.51	2.19	-4.10 (161)	***
- negative consequences on the economy	1.68	2.52	-2.41 (46)	**	1.52	2.20	-4.13 (161)	***
beliefs:								
- proliferation of nuclear weapons	3.71	3.30	.59 (45)		2.60	2.98	-1.19 (158)	
- serious consequences for the natural environment in general	4.29	5.02	-1.15 (45)		5.27	5.57	-.86 (159)	
- advantages for society in general	3.58	3.87	-.46 (45)		3.49	3.72	-.73 (159)	
- lower price of electricity	3.75	4.18	-.71 (44)		4.18	4.26	-.24 (156)	
- probability of a disaster contaminating an area of approx. 1400 square kilometers	4.38	4.00	.53 (45)		4.10	4.19	-.30 (159)	
attitude:								
- evaluation of using nuclear energy for large scale electricity generation	3.77	3.91	-.21 (47)		2.25	2.24	.05 (162)	
intentions:								
- signing a petition against	2.27	3.17	-1.60 (47)		3.39	3.45	-.18 (162)	
- demonstrating against	1.88	1.68	.39 (46)		2.61	2.84	-.73 (162)	
- supporting in conversations	1.81	2.17	-.82 (47)		1.92	2.04	-.44 (161)	

1) Asterisks denote significance levels: * = p .05 ** = p .01 *** = p .001; differences in desire for external information and reading in the newspapers are tested onetailed.

TABLE 2: Differences in correlations between individuals low and high in need for cognition: The results for group 1 and group 2

relationship between	group 1 need for cognition low	group 1 need for cognition high	Z_r	sign.[1)]	group 2 need for cognition low	group 2 need for cognition high	Z_r	sign.
- beliefs - attitude	.81	.77	.40		.66	.82	-2.24	*
- attitude - intention signing a petition against nuclear energy	-.31	.19	-1.89	*	.34	.41	-.53	
- attitude - intention demonstrating against nuclear energy	.59	.49	.47		.65	.75	-1.25	
- attitude - supporting nuclear energy in conversations	.31	.63	-1.49		.48	.55	-.66	

1) Differences in correlations are tested onetailed;
asterisks denote significance levels: * = p .05, ** = p .01, *** = p .001

Part Eleven
Tax Evasion

SOCIAL COMPARISON AND TAX EVASION IN A SHOP SIMULATION

Paul Webley, Henry Robben* and Ira Morris

Department of Psychology, University of Exeter
*Now at the Faculty of Law, Erasmus University Rotterdam

In recent years various aspects of tax evasion have been investigated experimentally. This paper reports two experiments which have employed this approach using members of the general public as subjects. In the first, the effects of social comparison, inequity, and audit occurrence were investigated. Neither of the social comparison situations (personal and categorical) had a significant effect, but the interaction between equity and social comparison came close to significance. In the second larger study social comparison was investigated in more detail but still no significant effects were found. Participants in the second study also completed a set of questionnaires based on the work of Hessing and Elffers [1]. Analysis of these demonstrated that tax evasion in the shop simulation was correlated with 'central' attitudes (e.g. alienation) but not the peripheral attitudes, a pattern similar to that found by Hessing and Elffers for documented tax evasion. It is concluded that experimental investigations of tax evasion have a useful role to play.

INTRODUCTION

Tax evasion has been of considerable interest to economists and psychologists for a number of years and a variety of investigative methods have been used. But recently, Hessing and Elffers [1] have cast doubt on the validity of studies which use self-reported tax evasion as a dependent measure. With self-reports, self-presentational concerns tend to predominate and so the incidence of socially proscribed behaviours such as tax evasion is underestimated. Their own approach, that of obtaining information about documented tax evasion [2] has much to commend it, but it is extremely time consuming and impossible to implement without exceptional co-operation from the revenue authorities. Experimental studies of tax evasion are a potentially valuable alternative, provided some of the problems of ecological validity can be overcome.

This paper describes two such studies, the first that have used members of the general public as subjects. Both investigate social comparison processes. In addition, Study 1 looks at the effect of equity and audit history, and Study 2 combines an experimental approach with the use of questionnaires to explore the determinants of evasion in a simulation and provide a check on ecological validity.

Social surveys have shown that tax evasion is associated with feelings of inequity [3] [4]. The idea behind this is that the perception of differences in tax treatment between oneself and another leads to feelings of unfairness and that these feelings give rise to behaviour which will restore an equitable relationship. Clearly we cannot be sure from survey work whether the reported feelings of inequity are mere rationalisations of tax evasion behaviour or actual determinants of it. The experimental evidence is equivocal. Spicer and Becker [5] demonstrated that inequitable fiscal treatment to one's disadvantage led to a higher percentage of taxes evaded and a favourable treatment had the opposite effect. However, Webley, Morris & Amstutz [6], in a more realistic and less transparent simulation, failed to replicate this effect.

Study 1 explores this issue further. Implicit in the idea of equity is the notion of comparing the position of other people with one's own. In Webley et al.'s study this notion was incorporated by investigating the effect of feed-back on performance. Although Webley et al. did not describe it as such, this is in fact a social comparison situation. Rijsman [7] argues that in these situations people are motivated to discriminate themselves in a positive sense from their competitors. According to Rijsman, a comparison on an individual level leads to different changes in performance than one on a categorical or group level. Empirically, on an individual level those who were told that they were in a superior position made little effort to improve their position further, whereas those in the inferior and equal conditions tried to improve their performance. On a categorical level, the picture reverses, that is, changes in performance are largest for the subjects in the superior condition. Since no differences are theoretically expected in the inferior and equal conditions only the latter and a superior condition are used in Study 1, along with a straightforward equity manipulation.

Study 2 investigates social comparison further by looking at all three levels of comparison (superior, equal and inferior). More crucially, it uses the work of Hessing and Elffers [1] as a basis for exploring the ecological validity of experimental studies of tax evasion. Briefly, Hessing and Elffers identified two groups of individuals; one comprising individuals who had been charged with evading taxes and whose cases had been settled, the other comprising individuals who had been carefully audited and found to have made accurate tax returns. The individuals were interviewed and a number of measures of attitudes, subjective norms and what Hessing and Elffers call 'central' attitudes obtained, in addition to answers about past tax evasion behaviour. Their results showed that only attitudes and subjective norms were correlated with self-reported tax evasion and that only 'central' attitude measures (alienation, tolerance of illegal behaviour, competitive orientation) correlated with documented tax evasion. Hessing and Elffers conclude, among other things, that future research must include data gathered from sources other than self-report. If tax evasion found in an experimental setting has the same predictors as documented tax evasion, then simulations have an important role to play in understanding this behaviour. Study 2 investigates this question.

STUDY 1: THE EFFECTS OF INEQUITY AND SOCIAL COMPARISON ON EVASION

Method

Subjects: Forty-eight members of the general public participated. Subjects were tested in many batches, one or two at a time at several locations. All subjects received refreshment and £ 1 for their trouble. Most were contacted initially by confederates.

Design: Four variables were investigated: equity (three levels), social comparison type (personal, categorical), nature of comparison (equal, superior) and audit occurrence (periods 1, 4, 7 and 11). The dependant measures were the overall percentage of income underdeclared and the number of periods in which income was underdeclared.

In the equity conditions, subjects were told that they would all receive a tax free starter's allowance of £ 2,200. However, in the negative inequity condition they were told that the average allowance was £ 3,600, in the equity condition that the average allowance was the same as theirs and in the positive inequity condition that the average allowance was £ 800. To make this information more salient to the participants, the allowance was continued in the second and third years. Although the amounts received decreased over the years, their position relative to the average allowance did not change.

In the personal social comparison conditions, participants were told that their performance would be compared with that of their direct competitor, Paul's. In the categorical social comparison conditions the performance of the co-operative to which individuals had been assigned was compared with that of another co-operative. These comparisons were in fact fictitious. Participants were told that they had either performed as well as or better than the other person / group with which they were being compared.

Subjects were informed that random audits would take place but no explicit information was given about the frequency of audits. Each subject was audited once. Audits took place either in the 1st, 4th, 7th or 11th period.

Procedure: The first part of the study consisted of the shop simulation, which on average took about 40 minutes. Subjects subsequently completed two brief questionnaires.

After some introductory information on how to operate the computer, subjects read the following instructions from the screen (they were also given a written version for reference).

> 'This is a simulation produced by Robben's Business Research to investigate behaviour in small businesses. You are to imagine that you set yourself up as a shopkeeper. You will have to make a series of decisions over a three-year period. For example, you will have to decide about the selling price of your products (soft-drinks and spirits), whether you want to buy any additional information, and whether to advertise or not. You will also have to report your income and pay tax on the amount reported. As a governmental subsidy, you will receive a tax free starter's allowance of £ 2,200 in the first year of your business. Every participant will receive an allowance, which is on average £ EQ. (The value of EQ obviously varied according to condition.)
>
> Your purpose in this simulation is to manage your business as successfully as possible.
>
> Your performance will be compared with that of your direct competitor called Paul's. The owner of that shop is in fact another participant in this simulation. The data of this person were collected on an earlier occasion. All the relevant data are stored in this computer so they can easily be compared with yours. (Obviously in the categorical comparison condition this paragraph referred to co-operatives.)
>
> Each year is divided into four quarters: Spring, Summer, Autumn and Winter. Each quarter you will be asked to do four things. These are
>
> 1. decide whether or not you want to buy information, and if so, what kind.
> 2. decide whether or not you want to advertise for that quarter, and if so, how much you will spend;
> 3. set your prices for the products you sell in that quarter;

4. make a tax return.

Information

Information is of six kinds and costs £ 50 per bit. You may buy only one bit of information per quarter. The following information is available:
1. market research on consumers.
2. forecasts of likely tax changes.
3. forecasts of trends in the market.
4. agency research on the effectiveness of advertising.
5. research on the seasonal effects on sales.
6. pricing in the retail business.

Advertising

Advertising costs £ 100 per unit. You may buy up to five units per quarter.

Prices

You may charge any price per product that you wish, but at high prices you will get too little custom, and at low prices you cannot cope with the demand.
In line with this, we have set a minimum and a maximum price for each product. Your selling price has to be set within that range.

Taxation

At the end of each quarter your total receipts will be calculated. You will be asked to report your taxable income for that quarter (receipts minus advertising and information costs). The tax rate during the simulation will be 35%. From time to time, audits will be conducted according to a random sample. If you underreported income then, for this period only, you will have to pay the amount of tax due plus a penalty. The maximum penalty is completely up to the discretion of the tax inspector.

The simulation is about to start. For your convenience, we summarise the different decisions you have to make in each quarter. First, you have to decide whether you want to buy information. Second, you have to decide whether you want to advertise or not. Third, you have to set your selling prices. Fourth, you will be asked to make a tax return. You can always refer to the written instructions if you need to.'

In each period subjects would be asked to make the four decisions mentioned above. So, for example, in one period a subject might pay for information about seasonal effects on sales, buy 2 units of advertising (at £ 80 a unit) and then set his price for soft-drinks at 30p and spirits at £ 6.

The following would then be displayed on the screen.

These are the results of your sales in the summer of year 3:

Product line	Your profit	Items sold	Profits per item
Soft-drinks	£ 2,000	10.000	£ 0.20
Spirits	£ 1,500	750	£ 2.00

It is year 3, summer.
Your balance sheet this summer is as follows:

Total profits	£ 3,500
Advertising costs	£ 160
Information costs	£ 50
Taxable income	£ 3,290

After the subjects had made their income declaration, there was a pause. The subject was then informed whether he had been audited or not, about his gross income, net income and total fines to date and then the next period began.

Results

The data were analysed using two three-way analyses of variance. For the percentage of income underdeclared there were no significant results. For frequency of underdeclaring the interaction between equity condition and type of comparison (personal, categorical) came close to significance ($F = 3.04$, d.f. = 2,36, critical value of $F = 3.32$) (see table 1a).

Table 1a

1A Mean number of periods (out of 12) that income was underdeclared as a function of equity and social comparison.

		Equity condition		
		Negative	Neutral	Positive
Personal Social Comparison	Equal	7.5	8.75	2.75
	Superior	9.0	8.5	2.25
	Average	8.25	8.63	2.5
Categorical Social Comparison	Equal	7.0	7.25	9.0
	Superior	3.0	3.75	5.25
	Average	5.0	5.50	7.13

To explore the effects of being audited, pre and post audit income declarations were compared using t-tests. No significant differences were found. A 2 x 3 x 4 mixed analysis of variance with type of comparison (2 levels) and audit occurrence (4 levels) as between group factors and year (3 levels) as a within groups factors found no significant effects for frequency of underdeclaring, although being audited in year 1 did appear to result in less evasion (see table 2).

Table 1b

1B Mean percentage of income underdeclared as a function of equity and social comparison.

		Equity condition		
		Negative	Neutral	Positive
Personal Social Comparison	Equal	13.58	27.46	4.49
	Superior	42.10	31.94	3.24
	Average	27.84	29.70	3.87
Categorical Social Comparison	Equal	22.77	22.00	17.36
	Superior	5.48	4.06	7.91
	Average	14.13	13.03	12.64

Table 2

Mean number of periods (out of 4) that income was underdeclared as a function of year and audit occurrence.

	Period in which audit occurred			
	1	4	7	11
Year 1	1.25	2.33	2.08	2.08
2	0.75	2.16	2.75	2.41
3	1.00	2.16	2.91	2.25

Discussion

The results of this experiment suggest that equity may not influence tax evasion, and is in line with Webley et al.'s [6] findings. This means that the survey and experimental evidence on equity and tax evasion do not match. This is actually encouraging, since Hessing and Elffers [1] found that equity of taxes was only correlated with self-reported evasion and not actual documented evasion. However, part of the reasons for failing to find an effect of equity is undoubtedly due to the difficulty of inducing feelings of inequity experimentally. Only ten subjects noticed a difference between their allowance and the average allowance and most subjects said they paid little attention to the information about allowances. So the equity variable clearly was not salient enough.

Social comparison had no significant effect. This cannot be attributed to weak manipulations. In the post-experimental questionnaire most subjects indicated that the comparison of their performance with others was not very important although some did say it evoked competitive feelings in them.

Perhaps the more important aspect of this study was that it was carried out on a non-student sample and so paved the way to the second study, which examined the ecological validity of experimental studies of evasion.

STUDY 2: THE CORRELATES OF TAX EVASION IN AN EXPERIMENTAL SETTING

Method

Subjects: Seventy-two members of the general public took part. Initially three hundred houses in a middle-class area of Exeter were leafleted inviting people to help in a study of small business behaviour. Subsequently, all these houses were visited by the third author to encourage participation. Subjects were tested individually in a room in one of the University's Halls of Residence. Subjects were rewarded with bottles of wine distributed after the study was completed.
Design: Two variables were investigated experimentally: social comparison type (personal, categorical) and nature of the comparison (inferior, equal, superior). In addition, questionnaires based on those used by Elffers, Vrooman and Hessing [2] were sent out two to three months after the experiment had been completed to obtain attitude, social norm and personality measures.
Procedure: The computer simulation was almost identical to Study 1 with the addition of an inferior social comparison condition. The questionnaire was sent to all 72 subjects - 65 returned completed questionnaires, a response rate of 90%. The questionnaire was split into three parts. The first combined a measure of alienation based on Srole's [8] scale (i.e. 'Most people really don't care what happens to the next fellow') with ten items drawn from Rundquist and Sletto's [9] measure of attitudes towards the law (e.g. 'Court decisions are almost always just'). The nineteen statements were presented in a strongly agree - strongly disagree format with five response categories. The second comprised three words/phrases which had to be rated on five bipolar adjectives drawn from the evaluative factor of the semantic differential. The words/phrases were 'competition', 'making false deductions on a tax return' and 'concealing income on a tax return'. The final part measured self-reported tax evasion ('Did you, when filling in your 1983/4 tax form understate your income or report any unwarranted deductions?') and perceived social support for tax evasion.

Results

The data from the simulation were analysed using a 2 x 2 x 3 mixed analysis of variance with type of comparison (2 types), nature of comparison (3 levels) as between groups factors and year (1, 2 or 3) as a within groups factor. Neither for the percentage of income underdeclared nor for the frequency of underdeclaring were there any significant results (see table 3).

Table 3
Mean number of periods (out of 12) that income was underdeclared as a function of type and nature of social comparison.

	Nature of comparison		
	Inferior	Equal	Superior
Personal Social Comparison	6.16	2.08	3.33
Categorical Social Comparison	2.75	4.25	2.25

The data from the questionnaires were more rewarding. Table 4 shows the correlations between the various measures and frequency of underreporting during the simulation. Two of the 'central' attitude measures were significantly correlated with simulated evasion. Only 5 individuals reported evading tax in either or both of the two previous years, so no correlations with self-reported tax evasion are shown.

Table 4

Correlations between tax evasion during the simulation and measures of attitudes, subjective norms and personality attributes.

Psychological Variables	Number of periods in which tax was evaded
Attitudes	
Underreporting income	0.052
False deductions	0.099
Subjective norms	
Social support	0.229
Personality attributes	
Alienation	0.284*
Attitudes towards law	-0.259*
Competitiveness	-0.114

Note: N=65; *p < .05

Discussion

Although the results from the simulation were non-significant, the pattern of results is very similar to those of Study 1. This suggests that a larger study might be able to demonstrate the effect of social comparison.

It was notable that the level of evasion in this and the previous study was much lower than in previous simulations (43 of the 72 subjects were completely honest). This is probably due to the fact that the tax declaration was embedded in a shop simulation (and so the purpose of the experiment was not obvious) and, that being members of the general public, subjects took the study more seriously than students tend to. Such a comparatively high rate of honesty will lessen the impact of the social variables that were manipulated. It appears that some subjects would remain honest regardless of their relative standing.

That the measures which predict tax evasion in the simulation are similar to those found to predict or not predict documented tax evasion [1] is extremely encouraging and lends credence to simulation studies. The one 'central' attitude variable which did not correlate significantly was rating of 'competition'. Respondents found this section of the questionnaire the most difficult to fill in, and many complained about the instructions for this part. So the lack of significance here is perhaps understandable. This suggests that experimental investigations of tax evasion can make a valuable contribution in that legal complexities are avoided and experimental control can be exercised. It is important to bear in mind however, that experimental studies must have their purpose disguised and elicit serious behaviour from subjects if the weaknesses associated with self-report are to be avoided.

Conclusions

Webley and Halstead [10], in reviewing experimental studies, concluded that 'for simulations to make a significant contribution to our understanding of tax evasion they must be considerably more sophisticated'. We believe that now simulations are good enough to be more widely used, and have a role to play in teasing out the causes of tax evasion. One problem is that embedding tax declarations in a shop or business simulation makes the task extremely time consuming. In a pilot version of the shop simulation subjects typically took over an hour to finish. Nonetheless, embedding tax declarations in this way is worthwhile because a small amount of good quality information is more valuable than a large amount of poor quality information.
The obvious next step is to devise a programme of research which uses a variety of methods to investigate tax evasion. In particular, a simulation study which used a group of known tax evaders would be informative.

REFERENCES

[1] Hessing, D.J. & H. Elffers, Economic man or social man?: A social orientation model for individual behavior in social dilemmas. In H. Brandstätter and E. Kirchler (eds.) Economic Psychology. Linz: Trauner, 1985.

[2] Elffers, H., J.C. Vrooman and D.J. Hessing, Non-experimental research in economic psychology: A field study of fiscal behavior. In H. Brandstätter and E. Kirchler (eds.) Economic Psychology. Linz: Trauner, 1985.

[3] Spicer, M.W. & S.B. Lundstedt, Understanding tax evasion. Public Finance, 31, 295-305, 1976.

[4] Wärneryd, K-E. & B. Walerud, Taxes and economic behaviour: Some interview data on tax evasion in Sweden. Journal of Economic Psychology, 2, 187-211, 1982.

[5] Spicer, M.W. & L.A. Becker, Fiscal inequity and tax evasion: An experimental approach. National Tax Journal, 33, 171-175, 1980.

[6] Webley, P., I. Morris, & F. Amstutz, Tax evasion during a small business simulation. In H. Brandstätter and E. Kirchler (eds.), Economic Psychology, Linz: Trauner, 1985.

[7] Rijsman, J.B., The dynamics of social competition in personal and social comparison situations. In W. Doise and S. Moscovici (eds.), Current issues in European social psychology, Cambridge: CUP, 1983.

[8] Srole, L., Social integration and certain corollaries. American Sociological Review, 21, 709-716, 1956.

[9] Rundquist, E.A. & R.F. Sletto, Personality in the depression. Minneapolis: University of Minnesota Press, 1936.

[10] Webley, P. & S. Halstead, Tax evasion on the micro: Significant simulations or expedient experiments? Journal of Interdisciplinary Economics, 1, 87-100, 1985.

A LINEAR STRUCTURAL MODEL FOR TAX EVASION MEASUREMENTS

Henk Elffers & Dick J. Hessing

Erasmus University Rotterdam

1. INTRODUCTION

In [2] we reported on the striking lack of correspondence between self-reported tax evasion behavior, on the one hand, and officially documented tax evasion behavior on the other. In the meantime, we have tried to understand this phenemenon and propose a conceptual model [4]. We utilized this model to complete a fuller analysis of variables associated with both types of measurement.

Two sets of variables have been distinguished:

(a) a number of *personal instigations* to tax evasion, e.g. variables such as dissatisfactions with various aspects of the tax system and social orientation.

(b) a number of *personal and situational constraints*, e.g. fear of punishment, social controls, and attitudes related to tax misdemeanour.

These sets make up a partial operationalization of the model in Hessing & Elffers [4].

By a straightforward inspection of correlation coefficients (based on 155 respondents in a contrast group design, in which the groups are defined with respect to documented tax evasion), we found remarkable results that will be published in Elffers, *et al.* [3].

Table I: Correlation pattern

	self-reported tax evasion	documented tax evasion
personal instigations	not correlated	correlated (average coeff. 0.20)
personal and situational constraints	correlated (average coeff. 0.22)	not correlated

These results have been replicated by Webley *et al.* [6].

The analysis as outlined above is rather crude while only using bivariate relationships between personal attitudes and dependent variables. We feel that a more refined multivariate analysis is required, in order to take into account:

(a) the interrelationships between explanatory variables and
(b) the fallibility of these variables as indicators of the underlying concepts in terms of which the dependency of tax evasion measurement is formulated.

In this paper we present such an analysis using a linear structural relationship modelling approach in two steps. First, we look into the multivariate structure of the dependent variables (confirmatory factor analysis), then we relate this factored structure to the dependent variables (structured model).

2. THE VARIABLES

Below we simply list the variables used; a more detailed description can be found in Elffers, *et al.* [3].

2.1. Explanatory variables.

personal instigations:

- DTA dissatisfaction with tax authorities
- CRI comprehensibility of tax rules and information
- COM attitude towards competition
- ANO anomia
- TOD tolerance of deviance

personal and situational constraints:

- CCE perceived certainty of being caught when evading
- SPC perceived severity of punishment when caught
- PFE perceived frequency of (non)evasion among relations
- PSS perceived social support for (not) evading
- AUI attitude toward underdeclaring income
- AFD attitude toward false deductions

2.2. Dependent variables.

- SR self-reported tax evasion
- DS documented tax evasion status

All explanatory variables are scales. The dependent variables are coded 0/1/2 for SR and 0/1 for DS.

3. FACTORING THE EXPLANATORY VARIABLES

From Hessing and Elffers [4] we derive our conviction that two separate common dimensions may be discerned: one for the instigation variables, IF, and one for the constraint variables, CF. Their relation is not clear beforehand (Figure 1, model F_1).

Figure 1: Factorstructure.
F_1: model without dotted arrow
F_2: model including dotted arrow

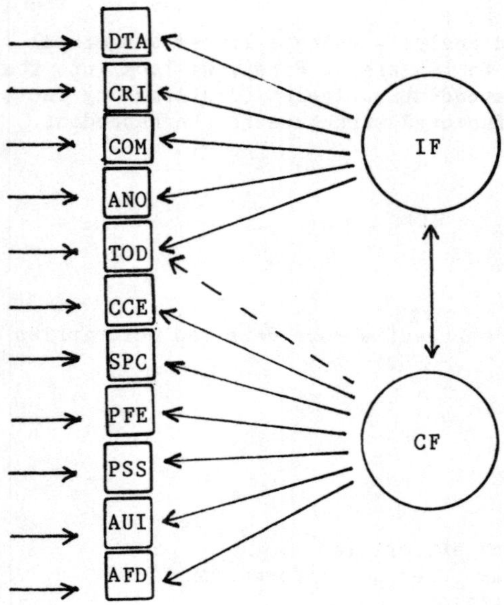

Estimation of this confirmatory factor model by the LISREL IV program [5] results in a rather poor fit (Table II). Inspection of residuals (or of Jöreskogs modification indices) suggests that model F_1 is not able to model the distinctly present correlations between the tolerance of deviance (TOD) variable and the constraint variables. Subsequently, we tried model F_2 allowing TOD to be also dependent on the constraint latent factor (Figure 1).
With hindsight this seems not too bad an idea, because TOD is indeed also conceptually related with deterrence type variables such as SPC or with the image of society as reflected in the attitudes with respect to deviant behavior: AUI and AFD.

Table II: Fit of factor models

Model	rho(IF,CF)	chi^2	df	p	Δchi^2	Δdf	p
F_1	0.29	71.41	43	0.004			
				]	13.33	1	0.000
F_2	0.15	58.08	42	0.051			
				]	1.63	1	0.202
F_3	0 (fixed)	59.71	43	0.046			

Model F_2 significantly improves on F_1 and displays a satisfactory fit, as well as a lack of systematically grouped residues.
It also shows that it is unnecessary to assume a non-zero correlation between the latent factors: model F_3 where this correlation is fixed at zero has an almost equivalent fit.

4. STRUCTURAL MODEL

Starting from F_3, we construct a structural model for the dependence of the behavior variables SR and DS (Figure 2). The main question to be solved is whether it is necessary to assume influence from the IF-factor on DS and from the CF-factor on SR.
We, therefore, compare two models: M_2, without these crossing influences (the model arising from Table I) and M_3 incorporating them.

Figure 2: Structural model
M_2: model without dotted arrows
M_3: model including dotted arrows

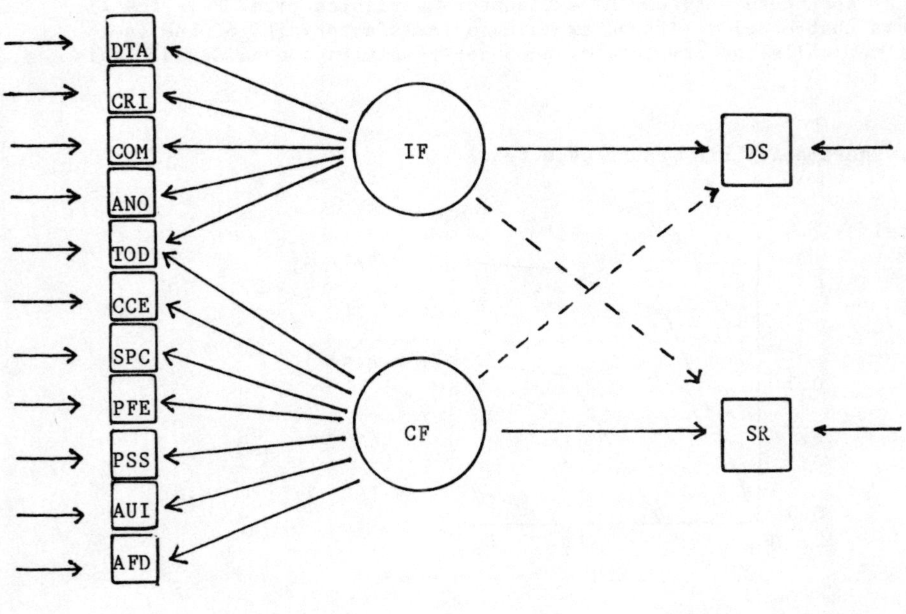

Model M_3 fits quite well, but in fact not significantly better than our favourite model M_2 (Table III).

Table III: Fit of structural models

Model	chi^2	df	p		Δchi^2	Δdf	p
M_2	84.58	64	0.044	]	5.33	2	0.070
M_3	79.25	62	0.069				

5. INCREMENTAL FIT

In order to check whether the structural model succeeds in explaining a considerable part of the dependencies between the variables, we look at a graph of the Bentler-Bonett incremental fit indices [1]. This index quantifies how much of the lack of fit of a minimal model M_ with respect to a hypothetical ideal model is accounted for by a serious model M. The following Bentler and Bonett conventional choice for a minimal model M_ is the model M_0 of complete independence between all variables. We, however, do not regard this as a serious baseline and we prefer to include fit indices with respect to M_1, the model that simply consists of a measurement structure between the explanatory variables (i.e. F_3). The fit graph shows that model M_2 indeed explains a satisfactory 51% of the lack of fit of M_1, while the complete M_3 does not result in a considerable gain here.

Figure 3: Incremental Fit Graphs (see text)

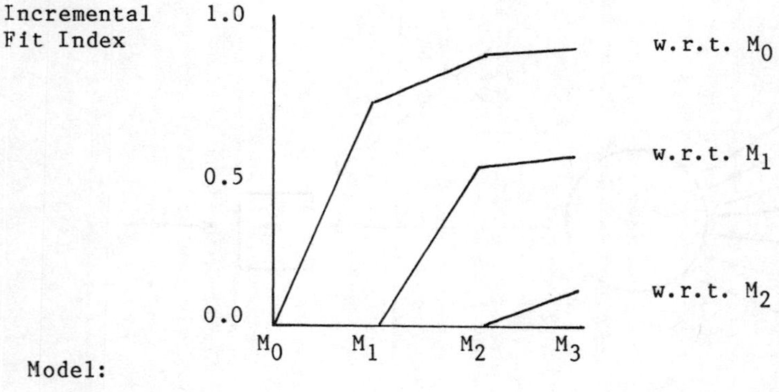

6. DISCUSSION

We may maintain our conclusion from Table 1 that two separate sets of social and psychological variables are associated respectively with self-reported and documented tax evasion behavior. We, moreover, see that

tolerance of deviance is not a pure indicator of these instigational or constraining complexes. Inspection of the estimated coefficients shows that the variable "competition" does not fit well within the model (that is, it does not get any substantial loading), though it has a distinct correlation with DS. May we infer that a third factor exists? The present set-up does not contain enough indicators for determining a third factor reliably, but in a later study we hope to tackle this problem.
Finally, we should notice that the explanatory force of the models remains humble: the determination of the dependent variables amounts to 20%.

7. REFERENCES

[1] Bentler, P.M. and D.G. Bonett, Significance tests and goodness of fit in the analysis of covariance structures, Psychological Bulletin, 88, 588-607, 1980.

[2] Elffers, H., J.C. Vrooman and D.J. Hessing, Non-experimental research in economic psychology, in: Brandstätter, H. and E. Kirchler (eds.), Economic Psychology, Linz: Trauner, 1985, p. 223-231.

[3] Elffers, H., R.H. Weigel and D.J. Hessing, The consequences of different strategies for measuring tax evasion behavior, Journal of Economic Psychology, 1987, in press.

[4] Hessing, D.J. and H. Elffers, Research in tax resistance, an integrative theoretical scheme for tax evasion behavior. This volume.

[5] Jöreskog, K.G. and D. Sörböm, LISREL VI Users Manual, Scientific Software Ltd, Chigago, 1983.

[6] Webley, P., H. Robben and I. Morris, Social comparison and tax evasion in a shop simulation. This volume.

RESEARCH IN TAX RESISTANCE
An integrative theoretical scheme for tax evasion behavior

Dick J. Hessing, Henk Elffers and Russell H. Weigel

Erasmus University Rotterdam - Amherst College, Massachusetts

Postbus 1738
3000 DR Rotterdam
The Netherlands

Amherst, Massachusetts 01002
USA

In recent years, policy makers as well as social scientists have begun to recognize that income tax evasion is a behavioral problem that seriously threatens the capacity of government to raise public revenue. If social science is to contribute to an understanding of tax evasion-behavior, the ideas and data generated to this point merit reexamination with respect to two issues: (a) the measurement procedures employed to assess tax evasion and (b) the types of variables associated with tax evasion in previous research.

1. THE MEASUREMENT OF TAX EVASION

Tax evasion refers to intentionally paying fewer taxes than the law requires. It is a deliberate act of noncompliance as distinguished from the consequences of inadvertant memory lapses, calculation errors, or inadequate knowledge of tax laws. With respect to income taxes, evasion typically occurs because taxpayers either underreport income or exaggerate deductible expenses when filing their returns.

Although a variety of procedures have been used to assess tax evasion in field settings, it is not surprising that, given the confidentiality requirements surrounding individual tax records, the bulk of the published studies rely on survey methods and assess tax evasion from respondents' verbal statements describing their past behavior. Since tax evasion behavior is both sensitive and potentially incriminating, self-reports of evasion would seem vulnerable to substantial underreporting whether motivated by self-presentation concerns or the anticipation of negative consequences. It is also clear that the few studies that have attempted to document respondents' tax evasion behavior have not produced measurement strategies that can be applied in future research efforts. For instance, Schwartz and Orleans' study [1] did not allow investigations of the social or psychological correlates of individual tax cheating. Studies by Clotfelter [2] and Witte and Woodbury [3] analyzed data from the Internal

Revenue Service. However, the measures they used assessed only those instances that could be detected in the normal course of an audit and could not distinguish between unintended errors and intentional underestimation of tax obligations. To overcome this limitation, Wallschutzky [4] compared a group of evaders (whose names were officially published) to a group of 'nonevaders' drawn from a random sample of registered voters. However, the non-significant differences that typified his comparisons of the two groups may have resulted from the likely contamination of the nonevader group with substantial numbers of undetected evaders.

Future research needs to address the problems associated with existing approaches to the measurement of tax evasion since no study to date has evaluated the degree to which self-reports and external assessments of tax evasion behavior covary.

Despite the seriousness of this limitation, it may be useful to critically examine the outcomes of past tax evasion research for clues regarding the variables that hold explanatory promise. Two general classes of variables will be considered in the following review: variables that instigate tax evasion behavior and variables that constrain such behavior (for a more thorough review see [5]).

2. INSTIGATING VARIABLES IN TAX EVASION BEHAVIOR

On an intuitive basis, it seems obvious that individuals would vary in the degree to which they are disposed toward tax evasion. Exposure to certain types of situational pressures might instigate evasion and certain personalities might be particularly prone to engage in this type of behavior. Nevertheless, motivational concepts are curiously absent from tax evasion research. The omission is likely a consequence of the dominant influence of economic models in this domain of inquiry. Such models [6,7] tend to view motivation as a given and behavior as primarily responsive to consequent costs and benefits. In other words, it is assumed that <u>all</u> taxpayers will declare as little of their income as possible and will be deterred only when the probability of detection and the severity of attendant punishment is high.

Since the explanatory value and sufficiency of economic models remains unproven, it would seem unwise to dismiss the potential of motivational concepts in tax evasion research. In this regard, three candidates appear promising.

2.1. Financial strain.

It has been suggested elsewhere [8] that persons experiencing "financial strain" would be more likely to engage in tax evasion behavior than would persons confronting less difficult financial circumstances. Nevertheless, two studies [9,10] found that respondents who reported an improvement in economic status during the previous five years, were <u>more</u> likely to admit evading taxes than those who reported a deterioration of their economic status during the same period. One implication that can be drawn from experimental findings [11] is alternative ways of operationalizing the strain variable deserve consideration. That is, instead of focussing on perceptions of deteriorating economic circumstances, future studies could examine the effects of other types of situationally induced strain such as the amount of income taxes owed by individuals after withholding. The prospect of a large out-of-pocket cost may produce strain and consequent evasion behavior regardless of the individual's overall estimates of his improving or deteriorating economic status.

2.2. Personal motives

One commonly held view is that tax evasion behavior is motivated by dissatisfaction with the tax system and beliefs that taxes are unfair. Empirical results with regard to variables such as dissatisfaction, equity, and fairness have not only been mixed, they would also, in our opinion, benefit from further refinement. For example, beliefs that the tax system is unfair may reflect individuals' convictions that they are overpaying taxes relative to what others pay, or relative to the value of the government services they receive, or relative to what they should pay if they were fully cognizent of the procedures available to reduce their tax obligation to the legal minimum. The possibility that some dimensions of perceived unfairness are especially likely to provoke compensatory behavior in the form of misrepresenting income or deductions remains to be investigated.

2.3. Personal orientation

Personality variables are typically invoked to explain why different people behave in distinctive ways when they encounter similar situational pressures, and more specifically, why some individuals are more prone to evade taxes than others despite similar opportunities and socioeconomic circumstances.

For example, some past research has documented the effects of individual differences in personal competitiveness on behavioral choices. In the present context, a competitively oriented individual might be disposed toward perceiving the confronting situation as an opportunity for attaining personal advantage versus the necessary fulfillment of a community responsibility. In this sense, tax evasion behavior may be instigated by central personality variables (e.g. motives, values, expectations) that influence individual willingness to cooperate with tax authorities. In view of the demonstrated value of incorporating such variables into explanatory frameworks for deviant behavior [12], they deserve attention in future studies of tax evasion.

3. CONSTRAINTS AGAINST TAX EVASION BEHAVIOR

3.1. Limited opportunity

Taxpayers vary in terms of the opportunities available to them to conceal income or declare unwarranted deductions. Greater opportunity is generally associated with self-employment and income sources not subject to withholding taxes. Studies, whether based on self-report or on documented evidence of tax evasion, suggest almost without exception the importance of differences in opportunity to evade. This consistent pattern of findings despite considerable variation in the procedures used to measure opportunity suggests the importance of this dimension for tax evasion behavior. Future investigators should attend to improving the precision with which this variable is measured. In this regard, it may be useful to develop reliable procedures for rating occupational categories with respect to their likelihood of obtaining cash payments, receiving income not subject to withholding taxes, eligibility for itemized deductions, etc. Scores on this type of opportunity scale could then be compared to objective assessments of the frequency and extent of tax evasion.

3.2. Threats of punishment

Probably the most widely studied idea in tax evasion research derives from both economic and sociological models of the deterrence of criminal behavior. Simply put, the idea is that fear of punishment inhibits criminal behavior. Fear of punishment, in turn, is typically conceptualized as a function of both the certainty of detection and the severity of the punishments if detected.

The results of several surveys have indicated that respondents acknowledgging some form of tax evasion were less likely than nonevaders to believe that such acts would result in apprehension and punishment. However, similar studies have not found evidence of such a relationship between perceived risk of punishment and reported noncompliance with tax laws.

3.3. Social disapproval

The types of negative consequences that attend certain behaviors include not only threats of legal sanctions, but also threats of disapproval from other significant people in the individual's reference group. Arguments about the importance of reference groups in providing sources of learning and support for deviant behavior have a considerable history in the social sciences (e.g. "differential association"). Presumably, the impact of personal associations is reflected in an individual's expectations regarding the approval or disapproval of certain types of behavior by significant others. Several investigators have assessed the relationship between perceptions of reference group standards and tax evasion behavior (for a review see [13]).

Although the results of these investigations are consistent with previous research on deviance, it should be noted that the magnitude of the correlations reported between measures of perceived social support and tax cheating is often quite modest. Moreover, it should be noted that all of these studies assessed tax evasion exclusively in terms of respondents' self-reports.

3.4. Personal controls

The configuration of attitudes that regulate any personal departure from normatively prescribed behavior has been described as a critical facet of the behavior process eventuating in deviance. As Jessor and his colleagues have argued, "a large part of what is meant by personal controls is contained in the notion of conscience or the Freudian concept of the superego, the cognitive agency which is the internalized repository for the socially defined norms or standards for acceptable conduct." [12, p. 106]. This conceptualization suggests a relatively direct approach to ascertaining whether an individual evaluates personal action tendencies in terms of such normative standards. In the present context, the personal manifestation of normative standards would be reflected in relatively intolerant attitudes toward tax evasion justified by reference to moral beliefs and community responsibilities. The existing survey data are compatible with this interpretation: admitted evaders were less likely than nonevaders to believe that tax evasion was wrong.

Attitudes toward tax evasion deserve further study for three reasons. First, past research has indicated that intolerant attitudes toward deviance can constrain the occurence of normatively proscribed behaviors [12]. Second, contemporary studies have consistently found significant correlations between tolerant attitudes toward tax evasion and self-reported noncompliance with tax laws. Third, since these attitudes explicitly specify the target behavior (i.e. tax evasion), they approximate the "attitude toward the act" measures that have exhibited considerable power in predicting behavioral variation in other research contexts [14].

4. A SOCIAL PSYCHOLOGICAL MODEL OF TAX EVASION

Although the importance of interdisciplinary theory is widely endorsed, conceptual frameworks emphasizing the interactive influence of social and psychological variables have emerged only rarely. Yet, as numerous investigators have stressed, every behavior is simultaneously personal and situational. Consequently, a full account of any behavior requires that analytic attention be directed at understanding the interplay between the situational influences and personal attributes that contribute to its occurence. Considering the explanatory leverage that such integrative theoretical schemes have exhibited in previous research on deviant behavior [12] and the conclusions of our review, a tentative social psychological model of tax evasion behavior is presented in Figure 1.

Our theoretical scheme draws heavily on the work of Jessor and his colleagues [12]. Indeed, the effort here is most accurately conceptualized as an attempt to accommodate the spirit of their general theory of deviance to the particulars of and existing data on tax evasion. Unlike previous explanatory models of tax evasion behavior [13], the theoretical framework suggested in Figure 1 specifies a set of variables in the social environment which are conducive to tax evasion and their logically analogous counterparts within the individual. By describing situationally defined instigations and constraints, the framework accounts for the concentration of evasion behavior among certain social groups, namely, those characterized by pronounced financial strain, self-interest norms, high opportunity, and limited legal and social regulatory controls. Location of an individual's position in terms of exposure to these social conditions yields an estimate of the probability that he or she will engage in acts of tax evasion. According to the model this probability is increased when it can be shown that the hypothesized effects of such exposure have occured; the individual actually possesses the psychological characteristics which are expected to flow from exposure to the conditions specified. It is, then, variation in these psychological attributes that accounts for behavioral differences among persons exposed to similar social conditions.

The linkages between the social and psychological elements of the framework are best illustrated if the five pairs of variables connecting the two domains are considered separately. First, financial strain is a situ-

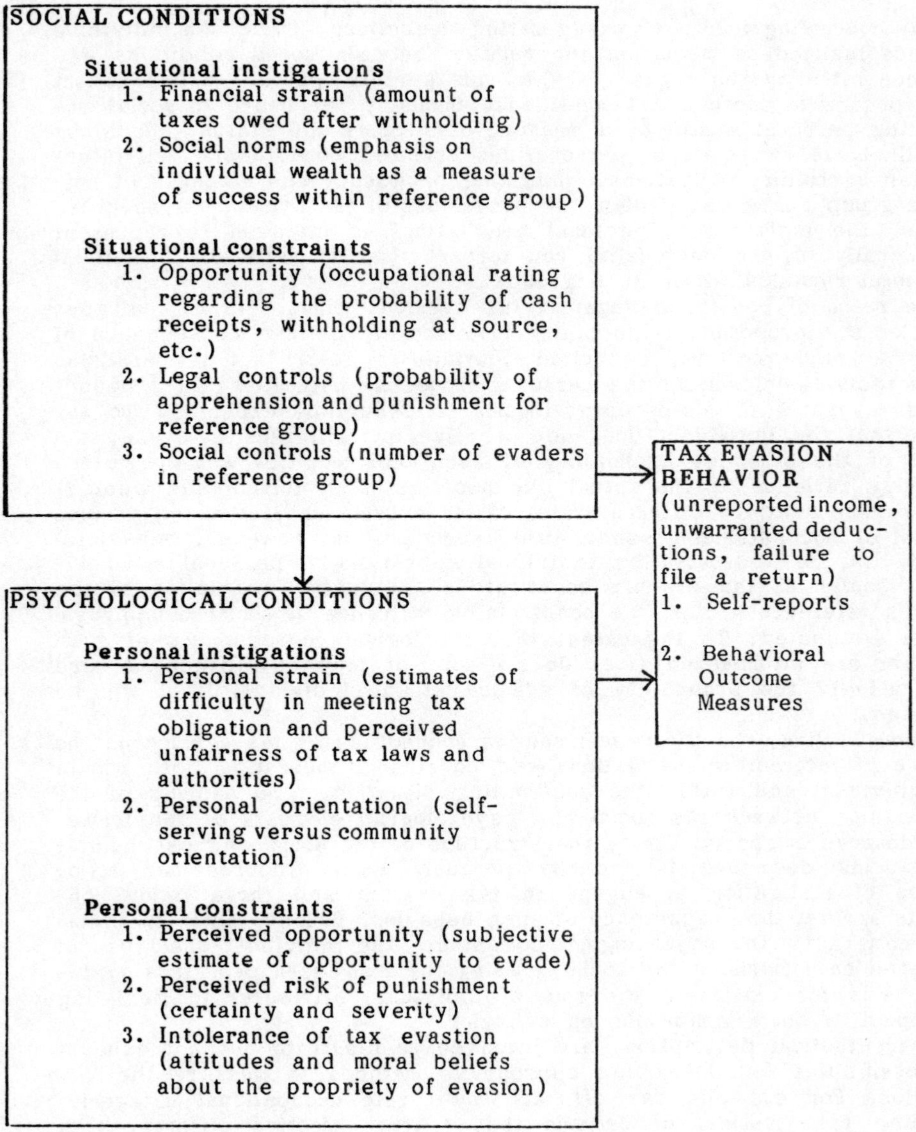

Figure 1. A social psychological model of tax evasion behavior

ational variable that has a direct impact on the likelihood of evasion by confronting the individual with the prospect of a large out-of-pocket expense. Exposure to situations characterized by financial strain, then, is expected to instigate higher rates of evasion among groups of individuals individuals so exposed. On the other hand, individual reactions to such exposure will not be uniform. Instead, reactions will depend, in part, on whether or not the situationally induced strain intensifies the individual's convictions that he is paying more taxes than he should, thereby motivating efforts to compensate for the perceived unfairness of the situation by concealing income or exaggerating deductions. Thus, the individual is conceptualized as mediating the relation between social conditions and deviance rates by the degree to which his personal characteristics reflect the exposure to those social conditions. Similarly, exposure to social emphasizing personal wealth as a measure of success and status, should be more likely to eventuate in personalities oriented more toward self-interest than community obligations. While the consistency and strength of reference group norms may explain the prevalence of tax evasion for specified groups, the individual's "personal orientation" is intended to represent the logically implied personality counterpart that accounts for individual behavioral variation within such groups.

In the realm of constraints against tax evasion, three sets of analogous variables are proposed. Opportunity is a socially defined consequence of access to cash receipts, deduction possibilities, etc. that is paralleled at the individual level by the person's subjective estimates of the opportunities available to misrepresent income or deductible expenses. To the extent that the individual does not perceive opportunities to evade, the impact of the objective availability of such opportunities will be muted. Similarly, variation in the actual likelihood of apprehension and punishment may account for different rates of tax evasion characterizing various national or occupational groups. Within such groups, however, behavioral choices will be moderated by individual appraisals of personal risk. Finally, insofar as tax evaders constitute a substantial proportion of the person's reference group, the constraining influence of social disapproval will be attenuated. To the extent that the logical consequences of such exposure are internalized (i.e. development of tolerant attitudes toward tax evasion), the probability of evasion at the individual level will be increased.

In general, then, the theoretical scheme conceptualizes tax evasion as the outcome of interacting instigations and constraints operating both within the individual and within the confronting situation. Two aspects of the relationships between the social and psychological elements of the framework deserve emphasis. First, the structure of the social and psychological domains described is formally parallel. Each proposes two major sources of instigation to engage in tax evasion and three major constraints against the occurrence of such behavior. Second, since the variables comprising the psychological domain are the individual analogues of the variables comprising the social domain, the framework permits a systematic basis for examining the role of individual attributes in mediating the impact of social conditions on behavior.

The parenthetical descriptions are intended to illustrate but not exhaust the possibilities for developing appropriate methods to measure the key variables. For example, tax officials could rate occupational categories according to a variety of criteria that reflect objective differences in situationally defined opportunity (e.g. access to cash receipts, proportion of income subject to withholding at source, eligibility for special deductions or credits). At the psychological level, survey respondents could provide subjective estimates of their perceived opportunity to successfully conceal income or declare unwarranted deductions. Once reliable instruments of these types are created, the separate and combined effects of objective opportunity and perceived opportunity can be assessed.

The proposed framework also underscores the need to attend more carefully to the measurement of the dependent variable - tax evasion behavior - in future research. Suspicions about the accuracy of self-reports will be diminished only by demonstrations that such reports are highly correlated with documented evidence of individual tax evasion behavior. Although the actions comprising tax evasion behavior cannot be directly observed, the outcome of these actions can be revealed by careful audits of individual tax returns. It is imperative that creative methods be developed for attaining such data, uncontaminated by instances of inadvertant error, without compromising individual confidentiality. Only then can the validity of self-reports and the plausibility of competing theoretical models be determined. To ignore this measurement task is to risk creating explanatory schemes that can account for what people say, but not what they do.

It is assumed that the variables proposed in the model are sufficient to explain tax evasion behavior; all other sources of influence, then, will be mediated by and reflected in one of the predictor variables specified. For example, a number of demographic variables such as age, sex, and social class or occupational status have exhibited significant correlations with admitted tax evasion in previous surveys. Since explanations of <u>why</u> these variables are related to tax evasion are rarely attempted, however, it appears that their frequent emergence in research efforts reflects their measurement convenience more than their explanatory value. From our perspective, the meaning of such demographic characteristics can be attributed to their links to the variables proposed in our theoretical scheme. In this sense, occupational status and the background characteristics confounded with it (e.g. age, sex, income) become crude approximations of the situational opportunities for evasion available to the individual. Similarly, knowledge of tax laws is assumed to increase the likelihood of evasion only to the extent that it increases perceived opportunity to evade, reduces the perceived risk of punishment, or yields tolerant attitudes toward tax evasion.

In the absence of supportive empirical data, the value of the proposed framework for explaining tax evasion behavior must remain tentative. On the other hand, it seems at least consistent with Nadel's description of a theory as a body of interconnected propositions "which serve to <u>map out</u> the problem area and thus prepare the ground for its empirical investigation by appropriate methods." [15, p. 1]. As such the proposed framework organizes a set of explanatory concepts that are compatible with the existing data from tax evasion research, provides some preliminary guidance for the development of measures capable of assessing the predictor variables specified, and clarifies the need for more careful examination of the correspondence between self-report and behavioral outcome measures of individual tax evasion behavior.

REFERENCES

[1] Schwartz, R.D. and S. Orleans, 1967. On legal sanctions. University of Chicago Law Review 34, 282-300.

[2] Clotfelter, C.T., 1983. Tax evasion and tax rates: An analysis of individual returns. Review of Economics and Statistics 65, 363-373.

[3] Witte, A.D. and D.F. Woodbury, 1983. The effect of tax and tax administration on tax compliance. Chapel Hill, N.C.: University of North Carolina, Department of Economics, Working Paper 83-1.

[4] Wallschutzky, I.G., 1984. Possible causes of tax evasion. Journal of Economic Psychology 5, 371-384.

[5] Weigel, R.H., D.J. Hessing, and H. Elffers, 1986.Tax evasion research: A critical appraisal and theoretical model. Journal of Economic Psychology, 7, in press.

[6] Allingham, M.G. and A. Sandmo, 1972. Income tax evasion: A theoretical analysis. Journal of Public Economics 1, 323-338.

[7] Becker, G.S., 1968. Crime and punishment: An economic approach. Journal of Political Economy 76, 169-217.

[8] Wärneryd, K. and B. Walerud, 1982. Taxes and economic behavior: Some interview data on tax evasion in Sweden. Journal of Economic Psychology 2, 187-211.

[9] Mason, R. and H.M. Lowry, 1981. An estimate of income tax evasion in Oregon. Survey Research Center, Oregon State University, Corvallis, Oregon.

[10] Vogel, J., 1974. Taxation and public opinion in Sweden: An interpretation of recent survey data. National Tax Journal 27, 499-513.

[11] Webley, P., I. Morris, and F. Amstutz, 1985. Tax evasion during a smallbusiness simulation. In: H. Brandstätter and E. Kirchler (eds.), Economic Psychology: Proceedings of the 10th Annual Colloquium of the International Association for Research in Economic Psychology, Trauner, Linz, Austria.

[12] Jessor, R., T.D. Graves, R.C. Hansen, and S.L. Jessor, 1968. Society, personality and deviant behavior: A study of a tri-ethnic community. New York: Rhinehart and Winston.

[13] Kinsey, K.A., 1985. Theories and models of tax cheating. Taxpayer Compliance Project Working Paper 84-2. Chicago, Ill.: American Bar Foundation.

[14] Ajzen, I. and M.Fishbein, 1980. Understanding attitudes and predicting behavior. Englewood Cliffs, N.Y.: Prentice-Hall.

[15] Nadel, S.F., 1957. The theory of social structure. New York: Free Press.

Part Twelve
Time and Time Preference

Time Preferences:

The expectation and evaluation of decision consequences as a function of time

Helmut Jungermann

Institut für Psychologie
Technische Universität Berlin
Dovestraße 1-5, D-1000 Berlin 10

Abstract

The concept of time preference is rarely used in psychology. The phenomenon, however, that peoples' preferences among options often depend on the time at which their consequences are to occur has been explored in various areas (e.g., personality theory, social psychology) under different names (e.g., deferred gratification, human impatience). The paper reviews some of the literature within a decision-theoretic framework.

The suggested conceptual framework has three major features: First, it is assumed that people prefer time-related consequences such that the time distribution is skewed either toward or away from the present. This is called a general time preference, implying as two special cases a positive time preference (a preference for the present over the future), and a negative time preference (a preference of the future over the present). Second, we conceptualize time preference as a theoretical concept rather than as a mental phenomenon. That is, people are not supposed to have a preference for time as such, but time is an inherent characteristic of options in uncertain situations. Third, the actual or perceived kind and scale of distribution of consequences over time are assumed to have an impact on the expectation and the evaluation of consequences and thus influence the choice among the options.

With these assumptions, the role of time can be disussed conveniently within a decision-theoretic framework, i.e., the analysis of peoples' expectations and evaluations can help to better understand the specific influence of time on choice.

Introduction

The psychology of human decision making has not paid much attention to the significance of time for an individual's choice. This research has produced a large body of knowledge about how probabilities of consequences and utilities of consequences influence human decision behavior, but little is known about the role of time as the frame for utilities and probabilities of future consequences and about the way in which the value of the outcomes of a particular option is assessed in relation to the time of their occurence. Decision theory assumes that a person's utilities and probabilities at any point in time reflect necessarily also his or her time preferences, and that therefore a separate study is not needed at all. However, the choice of an option and the outcome of it are, by definition, separated by a time-interval, and it is paradoxical that the time dimension has not been more actively investigated in decision research.

In economic theory the slope of an indifference curve - reflecting the marginal rate of substitution of present for future consumption - is assumed to correspond to the rate of time preference; generally, a preference of the present over the future is postulated (cp., for example, Maital 1982; Nijkamp and Rouwendal 1985). I suggest, in contrast, the use of a more general conceptualization of "time preference" that is independent of the notion of interesst and neutral with respect to the specific kind of preference. Such a conceptualization has been proposed by Yates (1972). According to Yates, "the generic form of the behavior in question involves a person confronted with a total amount of resources or gratifications (rewards or punishments) potentially available for his use or experience. His decision problem is to allocate or budget those resources or gratifications over a given amount of time or series of time periods in the future such that the budget is most pleasing to him" (p.4). That is, time preferences are preferred forms of allocation of potentially available resources, or preferences between consumption programs of dated goods. Yates then defines: "A person exhibits a general time preference if when confronted with a potential stock of resources to be allocated for consumption over intervals of time into the future, he allocates those resources such that the time distribution is skewed toward or away from the present. The former case is referred to as positive general time preference; the latter is known as negative general time preference" (p.5). This definition has two advantages: First, it allows for intertemporal consequences to be rewards or benefits as well as punishments or costs. Second, the significance of the totality of expected gratifications is emphasized.

Based on this definition of "general time preference" I will take a look at some theoretical and empirical work in psychology that is related, or can be related, to time preferences and their significance for decision making. (A more elaborate treatment of the issue is given in Jungermann and Fleischer 1985.)

Approaches to the study of time preferences in psychology

In 1911, the year in which Fisher (1930) published the basic ideas of his "impatience theory of interest" in an Italian Journal, Freud published his "Formulierungen über die zwei Prinzipien des psychischen Geschehens" (cp. Maital 1982). In this work he dealt with the principles that govern the regulation of human behavior and with the role of delay of drive impulses aiming at need satisfaction. The "pleasure principle" lets the organism seek the shortest way to satisfaction, but the "reality principle" modifies its influence: mechanisms like perception, thinking, and judgment mediate between drive impulse and action to satisfy the demand. The reality principle requires a delay of drive satisfaction, which eventually might bring about a satisfaction that otherwise would never have been achieved. Thus, whereas the pleasure principle works always towards a positive time preference, the reality principle can (though it must not) lead to a negative time preference.

Freud's "Formulierungen" were influenced by ideas of one of the fathers of modern experimental psychology, Gustav Theodor Fechner, who had published in 1848 already a paper "über das Lustprinzip des Handelns". But modern psychology did not get interested in the phenomenon of time preference until some 30 years ago.

Four major approaches may be distinguished: First, experimental research in animal psychology has produced many interesting studies on time-preferential behavior. The focus in these experiments is on the relation between externally delayed reinforcement and degree of learning, sometimes called temporal integration learning (e.g. Renner 1967; Ainslie 1975). Second, personality theory and in particular the psychoanalytic concept of "Ego power" have become the theoretical basis for a number of researchers (e.g. Singer, Wilensky and McCraven 1956) who argue that time-preferential behavior is due to an internal personality disposition (ego strength, delay capacity). Third, the work of Mischel and his collaborators (e.g., Mischel 1974) on delay of gratification is based on the psychology of social learning and motivation, in particular on expectancy x value models. These researchers try to measure time-preferential behavior more directly. In many studies subjects had to choose in a controlled laboratory situation between a low, but immediately available gratification (e.g., a sweet, a cigarette) and a greater gratification (of the same type) that was available after some specified period of time only. Finally, therapeutic approaches to "impulsive behavior" aim at supporting control of behavior (e.g., Thoresen and Mahoney 1974). A typical technique is called behavioral contracts: Therapist and client agree on a contract according to which a specific reward (e.g., money) will be given only if some specific behavior is shown that the client has great difficulties to show (e.g., nonsmoking).

It is difficult to make comparisons across the various approaches. They use different concepts, look at different behaviors, and use different methods. I will thus not try to make such a comparison. Rather, I will try to integrate some of the ideas and findings in a framework of my own.

Expectations, evaluations, and time preferences

Time preferences are explicitly expressed or implicitly revealed in specific kinds of choice situations. The distinctive feature of such situations is that the choice is between options the consequences of which differ in their distribution over time. In other words, there is no such thing as a preference for time, or some point in time, as such; we cannot ask people whether they have a time preference, for which time they have a preference, or how their time preferences are today. Rather, time is an inherent characteristic of the options at stake, since they are defined by consequences distributed over some period of time. But the actual or perceived kind and scale of distribution play a role for the expectation and the evaluation of consequences and thus influence the choice between the options.

o For example, a community might plan the reconstruction of a residential area which will significantly improve the quality of living in this area; the work will last several years and implies many inconveniences during that period for the residents. An old person might expect not to receive the benefits any more but only to suffer from the burdens, and thus prefer that the plan is deferred; a younger person, on the other hand, might expect his condominium to increase in value after the reconstruction and thus prefer a fast implementation of the plan. In terms of benefits, the older person exhibits a positive time preference and the younger person a negative time preference.

o The distribution over time also effects the evaluation of consequences: A scientific study shows that the disposal of nuclear waste will not create any problems for the first 500 years. A proponent of nuclear energy might take this as an argument in his favor since the very-long-range effects are really of minor importance in today's decisions; he would then exhibit a positive time preference. An opponent, on the other hand, might argue that the present generation should not have all the benefits and let future generations cope with the costs, and he might thus exhibit a negative time preference.

Expectations and evaluations of specific consequences are sometimes stored in our memory, i.e., they are part of our knowledge base. For example, we might know from experience that a friend will actually be able to pay some loan plus interest back in a year, or we have specifiable doubts. And we might know that we just hate going to the dentist and rather postpone an appointment than make it now. But in most choice situations, expectations and evaluations of consequences cannot directly be retrieved from memory but must be inferred from the available knowledge: The implications of the alternative options, i.e., the space of outcomes and their associated utilities, must be explored; the expolratory process comes to an end with some specific anticipation of outcomes and utilities, i.e., with specific expectations and evaluations.

There are many factors which have an influence on expectations and evaluations, of course. I will distinguish here external (environmental) and internal (personal) factors and discuss some of them in their significance regarding time preference. Table 1 shows the factors treated in the following sections:

Table 1: External and internal factors influencing time preferences via expectations and evaluations

	Expectations	Evaluations
External	- physical condition - reliability of sources - environmental situation	- socioeconomic status - culture and religion
Internal	- factual knowledge - time perspective - risk attitude	- drive and tension - state of wealth - experience and imagination

Expectations

The farther away in time some consequence of a decision is to occur, the more uncertain is it to occur. This uncertainty can be seen as due, on the one hand, to the actual number of possible events that can happen over time and prevent the occurence of the consequence, and, on the other hand, to our limited knowledge about the future. However, since the increasing possibility of alternative consequences is part of our knowledge we may simply confine our discussion to the increasing uncertainty as it is reflected in our knowledge. Björkman (1984) has speculated that our knowledge about the future may be seen as time-discounted, just as future values are assumed to be time-discounted: The present amount of knowledge is smaller the farther away the time it concerns; more specifically, the knowledge about the future decreases according to an exponential decay function. We assume that the uncertainty of potential consequences, which is largely dependent on the projected time of their occurence, plays a major role for the time preferences that people exhibit, and that this effect of expetations must be distinguished from the effect of evaluations.

In experimental studies (e.g., Mischel and Grusec 1967; Mischel, Grusec and Masters 1969) children did not prefer immediate punishment to deferred punishment, as was expected, and the investigators hypothesize that this result might reflect the children's subjective notion that the actual delivery of deferred punishment was less than certain. We find the same phenomenon also among adults, of course: For example, many people postpone the visit to a dentist (and thus defer certain punishment) even when they have great pain, because they hope that the pain might simply go away (and thus seem to hope that a continuation of the present punishment is less than certain). In general, the available studies do support the assumption of a monotonic relationship between delay time and benefits but not between delay time and costs.

Expectations are influenced by a number of factors from the environment and from within a person; three external and three internal factors will now be described briefly (see Table 1, left columne).

<u>External factors</u>: One external factor is, for example, the physical condition of an individual. An inverse relation exists between the age of a person and the probability that he or she will see the beneficial consequences of some option if these are distributed over a period of time extending his or her life expectancy, suggesting a positive correlation between age and positive time preferences in such situations. The opposite relation should hold for costs; for example, an old person might prefer not to have a dangerous medical operation that might result either in complete health or death tomorrow, and rather choose an alternative treatment (e.g., radiation) if the probability is low that he or she will live long enough anyhow to see the bad consequences resulting from that treatment.

Another external factor is the reliability of sources, i.e., the trust that rewards (and punishments) will actually be given; for example, Mahrer (1956) showed that with children the preference for delayed positive rewards increased with increasing certainty of attainment, and likewise the relative preference for immediate small punishments increased as the likelihood of larger alternative deferred punishments increased.

A further factor is the objective contingencies of the environmental situation as they exist, for example, for members of different social classes (Miller, Riessman and Seagull 1965).

<u>Internal factors</u>: An obviously very important internal factor is the factual knowledge a person has about the probabilities of consequences; for example, parents and children as well as experts and laypeople often have different time preferences simply due to the greater knowledge about the probable future.

A slightly different factor is a person's time perspective, i.e., how a person conceives the past and future life span and how well the perception of past and future events is organized; it seems that accuracy of time perception and longer, more coherent future time perspectives are associated with stronger delay tendencies (e.g., Mischel 1961; Siegmann 1961).

Finally, the risk attitude should influence the time preference of a person; a risk averse person should tend towards a positive time preference and a risk prone person should tend towards a negative time preference (regarding benefits).

<u>Regret</u>: So far I have assumed that a person, when faced with options that differ in the temporal occurence of their consequences, explores the possible implications and takes their uncertainties somehow into account when making a choice. This is a functional cognitive process to which not much conscious attention is paid. However, when the decision turns out badly the decision maker sometimes feels a regret related to that process. When the exploration was incomplete

and insufficient, one might ask: Why didn't I think one step further? Why was I so short-sighted? And when the exploration has led to incorrect and unjustified expectations, one might ask: How could I be so silly to expect that to happen? How could I forget all my experiences from the past?

The anticipation of regret, as well as the anticipated request of justification, might motivate people to use one of the strategies developed for supporting the exploratory process and to prevent potential regret. One such strategy is the construction of scenarios as action-event-sequences leading into the future; in order to generate expectations as complete and appropriate as possible one might combine a forwards and a backwards strategy in the construction process because it minimizes the possibility of 'holes' in the image of the future (Jungermann 1985).

An example: The role of expectations for time preferences and the impact for decisions has been discussed by Björkman (1984) and Svenson (1984) with references to an example of particular present importance: Large-scale hazardous technologies. The long-range consequences of actions (or non-actions) are hard to assess because they usually are far away in the future and are often vague and ill-defined. The limitations of cognition due to the longe time horizon prevents people from being fully aware of such consequences which are delayed and accumulate slowly. They are aware of the effects in the immediate future but unaware of more distal consequences. This circumstance is particularly serious when there are decision alternatives the positive consequences of which are large, distinct, and immediate, whereas the negative consequences are small, non-distinct, and delayed (e.g., nuclear power). Such alternatives will appear unduly attractive; the long-term effects cannot fully be assessed. On the other hand, alternatives with immediate negative consequences and delayed positive ones (e.g., investments for car catalysators) will appear unattractive.

If we base our decisions on our present preferences, we will regret these decisions some time in the future when our preferences will reverse. Awareness of the potential biases in our cognition of decision outcomes in the future is, of course, the first step in doing something about it: Technology assessment studies and information of the public about their results are strategies to reduce uncertainty about future benefits and risks on the one hand, and to make long-range consequences more salient in the public's perception on the other hand.

Evaluations

The value that people associate with consequences as a function of the time of their expected occurence is the key issue in the psychological study of time-preferential behavior. Preference for one distribution of benefits or costs, of rewards or punishments, over some other distribution is explained by the time-dependent values attached to these events. The general assumption is that time and value are negatively related, i.e., that the value of a commodity is discounted as a function of the time when it will be received. The general hypothesis is quite intuitive: Most people would prefer $ 100 immediately to $ 100 some time later; and similarly, most of us would find paying a fine of $ 100 in a month less unattractive than paying that fine today. On the other hand, although a person will usually prefer to being paid a dinner tonight rather than in a week, this preference might be reversed if the offer is made right after the consumption of an extensive dinner.

To explain time preferences by a discount function for value requires that the function between time and value is specified and factors are identified that modify the function.

The discounting effect has usually been represented as a simple exponential curve. However, based on data from animal behavior studies, Ainslie (1975) has proposed a competing model of the discounting effect according to which the curve is more concave than an exponential curve. We will discuss the relevance of the exact form of the function later; for the present purpose the assumption of a monotonic decreasing function in both models is a sufficient basis for discussing the arguments and findings related to the discounting effect.

The question is why a commodity to be received in the future is valued less than the same commodity to be received immediately, whether this is generally true or not, and which factors influence the evaluation of consequences depending on the time of their occurence.

There exists some empirical work on the effect of time delay on revealed or expressed evaluations of options from Mischel and his group (Mischel and Grusec 1967; Mischel, Grusec and Masters 1969; Mischel and Metzner 1962). They used behavioral choices as well as ratings of the relative value of options in their studies, and had adults as well as children as subjects. They found that the greater the period of delay, the lower was the probability that subjects would choose deferred rather than immediate rewards. With negative rewards, however, the lengths of delay periods had little effect on subjects' choices among deferred negative rewards. Interestingly, adult subjects generally preferred immediate rather than deferred punishment; one interpretation for this finding is that subjects thought that, if there had to be punishment, they might as well have it immediately.

Evaluations are contingent upon a numer of factors that may again be located more within the person or in the environment (see Table 1, right columne).

Internal factors: The internal factor most often discussed is drive and tension, i.e., an assumed natural tendency in organisms to reduce internal tension and thus to prefer in situations of tension a potentially satisfying object nearer in time to one that is farther away. The "pleasure principle" has been the most popular 'explanation' of (positive) time preference. It is not quite clear, however, how relevant the notion of the pleasure prinicple is for a discussion of time preferences. First, even on the organismic level we find exceptions from the rule. Animals, children and also adults find certain types of tension obviously very pleasant. The curiosity seeking behavior of organisms indicates that an increase of uncertainty and tension is sought rather than a reduction. The pleasure of anticipation and the pleasure of gambling are but two well-known examples. Second, it is open to what extent the pleasure principle works also on higher levels of needs than the biological level. It is somewhat difficult to apply the pleasure principle to the choice among payment schedules for a TV/Video Set. The problem is that there is nothing wrong with the pleasure principle as such, but what is pleasure? Immediate satisfaction of a need is obviously only a very specific case, and we have thus to look for other determinants of evaluation.

A second internal factor is the state of wealth of a person. Based on a number of studies on judgement and decision, Kahneman and Tversky (1979) have proposed that people code potential outcomes of a choice as positive or negative deviations (gains or losses) from a neutral reference point which represents the current state of wealth of a person. The value function is assumed to be S-shaped, concave above the reference point and convex below it, and it is steeper for losses than for gains. The displeasure associated with losing a sum of money is generally greater than the pleasure associated with winning the same amount of money, as is reflected in people's reluctance to accept fair bets on a toss of a coin. It varies therefore across individuals whether some future consequence will be evaluated as a gain or as a loss, and thus whether the time preference function will be positively skewed or negatively skewed.

A third factor is a person's experience and imagination, because the evaluation of future consequences of a decision is an anticipation of how satisfying or dissatisfying these consequences will be when they actually occur. This evaluation is not only dependent on a person's present biological tension and on the coding with respect to a reference point; it also depends strongly on the experiences a person has had previously with the same or similar consequences and on the person's ability to imagine how he or she will feel when the consequences occur. If a person has experienced the consequences before, he can retrieve his knowledge about his previous feelings; if he has not experienced them, he will have to infer his potential feelings. In any case, the farther away in time potential satisfactions and dissatisfactions are, the less salient are they and the more difficult is their imagination.

External factors: One external factor that has been investigated in several studies is the socio-economic status (e.g., Beilin 1956; Straus 1962). Unfortunately, the results are inconsistent and difficult to evaluate because different indicators for the socio-economic status and different definitions of delaying behavior were used across studies. One study using a comparatively complex measure of socio-economic status (family's income, possessions of certain items, and educational level of parents and grandparents) found only little relation between class and delaying tendencies as exhibited in a questionaire that included aspects like consumption, sex, and aggression (Straus 1962). Considering the variance in methods and results, support for the notion that there is a relationship between class and deferring behavior seems rather weak (Yates 1972).

Finally, I should mention culture and religion as well-known external factors determining time preference directly and strongly, usually towards a delay of immediate satisfaction. I will not elaborate on this issue here, however, since it has been treated extensively in the sociological literature, and also because there exist few empirical studies with generalizable results.

Regrets: When a decision turns out badly, a person might not only attribute this development to an incomplete or insufficient exploration of the potential outcomes, as was discussed in the previous section, but also or instead to flaws in his or her anticipation of satisfactions or dissatisfactions. If the anticipation was superficial one might ask: Why didn't I consider carefully what I would miss in the long run? Or, I knew it was going to be painful, but I did not realize how painful it would be! And if the anticipation was simply wrong one might ask: How could I have such illusions - I thought it would be wonderful while in fact it was awful! Unrealistic anticipation need not necessarily imply later regret, though: In many situations implying negative consequences unrealism is very healthy; for example, I better do not imagine the pain to be expected at the dentist, or I will cancel the appointment. In other situations, however, realistic anticipation can be essential: Ulysses anticipated realistically how he (and his fellowmen) would feel when the sirens would sing, and acted accordingly. The difference between the two situations is that, in the former, unrealistic anticipation helps achieving pleasure in the long run, whereas in the latter it is fatal in the long run. Janis and Mann (1977) have developed a technique by which subjects try to anticipate potential regret via mental rehearsal of how the present decision situation would look when viewed from a future point in time.

An example: An interesting study has been performed by Christensen-Szalanski (1984) on the impact that the discounting effect can have on the prescriptive validity of value-based decision techniques (e.g., Jungermann 1980). Based on Ainslie's work (1975) he presents a model which implies that a person's preference varies with the passage of time, and that during certain periods of time, a person's values may not be representative of his or her long-term preferences. The model suggests that the curve representing the discount effect of delay on a person's value is more concave than the exponential curve usually assumed (see Figure 1). Christensen-Szalanski's example is the value of a mother during childbirth: "Suppose the prospective mother values the option of delivering her child without anesthesia (represented in Fig. 1 as occuring at time t+2) as being substantially more important than avoiding the pain associated with hard labor (represented as occuring at time t). This preference would be evident in pre-labor (point a) when both options were in the distant future. Since the labor pains must necessarily occur before the delivery is completed, the model predicts that when the occurence of hard labor pain is quite immediate (point b), the mother's preference may suddenly reverse and for a very brief period of time she may prefer to avoid the hard labor pains. In essence, the mother is sacrificing a larger but delayed benefit (delivering her child without the use of anesthesia) for a smaller but more immediate benefit (relief from pain)" (p.49). An examination of the attitudes of eighteen pregnant women toward avoiding pain and avoiding anesthesia showed that most women preferred to avoid using anesthesia during childbirth when asked at one month pre-labor and during early labor. However, during active labor their preferences suddenly shifted towards avoiding pain. Their preference shifted again toward avoiding the use of anesthesia when

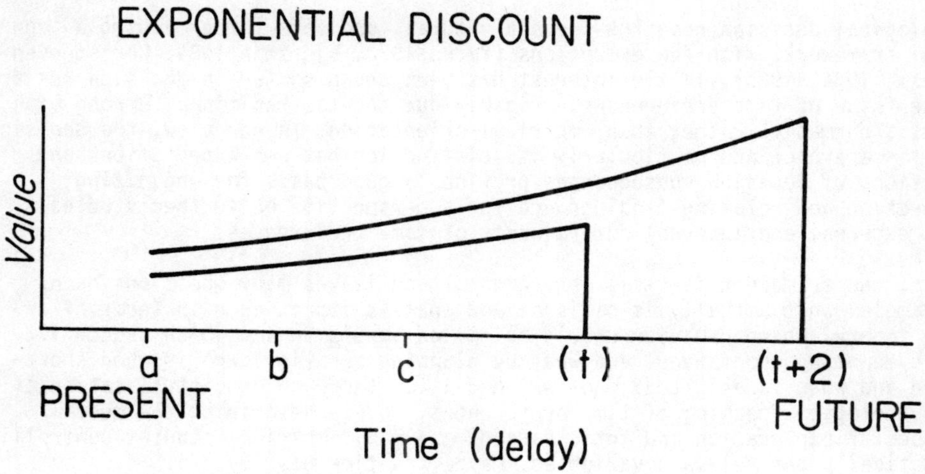

Fig. 2: Hypothetical effect of a delay assuming a hyperbolic rate of change (from Christensen-Szalanski, 1984)

asked one month later. The women's preferences at one month pre-labor were the best predictors of their post-partum preferences, while the preferences during active labor were unrelated to the post-partum preferences. This pattern of preference change is well-known to everybody who at least once in his life tried to stop smoking. It can be found in a number of other health-related choice situations (Christensen-Szalanski 1985). The results suggest that depending upon when a person's values are assessed, (1) they may not be representative of his or her long-term preferences, and (2) their use in value-based decision aids may not maximize the person's long-term satisfaction so much as maximize the probability that the decision will be based on the person's impulsive response. The results also show that distinguishing between current and long-term values can create a problem when determining whether people behave rationally (Jungermann 1983).

Conclusions

The phenomenon and the concept of time preference is not yet explored extensively in psychology. There is some descriptive research on delay of reward in various areas, but the results appear very context-dependent and can not be related to each other very well. Most studies were not concerned with time preferences as such but with other issues, and it is thus often impossible to isolate possible effects of time. Most importantly, there exists no theoretical framework to integrate the findings and to stimulate further research.

Psychological decision research seems a natural candidate for providing a conceptual framework. With few exceptions (Yates 1972; Björkman 1984; Christensen-Szalanski 1984, 1985), little interest has been shown so far in decision research for the issue of time preferences, probably due to its traditional strong bias towards a normative rather than empirical orientation. In our view, the decision-theoretic approach and particularly its distinction between expectations and evaluations of decision consequences provides a good basis for organizing, interpreting and relating findings and for a perspective on further studies on the external and internal determinants of time preferences.

However, the framework is still very general and leaves many questions open. For example, what actually is patience and what is impactience in terms of decision theory? Which behavior should be called impulsive and which prudent? What is meant by spontaneous and what by planning behavior? Who is when short-sighted and when far-sighted? What we need is a thorough conceptualization of the psychological meaning of time preferences, models describing the mental processes of exploration and anticipation, and many empirical studies controlling systematically the relevant variables. Maybe, as time goes by.....

References

Ainslie, G. (1975). Specious reward: A behavioral theory of impulsiveness and impulse control. Psychological Bulletin, 82, 463-496.

Beilin, H. (1956). The pattern of postponability and its relation to social class and mobility. Journal of Social Psychology, 44, 33-48.

Björkman, M. (1984). Decision making, risk taking, and psychological time: Review of empirical findings and psychological theory. Scandinavian Journal of Psychology, 44, 31-49.

Christensen-Szalanski,J.J.J.(1984). Discount functions and the measurement of patients values: Womens' decisions during childbirth. Medical Decision Making, 4, 47-58.

Christensen-Szalanski,J.J.J. (1985). Patient compliance behavior: The effects of time on patients values of treatment regimens. Social Science and Medicine.

Fechner, Th. (1848). Über das Lustprinzip des Handelns. Zeitschrift für Philosophie und Philosophische Kritik, 1-30, 163-194.

Fisher, I. (1930). The Theory of Interest. London: MacMillan.

Freud, S. (1911). Formulierungen über die zwei Prinzipien des psychischen Geschehens. In: S. Freud (1943). Gesammelte Werke. Bd. 8. London: Imago.

Janis, I. & Mann, L. (1977). Decision Making: A psychological analysis of conflict, choice, and commitment. New York: Free Press.

Jungermann, H. (1980). Speculations about decision-theoretic aids for personal decision-making. Acta Psychologica, 45, 7-34.

Jungermann, H. (1983). The two camps on rationality. In: R. Scholz (ed.), Decision making under uncertainty. Amsterdam: North-Holland, 63-86.

Jungermann, H. & Fleischer, F. (in press). As time goes by: Psychological determinants of time preference. In: G. Kirsch, P. Nijkamp & K. Zimmermann (eds.), Time preferences: An interdisciplinary theoretical and empirical approach.

Kahnemann, D. & Tversky, A. (1979). Prospect theory. Econometrica, 47, 263-291.

Mahrer, A.R. (1956). The role of expectancy in delayed reinforcement. Journal of Experimental Psychology, 52, 101-105.

Maital, S. (1982). Minds, markets, and money. New York: Basic Books.

Miller, S.M., Riessman, F. & Seagull, A.A. (1965). Poverty and selfindulgence: A critique of the non-deferred gratification pattern. In: L.A. Fermann, J.L. Kornblum & W. Haber (eds.), Poverty in America. Ann Arbor, Michigan.

Mischel, W. (1961). Delay of gratification, need for achievement and acquiescence in another culture. Journal of Abnormal and Social Psachology, 62, 543-552.

Mischel, W. (1974). Processes in delay of gratification. In: L. Berkowitz (ed.), Advances in Experimental Social Psychology. Vol. 7. New York: Academic Press.

Mischel, W. & Grusec, J. (1967). Waiting for rewards and punishments: Effects of time and probability on choice. Journal of Personality and Social Psychology, 5, 24-31.

Mischel, W., Grusec, J. & Masters, J.C. (1969). Effects of expected delay time on the subjective value of rewards and punishments. Journal of Personality and Social Psychology, 11, 3653-373.

Mischel, W. & Metzner, R. (1962). Preference for delayed reward as a function of age, intelligence, and length of delay interval. Journal of Abnormal and Social Psychology, 64, 425-431.

Nijkamp, P. & Rouwendal, J.(in press). Time, discount rate and public decision making. Paper presented at the conference on "Time Preference", Wissenschaftszentrum Berlin.

Renner, K.E. (1967). Temporal integration: An incentive approach to conflict resolution. In: B. A. Maher (ed.), Progress in Experimental Personality Research. Vol. 4. New York: Academic Press.

Siegman, A. W. (1961). The relationship between future time perspective, time estimation, and impulse control in a group of young offenders and in a control group. Journal of Consulting Psychology, 25, 470-475.

Singer, J. L., Wilensky, H. & McCraven, V. G. (1956). Delaying capacity, fantasy, and planning ability: A factorial study of some ego functions. Journal of Consulting Psychology, 20 335-383.

Straus, M. (1962). Deferred gratification, social class, and the achievement syndrome. American Sociological Review, 27, 326-335.

Svenson, O. (1984). Time perception and long-term risks. Canadian Journal of Operation Research and Information Processing, 22, 196-214.

Thoresen, C. E. & Mahoney, M. J. (1974). Behavioral self control. New York: Holt, Rinehart & Winston.

Yates, J. F. (1972). Individual time preference (delayed gratification) behavior: A review and a model. Unpublished manuscript. Ann Arbor, Michigan: University of Michigan.

THE TIME-SHAPE OF TRANSACTIONS: Relational Exchange, Repetition and Honesty

Gordon C. Winston, Williams College

1. INTRODUCTION

This paper analyses the "time-shape" of transactions. It focuses on when, within the ordinary analytical time unit, the events occur that make up a transaction and it thereby reveals incentives and characteristics of markets that are not apparent in the conventional representation.[1] Honesty, opportunism, a private market version of the classic free rider problem of public goods, all emerge as important aspects of transactions seen in time.

Transactions that take place in static, anonymous markets are usual in economic analysis. It is assumed that the separate events that make up any transaction -- agreement, performance, payment -- take place at the same time and that sellers and buyers don't recognize each other nor do they care to: neither personality nor history nor experience diverts analytical attention from price, product, and the static conditions of exchange. While that analysis has been powerful, most transactions don't happen that way: agreement typically precedes performance which doesn't coincide with payment and buyers typically buy from and sellers sell to the same people over and over again, developing important exchange relationships over time. Both of these time-specific departures from the conventional view -- both the time-shape of transactions and their relational quality -- importantly affect market behavior. This is the subject of a time-specific analysis of relational exchange.

The themes developed here derive mainly from the recent literature on relational exchange by Williamson (1979) and Goldberg (1980) and from my analysis of the timing of economic activities (1982). Earlier suggestions have been frequent if not developed: the importance of the temporal order of transactions events was central if implicit in Simon's model of the employment relationship (1951)[2]; Stigler's paper on information and search showed that repetition reduces search costs (1961); Akerlof's analysis of the asymmetric information that masks the sale of lemons showed that honesty is a necessary precondition to some desirable exchanges (1970); and Hobbes' Leviathan described the temporal vulnerability of the partners to a covenant, recognizing the problems created by the absence of an effective contract enforcement mechanism (1962). More recently, some of the flavor of the analysis has come through in Okun's distinction between "casual" labor markets and "auction" goods markets, on the one hand, and "career" labor markets and "customer" goods markets, on the other (1981).

Most relevant to the issues raised in this paper are the recent studies of "self-enforcing contracts" that have analysed the incentive structure created by a series of repetitive transactions -- those contract characteristics that encourage and those that discourage adherence to initial contract agreements. These studies identify some of the characteristics of transactions that induce even the most stridently self-interested of actors (Telser's article opens with advice from Machiavelli to The Prince) to resist the temptation of the immediate gains of reneging in favor of a larger long run gain of honest performance.

Telser's is an analysis of the gains of a one-shot exploitation of a trading partner's vulnerability relative to the gains of continued mutual performance. Klein and Leffler focus on asymetric information on product quality and the role that price in excess of costs can play in assuring high quality by creating an incentive for the honest representation of quality -- an incentive that is absent when price equals costs. Williamson generalizes the role of a "hostage" -- the voluntary creation of vulnerability -- as a way of guaranteeing honest and reliable performance with a trading partner.

The present paper extends that analysis in two directions. First, it uses a time-specific analysis to examine the incentive structure of the isolated, single transaction, thereby suggesting both some of the pressures and temptations of dishonest gain -- the private transaction free-rider problem -- and also the way transaction timing can attenuate opportunism without third-party intervention. This is in Section 3. In addition, by contrasting single-transaction behavior with repetitive-transaction behavior, Section 4 argues for the importance of repetitiveness, per se, as a characteristic of transactions (or, more generally, "events") that plays a large but largely unrecognized role both in disciplining market behavior and in determining the appropriateness of competing economic paradigms, notably neo-classical and Austrian presumptions. Repetition, it is suggested, tempers private opportunism in much the same way that competition has long been seen to [Hirschman]. Competition functions in social space much as repetition does in temporal space: reputation functions in both.

2. TIME IN ECONOMIC ANALYSIS

It is important to the understanding of these repetitive relational transactions to distinguish two quite different roles played by time in economic analysis:

> Time is a necessary dimension of any analytical structure, explicitly or implicitly. An analytical unit time must be specified or implied in order both to measure flow rates and to define the temporal range over which an economic process will be observed. In the same role, time dates stocks. This is an "analytical time" that establishes the temporal parameters of an analysis.
>
> In a quite different role, time defines the temporal perspective of the actor(s) -- the subjects of analysis -- with respect to the economic events and decisions in which they are involved. Uncertainty, information, expectations, irreversibilities, and more, are familiar issues in economic analysis that depend on the temporal positions of people in the economic process under observation. This aspect of temporality can be identified as a "perspective time."[3]

Two implications of this distinction are relevant to relational transactions.

First, essential though it is, the analytical unit time must always discard information. Indeed, the use of any analytical unit time loses *all* information about the timing of what goes on *within* it: the elementary time unit establishes a model's level of temporal abstraction. If the day is used as the unit time, for instance, information is retained about how much *accumulated* output is produced over the whole of any day -- and hence information about the timing of production *between* days -- but nothing can be said about *when, within* any day, that production is made. Similarly, if a year is used as the analytical unit time, all information about daily, monthly or seasonal variations is lost.[4] And so on. Events that actually happened with the time-shape pictured in Figure 1, could be understood only as an accumulated set of unordered events, 3As and 3Bs, when T is the analytical unit time.

```
_____________A B_______A B_____________________A B___time
             |-------------------- T ------------------|
```

Figure 1
Events in Unit Time

The second aspect is that information and uncertainty delineate these two very different uses of time in economics. If economic actors always knew what was going to happen, the distinction between analytical time and perspective time would loose its significance because the temporal position of the people in the economic process wouldn't matter. Distinctions between future, present and past might persist, but they would have little economic significance for all-knowing actors who would simply play out the known future by whatever rules prevailed. Hicks, to focus attention on the actors' temporal perspective, has appealed for an "economics in time," a relational or time-specific economics (1979).

3. RELATIONAL TRANSACTIONS IN TIME

Relational exchange analysis developed to identify the function of legal contracts. It was not originally set out as a time-specific model, but as a description of a neglected market phenomenon that depended on a small number of transactors and gave a rationale for the legal sanctions of formal contracts. Time-specific modeling of relational exchange, however, makes it apparent that a reason for that neglect is the fact that a conventional analytical unit time loses important temporal information; in this case, it is information about the timing and sequence of the events that make up a transaction and that alter transactors' incentives in time. This is revealed in the time-shape of even the simplest of transactions.

Consider the (two) participants in a market transaction as they move, with time perspective, t, through time; the movement of t along the time line in Figure 2. They traders pass through a sequence of transactions events and doing so changes their individual opportunity sets and constraints, systematically. These changes are the subject of relational exchange analysis.

In time-specific analysis, a single transaction is decomposed into the temporally ordered set of separate events that are seen by the two economic actors as they move through time. In a conventional analysis, those separate events would be encompassed by the unit time T and therefore not be seen to be ordered temporally: time would disappear from the analysis by construction. The two actors are assumed, as usual, to be motivated by self-interest -- though it will be seen that that assumption takes on more than usual significance in this time context.

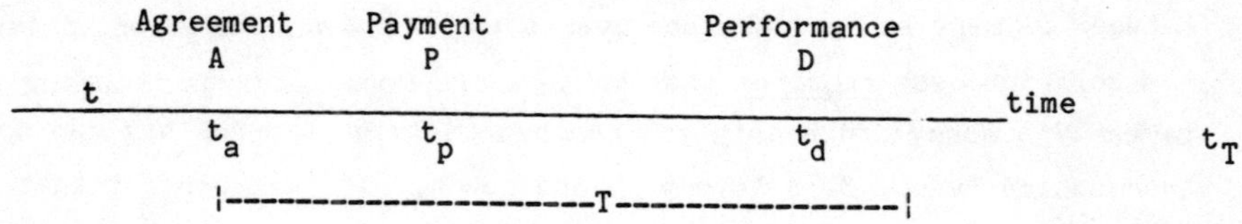

Figure 2
Unit Time and Relational Exchange

In the simplest single transaction, there are only the three events: an agreement (contract) event A at time t_a -- the mutual decision to trade -- a payment event, P, at t_p and a performance event -- delivery of the goods -- D, at time t_d. If these last two events are not simultaneous, if $t_p < t_d$, that fact changes the opportunities open to the two parties as they move (t) through time.

So "the transaction" does not look the same, and individually optimal behavior of self-interested actors is not the same, when viewed over the transaction in its entirety -- where it is an accumulated collection of unordered events in T -- as it does when it is seen to be time-shaped, an ordered series of events in time. Since conventional, time-indifferent, theory with unit time T can only view the whole of a transaction as a single event like A-and-P-and-D in unit time T, time-specific exchange analysis identifies the event timing that is usually obscured by temporal abstraction.

In the simplest transaction, buyer V and seller O agree (event A) that V will make a money payment to O (event P) in exchange for O's delivery of goods to V (event D). If events P and D are not simultaneous, then the self-interest of each trader along with the sequencing of those two transactions elements creates a quite basic problem of concern in relational exchange analysis. t_a is the moment of the agreement, A, to undertake the transaction and if payment, P, comes before delivery of the goods, D, so -- $t_a < t_p < t_d$ -- then Figure 2 describes the time-shape of the transaction events over which "now," t moves. Now, of course, is the same for both transactors.

The opportunities for self-interested actors clearly change as they move over the unit time $T(=t_T-t_o)$: they are different in the period before event P (V's payment to O: $t < t_p$); between that payment and event P (O's delivery of the goods to V: $t_p < t < t_d$); and in the time after event D ($t_d < t < t_T$). During the period before V's payment to O, $t < t_p$ -- that includes the moment of agreement to trade, t_a -- voluntary exchange assures that each party expects to gain from the complete transaction on the familiar ground that underlies the gains from trade.

Between payment and performance events ($t_p < t < t_d$), however, things change. O's self-interest requires that he take the money and run. During this period, he has V's money and hasn't yet reached the moment t_d of his own compensating transaction event, D, delivery of the goods. It is important that in an isolated two-person transaction, if O fails to exploit the time-specific vulnerability of V, he cannot be acting in his assumed self-interest: self-interest does not just allow O to behave opportunistically when he can, it requires him to do so. This is the basic problem identified in relational exchange analysis.

Of course, identifying the reasons why O typically doesn't abscond with V's money -- why transactions actually do take place -- is a primary point of this analysis. A naive V might get to this point in a transaction, but most of us aren't naive and we will put ourselves in the inherently vulnerable position between payment and performance ($t_p < t < t_d$) only when we have "protection of reliance" in the legal terms Goldberg uses -- some reason to believe that O won't take off with our money. An enforceable contract is one such way [Goldberg (1980)]; justifiable trust is another [Arrow (1974), Bok (1978), Schelling (1978)]; this time-specific formulation suggests that altering event timing is a third, and repetition is a fourth.

The particular transactions event sequence of this illustration -- payment-then-delivery -- is not central, of course, to the issue of relational exchange. If event P were the delivery of the goods and event D were the payment for them (ordinary trade credit or charge accounts), instead, then the vulnerable transactor, V, would simply be the seller and the potential opportunist, O, would be the buyer: all the rest of the simple case would remain including, crucially, O's incentive during $t_p < t < t_d$ to run, this time with V's goods instead of his money.[6]

Quite useful implications follow from the analysis of even this minimal transaction. One is that the obvious alternative to somehow protecting V's interest during his period of vulnerability is simply for him not to trade at all. That is clearly Pareto inefficient since it denies to both V and O the potential gains from trade. Arrow's (1974) functional justification of the role of codified behavior, including honesty, is much to this point as is Akerlof's appeal to honesty in face of the lemon principle in which mutually desirable trade is also precluded by opportunism (1970).

Another implication of the time shape of transactions is that if transactions events P and D -- payment and performance -- occured simultaneously, so that $t_p = t_d$, then the temporal situation, $t_p < t < t_d$, that is at the root of the problem of opportunism could not exist and there would be no period of vulnerability of either party to the transaction. Actual simultaneity of transactions events simply eliminates the problems and temptations described by relational exchange.[7] So, of course, does the illusion of simultaneity got by using a too-large analytical unit time, T, that represents transactions events as simultaneous even when they are not.

Finally, the asymmetry in the opportunities open to O and V that comes with time as they move through the transaction joins with the conventional requirement that each act in his own self-interest. Both are necessary to cause the problem identified by relational exchange.

The underlying difficulty of relational exchange transactions, it follows, would be eliminated:

a. if there were no trade;

b. if all transactions elements were in fact simultaneous;

c. if O's self-interest could be attenuated:

  i. by an altered objective function (trust-worthiness);

  ii. by external coercive legal authority (enforceable contracts) or

  iii. by O's hope for future -- repetitive -- transactions with V that would link self-control of his present opportunism to his potential future gains from trade.

More complicated relational transactions appear to have the same basic structure and therefore these same elements in their control.[8]

4. REPETITIVENESS PER SE

Now consider a series of transactions like the one analysed above that are repeated so that O and V are involved in an ongoing exchange relationship. The repetitiveness of economic events, it will be argued, has an analytical status that has been too little appreciated. Indeed, there are some striking parallels between large numbers of transactions in market space and large numbers of transactions in time -- between competitiveness and repetitiveness in transactions. The degree of repetitiveness of economic events is a characteristic that appears both to determine the empirical relevance of even the most textbookish of neoclassical market analysis and, when applied to relational transactions, to modify the incentives that a transactor (O) has to exploit his sequential advantage over his trading partner (V).

4.1 Repetitive Transactions and Neoclassical Theory

The most extreme version of conventional neoclassical market analysis includes assumptions of (a) perfect information, (b) rationality as maximization of an objective function and (c) an unchanged decision environment. It seems clear that these are not unreasonable assumptions when applied to highly repetitive transactions. They can be unreasonable when applied to transactions that occur with little regularity or are dominated by a changing environment [Nelson-Winter (1980)]. But that suggests the need for a greater sensitivity to repetitiveness as a characteristic of economic events that often determines the appropriateness of orthodox analysis.

The role of repetition becomes clear in considering an economic activity that occurs regularly in conjunction with a rhythmic geophysical time unit like the day -- say the decision on how to get to work.

a. Repetition ensures cognition and learning in the dullest economic actor so even "perfect knowledge" may not be an outrageous description of the conditions of decision: information about repetitive events is cheap and easy to process [Stigler (1961)];[9]

b. repetition allows the nice adjustments explicitly needed for optimization -- it is likely that all practical global, and not just local, optima will have been considered in deciding on a repetitive activity like how to get to work [Alchian (1950)];

c. repetition suggests that the event will occur many times without significant change in the decision environment, including tastes, prices, technologies, expectations, etc. and hence that behavior with respect to that event can be represented as in equilibrium. Simon's observation is relevant: that the relative rate of change in environment and speed of adaptation, together, determine the appropriateness of equilibrium analysis (1959); and

d. repetition makes expectations a reasonable guide to the future as they are based on a large amount of past information, including successful previous forecasts.

In the extreme, even a purely static equilibrium model will tell much about repetitive economic behavior. It can be argued that for repetitive events the economic decision is not made about an individual event -- how to get to work next Tuesday morning -- but about a class of events, getting to work.[10] The decision cost component of each transaction is small because it is spread over a large number of transactions events.

It seems necessary to reject the relevance, for the analysis of repetitive events, of highly abstract arguments that start with the fact that the future is unknowable as a first principle and then derive the implication that nothing therefore can be known [Lachmann (1976), Shackle (1958)]. Unless those analyses recognize crucial differences in the repetitiveness of economic events, their criticism is as limited as the scope of their target: it makes sense to underscore the deep existential uncertainty that surrounds unique decisions about unique events but it is inappropriate to extend it to repetitive events. Since a significant part of economic activity is repetitive, neoclassical economics would appear to remain a powerful tool of social analysis even if it were seen only as an economics of repetitive events; indeed, its power would be increased by the more appropriate definition of its range.[11]

4.2. Repetitive Transactions Attenuating Opportunism

Now turn back to the opportunism that emerges in a single relational transaction as described above. The problem is caused by the time sequence of transactions events that alters the relative opportunities of the transactors, seriatim, so that their assumed self-interest creates conficts, temptations, and vulnerabilities that can preclude all exchange. Repetitive transactions change that.

If a transaction of the simple type P-D is expected to be repeated over and over again between the same two people, the self-interest of O is no longer necessarily served by taking advantage of V during the period when V is vulnerable. Against O's incentive for opportunism during that period is set his self-interest in the gains from trade in future transactions with V.

With repetitive transactions, t_p is earlier than t_d for one transaction at the same time that t_p is later than t_d for the next. Only under the strictest single-transaction myopia will O have a clear incentive to take advantage of V during $t_p < t < t_d$ in a repetitive game. A time horizon that encompases future transactions with V reveals the possible gains that that opportunism will jeopardize; the myopic incentive may not survive.

So given repetition and awareness of the time-shape of transactions events, O's analytical unit time horizon will determine his optimal behavior -- the more encompassing is that time unit, the less relevant will be his myopic focus on the present transaction with its inherent opportunism and the more he will attend to his long-run advantage with its reduced opportunism.

Repetition, to be sure, cannot establish symmetry between V and O in even a long series of repetitive transactions. V is always vulnerable to O's opportunism during $t_p < t < t_d$ but O has no equivalent period of vulnerability to V. Yet both stand to lose the gains from trade if either should break off the potentially repetitive series of transactions. So even though an incomplete symmetry is established, the raw drive of O's opportunism that appears in a one-shot transaction (a used car; a set of encyclopedia) is tempered by the prospect of future trade. Honesty, as Arrow has argued, may pay: control of momentary self-interest, given repetitive transactions, may lead to longer run self-interest.[12]

This can be put more precisely with useful insights. Stick to the simple case of a series of P-D transactions between O and V. Then in the purest self-interest, O's incentive to take advantage of V during $t_p < t < t_d$, is measured by P_v, the price paid by V for the goods, D.[13] Assume that V will only be exploited once. O's gain at t from treating V honestly is,

$$(1)\quad H_o(t) = \sum_{i=1}^{n} \frac{G_i(t_i)}{(1+r)^{t_i-t}}$$

where n is the number of future transactions O expects to have with V, r is O's discount rate, an t_i is the timing and G_i the gain to O in money terms of an ith future transaction. Then the purest self-interest will keep O from taking advantage of V so long as

$$(2)\quad H_o(t) > P_v(t).$$

Ignoring any differences among the n future transactions, <u>honest-like</u> behavior[14] will be more attractive to the strictly self-interested opportunist the greater are:

a. $G_i/P_v(t)$, the advantage of his gain from a future trade relative to that of current opportunism,

b. n, the number of future transactions he expects to have with V,

c. t_i, the more proximate the time distribution of those transactions, hence the greater the present value of the

d. r, O's rate of discount or -- in psychological/sociological jargon -- ability to delay gratification: the lower, the more honest O will be.

Finally, an argument is encountered in discussion of finite sequential games to the effect that repetition of events is irrelevant in attenuating opportunism. For "the last" play of a repetitive game, the argument goes, incentives of self-interest can't be damped by prospects of future play and if that last transaction is thereby eliminated, the same thing becomes true at the next to the last. And so on. Anticipation of failure of cooperation induces a non-cooperative strategy and this temporal domino effect makes repetition incapable of disciplining any transaction, ever. But the argument appears to be a logical possibility with little relevance for actual market behavior. And most basically, it confuses analytical time and perspective time: the omniscient game theorist-observer may know when the finite series will end -- <u>which</u> is the last play -- but the actors whose strategic decisions are under examination can hardly be expected to: to know that there will be one last transaction is very different from identifying <u>which</u> transaction will be last (Telser).

4.3. Reputation and Honest-Like Behavior

The number of transactions in time and the number of transactors in market space interact. Even if O engages in unique, non-repetitive transactions in which his trading partners are different in each transaction ($V_1, V_2, \ldots V_n$), his temptations to opportunism in the vulnerable period of any one transaction may be reduced if <u>information</u> about his behavior can move at low cost from the current buyer (V_1) to potential future buyers (the V_i). This cheap information flow is most likely, of course, where there is a relatively small number of potential buyers and they are known to each other -- they have established information channels. Then even without the discipline of the prospect of repetitive transactions with V_1, the potential loss of <u>reputation</u> with other potential transactors will act in the same way to protect all the V_i during any period of vulnerability with O. O's calculation, again, weighs the gain of fleecing V_1 against the loss of gains from future trade with V_2, $V_3, \ldots$ consequent on his damaged reputation. People are more honest in small towns, except when they deal with tourists.

The equation above can be modified to reflect this aspect of reputation by making the gains from future transactions stochastic with the probability of any future transaction dependent on O's prior honest behavior and on the cost of information flows betwen the V_i. Then a change like urbanization that increases the costs of information flow among the V_i will reduce the honesty of transactions since it will reduce n, hence increase the frequency with which self-interested O's exploit vulnerable V's. But that less-honest behavior will be the consequence of altered opportunities for self-interested exploitation, not of altered preferences for honesty. To hope that these would long remain separate might appear vain, but the distinction seems useful nonetheless. (Indeed, people might well develop a heightened preference for honest behavior -- if, for instance, as more were victimized they became more appreciative of the sheer social value of honesty -- despite this increased respect for honesty, the objective data would still reveal less of honest behavior.)

4.4. Liars as Free Riders in Time and Space

Finally, note the striking parallel between the opportunistic traders in these private markets and the familiar free riders of public goods and cartel theories. One is a free rider in a time context, the other is a free rider in social or market space. Both, when asked to refveal their intentions, must be liars or abandon their self-interest.

In the usual market context, the free rider is one who misrepresents his own preferences or behavior in order to profit from the actions thus induced in others: he lies about his preferences for a public good, so that others will represent their preferences more honestly and he'll get the public good for free or he deceives his fellow cartel members into thinking he's going along with colluded pricing while he secretly shades price to increase his own sales. And so on. The behavior is familiar.

In time, the free rider of relational transactions is the opportunistic liar, O, who induces V to make decisions at t_a on the basis of false information so that those later decision will advantage O himself.[15] If he did not lie at t_a, he would have to either tell the truth that the goods would not be delivered -- thereby stopping the transaction and keeping V from becoming vulnerable -- or alternatively, he would have to deliver the goods. Either way, V escapes exploitation. Honesty eliminates the problem of temporal change in opportunity by modifying the pure self-interest of transactors. North (1981), Reder (1979), McPherson (1981) and Arrow (1974) have recently addressed this dimension of market behavior.

The extreme nature of the conventional presumptions about self-interest is apparent in this -- our assumption that markets not only can survive in the presence of pure self-interest, but that they actually depend for their efficiency on its unbridled employment. Yet the time-shape of transactions reveals that genuine self-interest precludes all non-simultaneous private transactions just as it destroys cartels and prevents honest revelation of preferences for public goods. This is useful, I think, not because it is a realistic description of private markets but because it underlines the unrealism of our conventional faith in unconstrained self-interest. Furthermore, in recognizing that self-interest creates much the same incentives in all transactions, yet private markets do function for plausible reasons, we may be guided in our search for plausible reasons why cartels endure and citizens are often honest in taxing themselves for public goods.

Repetition protects the vulnerable in much the same way as does the law or honesty. In order for there to be a transaction, V has to accept the truth of O's commitment before t_p and V won't likely do so if he's been burned by O before -- or if he knows by reputation of others who have. Legally enforceable contracts are also a way of guarding against liars in unique transactions just as legally mandated taxes are a way of guarding against liars about public goods in face of the same individual incentives to cheat.

FOOTNOTES

1. The last chapter of The Timing of Economic Activities introduced this analysis of transactions, repetition and honesty and argued for its more complete development. This paper is a beginning.

2. In the employment relationship, "The difficulty lies in the fact that, once agrement has been reached on w [the wage rate] and x [job duties]...the worker has no assurance that the employer will consider anything but his own profit in deciding what he will ask the worker to do." [Simon (1951)]

3. In a third role, time is a scarce resource whose allocation, like that of any scarce resource, is subject to economic analysis. This, of course, is time-allocation analysis: time treated as a THING, a "commodity time." The present discussion of relational transactions will not be concerned with commodity time.

4. The abstraction inherent in any unit time is not an analytical problem confined to discrete time. In continuous time, the same thing appears as a vague specification of variables. What is called "continuous time analysis" really isn't if it leaves out any of the temporal details of time-shaped processes. But it always does -- as indeed it must, in order to make any sense at all.

5. Kornai's analysis of transactions includes a much richer transaction sequence, starting before t_a. But his purposes are different (Kornai, 1971).

6. One might pursue the fact that to the extent that payment B is expected during $t_p < t < t_d$ even with probability less than one, the incomplete transaction is itself an asset to V as an account receivable.

7. Harvey Leibenstein pointed out to me that transactions with kidnappers are especially freighted with distrust, hence often elaborately contrived to assure simultaneity of performance and payments events. The Iranian hostage transaction of 1981 was an international example of such distrustful simultaneity.

8. So Goldberg's analysis emphasizes the role of contracts in, for instance, a firm's installation of expensive and durable capital in order to provide a flow of product to a given buyer. In the product market, the seller is vulnerable to

the buyer's opportunism after the plant is built but before all the goods deliveries have been made.

9. Even the classic psychological motive for self-induced misinformation -- the reduction of cognitive dissonance -- is less likely to survive repetitive events as repetition multiplies the costs of self-deception.

10. Such decisions have much of the character of stocks in a static model rather than flows: their representation as human capital is apt. The relevance of class decisions is often rejected in analysis of economic behavior [Mises (1949); Lachmann (1976)].

11. Nelson and Winter (1980) have argued that because any theory is partial in its applicability, it is important to be clear about what it is applicable _to_ -- about its range of relevant phenomena. The implication is that a theory can be strengthened either by extending its explanatory power _per se_ over a given set of phenomena _or_ by more accurately defining the set of phenomena over which is it seen to apply. The emphasis here on the role of repetition in conventional theory is intended to do the second, to strengthen the power of that neoclassical analysis by restricting its range of applicability.

12. Simon described "long run rationality," as "rationality when a relationship of confidence between employer and worker can be attained. The fact that [it costs more without that confidence and trust] shows that it 'pays' the employer to establish this relationship." (Simon, 1951)

13. This formulation, too, is general and does not depend on the sequence of transactions that makes V vulnerable -- whether V is buyer or seller -- so long as the value of the goods is not dependent on this transaction. If O runs off with the goods instead of the money, they both have the same value, P_V.

14. It seems useful to remain agnostic on whether this _is_ honest behavior.

15. This analysis, indeed, might represent a degenerate case of Akerlof's lemon principle. The information asymmetry here lies in the fact that the Opportunist knows whether he's going to go through with the transaction but the Vulnerable one doesn't -- if they both knew, of course, there would be no relational exchange problem because the transaction would take place either without a hitch or not at all. So the "lemon" in this case isn't a slightly rusted car or one with a bad transmission, it is nothing, no transaction. Clearly, a world of self-interest not only precludes all non-simultaneous transactions, but

eliminates asymmetric information of this sort since both potential traders know what will happen and that knowledge precludes all transactions.

REFERENCES

Alchian, Armen A. 1950. "Uncertainty, Evolution, and Economic Theory." Journal of Political Economy 57: 211-21.

Arrow, Kenneth J. 1974. The Limits of Organization. New York: W.W.Norton.

Akerlof, George A. 1970. "The Market for 'Lemons': Quality Uncertainty and the Market Mechanism." Quarterly Journal of Economics (August 1970): 488-500.

Bok, Sissela. 1978. Lying: Moral Choice in Public and Private Life. New York: Pantheon.

Frisch, Ragnar. 1965. Theory of Production. Dordrecht: D. Reidel.

Goldberg, Victor P. 1980. "Relational Exchange: Economics and Complex Contracts." American Behavioral Scientist 23: 337-52.

Hicks, J.R. 1979. Causality in Economics. New York: Basic Books.

Hirschman, Albert O. 1977. The Passions and the Interests: Political Arguments for Capitalism before Its Triumph. Princeton: Princeton University Press.

Hobbes, Thomas. 1962. Leviathan or the Matter, Forme and Power of a Commonwealth Ecclesiasticall and Civil. New York: Collier.

Klein, Benjamin, and Keith B. Leffler. 1981. "The Role of Market Forces in Assuring Contractual Performance." Journal of Political Economy, 89:615-641.

Kornai, Janos. 1971. Anti-Equilibrium: On Economic Systems Theory and the Tasks of Research. Amesterdam: North-Holland.

Lachmann, Ludwig M. 1976. "From Mises to Shackle: An Essay on Austrian Economics and the Kaleidic Society." Journal of Economic Literature 16: 54-62.

McPherson, Michael S. 1984. "Limits on Self-Seeking: the Role of Morality in Economic Life." In Colander, David (ed.) Neoclassical Political Economy. Cambridge: Ballinger Publishing Company.

Mises, Ludwig von 1949. Human Action: A Treatise on Economics. New Haven: Yale University Press.

Nelson, Richard R., and Winter, Sidney G. 1980. "Firm and Industry Response to Changed Market Conditions: An Evolutionary Approach." Economic Inquiry 18:179-202.

North, Douglass C. 1981. Structure and Change in Economic History. New York: W.W. Norton.

Okun, Arthur M. 1981. Prices and Quantitites: A Macroeconomic Analysis. Washington: The Brookings Institution.

Reder, M.W. 1979. "The Place of Ethics in the theory of Production." In Economics and Human Welfare: Essays in Honor of Tibor Scitovsky, edited by M. Boskin, pp. 133-46. New York: Academic.

Schelling, T.C. 1978. Micromotives and Macrobehavior. New York: W.W.Norton.

Shackle, G.L.S. 1958. Time in Economics. Amsterdam: North-Holland.

Simon, Herbert A. 1951. "A Formal Theory of the Employment Relationship." Econometrica 19: 293-305.

_______________ 1959. "Theories of Decision-Making in Economics and Behavioral Sciences." American Economic Review 49: 253.

Stigler, George J. 1961. "The Economics of Information." Journal of Political Economy 69: 213-25.

Telser, L.G.. 1980. "A Theory of Self-enforcing Agreements." Journal of Business. 53:27-44.

Williamson, Oliver E. 1979. "Transactions-Cost Economics: The Governance of Contractual Relations." The Journal of Law and Economics 22: 233-61.

___________________. 1985. The Economic Institutions of Capitalism: Firms, Markets, Relational Contracting. New York: The Free Press.

Winston, Gordon C. 1982. The Timing of Economic Activities: Firms, Households and Markets in Time-Specific Analysis. Cambridge: Cambridge.

Part Thirteen
Behavioural Labour Economics

THE INDUSTRIAL RELATIONS SYSTEMS MODEL AS AN ANALYTICAL TOOL*

Noah M. Meltz

Centre for Industrial Relations
University of Toronto
123 St. George Street
Toronto, Ontario, Canada
M5S 1A1

> Another qualification for Post Office management, at least in Toronto, was to be a cuckoo. This term dates back to 1924 when the old Dominion Postal Clerks Association tried to organize a national strike. Other centres backed down, and the Toronto strikers were isolated and broken. From that day, every Toronto clerk who had crossed the picket line was a cuckoo, and every new postal worker was told who they were. Even thirty-five years later if you were talking to an older man at your case and the call of "cuckoo" ran down the isle, the conversation ceased and from that moment the fellow ceased to exist.
>
> Joe Davidson, by Joe Davidson and John Deverall, 1978.

I. INTRODUCTION

It has long been recognized that industrial relations represents a field of study which is shared among a number of disciplines including economics, psychology, sociology, history, law, political science and administrative science. In spite of, or perhaps because of, the extensive shared jurisdiction, industrial relations has not yet fully established itself a separate discipline. While there are a large number of scholars engaged in research in this field, few universities have departments of industrial relations. Instead industrial relations is usually taught within economics departments or in business schools. The exceptions are a few Schools of Industrial Relations (Cornell, Illinois), departments (such as at Montreal and Laval) and a very small number of programs and centres.

One of the reasons which has been offered for the lack of full discipline status is the absence of a unifying theoretical framework Heneman [8]. Another suggested explanation is the lack of a specific set of analytical tools. Both of these views have been disputed by Adams [1] and Laffer [11] and others who point to the industrial relations systems model developed by John Dunlop [6]. The purpose of this paper is to examine the evolution of what Dunlop proposed as a unifying theoretical framework and assess its value as an analytical tool. The conclusion is that the basic concept of the model together with the subsequent modifications does provide a fundamental analytical tool for industrial relations which can act as a link with other disciplines and a point of departure for testing specific hypotheses. The paper is organized into four sections: the industrial relations systems model, the model as an analytical tool, systems theory versus other theories, and the implications of the model for industrial relations.

2. THE INDUSTRIAL RELATIONS SYSTEMS MODEL

In publishing Industrial Relations Systems in 1958 John Dunlop set out to provide a theoretical basis for the field of industrial relations that would be on the same logical plane as an economic system. There were mounds and mounds of facts which he proposed to analyze through a systematic framework. While Dunlop did not attempt to summarize his framework in a schematic diagram, his book prompted subsequent authors, both supporters and opponents to present his views in diagram form. Chart 1 from Craig [5] is one such example. The central features of Dunlop's Industrial Relations System are: actors, ideology, contexts (the independent or explanatory variables) and rules (the dependent variables or outputs to be explained).

Criticisms of Dunlop's framework included its lack of predictable relationships or testable hypotheses, the more macro emphasis instead of micro (organization level) considerations, and the virtual absence of such subjects as interpersonal relations [2]. Subsequent work has modified the framework in an effort to take into account the criticisms. Recent examples are included in Kochan [10], Anderson and Gunderson [3] and Craig [5]. The diagram in Craig [5] is somewhat more detailed and is presented in Chart 2. The central features of each framework are environmental contexts (inputs), actors, converson processes and outputs.

In spite of almost thirty years of debate over Dunlop's model and the variations, there has been limited application although the basic approach is beginning to influence the way of organizing industrial relations material, specifically industrial relations textbooks.

3. THE MODEL AS AN ANALYTICAL TOOL

Two specific issues will be considered in using the systems model as an analytical tool: (1) the model as a link with other disciplines, and (2) the model as a point of departure for testing specific hypotheses.

3.1 Link with other Disciplines

The major link between the systems model and other disciplines is provided by the environmental subsystems. In general these subsystems have particular disciplines underlying them: economics, political science, law, sociology and psychology. Appendix 1 briefly summarizes the differences in objectives and methodology of industrial relations and the environmentally based disciplines. Depending on the particular issue which is identified, one or more of the subsystems will be relevant. As an illustration several current industrial relations issues are examined to indicate which environmental subsystems are relevant. The issues are: voluntary or imposed incomes and price restraint to control inflation; equal pay for work of equal value (comparable worth between work performed by men and women); legislation to impose a first contract if union and management are unable to reach an agreement; and factors responsible for the growth or decline of union membership.

The subject of income and price restraint involves all of the subsystems. There are both macro and micro economic forces underlying inflation as well as social and psychological considerations in the extent to which society is prepared to attach a high priority to reducing inflation. Macro economic policies can be implemented by monetary and fiscal decision-makers. The legal system comes in if forced restraints are introduced. While the economic and the social subsystems are perhaps the most important, in the case of income and price restraint, the industrial relations system is almost equally important because of the scope of decision-making on this subject [12]. How are large wage increases based on firm-specific productivity growth to be prevented from setting a pattern which could affect wages in firms with limited productivity growth? Here actions of labour and management are clearly crucial to the restraint of both incomes and prices. To study these actions requires an understanding of the relations among the actors and the economic and social subsystems along with the pivotal role of the political subsystem. In the case of controls, the role of the political subsystem is strengthened because the focus of the actors is shifted to the political arena and away from the conversion mechanism (the negotiation process). Since each of the subsystems has a major discipline underlying it, and two in the case of the social system (psychology and sociology), the link between the disciplines at a macro level is through the subsystems. For other problems there are also links to disciplines through the conversion mechanisms such as through economic, psychological and sociological theories of bargaining.

The equal pay issue has a base in the social system to the extent that society identifies it as a priority item. There are also aspects of the economic system which are relevant in terms of market forces and how higher wages for women will affect their own versus male employment prospects. Again we are considering a political decision which is implemented through the legal subsystem. Industrial relations aspects are involved through the effect the provisions of equal value legislation have on collective bargaining outcomes as well as the attitudes of unions (and managment) as actors in the system. Unions are likely to be in an ambivalent position since their general approach has been to foster equality, but in specific cases, unions made up primarily of males may feel threatened with a reduction in future job opportunities or potential future wage increases. In addition, unions may be concerned that administrative job evaluation procedures may replace collective bargaining as a mechanism for wage determination.

First-contract legislation is a more narrowly focussed issue in which the political and legal subsystems are the most crucial though social attitudes are a conditioning element. For the industrial relations system such legislation or its absence have a major impact on the conversion process relating unions and management. First-contract legislation clearly strengthens the hand of unions in dealing with an obstinate management.

The growth or decline of unions is affected by all the subsystems but the most direct impact recently has been from the political and legal subsystems [13], [14], [17]. Legislation favourable to the formation of unions and strong enforcement of the legislation by labour relations boards has been identified as a primary factor in growth (and in decline in its absence). This raises the question of why legislation differs, a question that can be addressed by political scientists as well as by economists, in their public choice perspective. Differences of social attitudes are clearly underlying factors. The strength of the union movement in general clearly affects the interaction with management in the conversion process and thereby in the outcomes of the industrial relations system.

3.2 Specific Hypotheses to be Tested

A criticism of the systems model is its lack of predictable relationships or testable hypotheses. While the criticism is valid as a generalization, it misses the mark in terms of the objective of the model. Being a global framework the model is not intended in and of itself to provide testable hypotheses. For example, the standard global model of the economic system allocating scarce resources for competing ends is also not "testable" in and of itself. What is important is whether the framework provides a point of departure for formulating testable hypotheses.

Judged by the same standards as an analogous model in other disciplines the systems model does provide a basis for formulating testable hypotheses as can be shown for each of the issues discussed earlier. In the case of income and price restraint, simulations have been prepared to explore the impact of separate and combined restraints on the consumer price index [12]. For comparable worth one could hypothesize and subsequently test the proposition that the greater the percentage of women in a union the more favourable the union is to comparable worth legislation. First-contract legislation should tend to reduce the duration of first-contract strikes and possibly even reduce the incidence of first contract strikes. Legislation favourable to union growth (or at least not inimical to union growth) and perceived strong enforcement of the provisions of such labour relations acts would tend to foster a higher union density rate (percent of labour force belonging to unions).

The central point is that specific hypotheses can be formulated using the industrial relations systems model as a starting point. The particular hypothesis depends on the subject being explored and the level of aggregation under consideration (establishment, firm, industry, economy). These in turn affect the extent to which the hypothesis is confined to industrial relations issues or relates to other disciplines.

4. SYSTEMS THEORY VS. OTHER IR THEORIES

There are a number of other major paradigms in industrial relations beside systems theory [4] [15] [16]: including Marxist Theory and the Unitary Theory. Marxist Theory postulates the impact of the separation of labour from capital in the capitalist system and the creation of classes. The result is an unceasing power struggle which is a central feature of industrial relations [9]. This approach can certainly be assessed within the Systems model by making certain assumptions about the political system and the goals, values and power of unions and management. Hypotheses to test Marxist theory can be fitted into the industrial relations systems model.

The Unitary Theory postulates that there is a unity of interest between workers and management such that unions are superfluous and an interference with productive relations between management and unorganized workers [7]. What is in the interests of management is the interest of its workers. Again hypotheses to test this theory can flow from the Systems model. A breakdown in what the Unitary Theory postulates as a fundamental harmony of interests would result from inappropriate personnel policies by management. As the old industrial relations adage suggests: management gets the union it deserves. This could be tested by examining management's attitudes and practices towards its workers prior to unionization on such subjects as impartiality versus favourtism, trust versus mistrust, comparability of wages and benefits between this and related organizations.

Both the Marxist and Unitary theories can be contained within the Industrial Relations Systems model. Only the underlying assumptions and the outputs change.

5. IMPLICATIONS FOR INDUSTRIAL RELATIONS

The implication of using the industrial relations systems model as an analytical tool is that initially it should be thought of as a check list. Beginning with the various environmental subsystems (or contexts as Dunlop terms them), consideration must be given to possible interrelations with the particular issue being examined. Since the primary focus is industrial relations, this means that the focus is on the actors, the conversion mechanisms and the outcomes. However, because the contexts can be so important, initial consideration has to be given to their particular impact on the major industrial relations subjects.

Does this mean that industrial relationists (to use Laffer's [11] term) have to also be economists, psychologists, sociologists, etc.? While the answer is no, it is important that they understand the differing perspectives adopted by the other disciplines and for which issues it would be appropriate to draw from particular disciplines.

One of the fears of industrial relationists is that they will be viewed as second rate economists, second rate psychologists or second rate sociologists. The answer lies in the essence of research and practice in industrial relations. As Heneman [8] said, the test of their contribution is whether they can do it better. That is, whether a total focus on all aspects of the employment relationship produces more complete explanations and better predictions in the IR field. The suggestion of this paper is that the systems model provides the appropriate vehicle to use as an organizing framework within which to conduct analysis of industrial relations developments. While the field does overlap with a number of disciplines including economics and psychology, there is a synergistic result which justifies the separate discipline of industrial relations. For this approach the systems model is the most logical organizing framework.

FOOTNOTES

*The author would like to acknowledge the comments received from Roy Adams, Jean Boivin, Alton Craig, Donald Carter and Morley Gunderson.

REFERENCES

[1] Adams, Roy J. Competing Paradigms in Industrial Relations. Relations Industrielles/Industrial Relations 38, No. 3 (1983):508-531.

[2] Adams, Roy J. Dunlop After Two Decades: Systems Theory as a Framework for Organizing the Field of Industrial Relations. Faculty of Business, McMaster University, Hamilton, Ontario. Working Paper Series No. 142, December 1977.

[3] Anderson, John C. and Morley Gunderson. Union-Management Relations in Canada. (Addison-Wesley, Don Mills, Ontario, 1982)

[4] Cox, R.W. Approaches to a Futurology of Industrial Relations, International Institute for Labour Studies, Bulletin 8 (1971): 139-164.

[5] Craig, Alton. The System of Industrial Relations in Canada, (Prentice-Hall, Canada, Scarborough, Ontario, 1983). See also revised edition, 1986.

[6] Dunlop, John. Industrial Relations Systems, (Henry Holt, New York, 1958)

[7] Fox, Alan. Industrial Sociology and Industrial Relations, Research Paper No. 3, Royal Commission on Trade Unions and Employers' Associations, (Her Majesty's Stationery Office, London, 1966)

[8] Heneman, Herbert G. Jr. Toward a General Conceptual System of Industrial Relations: How Do We Get There? in: Somers, Gerald G. (ed.) Essays in Industrial Relations Theory (The Iowa State University Press, Ames, Iowa 1969)

[9] Hyman, R. Industrial Relations: A Marxist Introduction. (MacMillan Press, London 1975)

[10] Kochan, Thomas A. Collective Bargaining and Industrial Relations. (Richard D. Irwin, Homewood, Illinois 1980)

[11] Laffer, Kingsley. Is Industrial Relations an Academic Discipline? The Journal of Industrial Relations 16, No. 1 (1974), 62-73.

[12] Maital, Shlomo and Noah M. Meltz. Labor and management attitudes toward a new social contract: A comparison of Canada and the United States in: Maital, S. and Lipnowski, I. (eds) Macroeconomic Conflict and Social Institutions, (Ballinger, Cambridge, Mass. 1985).

[13] Meltz, Noah M. Labor Movements in Canada and the United States in: Kochan, T.A. (ed) Challenges and Choices Facing American Labor. (The MIT Press, Cambridge, Mass., 1985)

[14] Rose, J.B. and Chaison, G.N. The State of the Unions: United States and Canada. Journal of Labour Research (Winter 1985), 97-112.

[15] Shalev, M. Industrial Relations Theory and the Comparative Study of Industrial Relations and Industrial Conflict. British Journal of Industrial Relations 18, No. 1 (March 1980) 26-41.

[16] Shienstock, G. Toward a theory of industrial relations, British Journal of Industrial Relations 19 (July 1981) 170-189.

[17] Weiler, Paul. Promises to keep: securing workers' rights to self-organization under the NLRA. Harvard Law Review (June 1983) 1769-1827.

[18] The World Book Encylopedia, 1978 edition. (Childcraft International, Chicago, 1978)

APPENDIX 1

Central Focus of Industrial Relations, Economics, Psychology and Sociology

INDUSTRIAL RELATIONS	ECONOMICS	PSYCHOLOGY	SOCIOLOGY
Nature of the employment relationship and the wide range of factors that influence the relationship. The choices made by employers and employees not only on wages and benefits but on accepting or leaving a job. An interest in the process which influences the terms and conditions of work.	How goods and services get produced and how they are distributed.	Why human beings and animals behave as they do.	Study of individuals, groups and institutions that make up human society. Deals with the predominant attitudes, behaviour and types of relationships within a society.
	Labour economics: concerned with wages and hours, labour unions, government labour policies. Effects of unions and investment in human capital on wage determination process. The role of labour market variables and economic conditions in society on decision-making behaviour of individuals, unions and firms.	Industrial psychology: study of people at work, ie to understand how workers behave on the job, why they behave as they do, and how to make jobs more rewarding to workers, industry and society.	Industrial sociology study of the behaviour of work groups, the role and determinants of conflict in labour organizations and society.

Sources: [3], [18].

Quality Circles and Corporate Identity
- towards overcoming the crisis of taylorism -

Gerd Wiendieck

a b s t r a c t

In many economic organizations taylorism has over the years created bureaucratic inflexibilitities and the inability to adjust. This organizational burden has recently stimulated the development of new concepts of work organization, which basically imply the reopening of the tayloristically reduced scope of individual action by some means of decentralization of decision making. The concept of 'Quality Circles' can be seen as an organizational tool to overcome the tayloristic inflexibilities by stimulating small group problem solving activities and by creating a sense of responsibility and loyality among its members. The increased degree of freedom, inevitably connected with Quality Circles have, on the other hand, created new problems of organizational control and interpersonal conflict. It is argued, that these problems can partly be dealt with by means of some measures of normative control, such as 'Corporate Identity' wich implies the establishment of commonly accepted values, which tend to give both, guidance and security of action.

Quality Circles and Corporate Identity

The crises of western economies in the 70s stimulated a rather hectic search for instant remedies. Since at the same time the Japanese economy was stable and prosperous, it was understandable that European Managers searched all over Japanese factories for an explanation for their extraordinarily high standard of productivity and product quality. Soon the so-called 'Quality Circles' were spotted and immediately imported into Western Germany, regardless of their specific cultural backing in Japanese societies. Meanwhile, more than 50% of the 100 biggest companies in Western Germany operate with Quality Circles (QC) or familiar concepts (BUNGARD & WIENDIECK 1986, 12).

The principle idea of QC is simple and makes sense: A group of workers meet at regular intervals in order to discuss their own work problems, to look for solutions and to implement them as far as possible. In fact this concept is so simple and banal that it becomes difficult to understand the amount of excitement, both approving and rejecting, it created within the organizations. And perhaps it is the banality of the idea which induced the scientific community to almost completely overlook the concept of QC. At least up to now there have been very few sincere psychological discussions of this simple concept and its impact on traditional organizations.

The revolutionary aspect of the concept can only be understood, once the principles of tayloristic organizations have been mentally incorporated so that they give the impression of being both normal and normative, hence even imagining a non tayloristic work organization is made difficult. The concept of QC is in fact contradictory to tayloristic principles and can in this way be regarded as having broken free of its narrow boundaries.

Irrespective and independent of this another concept can be found in recent discussions between western management circles: The concept of 'Corporate Identity' (CI). The idea behind this concept is also quite simple: Create a stable and unmistakable image of the organization which offers a vision instead of mere goods or salaries. The total appearance - from the letter head to the entrance hall and from the workers clothing to the secretaries way of smiling - should be put under one single heading and hence become operative in a twofold way: The externally directed marketing strategy of attracting customers by means of a central idea instead of selling commodities and secondly the internally directed organizing principle of workers beeing guided by values instead of being pushed by superiors. After Frederik HERZBERG's work on job motivation this idea was partly reactivated on a temporary basis in the concept of job enrichment or management by objectives, but soon became forgotten within the still booming period of rational management philosophies. These seemed to suggest that nearly every organizational objective could easily be met as long as there was a rational management with clear cut structures, strict regulations and tight supervision. Thanks to PETERs and WATERMAN's book 'In search of excellence' managers became reminded of the fact that man does not behave so rationally and that his management by external reinforcement schedules is limited. He is much more guided by values and self-determination than management dared to admit since this admittance seemed to indicate managements impotency whereas it actually refers to the boundaries of tayloristic principles.

In accordance with this line of reasoning we argue that both - until now independently discussed - concepts of 'QC' and 'CI' are in fact close relatives since they are both offsprings of a crisis of Taylorism and will jointly pawe the way for providing a solution. This would mean an increase in organizational stability and flexibility simultaneously. Only at first glance does this seem to be contradictory. But just as a technician requires an elastic material to construct highly loaded elements in order to improve overall stability, here the brittle structure of traditional hierarchical systems should be replaced by a more elastic one, which does not draw its potential for survival from monumental stiffness but from decentralized units capable of development. A slightly different aspect of this idea had previously been put forward by Herbert SIMON (1962) who illustrated the avantages of an organization consisting of hierarchically interconnected subunits by a story about two watchmakers called Hora and Tempus. Both craftsmen, equally diligent and eager were building watches consisting of 1000 pieces each. Both were occasionally interrupted by customers asking for the state of completion of their watches. But the effects of these telephone calls were tremendously different. While Hora could easily manage these disturbances Tempus could not and had finally to give up his business. The reason was simple: Their watches were constructed differently: Whenever Tempus had to stop and to put his partly assembled watch aside it completely fell apart so that he had to start right from the beginning again. Horas watches were equally complex, but constructed in a way that they consisted of different subunit of 10 pieces each. Ten of these subunits were then assembled into bigger subunits and so forth. While the constructive difference is a minor one, the consequences are tremendous: Whenever Hora was interrupted only a amall fraction of his work was affected. This picture symbolizes one of the advantages of a decentralized organization, consisting of different and independent subunits hierarchically interconnected into an organization capable of flexible response to external challenges. This organization draws its stability from the independence of its subunits and its flexibility from the looseness of their interconnections. Obviously, a harmonious equilibrium between flexibility and stability or independence and interconnection must be maintained. This is the dilemma of hierarchy.

- The dilemma of hierarchy -

In general, hierarchical systems are characterized by a particular form of division of labour: The higher echelons are in charge of defining the goal while the lower charges have to execute orders. This system runs into a specific dilemma: The realization of superordinate goals is both made possible and endangered by the active contribution of members of the lower echelons. They must not be regarded as mere objects or tools but as individuals whose task it is to transform the abstract management instructions into deeds by adding their own concrete will.

Their individual will could, on the one hand, undermine the system if it becomes too vigorous or on the other, cease all activities once it is too minor. In the latter case, management would have to fully specify its intentions considering every trifle and would soon be overburdened by trivialities. So the hierarchical organization has to maintain a delicate balance between planned structures on the one side and spontaneous developments on the other. It is an equilibrium between the opposite evils of torpid bureaucracy and uncontrollable chaos (BAHRDT 1958, 56). This equilibrium is far from beeing a stable one. It rather seems to be permanently endangered by both internal and external forces. It is therefore more adequate to call it a 'delicate balance'. It is our conviction, that this balance had gradually been destroyed by the long lasting and dominant influence of tayloristic principles of the so-called 'scientific management'. The destruction of this balance in favour of an inflexible structure was an unwanted and unnoticed side-effect. Because of the tayloristic efficiency in rising productivity the negativ side-effects could develop without creating to much attention until they reached a new quality: The double problem of organizational torpidity and individual apathy.

- The 'one-best-way principle' -

The central idea behind Taylorism is the conviction that there is only one best way for every job and that it is vital to find this one way and to adhere to it relentlessly. There can be no doubt that adherence to this rule resulted in an enormous increase in productivity. This effect was actually so overwhelming that the unwanted side-effects of this one-best-way-principle were easily overlooked or even repressed. For Taylor it was self-evident that management should not be dependent on the casualness of individual knowledge or experience. Hence centralized bureaus were installed to systematically analyse jobs, collect the existent knowledge and to concentrate it into general rules and to strictly regulate, control and supervise the particular way a certain job has to be executed. As a consequence of this, the individual experience and competence became increasingly superfluous.

- The double division of labour -

This principle implies a double form of division of labour. Firstly, in a functional sense, the division of planning and execution and secondly, in a hierarchical sense, the devision of centralized and subordinate power holders which tend to be put under tutelage. Since the division of labour necessarily implies coordination of labour there are consequences both for the organization and the individual. The high degree of division of labour meant standardisation and simplification of jobs but also required a complex system of management control, coordination and supervision. Job simplification and organizational complexity are just two sides of the same model. Furthermore, the locus of control has moved from the individual worker to a central management agency. The loss of individual control corresponds with the perfection of organizational control.

Tab.1: Consequences of tayloristic principles of organization

	Division of labour (Person)	Coordination of labour (Organization)
Functional division of labour	Simplification of work tasks (Partialisation)	Complication of organization (Line-staff-system)
Hierarchical division of labour	Reduction of individual control ('Tutelage')	Perfection of central control ('Domination')

- The bureaucratic torpidity -

As a result of this organizational development the individual scope of action shrank in a threefold manner: The task variability, the job responsibility and the chance for social interaction diminished. It is not at all astonishing that job motivation and job competence vanished as well. Subtle forms of job refusal and work denial developed and stimulated further dirigistical measures of control in order to compensate these negative effects. A vicious circle of dirigism and lethargy originated, which could psychologically be understood as reactance behaviour due to an organizational reduction of freedom (WORTMAN & BREHM 1975). THORSRUD and EMERY (1982) have vividly described this circle and recently we could prove its existence ranging over several hierarchical levels (WIENDIECK 1986, 219).

And again we find an interaction between the individual and the organization. The individual lethargy corresponds with the organizational torpidity. It looks as if the old Leninistic wisdom that confidence is good, but supervision is better was expanded by a tayloristic superlative that suppression is best. There can be no doubt that taylorism had the latent function of stimulating the development of a torpid, bureaucratic organization, whose members were only as competent and motivated as was absolutely necessary for their minimized span of control. These organizations were by all means capable of executing routine jobs but failed largely or completely as soon as creativity, flexibility and loyalty were needed. This organizational system produces a particular style of leadership, although this could be more appropriatly termed 'supervision'. It was both characteristic and unmasking to find that quite often these leaders were (placed) in a slightly elevated room designed to facilitate the overall supervision of their subordinates. Leadership lost its functions of defining objectives and maintaining group structures and was thereby reduced to a mere supervision of normative behaviour.

- The new look -

Social, economic and technological developments of the last decade led tayloristic principles and leadership philosophies become absolete. Nowadays, innovative power and flexibility are needed. A social change of values strengthened the desire for integrated and challenging jobs, which allow and demand for participation and joint actions. Secondly, we could observe an increase in economic competition coupled with a modification from a dominant price competition towards a dominant quality competion and thirdly there was an acceleration of technical rationalisation which led to the installation of so-called 'intelligent machines'. These intelligent machines become more and more interconnected into an integrated system of computer aided design, manufacturing and quality control. This system requires human skills which could not develop under the tight tayloristic system of control: Competence coupled with independence and a sense of responsibility.

Although these social, economic and technical developments are different in nature, their effects accumulated and produced an organizational crisis, deep enough to stimulate a sincere search for a remedy to increase flexibility without causing chaos.

The direction in thinking is to widen the previously reduced scope of action and to decentralize decision making in order to stimulate motivation and a sense of responsibility. This line of reasoning interprets man as an active and conscious human being, who wants to construct his environment according to meaningful criteria and to improve his own abilities and experience at the same time. The necessary prerequisite for this chance of creation and growth is the existence of a relatively wide scope of action which stimulates the exploration of new patterns of behaviour and a feed-back process which provides the information necessary for learning and cognitive processing. It was in particular HACKER (1978, 82ff.) who pointed out the importance of this informative feed-back process; since it was only this which permitted the development of an adequate image of the work process and the organizational environment. HACKER calls it an 'Operative-image-system' (OAS-Operatives Abbild System) which allows for adequate decision making. The term 'adequate' here implies a time perspective: Those who are permanently caught offguard by the sudden accurance of problems can only spontaneously interfere in a fire-fighting way but cannot operate in an anticipative and preventive manner so as to minimize the possibility of a problem arising in the first place and hence reduce the amount of disruption. This is why it is vital to increase simultaneously both, the scope of action and the transparency of modern work processes. This may be commonplace, but as long as we hear workers say: "I don't know why we have to do it this way either, I suppose we always did it this way" this plea hasn't been really understood. This argument becomes even more meaningful as the complexity of the production and administration processes rises. While the effect of a hammer hitting a nail is abvious to everybody, the technical processes of a CNC-controlled machine is far beyond our direct imagination. Therefore, transparancy is vital in restoring security of action, which otherwise tended to vanish when simply widening the scope of action.

QC are an attempt to restore a worker's control over his own work and at the same time to guide his learning process by the group he belongs to. Normally the group meetings are moderated - neither directed nor controlled - by the supervisor of the workers. Within the QC he ceases to be the boss and becomes a group member or facilitator; a linking pin between the autonomous group and the formal organization. So the QC partly forms a parallel organization, which, although dependent on the dominant organizational structures, also interferes with them thereby creating conflict.

- Conflict and the loss of control -

This conflict inevitably produced by quality circles can be seen in a threefold way, on the individual, the interpersonal and the organizational level.

On the individual level, we have quite frequently observed that workers or foreman who were used to obeying orders, ran into difficulties of insecurity when self-determination and responsibility was expected. The widened scope of action not only meant freedom to decide but also responsibility. So new demands originated that not all of the workers and foreman were eager to accept. Failure could no longer be that easily explained by external constraints or inadequate orders by superiors. The organizational structure lost parts of its behaviour guiding and its behaviour excusing power. This is the individual risk, inevitably connected with the chance of a more self-determined work. And again there is a counterpart to this ambivalence on the management level.

There can be no daubt that the installation of QC activated worker's individual motivation and loyalty which had previously been suppressed by a shortsighted and unimaginative adherence to the tayloristic principles of clear cut structures, strict control and tight supervision. Often exactly those managers who used to complain of workers inactivity and lethargy are now alarmed or even shocked by workers initiative and self-determination after QC have been created. These managers fear the loss of control, which for them means losing face or prestige. This is the individual aspect of the previously mentioned dilemma of the hierarchical organization. As decision making processes become decentralized the central hierarchical influence tends to decrease. The tight organizational systems softens and principally runs the risk of control loss. Frequently, this will reactivate some restorative processes; soon middle and lower management personal come to the forefront who have from the outset opposed these new organizational developments but never dared to mention them aloud since top management was obviously firmly in favor of the installation of quality circles. There are some companies that eventually abolished quality circles, because they feared individual arbitrariness and organizational chaos.
So the possibility of conflict which had previously been covered by the excitement over the increased flexibility, now becomes apparent.

- Normative control instead of tayloristic dirigism -
It is obvious that taylorism was not only geared towards an increase in productivity by means of standardizing all working methods but also toward the stabili-

zation of domination by centralising power. So we must ask whether the conquest of taylorism and the rise of flexibility can only be obtained at the cost of a loss of organizational control. It was fundamentally this question which gave rise to the discussion of leadership philosophies and the concept of corporate identity. And it is by no means accidental that companies that discuss or implement concepts like QC are at the same time interested in the concept of corporate identity. There seems to be a common cause.

The concept of corporate identity aims at giving members of the organization some commonly accepted guidelines which secure stability of action without beeing externally suppressive.

The experiments of LITWIN & STRINGER (1968) on the management of organizational climates showed that the rather divergent values such as 'flexibility and innovation' or 'order and regularity' could be successfully implanted within the organization as long as all managers and superiors agreed to consistently behave according to the guidelines. This does not mean that any value could be established since they require acceptance in order to become operative. So, this system of normative control is by no means as subtly form of new taylorism, but should be conceived more in terms of an analogy of the political change from despotism to democracy. The requirement of variety and vividness didn't abolish rule, it merely served to transform it. The system of control changed its basis from reactive obedience to active acceptance.

- Normative control and interpersonal conflict -

And yet there is another reason for a joint discussion of Quality Circles and Corporate Identity. Besides the need to preserve control in order to stabilize organizations there is a further possibility of conflict, this time on an interpersonal level. It is now obvious that a dirigistic style of leadership does not fit into the concept of a widened scope of action. And again the argument holds that freedom of decision implies individual responsibility and that this is true not only for subordinates but for superiors as well. Under the tayloristic principle not only the subordinate was tied into a rigid system of regulations, but the leaders as well, which led, as previously mentioned, to reducing leadership functions toward mere supervision. So even the leaders could easily explain or excuse their behaviour by external contraints, which did not leave him any alternatives. This in fact minimized interpersonal conflicts. Finally, the superiors simply performed their organizational duties, and their subordinates had to accept this situation. As the system opens up and allows for decentralized decision making, the external organizational legitimacy of leadership behaviour tends to vanish. Thus a conflict, could arise, which may undermine or even destroy the chance for organizational flexibility and individual growth.

If two people hold different views, a conflict arises, which shows two aspects, an informational one and an interpersonal one. Let us say that the other view is not only different from mine, but is one of a different person. To accept this other view may resolve the informational conflict, but may activate the interpersonal one since the acceptance of this view could by myself and others be misunderstood as submission. And this tends to make the acceptance of the other view an unlikely event. Obviously we are often prepared to follow facts but refuse submission. We do not hesitate to give way to a tree that had fallen on the pavement but we become angry if a group of people blocks our path. MOSCOVICI & RICATEAU (1973) could experimentally prove this effect, which can easily be observed in everyday life interaction. Quite often, the readiness for the acceptance of another opinion arises, as soon as the other person leaves the site of interaction or after a certain period of time has elapsed, i.e. generally after a disassociation between person and opinion has taken place. The underlying conflict stems from the specific attribution style of the subordinate. If he views the superiors orders as a result of external necessities he tends to accept, but if he views them as a result of his personal peculiarities, he tends to reject them.

This pattern of attribution is - as the attribution theory (KELLEY 1973) tells us - a likely one, if the superior expects a particular pattern of behaviour from his subordinate regardless of the objective job necessities and secondly if the superior's orders are rather unique. If, on the other hand, all superiors act in a similar way and in accordance with the specific work situation, their behaviour psychologically takes on a different meaning. It appears to be disconnected from a particular superior but is in line with the overall organizational objectives. So the interpersonal part of the possible conflict becomes less vital and hence rejective tendencies diminish. A commonly accepted corporate identity provides values which guide and align behavior and thereby restore some kinds of organizational control, which even furthers loyalty and mobility.

That is why the principle of decentralization of power, for example, by means of Quality Circles on the one hand and the principle of normative control, for example by means of corporate identity instead of dirigistic supervision, on the other hand are necessary, joint elements of an organizational system which tries to overcome the bureauaucratic torpidity without losing control or being locked in interpersonal conflicts.

- Summary -

A simple graph may take the role of a summary and hopefully illustrate and illuminate the overall argumentation

Taylorism and its consequences

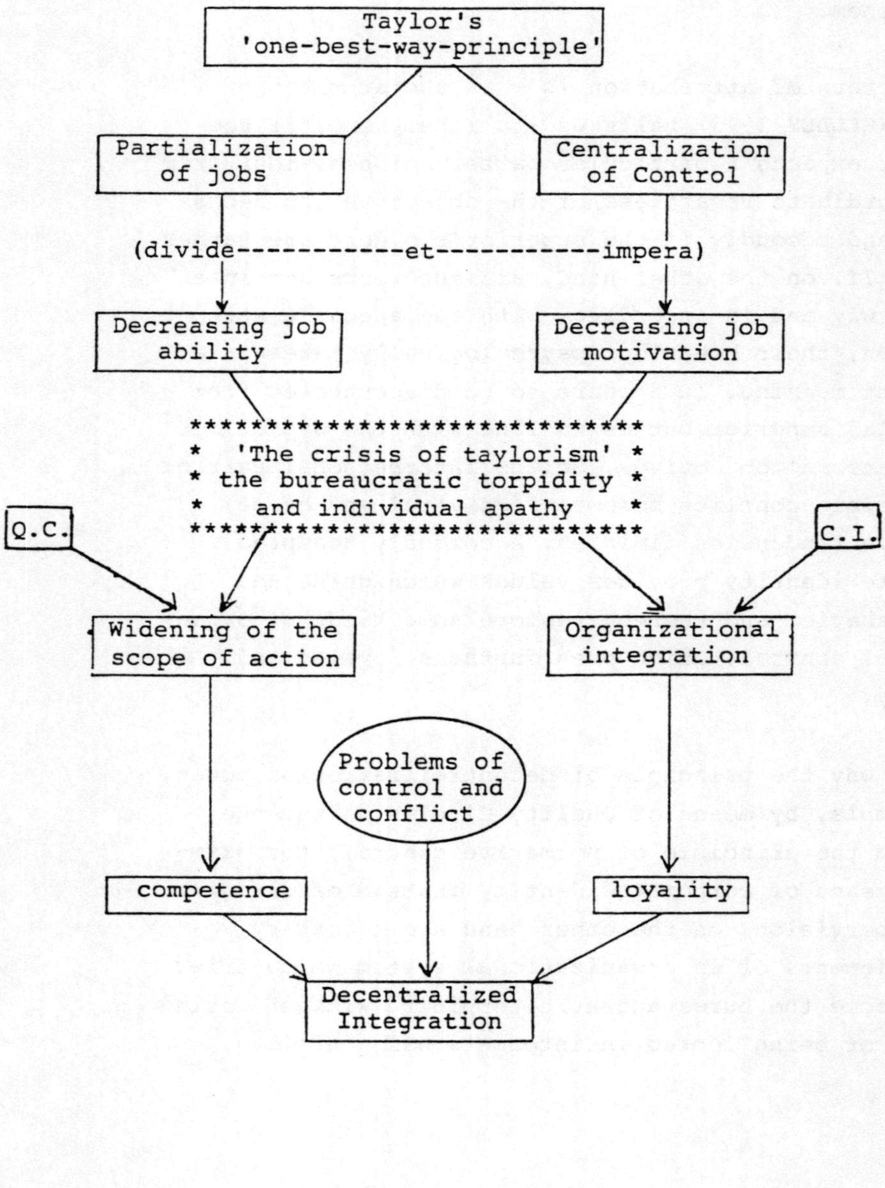

References:

BARTDT; H.P.: Industriebürokratie. Versuch einer Soziologie des industrialisierten Bürobetriebes und seiner Angestellten. Stuttgart 1958.

BUNGARD, W. und WIENDIECK, G.(Hg.): Qualitäts-Zirkel als Instrument zeitgemäßer Betriebsführung. Verlag Moderne Industrie, München 1986.

HACKER, W.: Allgemeine Arbeits- und Ingenieurpsychologie. Huber-Verlag, Bern 1978.

HERZBERG, G., MAUSNER, B. und SNYDERMAN, B.: The motivation to work. New York 1959.

KELLEY, H.: The Process of Causal Attribution. In: American Psychologist 1973, 28, S.107-128.

LITWIN, G. H. und STRINGER, R.A.jr.: Motivation und organizational climate. Harvard University, Boston 1968.

MOSCOVICI, S. und RICATEAU, P.: Konformität, Minderheit und sozialer Einfluß. In: MOSCOVICI, S.(Hg.): Forschungsgebiete der Sozialpsychologie. Bd.1, Fischer Athenäum, Frankfurt a.M. 1973, S.155-214.

PETERS, T.J. und WATERMAN, R.H.: In Search of Excellence Lessons from Americas Best-Run Companies. Harper & Row, New York 1982.

SIMON,H.A.: The architecture of complexity. In: Proceedings of the American Philosophical Society 1962, 106:467-482.

THORSRUD, E. und EMERY, F.E.: Industrielt demokrati. Oslo 1964.

WIENDIECK, G.: Warum Qualitätszirkel? Zum organisationspsychologischen Hintergrund eines neuen Managements-Konzepts. In: BUNGARD, W. und WIENDIECK, G.(Hg.): Qualitäts-Zirkel als Instrument zeitgemäßer Betriebsführung. Verlag Moderne Industrie, Landsberg 1986, S.61-74.

WIENDIECK, G. Widerstand gegen Qualitätszirkel. Eine Idee und ihre Feinde. In: BUNGARD, W. und WIENDIECK, G.(Hg.): Qualitäts-Zirkel als Instrument zeitgemäßer Betriebsführung. Verlag Moderne Industrie, Landsberg 1986a, S.207-221.

WIENDIECK, G.: Handlungsspielraum und Führungsphilosophie. - Zur Organisationspsychologie der Entscheidungsdezentralisierung. In: Gruppendynamik 1986, 2, S.26-37.

WORTMAN, C. und BREHM, J.W.: Responses to uncontrollable outcomes. An Integration of reactance theory and the learned helplessness model. In: BERKOWITZ, L.(Hg.): Advances in experimental social psychology. Bd.8, Academic Press, New York 1985.

Worker Participation: Paths to Higher Productivity and Well-Being

by

John F. Tomer

Department of Economics and Finance
Manhattan College
Riverdale, N.Y. 10471

Tel: (212) 920-0462 (w)
(518) 273-1851 (h)

Practically everyone agrees that the reasons for introducing greater worker participation are to increase productivity and worker well-being. However, as evidenced by the specific organizational changes being made and the organizational ideals involved, there is much diversity with respect to the desired paths to increasing participation. This paper develops a theoretical framework enabling us to think clearly about the relative merits of different worker participation approaches. Because increased worker participation generally leads to increased X-efficiency, it is useful to conceive of the process as involving organizational capital formation, and thus, a shift outward of the production possibility frontier. Moreover, increased worker participation that leads to increased worker well-being shifts the worker well-being possibility frontier outward. An organization will have reached the ultimate participative ideal, Theory Z management, when 100% of both the X-efficiency improving and worker well-being improving organizational innovations have been made. Different types of worker participation can be compared by assessing the extent to which they measure up to the Theory Z ideal.

This paper, a summary of a longer paper with the same name, was presented at the International Conference on Economics and Psychology on July 11, 1986 at the Kibbutz Shefayim, Israel.

Introduction

Around the world, many different paths to increased worker participation are being trod. Not only do enterprises differ in the specific organizational changes being made, but their organizational ideals or models differ. These differences are reflected in a variety of literatures related to worker participation. Despite these differences, everyone seems to agree on the two main reasons for introducing greater worker participation: increased productivity and increased worker well-being. The problems arise when we begin to think about how increased worker participation is induced by changes in particular organizational features and why these should lead to improved productivity and well-being. The purpose of this paper is to develop a theoretical framework enabling us to think clearly about the relative merits of these different approaches to worker participation. The view here is that firms making organizational changes to increase worker participation are making a kind of intangible human capital investment, i.e., an investment in organizational capital, enabling a flow of future benefits in the form of higher productivity and worker well-being. Thus, the process of increasing worker participation is inherent to the process of economic growth.

The Meaning of Worker Participation

Full worker participation occurs when a worker is able to experience his full human potential at work. Five general aspects of worker participation are identified: 1) influence over what goes on at the workplace, 2) influence with respect to major decisions, 3) feeling part of the organization, 4) ability to make a real contribution through the exercise of discretion and the taking of responsiblity, and 5) experience of cooperative work relationships. It should be noted that the term worker participation is more commonly used in a narrower sense to denote workers' participation in roles usually reserved for management. The relationship between participation and a variety of organizational features is considered below.

Organizational Forms Associated With Worker Participation

There is no unique way to classify the different organizational forms associated with worker participation. Fusfeld's (1983, pp. 772-774) spectrum of four institutional forms emphasizes the social division of labor among workers, managers and owners. First is "the pure capitalistic firm [in which] authority is exercised exclusively by the owners. The second institutional form is the capitalistic firm in a system of collective bargaining" where workers periodically attempt to reach agreements with managers and/or owners to resolve certain of their conflicts (pp. 772-773). The third form, the participatory firm, involves a shift in the structure of power to workers in that workers 1) take over some of the managerial functions at the workplace level and 2) take on a number of functions of owners and/or management at the peak of the organization. Organizational changes consistent with the former include "quality circles, job enrichment and other quality of work life programs; those consistent with the latter include employee stock ownership plans and worker representation on boards of directors such as "codetermination." The fourth institutional form is the labor-managed or self-managed firm. In it the ownership of assets is separated from the management function; laborers exercise managerial control at all levels and have the right to the firm's economic profit.

Jaroslav Vanek's (1975, pp. 13-16) classification of organizational forms is the most comprehensive. His first order distinction concerns control; firms are 1) self-managed if they are dominated by members who work in the organization and 2) capital controlled (dehumanized) if they are dominated by and serve the objectives of those who own capital.

David Ellerman (1984) classifies firms according to their legal structure. He focuses on three rights, 1) voting rights, 2) the right to the firm's economic profit, and 3) the right to the firm's net book value; also, he considers who exercises these rights and whether they are 1) personal (nontransferable) or 2) property rights. In the conventional capitalist firm all these rights are property rights and are owned by the shareholders. In a producer or worker coooperative (e.g., Mondragon), voting and economic profit rights are the personal rights of worker-owners; whereas the net book value rights are a type of property rights with restricted transferability. In Ellerman's view, the legal structure of the worker cooperative is superior to not only the capitalist corperation but employee-owned corporations, traditional worker cooperatives, and Yugoslav-type self-managed firms.

The common element running through these and other classifications is that the organization's form (e.g., the formal division of labor, the dominant pattern of influence, the legal structure, or the property rights in ownership) is the key to attaining the desired participation.

Ideal Organizational Behavior

In contrast to the above view is the view that changing the organization's culture, i.e., organizational development (OD), will unlock the door to increasing desired types of worker participation. To shorten the exposition, the focus here will be on Blake and Mouton's approach known as Grid OD, an approach which integrates the insights of most of the behavioral theorists and epitomizes OD.

The basis for Grid OD is that business excellence is unlikely to be achieved simply by using sound corporate logic and using valid business skills and techniques if "conflict is not faced,... creativity is stifled, or where dedication and commitment are low, and under circumstances where people do not have a sound approach to critique and learning. The critical ingredient -- motivated people -- is missing" (Blake and Mouton 1969, p. 75). Accordingly, Blake and Mouton advocate systematically changing the thinking and behavior of managers in an organization so that management will be characterized simultaneously by high concern for production (getting results) and high concern for people, i.e., the 9,9 leadership style. The 9,9 style "is a goal-centered, team approach that seeks to gain optimum results through participation, involvement, commitment, and conflict solving of everyone who can contribute (Blake and Mouton 1985, p. 13). In Blake and Mouton's (1969, pp. 88-91) view, it is not participation per se that leads to high motivation and commitment; only participation of a 9,9 character will do.

Towards an Integration

Will the desired participative behavior follow when appropriate organizational forms are introduced? Or are the institutional forms secondary to the psychological quality of people interactions? One author has taken an integrated approach to worker participation, i.e., one in which cultural and structural factors are given more or less equal emphasis.

According to Richard Walton (1985), the workplace participation ideal is the "commitment strategy" which contrasts dramatically with the traditional or "control strategy." The control strategy follows largely from the ideas of Frederick Taylor and emphasizes 1) small fixed jobs, 2) low motivation and skill expectations, 3) labor as a variable cost, 4) managerial control necessitating a substantial hierarchy with top-down communication, and 5) adversarial relations with unionized workers. On the other hand, in the commitment strategy

> "... jobs are designed to be broader than before, to combine planning and implementation, and to include efforts to upgrade operations, not just maintain them. Individual responsibilities are expected to change as conditions change, and teams, not individuals, often are the organizational units accountable for performance. With management hierarchies relatively flat and differences in status minimized, control and lateral coordination depend on shared goals, and expertise rather than formal position determines influence" (Walton 1985, p. 79).

A Unified Worker Participation Framework

For the purpose of comparing different types of worker participation with respect to their likely effects on the organization's productivity and worker well-being, what is needed is a unified framework which 1) utilizes insights regarding both organizational form and behavior and 2) builds on the dimensions of Tomer's (1985) implicit psychological contract spectrum as well as the organizational dimensions in the frameworks of Walton and others. Table 1 displays the essential elements of this unified worker participation framework. It shows the twelve dimensions of the individual-organization relationship. A knowledge of the characteristics of a particular firm's organization and management, particularly the quality and quantity of its worker participation, would enable one to locate this firm along each of the dozen left to right spectrums. From the location, one can get a real sense of how productive and "human" the firm's organization is by comparison to the ultimate participative ideal, Theory Z. Theory Z is the ultimate participative ideal in the sense that the organization's features are as motivating and need satisfying as it is possible for an organization to be (see Maslow 1971, pp. 270-286). It corresponds closely to Walton's (1985) "comprehensive commitment strategy." The participative dozen are intended to be the necessary and sufficient dimensions along which a firm's organization must develop to attain the ultimate participatory ideal over a long period of time.

As indicated by comparing columns 2 and 3 of Table 1, Z management is very different from A or traditional American management (basically the same as Walton's control strategy). To illustrate further the unified framework, the characteristics of "ideal Japanese management" and an "ideal producer cooperative" are listed in columns four and five of Table 1.

The above strongly suggests the <u>worker participation hypothesis</u>: companies whose management and organization are further to the right on the twelve individual-organization dimensions of the spectrum will have higher productivity and worker well-being than other companies, other things being equal. The worker participation hypothesis can be elucidated by imagining two corporations, A and Z, with the same endowments of tangible capital goods, individual human capital, and technology. Corporation Z with Z management is hypothesized to have dramatically higher productivity and worker well-being as a result of the very significant differences between it and corporation A (using A management) along the participative dozen dimensions.

<u>Worker Participation and X-Efficiency</u>

It follows directly from the worker participation hypothesis that firms closer to the Theory Z ideal will have higher X-efficiency, i.e., higher productivity stemming from superior organization. This is very important, because the possible percentage gains in productivity from X-efficiency improvements are much greater than those related to allocative efficiency as Vanek (1970, pp. 253, 237) has noted.

Table 1 Unified Worker Participation Framework

	Five Elements of Participation	Dimensions of Individual-Organization Relationship	Organizational "A" Management or "Control Strategy"	Behavior Models' Characteristics "Z" Management or Fully Participative Firm	Ideal Japanese Management	Mondragon Cooperatives
To partici-pate: to take part; join or share with others	(1) Influence over what goes on at workplace	(1) Duration of Association and Employment Security	Employee is Variable Factor of Production, esp. hourly employees	"Lifetime," Secure →	→	→
		(2) Basis of Association or Attachment to Organization	Fixed, Defined Job Assignment	Member of Community →	→	→
		(3) Contribution/Commitment Expected from Employee	Minimum stable performance on deskilled jobs, separating doing from thinking	High, Varying Responsibilities; Emotional, Spiritual Commitment Expected →	→	→
	(2) Influence with respect to major decisions	(4) Relationship to Principal (Employer)	Agent to accomplish owner(s)' purposes [1,2]	Established Procedures for sharing in goal determination and major decision making	Shared Goals, Consenus Decision Making[3]	Shared Goals, Worker Representatives decide on Managers, Policies
		(5) Internal Control of Employees	Management directives top-down controls, rules	Implicit Control through Internalized Goals →	→	→
	(3) Feeling Part of the Organization	(6) Leadership Style	Authoritarian, Adversarial	Develop Teams, Supportive and Facilitative with respect to Problem Solving →	→	→
		(7) Superordinate Goals, Values of Organization	Goals usually financial, if any; values reflect owner(s)	Clear Goals and Strong, Humanistic Values Predominate →	→	→
	(4) Ability to make real contribution through the exercise of discretion and the taking of responsibility	(8) Rights of Workers to appeal with respect to disputes & grievances	None; if union, grievance procedures	Guarantee of Appeal to Independent Body in disputes and grievances	?	?
		(9) Employees' Sharing in Gains/Profits	Only external owners and/or top management share in profits	Members' rights to all economic profits from firm's operations[4]	Bonuses, Collective Compensation	Members' Share in Profit Individually and Collectively
	(5) Experience of Cooperative Work Relationships	(10) Relationship of Organization to Community/Society	Agent with respect to specific transactions	Goals Integrated with Societal Goals; Service to Society is Goal →	→	→ Also Financial Contribution
		(11) Employee Status/Income Differentials	Status and income differentials emphasized	Low Differentials, Advancement with Seniority and Performance →	→	→
		(12) Organization's Sharing of Information with respect to firm's status and tasks	Information distributed on "need to know" basis	High Degree of Information Sharing →	→	→

Notes: [1] If union, adversarial negotiation
[2] Employee inputs allowed on narrow agenda in prescribed format
[3] De Facto ownership due to formal ownership by affiliated institutions
[4] This is separate from scarcity returns to the contributors of capital (whether they are members or external to the organization).

Jaroslav Vanek (see, e.g., 1970, pp. 234-279) and an increasing number of other economists have argued that labor-managed firms, producer cooperatives, and firms with a variety of forms of worker participation are likely to be higher in X-efficiency than their nonparticipative counterparts. A key argument is that worker participation can contribute to better alignment of the priorities and goals of individuals and organizations as well as reducing opportunism and increasing trust, especially between workers and managers (Bradley and Gelb 1981, pp. 216-217). Because these workers are to a greater extent "working for themselves," there will not only be greater self-control but greater horizontal control, i.e., monitoring and mutual encouragement between workers (see, e.g., Bradley and Gelb 1981, pp. 216-217 and 1982, p. 255; Vanek 1970, p. 245; Levin 1982, pp. 46-47; Cable and FitzRoy 1980a, p. 103; and Tomer 1985, chapter 7). Greater worker participation will also improve vertical control, because it reduces resistance to traditional hierarchical control by inhibiting "attitudes, informal agreements and collective understandings which serve to frustrate attempts at vertical control" (Bradley and Gelb 1981, pp. 216-217; see also Bradley and Gelb 1982, p. 255 and Cable and FitzRoy 1980a, p. 103). This improved horizontal and vertical control "permits reduction in the number and cost of supervisory personnel" (Fusfeld 1983, p. 769; see also Bradley and Gelb 1981, p. 216; Levin 1982, p. 46; and Tomer 1985, chapter 7).

Cable and FitzRoy (1980a, pp. 102-104) argue that profit sharing is more X-efficient in the presence of worker participation because the latter should increase "workers' awareness of a reliable connection between their individual exertions [efforts] and received profit shares, and reduce fears that managerial opportunism will deprive them of the fruits of their extra labour" (see also Bradley and Gelb 1981, pp. 216-217). But the single most important argument is that "the psychological effects of participation ... stimulate greater effort" (Fusfeld 1983, p. 769; see also Vanek 1970, pp. 234-279). It is the latter argument that Tomer (1981b, 1985) has developed in considerable detail by building on the economic framework of Leibenstein (1966) and utilizing insights from the organizational behavior literature.

The various arguments above explaining why participative organizational features are X-efficient apply in a variety of ways to explaining why an organization with Theory Z features along all twelve participative dimensions would have the highest possible X-efficiency. The essense is that workers' feelings of participation will be greatest in an organization with Theory Z features along all twelve participative dimensions.

X-Efficiency and Economic Growth

The Production Possibility Frontier

When organizational change increases potential output, perhaps due to increased worker participation, organizational capital formation occurs. This greater endowment of intangible capital produces a shift in the production possibility frontier (PPF) because of the greater X-efficiency (Tomer 1981, p. 4). Thus, if one of two otherwise equal firms makes an investment in enhancing the participative qualities of its organization, the investing firm's potential output will be higher than its twin, presuming a positive rate of return on the investment.

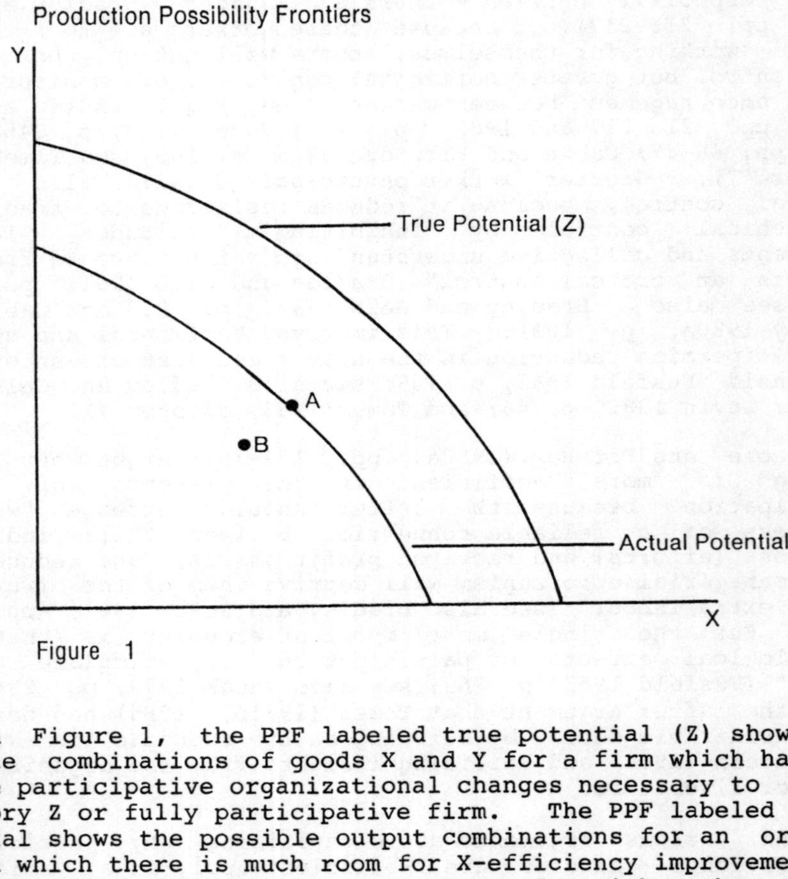

Figure 1

In Figure 1, the PPF labeled true potential (Z) shows the possible combinations of goods X and Y for a firm which has made all the participative organizational changes necessary to become a Theory Z or fully participative firm. The PPF labeled actual potential shows the possible output combinations for an ordinary firm in which there is much room for X-efficiency improvement via organizational investment. In accord with the worker participation hypothesis, firms which move further to the right on the participative dozen dimensions will increase their production possibilities, and the actual potential frontier will move closer to the true potential (Z) frontier.

<u>The Worker Well-being Possibility Frontier</u>

Organizational change, particularly change in worker participation, affects not only potential output but worker well-being. <u>Worker well-being</u> is defined in relation to Abraham

Maslow's (1970, chapter 11) hierarchy of human needs, which starts on the low end with material needs, proceeds to social needs, and ends with self-actualization needs. To the extent that an organization's features enable a worker to satisfy these human needs, the organization contributes to his well-being. Since in developed societies most organizations do reasonably well in enabling workers to satisfy their material needs, differences among organizations in worker well-being will largely be related to how well they enable workers to satisfy their higher needs. A worker's ability to satisfy his higher needs is presumed to depend 1) on the nature of his organizational participation and 2) his income from work.

When worker well-being is increased as a result of organizational change (and organizational capital formation), it is fruitful to think of this as shifting the *worker well-being possibility frontier* (WWPF) and involving an increase in W-efficiency (defined below). The WWPF plays a role similar to the PPF except that it relates to possible levels of worker well-being, not production, given the state of the organization, technology, and factor endowments. Any point on the frontier represents the possible levels of well-being of two workers, V and U, or two classes of workers. The WWPF labeled true potential (Z) in Figure 2 shows the possible well-being combinations for a fully participative or Theory Z firm, one with the highest possible W-efficiency. *W-efficiency* refers to the degree to which worker well-being in an organization is at its potential. The WWPF labeled actual potential shows the possible well-being combinations for a typical firm in which there is considerable room for increased worker well-being through organizational investment. In line with the worker participation hypothesis, a typical firm which moves to the right on the participative dozen dimensions will increase the well-being possibilities of workers, and its actual potential frontier will move closer to its true potential frontier.

The Production/Well-being Grid

Although organizational change might affect only X-efficiency or only W-efficiency, it ordinarily affects both, though not necessarily to the same degree. The *production/well-being grid* shown in Figure 3 provides a way to summarize the above theory concerning potential production and worker well-being. The vertical axis measures actual potential production as a percent of true potential production (or the X-efficiency percentage), and the horizontal axis measures actual potential worker well-being as a percent of true potential worker well-being (or the W-efficiency percentage). At the northeast corner of the grid is the Theory Z participative ideal with 100 percent of potential production and worker well-being. One hundred percent of all possible X-efficiency and W-efficiency improving organizational changes have been made. The figure bears a resemblance to Blake and Mouton's Managerial Grid in that their grid's optimum, the 9,9 concern for production and people, is also located at the northeast corner; furthermore, like the

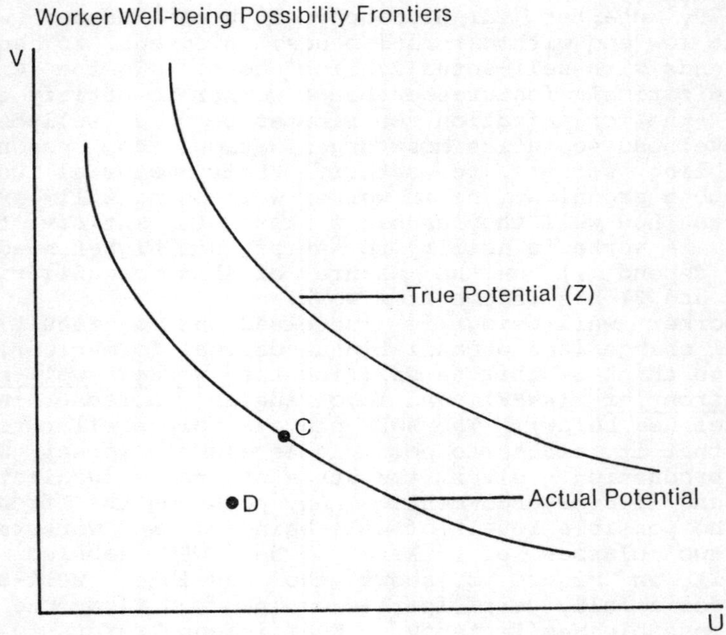

Figure 2

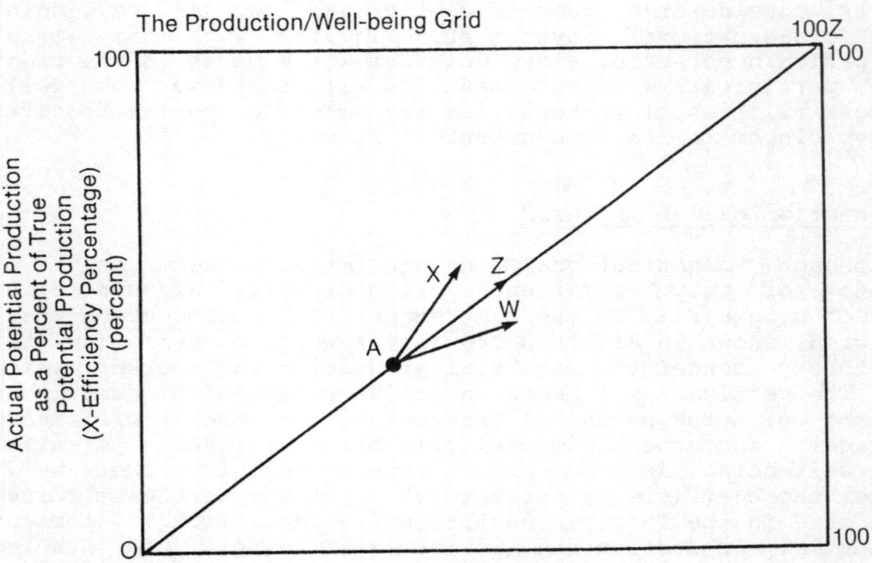

Figure 3 Actual Potential Worker Well-being as a Percent of True Potential Worker Well-being (W-Efficiency Percentage)

Managerial Grid, it facilitates thinking about the organizational gap between actual and potential and how to close it. Suppose point A on Figure 3 represents typical American management or Walton's control strategy. The distance from A to Z is suggestive of the room for improvement through organizational capital formation.

Conclusion

Increasingly, both theory and empirical findings lead to the conclusion that higher productivity and worker well-being are possible through organizational change which introduces greater worker participation. The empirical findings are particularly clearcut on the relationship between participation and productivity when more than one type of participative feature is involved. Despite the consistency of these findings, a few caveats should be cited. First, there are limits to the ability and willingness of employees to participate. Some people don't respond as well to participation opportunities as others or only respond well with the benefit of appropriate types of training, socialization, and experience. Moreover, developing a more participative organization is inevitably a process which takes considerable time, thought and commitment. The risk of failure is very real. More than in most kinds of innovation the personal qualities of the firm's leaders are critical to the success of organizational change.

The unified worker participation framework (Table 1) with its twelve participative dimensions is at the heart of this chapter's attempt to integrate the diversity of theory and findings in the fields of economics and organizational behavior. The use of a very broad definition of participation and a comprehensive set of organizational features makes it possible to understand more clearly the relationship among the many types of organizational attributes and worker participation. The approach is, thus, counter to the tendency in much of the worker participation literature to use an overly narrow conception of participation and the organizational features giving rise to it. In the view developed here, purposeful changes in any of an organization's participative dimensions add to the stock of organizational capital, thereby making possible greater productivity and worker well-being. Theory Z management is the ultimate participative ideal reflecting the highest possible productivity and worker well-being achievable through organizational change given the firm's other factor endowments.

This perspective leads to greater awareness of 1) the organization-related gap between actual and potential productivity (or worker well-being) and 2) the diversity of ways to close the gap. It helps us see that Japanese managers typically have done more to close the gap than American managers. It helps us to see that West German Codetermination is a step in the direction of closing the gap, but not an ultimate answer. It also suggests that organizational obsolescence may be a major factor explaining why the U.S., in many sectors, has been losing competitive advantage in international trade. There is, of course, evidence that U.S. corporations are now stepping up their organizational investments with the intent of making their organizations more participative. With any luck and a little help from macroeconomic policymakers, the U.S. should as a result begin to experience greater economic growth with faster growth in productivity and worker well-being.

References

Bernstein, Paul. 1980. Workplace Democratization: Its Internal Dynamics. New Brunswick, N.J.: Transaction Books.

Blake, Robert R. and Mouton, Jane S. 1969. Building a Dynamic Corporation Through Grid Organization Development. Reading, Mass: Addison-Wesley.

Blake, Robert R. and Mouton, Jane S. 1985. The Managerial Grid III Houston, Texas: Gulf.

Bradley, Keith and Gelb, Alan. 1981. "Motivation and Control in the Mondragon Experiment." British Journal of Industrial Relations, 19(2), 211-231.

Bradley, Keith and Gelb, Alan. 1982. "The Mondragon Cooperatives: Guidelines for a Cooperative Economy." in Jones and Svejnar (1982).

Cable, John and FitzRoy, Felix. 1980a. "Productivity, Efficiency, Incentives, and Employee Participation: Some Preliminary Results for West Germany." Kyklos, 33(1), 100-121.

Conte, Michael. 1982. "Participation and Performance in U.S. Labor-Managed Firms." in Jones and Svejnar (1982).

Ellerman, David P. 1984. "Theory of Legal Structure: Worker Cooperatives." Journal of Economic Issues, 18(September), 861-891.

Fusfeld, Daniel R. 1983. "Labor-Managed and Participatory Firms: A Review Article." Journal of Economic Issues, 17(September), 769-789.

Garson, G. David. 1977. "Models of Worker Self-Management: The West European Experience." in Garson, G.D., ed. Worker Self-Management in Industry: The West European Experience. New York: Praeger.

Jones, Derek C. and Svejnar, Jan, eds. 1982. Participatory and Self-Managed Firms. Lexington, Mass.: Lexington Books.

Leibenstein, Harvey. 1966. "Allocational Efficiency versus X-Efficiency." American Economic Review, 56(June), 392-415.

Levin, Henry. 1982. "Issues in Assessing the Comparative Productivity of Worker-Managed and Participatory Firms in Capitalist Societies." in Jones and Svejnar (1982).

Levitan, Sar A. and Werneke, Diane. 1984. "Worker Participation and Productivity Changes." Monthly Labor Review, 107(September), 28-33.

Maslow, Abraham H. 1971. The Farther Reaches of Human Nature. New York: Penguin Books.

Pryor, Frederic L. 1983. "The Economics of Production Cooperatives: A Reader's Guide." Annals of Public and Cooperative Economy, 54(2), 134-172.

Simmons, John and Mares, William. 1982. Working Together: Employee Participation in Action. New York: New York University Press.

Stephen, Frank H., ed. 1982. The Performance of Labor-Managed Firms. New York: St. Martin's Press.

Thomas, Henk and Logan, Chris. 1982. Mondragon: An Economic Analysis. London: George Allen and Unwin.

Tomer, John F. 1981a. "Organizational Change, Organizational Capital and Economic Growth." Eastern Economic Journal, 7(January), 1-14.

Tomer, John F. 1981b. "Worker Motivation: A Neglected Element in Micro-Micro Theory." Journal of Economic Issues, 15(June), 351-362.

Tomer, John F. 1985. "Working Smarter the Japanese Way: The X-Efficiency of Theory Z Management." in Kleindorfer, Paul. ed. The Management of Productivity and Technology in Manufacturing. Philadelphia, Pa.: Plenum.

Vanek, Jaroslav. 1970. The General Theory of Labor-Managed Market Economies. Ithaca, N.Y.: Cornell University Press.

Vanek, Jaroslav. ed. 1975. Self-Management: Economic Liberation of Man. Baltimore, Md.: Penguin Books.

Walton, Richard E. 1985. "From Control to Commitment in the Workplace." Harvard Business Review, 64(March-April), 76-84.

Williams, Ervin. ed. 1976. Participative Management: Concepts, Theory and Implementation. Altanta, Georgia: School of Business Administration, Georgia State University.

Zwerdling, Daniel. 1980. Workplace Democracy: A Guide to Workplace Ownership, Participation, and Self-Management Experiments in the United States and Europe. New York: Harper Colophon Books.

Part Fourteen
Choice Under Uncertainty

A PILOT EXPERIMENTAL INVESTIGATION INTO OPTIMAL CONSUMPTION UNDER UNCERTAINTY

JOHN D. HEY

University of York

We have an apparent paradox: on the one hand, predictions of theories of economic behaviour under uncertainty based on Subjective Expected Utility (SEU) theory appear to fit the (aggregate) facts quite well; on the other hand, experimental investigations into individual behaviour under uncertainty frequently reveal systematic departures from the predictions of SEU theory. Aggregation alone does not appear to resolve this paradox. What does? This paper suggests an answer.

Consider, for an excellent example, the implications of the life-cycle-permanent income theory of consumption under uncertainty advanced in a famous paper by Hall (1978) in a fairly recent issue of the JPE. One of the predictions of this theory (combined with a few relatively innocuous assumptions) is that consumption follows a random walk with trend. Using quarterly data for the U.K. for the period 1970 III to 1982 II we obtained the following:

$$C_{t+1} = \underset{(1.6)}{944} + \underset{(27.3)}{0.947}\, C_t + e_{t+1}. \qquad R^2 = .943,\ DW = 2.25,\ n = 47$$

(t-statistics in brackets).

Hall, using U.S. data, gets even more impressive results; over the period 1948 I to 1977 I using quarterly data once again, he obtained the following:

$$C_{t+1} = -0.014 + \underset{(337)}{1.011}\, C_t + e_{t+1} \qquad R^2 = .999,\ DW = 1.70,\ n = 120$$

(t-statistics in brackets).

Moreover, in neither case are the coefficients of additional lagged explanatory variables significant (with the possible exception, in the case of the U.S., of the coefficient of the lagged stock exchange index). These empirical findings constitute a remarkable vindication of the theory. Yet the theory is based upon Subjective Expected Utility theory - which has come in for much criticism in the recent past, mainly because of the empirical findings of laboratory-type experiments. (See, for a useful survey, Machina (1983).) So we have an apparent paradox, which aggregation does not seem to resolve.

Let us look at the theory in more detail. Consider a discrete random-horizon model, in which the (uncertain) income stream is denoted by

$Y_1, Y_2, \ldots, Y_t, \ldots$ and the consumption stream by $C_1, C_2, \ldots, C_t, \ldots$ Let the individual's wealth at the beginning of period t be denoted by W_t, and let r_t denote the (certain) rate of return on wealth held at the end of period t (r_t equals 1 plus the rate of interest). Let us, for simplicity, assume that the individual's objective, as viewed from the beginning of period t, is to maximize

$$E_t \sum_{\tau=t}^{\infty} \rho^{\tau-t} U(C_\tau) \quad (1)$$

where E_t is the expectation as viewed from the beginning of period t, and where U(.) is the individual's (per-period) utility function. The parameter ρ is the (assumed constant) product of the individual's discount factor and the probability that the individual will be alive next period given that he or she is alive this period.

We must now make some assumptions about <u>timings</u>: we assume that income in t, Y_t, is known <u>before</u> the decision on C_t, consumption in t, is made. Furthermore, let us assume that W_t <u>includes</u> Y_t. Finally, let us assume that C_t is chosen at the <u>beginning</u> of t, immediately after Y_t is revealed. We thus have

$$W_{t+1} = r_t(W_t - C_t) + Y_{t+1}. \quad (2)$$

We must now determine the individual's optimal consumption strategy. To this end, let us introduce $V_t(W_t)$ to denote the <u>maximal value</u> of (1), that is, of expected lifetime utility (as viewed from the beginning of period t). Obviously this depends on W_t, the individual's wealth at the beginning of period t. (It also depends on the various parameters of the problem, <u>plus</u> the joint distribution of $Y_{t+1}, Y_{t+2}, \ldots$.) Thus, definitionally, we have

$$V_t(W_t) = \max_{C_t, C_{t+1}, \ldots} \left\{ E_t \sum_{\tau=t}^{\infty} \rho^{\tau-t} U(C_\tau) \right\}. \quad (3)$$

From this, it follows that

$$V_t(W_t) = \max_{C_t} \left\{ U(C_t) + \rho E_t V_{t+1}(W_{t+1}) \right\}, \quad (4)$$

where W_{t+1} is given by (2).

The optimal choice of C_t, which we denote by C_t^*, is determined by the maximization of the term in curly brackets on the right hand side of (4). The first-order condition is

$$U'(C_t^*) = \rho r_t E_t V'_{t+1}[r_t(W_t - C_t^*) + Y_{t+1}]. \tag{5}$$

(The second-order condition is automatically satisfied if U(.) is concave.)

We also have definitionally from (4) that

$$V_t(W_t) = U(C_t^*) + \rho E_t V_{t+1}[r_t(W_t - C_t^*) + Y_{t+1}]. \tag{6}$$

If we now differentiate (6) with respect to W_t (noting that C_t^* is a function of W_t), and if the optimality condition (5) is used to simplify the resulting expression, we get

$$V'_t(W_t) = \rho r_t E_t V'_{t+1}[r_t(W_t - C_t^*) + Y_{t+1}] = U'(C_t^*). \tag{7}$$

From this, we get trivially that

$$V'_{t+1}(W_{t+1}) = U'(C^*_{t+1}). \tag{8}$$

Substituting this in (5) yields

$$U'(C_t^*) = \rho r_r E_t U'(C^*_{t+1}), \tag{9}$$

from which it follows that

$$U'(C^*_{t+1}) = (\rho r_t)^{-1} U'(C_t^*) + u_{t+1} \quad \text{where } E_t(u_{t+1}) = 0. \tag{10}$$

This, of course, implies that (under the optimal strategy) the marginal utility of consumption follows a random walk (with trend $(\rho r_t)^{-1}$).

Finally, if marginal utility is (approximately) linear, and if $r_t = r$ (all t), then we get (approximately) that

$$C^*_{t+1} = \alpha + \beta C_t^* + \varepsilon_{t+1} \quad \text{where } E_t(\varepsilon_{t+1}) = 0. \tag{11}$$

This is the famous Hall result, quoted and tested above.

An interesting special case occurs when $r_1, r_2, \ldots, r_t, \ldots$ are all identical, when $Y_1, Y_2, \ldots, Y_t, \ldots$ are identically and independently distributed, and when the utility function is

$$U(x) = -\exp(-Rx), \tag{12}$$

that is, when the individual displays constant absolute risk aversion. In this case it can be shown (see Hey (1980) for details, though note the slight differences in assumptions about timings) that the optimal consumption strategy is linear in wealth:

$$C^*(W) = a + bW. \tag{13}$$

Moreover, the parameters a and b can be shown to be given by

$$b = (r - 1)/r \tag{14}$$

and

$$\rho r E\{\exp[R(r - 1)(a - Y/r)] = 1 \tag{15}$$

respectively.

If each Y is normally distributed with mean μ and variance σ^2, (15) can be further simplified to yield:

$$a = \mu/r - R(r - 1)\sigma^2/(2r^2) - \log(\rho r)/[R(r - 1)]. \tag{16}$$

We report this special case since many applied consumption function studies adopt formulations which are linear in wealth. This special case provides theoretical support; the data often provide considerable empirical support. (A discussion of alternative specifications - particularly relating to the stochastic specification of the income stream - and their implications can be found in Hey (1984).)

The above theory of optimal consumption under uncertainty, whether (indirectly) tested in the general form of (11) or (directly) tested in the special case of (13), performs remarkably well when confronted with data. This is all the more surprising when it is recalled that the above theory is constructed on the foundation of Subjective Expected Utility theory (combined with backward induction); a theory which has come under increasing criticism as of late.

Much of this criticism has originated from a series of laboratory-type experimental investigations which have examined the validity or otherwise of the axioms (and some simple implications) of Subjective Expected Utility theory. SEU theory has emerged with some discredit from these investigations.

It is, however, a long way from individual experimental investigations into the validity of SEU theory to aggregate empirical investigations of the implications of that theory. Without further information, it is difficult, if not impossible, to determine where along the spectrum the paradox referred to above becomes resolved.

We decided, therefore, to try to shed some light by adopting a middle path: by carrying out some exploratory experimental investigations into optimal consumption under uncertainty itself. This is part way along the spectrum of the paragraph above.

Clearly a direct experimental investigation of the consumption story told above is almost impossible to implement (and certainly impossible to implement cheaply and legally!). So instead we decided to conduct an experimental investigation into a problem with exactly the same structure as the consumption story, though with different details. We present below some relevant excerpts from the instructions given to the subjects taking part in this experiment. (The full instructions are obtainable on request.)

> "The experiment consists of a random number of periods. In each period, you will be given a certain income denominated in tokens. These will be added to any tokens you have accumulated from earlier periods. In each period, you must decide how many of your stock of tokens to convert into money. Your payment for taking part in the experiment will be the amount of money converted from tokens in the (randomly-determined) FINAL PERIOD of the experiment. (Any money converted in preceding periods is lost.)
>
> "The number of periods for which the experiment continues is determined at random. To be specific, while the experiment is continuing there is a 1 in 10 chance that any period will be the last. Note carefully that whether any period is the final one or not has nothing at all to do with your decisions in that or any preceding period. Also note again that your payment is the amount of money converted in the final period, whenever that is.
>
> "The conversion scale from tokens into money is pictured in the Figure appended to the instructions. [...]
>
> "Any tokens you do not convert will be credited to a tokens account which will be maintained in your name. This account earns interest at 12% per period. ... You can, if you wish, run an overdraft on your tokens account; this will also incur interest at 12% per period. [...] (The maximum permitted overdraft is 40 tokens; [...].)
>
> "The income in tokens will vary randomly from period to period. You can obtain information from the computer about the likely values of future incomes. You can ask the computer what proportion of future token incomes will be greater than some specified value, and you can ask the computer what proportion will lie between two specified values."

As the subject could discover, if he or she so wished, the token incomes in each period were independently and identically normally distributed with mean $\mu = 10$ and standard deviation $\sigma = 4$. The conversion scale from tokens x into money U (using a rather suggestive notation) was

$$U(x) = 30[1 - \exp(-.022314x)]. \qquad (17)$$

Note that this is of the form of (12), with $R = .022314$. Note too that the monetary value of the mean token income is £6. (95% of the time, the token income is between 2.16 and 17.84; the monetary values of these end-points are £1.41 and £9.85 respectively.)

The beauty of the above experimental set up is that, under one assumption, it is identical in structure to the optimal consumption problem discussed earlier. The one assumption that we need is that the subject is risk-neutral (or, at least, approximately so) over the range of possible monetary outcomes of the experiment. In essence, this means we require subjects to be risk-neutral for winnings of between £0 and £15.

If this is the case, then the problem is indeed identical. The subject's problem is to choose a conversion strategy C_1, C_2, ... which maximises his or her expected winnings, which are, as viewed from the beginning of period t:

$$(1 - \rho)E_t \sum_{\tau=t}^{\infty} \rho^{\tau-t} U(C_t) \tag{18}$$

where U(.) is given by (17) and where $\rho = .9$. (This is the probability that the experiment will continue into period (t + 1) given that it was still continuing at period t; in contrast, the probability that this current period will be the last is $.1 = 1 - \rho$. Note that subjects were told that "... while the experiment is continuing, there is a 1 in 10 chance that any period will be the last".)

Compare (18) with (1); they are indeed identical (except for the innocuous extra term $(1 - \rho)$ in (18)).

Furthermore, under the specification that the token incomes (Y_1, Y_2, ..., Y_t, ...) are identically and independently normal with mean 10 and standard deviation 4, and under the particular specification that the conversion scale takes the form of (17) (that is, the form of a constant-absolute-risk-aversion utility function with risk-aversion index R = .022314), it follows (maintaining our assumption of the risk-neutrality of the subject) that our experimental set-up is identical with the special case of the optimal consumption problem that was discussed above. The parameters are clearly as follows:

$$\left.\begin{array}{ll} \mu = 10 & R = .022314 \\ \sigma = 4 & r = 1.12. \\ \rho = .9 & \end{array}\right\} \tag{19}$$

We see immediately therefore that the <u>optimal</u> conversion (consumption) strategy is given by (substitute (19) into (13), (14) and (16) above)

$$C^* = 5.936 + .107W. \tag{20}$$

So the subject's optimal strategy is to convert each period the number of tokens determined by (20), where W is the (post-income) stock of tokens.

We carried out a pilot investigation using 14 subjects. All were economists, either staff or postgraduate students. They performed the experiments individually, using a VDU. They were given the written instructions in advance, and had the opportunity to discuss any ambiguities or confusions before they were left on their own to carry out the experiment. No subjects appeared to have any difficulties in understanding or carrying out the experiment. (The time taken to complete the experiment varied from subject to subject; usually it was around half-an-hour.)

In addition, they were asked to "think aloud" and to record their thoughts on a tape-recorder, which was left switched on throughout the experiment. The idea behind this "protocol analysis" was to have available some supplementary material with which to interpret the raw data.

The actual operation of the experiment was exactly as described in the instructions. Accordingly, the number of periods for which the experiment continued varied considerably from subject to subject: for some, it terminated after 1 period; for others it went on for 19 periods. Table 1 gives the raw data. Some brief comments on the subjects' behaviour and on their tape-recordings may be of interest. [My comments in square brackets.]

Subject 1 Never found out the mean income (despite the easy-to-use interrogation option); deliberately followed what he termed a "1 in 10 rule", though the rationale for this was not clear. [Showed some confusion about likely values of token incomes.]

Subject 2 Found the median, and then checked whether the distribution was symmetrical; argued that "the appropriate strategy is to select the same value of conversion each period. The problem is then to find the appropriate level ... Set conversion equal to expected income each period. Given symmetry, this seems to be sensible. I might modify this as I go along. But let's see if it works". [In the event, he never got the chance! His rule has some obvious attractions, but ignores interest and the stopping probability.]

Subject 3 Establishes 10 is median; checks periodically later to see whether distribution changes. [It doesn't.] Convinced himself that experiment was most likely to end between periods 5 to 10 [despite being told that probability of stopping is same at all times]; then gets rather confused when experiment continues after period 10. Eventually settles down to rule of "convert 10 [mean] plus or minus a little bit depending on current stock of tokens".

Subject 4 Found out 10 is mean; argues that "the experiment will finish between the 5th and 15th period" [cf. S3]; so plans to build up big balance, and then run it down between period 5 and 15 [but doesn't get the chance, much to his disgust!].

Subject 5 Displayed some confusion about meaning of interrogation option.

Subject 6 Displayed considerable confusion about meaning of interrogation option; but nevertheless took some reasonable decisions. [Very odd case this: his tape-recording was largely (unintentional, I presume) gibberish.]

Subject 7 Checks computer's addition! [every now and again, the computer lost or gained a penny because of rounding]; eventually settles down to a strategy of converting roughly half the stock, the idea being to try to move towards a position where the "starting balance is roughly constant".

Subject 8 Deliberately "went for broke". This is a problem I had anticipated: without any constraint on the overdraft, it would seem optimal* to borrow increasingly large amounts. Hence the imposed 40 overdraft limit. The computer implemented the rule in the instructions that the individual would be paid nothing if the overdraft ever exceeded 40.

Subject 9 Established median as 10; strategy varied considerably throughout the experiment; like other subjects he was under the illusion that the experiment would stop somewhere between the 5th and 15th period; from period 16 onwards he became increasingly confused!

Subject 10 Worked out that the maximum token income was about 20; in period 3 [which turned out to be the last] chose conversion so as to leave stock of 10. [Why?]

Subject 11 Establishes median as 10, but gets the impression [perhaps from the instructions?] that the distribution is skewed, with a mean of 8 or 9, but eventually corrects this misimpression; adopts a strategy of converting a couple less than income till balance up to a "satisfactory level" which he eventually [rather arbitrarily] decides is 20.

Subject 12 Does not get the chance to develop a strategy.

Subject 13 "What I'm going to try and do is to go for the big one ... spend a few periods risking being killed ... Because of the tailing off, I'm not going to go on accumulating for ever ... perhaps stop at 40 or so ... no, that's too high ..." [Very risky strategy - clearly violates my assumption about risk-neutrality; but see later.]

Subject 14 No coherent strategy developed.

It will be noted from Table 1 that integral amounts were converted in almost all cases. Furthermore, very few subjects really exploited the interrogation option (revealing details of the income distribution) to the full. I suspected that many subjects simply could not cope with more information over and above that of the mean value.

How close are the actual strategies to the optimal strategy (namely, that given by (20) above)? Table 2 gives the results of regressing C_t on W_t (where meaningful).

---

* This is a strange curiosum which I have not been able to resolve. With unlimited borrowing allowed, it would surely maximise utility to consume (convert) an infinite amount each period. If so, what is "optimal" about the Hall condition?!

A glance at this Table will reveal immediately that the behaviour of virtually all the subjects departs significantly from the optimal strategy. (All the estimated intercepts are significantly different from 5.936 at the 5% level, and all the estimated slopes - with the exception of that for subject 9 - are significantly different from .107 at the 5% level.) The most striking features of Table 2 are the facts that, with one exception, all the estimated slopes are <u>higher</u> than the optimal slope, and, with two exceptions, that all the estimated intercepts are <u>lower</u> than the optimal intercept. (The one exception is subject 1, who displays rather strange behaviour; and the two exceptions are subjects 8 and 9, both of whom, though to differing extents, try to "go for broke".) So there is evidence of <u>systematic</u> departure from the predictions of SEU theory - just as in earlier experimental studies.

How do our experimental results compare with the (U.K. and U.S.) aggregate level regressions reported on our opening page? Table 3 gives the results of regressing C_{t+1} on C_t (where meaningful).

It is apparent that these depart quite markedly from the aggregate level regressions. However, we should note that the assumption that enables (11) to be derived from (10) does <u>not</u> hold in this particular case: given our utility (conversion) function (17) it is <u>not</u> true that marginal utility is (approximately) linear.

So the behaviour of the subjects appears to differ quite significantly from that predicted by the theory. But is that really the case? The theory assumes that people optimize - that is, that they try and maximise expected utility. In the context of this experiment, the theory assumes (under the continuing presumption that the subjects are risk-neutral in the relevant range) that the subjects try to maximise their expected winnings. Is <u>this</u> true or not?

An obvious test is to examine the implications of the apparent actual strategies. To this end, we simulated the implications of following strategies of the form

$$C_t = \hat{a} + \hat{b} W_t$$

where $(\hat{a}, \hat{b})$ are as revealed by the subjects, and are as estimated in Table 2. (We ignored <u>our</u> uncertainty about the 'actual' values of $\hat{a}$ and $\hat{b}$, and ignored any conscious or unconscious stochastic component of consumption; these are obviously matters for further investigation in a more comprehensive and systematic study.) Table 4 reports the implications in terms of the expected winnings following a strategy of the form $C_t = \hat{a} + \hat{b} W_t$. (Ignore the column headed CEG for the moment.)

The expected winnings following the optimal strategy are £6.06; five of the nine subjects listed in Table 4 'had' strategies which implied expected winnings of at least 99% of this maximum! Even the worst strategy implied expected winnings of 93.7% of the maximum. These are interesting findings.

It could, of course, be retorted that these are not *surprising* findings given the particular values of the parameters chosen for the experiment. Indeed, one can guarantee expected winnings of £6.00 simply by converting 10 tokens (the mean token income) each period. The reason why the maximal expected winnings are only slightly higher than this is the fact that the 'discount factor' ρ and the rate of return r are almost the reciprocals of each other, so that ρr is almost unity (1.008 to be precise). The more ρr departs from unity, the greater the departure of the maximal expected winnings from the converted value of the mean token income. (If ρr significantly exceeds 1 then *either* the individual puts a lot of weight on the future, *or* the rate of interest is very high; either of these implies high rewards from saving. The converse, of course, is true if ρr is significantly less than 1.)

From listening to the tape-recordings, it is clear that subjects tended to ignore both ρ and r. It is possible that this was because they almost "cancelled each other out". Some subjects hinted that they would have taken them into account, in the manner described in the paragraph above, if ρr was significantly different from unity; but further experimentation would be needed to verify this.

It also appears to be the case that the graph of expected winnings, when plotted against a and b, is very flat-topped, so that expected winnings are not particularly sensitive to the chosen values of a and b. So the chosen values could be a long way from the optimal values, yet the actual expected winnings could be very close to the maximal expected winnings. *Thus the subject's behaviour could in fact be very close to optimal without it appearing so* (as measured by $\hat{a}$ and $\hat{b}$).

This gives us a clue as to the resolution of our paradox: just as in earlier experiments, *behaviour* appears to depart significantly and systematically from optimal *behaviour*. Yet the *implications* of the actual behaviour, *in terms of the objective function*, are very close to the *implications* of optimal behaviour.

(We perhaps ought to comment at this stage on the validity of our underlying assumption that subjects were (approximately) risk-neutral in the relevant range. To check on this, we asked subjects two questions which should shed light on their attitude to risk. Effectively the two questions asked for the certainty equivalents of two gambles, one which had a 50-50 chance of paying out £100 or nothing, and one which had a 50-50 chance of paying out £10 or nothing. The column headed CEG in Table 4 lists the subjects' answers to the second question. A figure of 5.00 indicates risk-neutrality in the relevant range, while a figure less (greater) than 5.00 indicates risk-aversion (-loving). This column reveals that subjects 6 and 8 were risk-neutral, and subjects 7, 10 and 11 were approximately so. For the other subjects, the departure of their behaviour from optimality could therefore be rationalised in terms of the departure from neutrality of their attitude to risk. But further investigation into this hypothesis is clearly necessary.)

Let us also note another preliminary finding: the theory predicts that C is a function of W; the evidence agrees with this. Moreover, in the special case under investigation, the theory predicts that C is a linear function of W; the evidence does not disagree with this. True, the estimated parameters are 'wrong' in the sense that they appear to differ significantly from the optimal parameters, but the tape-recordings do suggest that these parameters are sensitive to the underlying parameters of the problem. If they are sensitive in the way that the theory predicts, then the apparent paradox is resolved. This indicates the way to proceed in a full-scale experimental investigation. That, however, must await another day - and a further injection of research funds!

So we have two clues as to the resolution of our paradox: first, behaviour may appear to depart from optimal behaviour, but only because the objective function is very flat-topped (indeed, the actual outcome may be very close to the optimal outcome); second, and as a consequence, the parameters of behaviour may be wrong (though the underlying structure may be correct); however, they may well be sensitive to the underlying parameters of the problem in the way that theory predicts. So the theory may be right - though perhaps not quite for the right reasons.

References

Hall, R. E. (1978), "Stochastic Implications of the Life Cycle-Permanent Income Hypothesis: Theory and Evidence", Journal of Political Economy, 86, 971-987.

Hey, J. D. (1980), "Optimal Consumption under Income Uncertainty: An Example and a Conjecture", Economics Letters, 5, 129-133.

Hey, J. D. (1984), "Optimal Consumption when Income Follows a Markov Process", Bulletin of Economic Research, 36, 109-118.

Machina, M. J. (1983), "The Economic Theory of Individual Behavior Toward Risk: Theory, Evidence and New Directions", Institute for Mathematical Studies in the Social Sciences, Economics Series, Technical Report no. 433.

Table 1: Raw data

Subject	t	W_t	C_t
1	1	9.80	1.00
	2	21.89	2.00
	3	34.42	3.00
2	1	12.43	10.00
3	1	11.95	0.00
	2	24.07	5.00
	3	29.56	10.00
	4	38.70	15.00
	5	33.55	15.00
	6	34.66	20.00
	7	26.09	10.00
	8	27.60	13.00
	9	29.37	12.00
	10	20.15	10.00
	11	22.36	11.00
	12	19.36	10.00
	13	15.49	10.00
	14	13.31	7.00
4	1	12.07	0.00
	2	16.12	0.00
5	1	8.58	4.00
	2	18.23	10.00
	3	22.47	12.00
	4	17.97	10.00
	5	17.36	10.00
	6	21.12	15.00
6	1	8.74	4.00
	2	13.91	6.00
	3	9.72	4.00
	4	18.48	6.00
	5	13.75	7.00
	6	13.93	5.00
	7	19.15	3.00
	8	28.37	8.00
	9	32.92	12.00
	10	28.39	10.00
	11	23.31	10.00
	12	25.30	10.00
	13	22.98	10.00
	14	21.01	6.00
	15	27.76	10.00
	16	26.44	10.00
	17	35.19	10.00
7	1	12.22	8.00
	2	15.24	9.00
	3	22.15	12.00
	4	22.04	12.00
	5	23.18	13.00
	6	21.56	10.00
	7	31.28	16.00
	8	25.22	13.00
	9	20.78	10.00
	10	21.75	10.00
	11	27.17	13.00
	12	21.47	10.00
	13	18.43	9.00
	14	19.44	9.00
	15	26.34	13.00
	16	29.50	14.00
	17	30.46	14.00
	18	26.29	13.00
	19	22.48	10.00
8*	1	7.41	18.00
	2	-2.36	17.00
	3	-15.67	16.00
	4	-23.34	12.00
	5	-28.24	7.00
	6	-30.71	5.00
9	1	7.84	0.00
	2	17.99	10.00
	3	12.68	12.68
	4	13.42	13.42
	5	10.39	15.00
	6	4.42	15.00
	7	1.07	20.00
	8	-13.10	6.00
	9	-16.09	15.00
	10	-21.36	0.00
	11	-17.34	6.00
	12	-19.89	14.00
	13	-32.05	0.00
	14	-29.19	0.00
	15	-23.36	0.00
	16	-9.12	15.00
	17	-17.95	7.00
	18	-11.92	15.00
	19	-20.23	6.00
10	1	11.75	4.00
	2	10.45	4.00
	3	16.43	6.43
11	1	8.16	5.00
	2	14.91	8.00
	3	19.54	10.00
	4	22.63	12.00
	5	16.04	10.00
12	1	9.73	2.00
13	1	8.87	2.00
	2	16.99	2.00
	3	28.81	2.00
	4	33.90	2.00
	5	44.90	2.00
14	1	7.56	11.00
	2	7.41	9.00

* subject was paid nothing since overdraft exceeded limit of 40.

Table 2: Regressions of C_t against W_t by subject

Subject	INTERCEPT estimate	INTERCEPT standard error	SLOPE estimate	SLOPE standard error	R^2	DW	n
1	0.210	0.002	.0812	.0008	.9999	3.00	3
3	-0.742	2.714	.4575	.1046	.6145	0.80	14
5	-1.989	2.460	.6898	.1354	.8665	0.98	6
6	1.383	1.166	.2910	.0506	.6876	1.63	17
7	1.981	0.982	.4127	.0418	.8515	1.31	19
8	17.506	1.650	.3233	.0794	.8057	1.07	6
9	10.841	1.546	.2191	.0883	.2658	1.75	19
10	-0.810	1.210	.4364	.0922	.9573	2.11	3
11	1.349	1.166	.4706	.0687	.9399	0.94	5

OPTIMAL STRATEGY

5.936	.1070

Note re. subjects omitted from this table:

(a) subjects 2 and 12 survived only 1 period;

(b) subjects 4 and 14 survived only 2 periods;

(c) subject 13 put C_t = 2 for all t (=1, ..., 5).

Table 3: Regressions of C_{t+1} against C_t by subject

Subject	INTERCEPT estimate	INTERCEPT standard error	SLOPE estimate	SLOPE standard error	R^2	n
3	6.895	2.379	.4139	.2017	.2769	13
5	10.000	3.910	.1522	.4077	.0444	5
6	3.791	1.692	.5482	.2107	.3259	16
7	9.021	2.668	.2289	.2269	.0598	18
8	-4.137	3.247	1.1098	.2281	.8921	5
9	8.679	2.666	.0845	.2368	.0079	18
11	6.729	2.575	.3738	.2822	.4673	4

Note re. subjects omitted from this table:

(a) subjects 2 and 12 survived only 1 period;

(b) subjects 4 and 14 survived only 2 periods;

(c) subjects 1 and 10 survived only 3 periods;

(d) subject 13 put C_t = 2 for all t (=1, ..., 5).

Table 4: Expected winnings of the 'actual' strategies

Subject	$\hat{a}$	$\hat{b}$	EXPECTED WINNINGS*	CEG
1	0.210	.0812	5.69	3.00
3	-0.742	.4575	6.00	7.00
5	-1.989	.6898	5.95	2.00
6	1.383	.2910	6.02	5.00
7	1.981	.4127	6.03	4.00
8	17.506	.3233	5.68	5.00
9	10.841	.2191	5.88	7.00
10	-0.810	.4364	6.00	4.30
11	1.349	.4706	6.01	4.80
OPTIMAL	5.936	.1070	6.06	5.00

* Note: These are simulated figures, each based on 5,000 repetitions; they are, therefore, subject to some sampling error.

THE ST. PETERSBURG PARADOX AND THE EXPECTATION HEURISTIC

Michel TREISMAN

Department of Experimental Psychology, University of Oxford, South Parks Road, Oxford OX1 3UD, England*

The St. Petersburg paradox refers to a gamble which can be shown to have an infinite expected utility, but which we would expect gamblers to be normally unwilling to pay more than a small sum to play. The explanations that have been offered for the paradox are briefly reviewed, and an alternative explanation is put forward. This postulates that when faced with what are to them mathematically complex problems, lay people apply a heuristic that is described herein, and that is referred to as the "expectation heuristic". The expectation heuristic involves the analysis of a complex problem into a series of subproblems. These are solved individually and the solutions found are combined in a simple way to give a solution for the problem as a whole. It is shown that this strategy will account for the St. Petersburg paradox.

*This work was performed while in receipt of support from the Medical Research Council of Great Britain. Requests for offprints should be addressed to M. Treisman, Department of Experimental Psychology, University of Oxford, South Parks Road, Oxford OX1 3UD, England.

1. INTRODUCTION

A number of interesting things were happening in 1738. David Hume was preparing to bring out his book, "A Treatise of Human Nature" [1], in the following year. And Daniel Bernoulli [2] published a discussion of a problem devised by his cousin Nicolas Bernoulli. Daniel Bernoulli's paper was important not only because of the intrinsic interest of the problem, but also because of its historic role in the development of the concept of utility. However, I shall mainly be concerned with attempting to understand the modes of thought that lead to the St. Petersburg paradox. This problem, which is still a source of discussion, bears this name because it was discussed by Bernoulli in a scientific journal published in St. Petersburg. In fact, the paradox has outlived St. Petersburg.

In this problem (slightly simplified) we have two protagonists, Peter and Paul. Peter offers Paul the opportunity to play a game that goes as follows. Peter tosses a fair coin and continues to do so until it falls heads. If it falls with the head uppermost on the first toss, he pays Paul 2 ducats and the game ends. The probability that this will happen is 1/2. Thus if we start to build up an expression for Paul's expected return, the first term will be $1/2(2) = 1$.

Of course, with probability 1/2 the first toss may result in a tail. If so, Peter tosses the coin a second time. The probability of a head on the second toss but not before is $(1/2)^2$. If the coin falls heads on this toss, Peter gives Paul 4 ducats and the game ends. In general, the value of the payment received when the first head occurs on toss n is given by the expression $V_n = 2^n$. For a head on the first toss this gives a payment of 2 ducats; for a head on the second toss, 4 ducats; and successively, 8, 16, 32, 64... Similarly, the probability that the first head occurs on toss n is $(1/2)^n$. It follows that the expected value of the return from this game is

$$E(V) = \sum_{n=1}^{\infty} p_n V_n = \sum_{n=1}^{\infty} (1/2^n)\, 2^n = 1 + 1 + 1 \ldots = \infty .$$

Thus the game offers Paul an infinite expected value. If Paul plays the game often enough there is no limit to the fortune he can win. Nevertheless, and this is the paradox, if a person is given the right to play this game, it has to be admitted, as Bernoulli [2] puts it, "that any fairly reasonable man would sell his chance, with great pleasure, for twenty ducats". If Paul were offered this sum for his place at Peter's gaming table, he would be likely to accept. Why should it seem rational to Paul to sell an infinite expected value for 20 ducats?

This problem led Bernoulli to introduce the concept of utility and to propose that the solution to the paradox was that Paul calculated not expected value but expected utility. If utility were a negatively accelerated function of value, this would take into account the decreasing satisfaction that will accrue to Paul with each monetarily equal increment to the magnitude of his fortune, as his fortune grows larger. If Paul calculates an expectation based on utility, it can be shown that the resultant expected utility will be a small finite quantity. Thus when the utility of the selling price exceeds this small expectation, it will make sense for Paul to sell his place at the gaming table.

The paradox raised two issues for decision theory: the normative - how ought Paul to make such a decision? - and the descriptive - how in fact does he? Bernoulli's argument showed that expected value cannot be the basis that Paul employs in practice for making this decision. However, Bernoulli's approach did not distinguish between these two questions, the normative and the descriptive. He assumed by implication that a normative account resting on calculation of an expectation could be found that was also descriptive, and purported to offer such an account. The importance of the paradox for him was that it demonstrated that the normative approach based on finding an expectation broke down when expected value was the expectation calculated: expected value did not predict what Cramer called the "vulgar evaluation" [2]. Bernoulli believed that an adequate inclusive account could be established if expected utility were substituted for expected value: this would provide the basis for a normative account that would also be descriptive.

2. DIFFICULTIES WITH THE EXPECTATION APPROACH

Over the years, numerous objections have been made to Bernoulli's approach, and alternative explanations have been offered: Vlek and Wagenaar [3] list nine such explanations. These tend to be ad hoc, involving the assumption that underestimation of small probabilities occurs, or mistaken assessments or combination of both probabilities and payoffs, and these explanations have not been widely accepted. It is surely unsatisfactory if when we analyse the St. Petersburg game we must assume that subjects underestimate small probabilities, but when we analyse choices between gambles we are required to assume that subjects employ "decision weights" which effectively overestimate small probabilities, as Kahneman and Tversky [4] found it necessary to assume in their theory for this situation, prospect theory. Another alternative explanation, put forward by Lopes [5], proposes that a model of rational choice should include multiple decision criteria, one of which will be expected utility, but another may be the probability of showing a positive gain in a limited period.

Of the objections that can be made to the expectation approach three are of especial interest. First, expected value fails as an explanation not only because of the paradox that a finite selling price is preferred to an infinite expectation, but also because it is possible to modify the original game slightly so as to produce variants such that individuals prefer one variant to another, but expected value does not accurately predict our preferences among these variants. This was pointed out by Lopes [5] who compared four different versions of the game and suggested that people's intuitive preferences between these variants did not correspond to the ordering predicted by their expected values. She considered the following games:

1. The standard game, with the return V_n given by 2^n; i.e., successive returns are given by 2,4,8,16...dollars.

2. Standard game for $n \leqq 20$; for $n \geqq 20$, $V_n = \$2^{20} = \$1,048,576$.

3. A similar game but with V_n based on units of \$1.99; successive returns are V = 1.99, 3.96, 7.88...dollars.

4. The standard game but with V_n based on a unit of 2 cents; V = 2,4,8,16...cents.

Lopes surmised, and it seems plausible, that most people would consider the standard \$2 game, the same game with increase in reward curtailed above n = 20, and the \$1.99 game to be roughly equivalent, and the 2 cent game to be worth considerably less. But the expected values of these games are:

	E(V)
1. Standard game, with \$2 unit:	Infinite
2. Standard game with V non-increasing above n = 20:	\$21
3. Standard game but with \$1.99 unit:	\$200
4. Standard game, with 2 cent unit:	Infinite

If people calculate expected values and choose on that basis, as the original normative theory requires, they should prefer games 1 and 4 to games 2 and 3, which contradicts the implications of these expectations.

A second difficulty for the expectation approach is that although utility was to prove a concept of such importance, it does not actually provide a solution for the original paradox that engendered it, because, whatever function is taken for utility, a modified game can be devised that reinstates the original paradox. If the utility function is u = f(V), we define a new game in which

$$V_n = f^{-1}(2^n)$$

- then $u_n = 2^n$. For example, consider a utility function which is a logarithmic function of value:

$$u_n = \log_2 V_n.$$

In the original paradox V_n was 2^n. We define a new version of the game in which the rewards are given by

$$V_n = 2^{2^n}.$$

Now the utility of the nth reward is

$$u_n = \log_2 V_n = 2^n,$$

and consequently the expected utility is:

$$(1/2)2^1 + (1/2^2)2^2 + (1/2^3)2^3 + \ldots = 1 + 1 + 1 + \ldots = \text{infinity}.$$

In place of the previous returns 2,4,8... we now have 4,16,256...and although we may anticipate that Paul will value this game somewhat more highly than the standard version, he should still be ready to sell out for quite a low sum [6].

A third difficulty may also be proposed. It is presented by what might be named "the martingale paradox". A martingale is a scheme gamblers use in laying bets, in the belief that it offers a good prospect for making continuing wins. The principle is that on each trial the gambler wagers sufficient to cover his losses up to that point and also make a small gain. Suppose that the gambler is betting at even odds on tosses of a fair coin. If it falls tails he loses his stake; if it falls heads he wins an equal amount. The gambler wagers $1 if he has just won (a head came up), but he doubles his last stake if he has just lost (a tail came up). If a series of 0 or more tails followed by a head is referred to as a run, the stake when the head comes up is then sufficient to cover the gambler's previous losses on that run and also win him an additional $1. For example, successive wagers, outcomes and payoffs might be as follows:

Trial:	1	2	3	4	5	6	7	8	9	10	11	12
Outcome:	H	T	T	T	H	H	T	T	H	T	H	H
Stake:	1	1	2	4	8	1	1	2	4	1	2	1
Payoff:	1	-1	-2	-4	8	1	-1	-2	4	-1	2	1
Gain per run:	1	-1	-3	-7	1	1	-1	-3	1	-1	1	1
Total gain:	1				2	3			4		5	6

A martingale may be described as a series of dependent random variables whose conditional means satisfy

$$E(S_{n+1} \mid S_0, S_1, \ldots S_n) = S_n,$$

where S_0 is the gambler's initial fortune and S_n is his capital after n plays [7]. Then the expectation $E(S_n) = E(S_0)$ and is unchanged forever. If we let S_n be his fortune relative to his original capital, then $E(S_n) = S_0 = 0$. The martingale paradox lies in this, that whereas the expected value of the St. Petersburg game is infinite yet Paul will sell his right to play it for a small sum, the expected value of a martingale is zero yet gamblers enthusiastically rediscover and precipitately embrace this strategy all the time, notwithstanding also that the probability that a run of tails will occur that is sufficiently long to exhaust the gambler's fortune and bankrupt him approaches one, if the game continues long enough.

Bernoulli's concept of utility led to an important extension of normative theory, but these observations suggest that it cannot represent Paul's process of thought. But if the normative theory will not work as a descriptive theory, what account of subjects' thought processes can we offer that will explain their preferences between these gambles? Can we diagnose the implicit non-normative argument that leads the average person to an almost automatic scepticism about the value of this game?

3. HEURISTICS AND THE EXPECTATION HEURISTIC

One year after Bernoulli published his paper, in 1739, Hume published his book, A Treatise of Human Nature [1]. Among many other observations, he noted that our assessments of causal relatedness or probability may be influenced by factors other than frequency of association. One such factor he called "resemblance". He argued, for example, that our expectation that if a moving ball strikes a stationary ball the moving ball will communicate its motion to the latter, "is founded on the relation of resemblance betwixt the cause and effect, which ... binds the objects in the closest and most intimate manner to each other ... Resemblance ... has the same or a parallel influence with experience (p. 113)." Another important factor was that an observation "that is recent and fresh in the memory affects us more than one that is in some measure obliterated... Thus a drunkard, who has seen his companion die of a debauch, is struck with that instance for some time, and dreads a like accident for himself; but as the memory of it decays away by degrees, his former security returns, and the danger seems less certain and real (pp. 143-4)."

More recently, these factors affecting judgment have been rediscovered and re-named the "representativeness heuristic" and the "availability heuristic" [8]. What type of process of thought is a "heuristic"? It has been described as a "cognitive or perceptual bias" [9], as "rules learned through induction" [10], or as "any guiding principle for transforming information to solve a problem" [11]. Such definitions indicate that resemblance, for example, provides a cue that may bias a judgment, but they do not specify the process of thought that is so biased. A stronger and more interesting use of the term "heuristic" can be derived from computer programming terminology. This distinguishes two computational approaches to solving a problem. The first is to employ an algorithm. This is a defined procedure which can be carried out in a finite number of steps and the result of which will be the solution to the problem. When an algorithm is not known or is not feasible, a heuristic may be employed. Like an algorithm, this is a procedure consisting of a defined sequence of steps, although their number may be indefinite. It differs from an algorithm in that it does not guarantee to conclude with the correct answer; it only offers an acceptable probability of doing so.

In relation to the decision problem, we might propose that the subject applies a procedure whose relation to the calculation of expected value is that of an heuristic to an algorithm. Some particular mode of reasoning is followed which often but not always leads to a good decision. What process of reasoning does the subject follow that leads to the St. Petersburg paradox?

I suggest that the subject applies, in this case, and in other similarly complex problems, a heuristic that I call the "expectation heuristic". This proceeds by breaking up a problem into a small number of soluble constituent problems, finding the solution for each component as the expectation of that component, and combining these solutions linearly to give an answer for the problem as a whole. In some cases this procedure will lead to the correct solution, in others to an erroneous result. But because it will frequently be useful, and it offers an approach to problems that may seem otherwise intractable, lay persons may use it despite the errors.

To illustrate the expectation heuristic, consider the following simple problem. Philip tosses a fair coin three times, and receives 1 ducat for each head that turns up. How many ducats can he expect to receive?

Let the probability of a head be p and of a tail q. Since the coin is fair, $p = q = 1/2$. We can represent the situation by a probability tree.

There are eight terminal branches, representing eight different sequences, HHH, HHT,...TTT. To calculate expected value correctly, we should identify each sequence, find its probability and corresponding payoff, and compute the expected value by combining these eight products. For people who lack an appropriate notation to apply to the problem, and have not been taught the theory of its solution, this may seem a very complex task. It will become increasingly complex, for anyone who has not mastered the mathematics of the situation, as the number of tosses and thus the number of sequences to be considered lengthens.

If the expectation heuristic is applied to this problem, all that is necessary is to find the expectation for each toss. The expected value for the first toss is $E(V_1) = p1 + q0 = 1/2$, since $p = 0.5$. The second toss has the same two alternative outcomes and an identical expected value: $E(V_2) = 1/2$. Similarly, for the third toss. Thus the solution for the problem as a whole is $E(V_1) + E(V_2) + E(V_3) = 1.5$, and this is the correct solution.

But this simple procedure is a heuristic and cannot be guaranteed to be correct all the time. Consider the following similar problem: the coin is tossed three times and the reward is (Number of Heads)^2. The exact solution found from the possible sequences, as shown in the figure, and their outcomes is 3. But if we apply the expectation heuristic we must calculate the expectation for each toss and sum these values. The expectation for the first toss is $E(V_1) = p1^2 + q0 = 1/2$. Toss 2 has the same expected value: $E(V_2) = 1/2$. Similarly, $E(V_3) = 1/2$. Thus the solution given by the heuristic is $E(V_1) + E(V_2) + E(V_3) = 1.5$. Of course, this is a gross underestimate of the true value, which is 3.

I suggest that if the St Petersburg game is presented to a lay person, he or she applies the expectation heuristic, and analyses the problem presented by this game into the following subproblems. He asks first, On what trial n^* can I expect to see the first head? He asks second, What is the return on a game which ends on trial n^*? And he takes the answer to this question as his estimate of the expected value of the game.

The value of n^* is given by

$$n^* = \sum_{n=1}^{\infty} np^n = p/(1-p)^2 = 2.$$

So the expected return given by the heuristic will be

$$E_{eh}(V) = 2^{n^*} = 4 \text{ ducats.}$$

4 is a poor approximation to infinity. But if Paul proceeds in this way when assessing the opportunity Peter has offered him, it is easy to see why he would be prepared to sell his place for 20 ducats. It is, of course, not necessary for Paul to sum the series above to find n^*. If he has played a number of such games past experience will tell him that n^* is likely to be a small quantity, giving a small estimated return.

The present suggestion explains Bernoulli's original paradox without requiring the application of the utility hypothesis. The expectation heuristic can also be applied to Lopes' (1981) four games. It gives the following expected values:

	E(V)	E_{eh}(V)
1. Standard game, with $2 unit:	∞	$4
2. Standard game with V non-increasing above n = 20:	$21	$4
3. Standard game but with $1.99 unit:	$200	$3.96
4. Standard game, with 2 cent unit:	∞	4 cents

If people calculated correct expected values and chose on that basis, as the normative theory would require, they would prefer games 1 and 4 to games 2 and 3. But if they apply the expectation heuristic they will find games 1, 2, and 3 roughly equivalent, and game 4 considerably less attractive. As Lopes [5] pointed out, it is these choices that seem intuitively plausible.

Earlier I pointed to a third difficulty, the paradoxical popularity of the gambling scheme known as a martingale. But if gamblers apply the expectation heuristic, it is possible to understand this. In a martingale, the gambler wagers sufficient on each toss of a coin (or other bet) to cover his losses up to that point and also make a small gain. Suppose that the gambler wagers $1 on the first toss of a fair coin. If the coin falls tails he loses his stake; if it falls heads he wins $1. The gambler wagers $1 after a win, but doubles his last stake after a loss. This procedure has a constant expectation, and in the case of tosses of a fair coin, this expectation will be zero. Furthermore, if the gambler's initial fortune is finite, it is certain that sooner or later it will be exhausted. Ruin is inevitable. Nevertheless, this scheme is often embraced with enthusiasm.

But as I have argued above, finding the expectation of a long series of tosses is not a calculation that the average person is readily capable of making. What does he do instead? I suggest he first notes the way gains will accumulate over a short run of trials, for example, as in this sequence:

Outcome:	H	T	T	T	H	H	T	T	H	T	H	H
Payoff:	1	-1	-2	-4	8	1	-1	-2	4	-1	2	1
Gain per run:	1	-1	-3	-7	1	1	-1	-3	1	-1	1	1
Total gain:	1				2	3			4		5	6

He observes that his winnings go up by $1 for each head. He then asks, first, what is the expected number of heads in a sequence of length N? The answer is N/2. Second, what are his expected winnings for a sequence with the expected number of heads? The answer is $N/2, reduced by any loss on the last toss if it is a tail. Since the expected number of tails before the first head, on runs on which there is at least one tail, is two, the gambler is likely to consider that this loss will be negligible. If this is the result delivered when he applies the expectation heuristic, it is clear enough why a gambler should find the martingale so attractive.

Although the St. Petersburg paradox has been a mainstay of discussion about utility for almost two and a half centuries, the present argument brings us to the conclusion that this and other such paradoxes are not to be explained by finding the right utility function, but by understanding how people actually reason about uncertain situations of this sort. To understand this we apply the idea of an approximate calculation, or heuristic, a procedure that can be specified in detail. We assume that most people employ, probably unconsciously, a crude approximation to the calculus of expectations, and their resulting preferences are such as would be delivered by this heuristic. Whether the heuristic is applied to calculate an estimated expected value for the St. Petersburg game, or an estimated expected utility does not much matter, since we will arrive at the same conclusion in either case.

REFERENCES

[1] Hume, D. A Treatise of Human Nature. Vol. 1. Originally published 1739. (Dent, London, 1911).

[2] Bernoulli, D. Specimen theoriae novae de mensura sortis. Commentarii Academiae Scientiarium Imperialis Petropolitanae, 6 (1738) 175-192. Translated by L. Sommer. Exposition of a new theory on the measurement of risk. Econometrica, 22 (1954) 23-36.

[3] Vlek, C. and Wagenaar, W. A. Judgement and decision under uncertainty. In J. A. Michon, E. G. J. Eijkman and L. F. W. de Klerk (Eds.), Handbook of Psychonomics, vol. 2. (North-Holland, Amsterdam, 1979).

[4] Kahneman, D. and Tversky, A. Prospect theory: An analysis of decision under risk. Econometrica, 47 (1979) 263-291.

[5] Lopes, L. L. Decision making in the short run. Journal of Human Experimental Psychology: Human Learning and Memory, 7 (1981) 377-385.

[6] Savage, L. J. The Foundations of Statistics. (Wiley, New York, 1954).

[7] Grimmett, G. and Stirzaker, D. Probability and Random Processes. (Clarendon Press, Oxford, 1982).

[8] Tversky, A. and Kahneman, D. Judgment under uncertainty: Heuristics and biases. Science, 185 (1974) 1124-1131.

[9] Tversky, A. and Kahneman, D. Belief in the law of small numbers. Psychological Bulletin, 76 (1971) 105-110.

[10] Einhorn, H. J. Learning from experience and suboptimal rules in decision making. In D. Kahneman, P. Slovic, and A. Tversky (Eds.), Judgment under uncertainty: Heuristics and biases. (Cambridge University Press, London, 1982) pp. 268-283.

[11] Nisbett, R. E., Krantz, D. H., Jepson, C. and Fong, G. T. Improving inductive inference. In D. Kahneman, P. Slovic, and A. Tversky (Eds.), Judgment under uncertainty: Heuristics and biases. (Cambridge University Press, London, 1982) pp. 445-459.

Framing and Communication Effects on Group Members' Responses to Environmental and Social Uncertainty

David M. Messick, Scott T. Allison, and Charles D. Samuelson

University of California, Santa Barbara

Correspondence:

David Messick

Department of Psychology

University of California

Santa Barbara, CA 93106

This research was supported by Grant No. BNS83-02674 from the National Science Foundation to the first author.

Abstract

In many group decision making settings, members must consider two sources of uncertainty, environmental and social. Environmental uncertainty refers to environmental variables that determine which group action is best, while social uncertainty centers on how other group members will respond. The present study investigated members' responses to these two types of uncertainty using a 2 X 2 (Framing X Communication) factorial design. The group decision making task was framed as either a take-some task, in which members where to request money, or as a give-some task, in which members were to return money already in their possession. Moreover, members were either permitted to communicate with each other prior to making their decisions or they were denied the opportunity to communicate. The results revealed that communication significantly reduced environmental and social uncertainty by enhancing group coordination and performance. Specifically, members of groups that were allowed to communicate were more likely to make optimal decisions and were less likely to vote for a superordinate authority who would control future group decisions than were members of groups that were not permitted to communicate. Framing had no effects on members' choices. Some implications of these findings for future work on framing and communication effects on group decision making are discussed.

Framing and Communication Effects on Group Members' Responses to Environmental and Social Uncertainty

When a member of a group needs to make a decision the goal of which is to help achieve some group goal, there are two sources of uncertainty that the member must consider. The first of these is uncertainly concerning the task environment. What are the relevant environmental variables that will determine which group action is best? The second source of uncertainty concerns the behavior of the other group members. How can one member make a sensible decision in ignorance of the decisions made by the other members? The first source of uncertainty, which may be thought of as environmental uncertainty, is an important determinant of optimal group behavior and has been discussed, for instance, by Roby (1968). The second source of uncertainty is, or ought to be, an important factor influencing an individual's decision since the individual group member must cope not only with the environmental but also this social uncertainty. If a group needs to raise some fixed amount of money in order to win a contest, one needs to know where the group total stands with regard to the goal to determine how much more money, if any, needs to be raised to meet the goal. The problem that is raised by the environmental uncertainty is the problem of optimality or efficiency, while the problem raised by social uncertainty is, as Schelling (1960) has noted, coordination. One general point of this paper is to highlight the difference between these two types of uncertainty.

Because our experimental task is novel, it will be most efficient if we describe it before discussing the hypotheses underlying our manipulations. The subjects in this study participated in groups of four. They were told that there was a certain amount of money that the experimenter was going to make available to them and all that they had to do was to request, individually and anonymously, how much of the money they, as individuals, wanted. So long as the total amount requested did not exceed the amount available, each subject got what he or she asked for. If the total group request exceeded the amount available, no one received anything. Thus, the sources of uncertainty for a subject were (1) how much money is available (environmental uncertainty) and (2) how much the other three group members request (social uncertainty). Both sources of uncertainty were amplified by telling the subjects that the amount of money available would depend on the flip of a coin that they would witness after having made their decisions.

<u>Task Analysis</u>

The subjects were told that the amount available to the group would be either \$16 or \$32 and that the amount would be determined by a coin toss. Thus, if the <u>group</u> requested a total of \$16 or less they would receive that amount with certainty. If they requested an amount between \$16 and \$32, they would receive their request with a probability of one half. Thus, the group has two choices that are equally good in terms of expected dollar outcome.

The first is for the group to request \$16 and the second is to request \$32. The expected outcome in both cases is \$16, but requesting \$32 is risky with respect to the environmental uncertainty while requesting \$16 is not.

How can the "group" request \$16, however, if the group members, whose maximum request is \$8, cannot coordinate their individual requests? An individual group member has to consider the social uncertainty in addition to the environmental uncertainty. From this perspective, the situation is somewhat different. Each subject may be risk-averse and prefer to request \$4 rather than the risky \$8, but if only one member of the group should decide to request the \$8 while the others have requested \$4, then the total will exceed \$16 and the expected payoff to those who asked for only \$4 will be halved. In fact, it is easy to show that, in terms of expected dollar return, requesting \$8 dominates any other amount. Considering both types of uncertainty, it is optimal for the individuals to request \$8. However, if the social uncertainty could be reduced or eliminated, requesting either \$4 or \$8 could be optimal, depending on the groups' risk preferences.

Theoretical Considerations

Recent work on the nature of human preference in risky situations suggests that people are risk-averse for gains but risk-seeking for losses, at least over some part of the range (Kahneman & Tversky, 1979, 1984). This means that when contemplating options that would add to their wealth, people tend to prefer a sure amount rather than a gamble whose expected value equals the sure amount. Most people would choose a sure $500 to a fifty-fifty chance of getting $1000 or nothing. For losses, this preference tends to reverse. Most people would prefer to risk loosing $1000 (or nothing) rather than accepting a sure loss of $500. One of the goals of this study was to look for evidence of this same relationship in this group decision making task.

The task as it was described in the previous section is one in which the subjects can only win. Hence, the payoffs are all in the domain of gains. Half of the subjects were confronted with a task that had an identical payoff structure to the one described above, but in which the outcomes were framed in terms of losses. In this case, when the subjects entered the experimental room they were given $8 in cash. They were told that the money was theirs to keep but they might need to return some of it in order to be able to have the remainder. These subjects were told that if the group returned 16 dollars or more, then each member would be entitled to keep whatever amount he or she had remaining, regardless of the coin flip. But if the group total was less than 16 dollars, members could keep whatever cash they had left if the coin flip resulted in heads but would be allowed to keep nothing if the coin flip was tails. This version of the task we called the <u>give-some</u> task to contrast it to the <u>take-some</u> task described earlier. The payoff structure for the two tasks is identical, with the amount being <u>taken</u> in the take-some task being the equivalent to the amount being <u>kept</u> in the give-some task.

If the subjects in the give-some task frame the amount that they have to return as a loss, and if they are risk-seeking for losses, then there should be a strong propensity for these subjects to refuse to return any of the $8 and to take the chance of keeping it all. The risky option of returning nothing should be more attractive than the less risky option of returning $4. In the take-some task, in contrast, the subjects' risk-aversion should make the less risky option more attractive. The social uncertainty which should lead one to favor the $8 option should, at most, create a conflict between the two strategies. In any case, we would expect to see a greater preference for the risky option in the give-some than in the take-some condition.

One way of reducing the social uncertainty is via communication. If the group members can discuss their choices with each other prior to making their decisions then the information that they get from the others could have a number of effects (Messick & Brewer, 1983). In the present context, those effects could include the following consequences. First, through discussion, the group members are likely to realize that there is no reason for any individual to request an amount different from either $4 or $8 if the person wants to maximize his or her expected return. Second, all members of the group should request (or keep) the same amount. It is sub-optimal, from the group level, for some of the members to ask for $4 while others ask for $8. If at least one person is going to ask for $8, then all should do so. Thus, the need for the coordination of responses is highlighted and the ability to do so is afforded by communication. Finally, communication should enhance the trust existing among the group members (Dawes, McTavish & Shaklee, 1977). If the members are risk-averse but are reluctant to ask for (retain) $4 for fear that one or more members may ask for (retain) $8, the increased trust may reduce this perceived risk and allow a higher proportion of groups to opt for the environmentally riskless option. On the other hand, the communication may also underscore the superiority of asking for $8 in preference to asking for $4.

With regard to the individual's choices, we can summarize the expected effects of communication as follows: (1) Groups allowed to communicate should show superior coordination to groups that can not; (2) Groups allowed to communicate should have fewer sub-optimal choices (ones other than $4 or $8) than non-communicating groups; and (3) Communicating groups, especially in the take-some version of the task, should show greater risk-aversion, due to increased trust, than non-communicating groups.

One final issue that was probed by this study relates to our continuing efforts to understand the circumstances under which members of a group will be willing to change the decision-making structure of the group itself (see, for instance, Messick, 1984; Samuelson & Messick, 1986). In previous experiments using a somewhat different task, we have found that subjects will prefer to change the decision-making structure of a group when the group does not efficiently cope with the task at hand. In this experiment, as we have done in previous ones, we told the subjects that they might have a chance to repeat the task. They were further told that they had the choice of doing the task as they had done it the first time, with each group member making a private decision, or they could, if they wished, elect a leader who would make a decision that would be binding on all group members. The leader would decide on a total amount to take (return) and would also specify how much each member would receive from (contribute to) that total amount.

We had two hypotheses about the effects of framing and communication on this preference for structural change, for electing a leader. First, the leader would act as a way of achieving the coordination that the group needs to be effective. However, groups that communicate will already have a means of coordinating their decisions so they should experience less need for a leader than groups that cannot communicate. Thus, groups without communication should show a stronger preference for a leader than groups with communication.

One prediction with regard to framing effects focussed on the type of power that a leader would have in the take-some and give-some tasks. In the take-some task, the leader will take some number of dollars and allocate gains to the others. In the give-some task, the leader will decide how much the group should contribute and will then take the appropriate amount from the $8 that each of the other members has. Our hypotheses, adapted from Thurow (1980), is that people are more willing to accept a leader who has the authority only to increase their wealth, than a leader who has the authority to reduce their wealth. Thus, we predicted that subjects in the take-some task, especially with no communication, would be more eager to have a leader than subjects in the give-some task. A previous study by Rutte, Wilke, and Messick (1985) found support for this prediction.

Method

Subjects

Eighty subjects, in twenty groups of four persons each, participated in the experiment. Each group was homogeneous in terms of gender. Fifteen of the groups were composed of females, five were composed of males.

Design

The study was a 2 x 2 factorial, with two levels of task type (take-some, give-some) crossed with two levels of group communication (communication, no-communication). Each of the twenty groups of subjects was randomly assigned to one of the four experimental conditions.

Procedure

As each subject arrived at the experiment, he or she was instructed to sit at any one of four semi-private desks. The desks were arranged so that subjects could see each other but not each others' desk-tops. When all four subjects arrived, the experimenter began reading the instructions. Subjects were told that during the experiment there was a chance that they might win some money, and that whether or not they did depended on their own behavior, the behavior of the others in their group, and the outcome of a coin flip. The experimenter emphasized that everyone's choices during the experiment would be kept completely confidential.

In what constituted the take-some condition, one half of the groups were verbally instructed that each member, privately, was to request in writing any amount of cash in integer dollar amounts up to and including eight dollars. Subjects were informed that after they made their requests a group total would be computed and a coin would be flipped. If the group total was sixteen dollars or less, each member would receive the amount he or she requested regardless of the coin flip. But if the group total exceeded sixteen dollars, members would receive their requests if the coin flip resulted in heads but would receive nothing if the coin flip resulted in tails.

In the give-some condition, subjects received eight one dollar bills each the moment they arrived at the experiment. They were told that each member, privately, was to return to the experimenter any amount of money from zero to the entire eight dollars. Subjects were informed that after they returned this cash, a group total would be computed and a coin would be flipped. If the group returned sixteen dollars or more, each member would be entitled to keep whatever amount he or she had remaining, regardless of the coin flip. But if the group total was less than sixteen dollars, members could keep whatever cash they had left if the coin flip resulted in heads but would be allowed to keep nothing if the coin flip was tails.

After subjects received these verbal instructions, they were presented with two numerical examples that illustrated how the task worked. In the first example subjects were shown the consequences of their group requesting more than or returning less than sixteen dollars, while in the second example subjects were informed of the consequences of requesting less than or returning more than sixteen dollars. Subjects were then encouraged to ask questions to ensure their understanding of the task.

The communication manipulation was then introduced. Groups who were permitted to communicate were led into small room containing a table and four chairs. Once seated, these members were told that they could discuss the task among themselves. The length of the discussion was left entirely up to the group. A written copy of the instructions, exactly as the experimenter had read them, was left for the group to examine if they wished during the discussion. The experimenter then left the room, When subjects finished discussing the task, they returned to their original semi-private desks.

Group members in the no-communication condition, after hearing the experimenter's original verbal instructions, were then each provided with a written copy of the instructions and were told to think about the task for about five minutes. Subjects were instructed to remain seated and to refrain from communicating with the other members during this five minute period.

At this point, the experimenter handed each subject a plain envelope in which the subject could return money (in the give-some condition), or a piece of paper on which dollar values ranging from one to eight were printed for subjects to request money (in the take-some condition). These envelopes or papers were then collected by the experimenter; at which time subjects were asked to complete a short post-experimental questionnaire.

One of the questions on this questionnaire stated that the subjects might have a chance to do the experiment a second time. They were told that they could repeat the task as they had just done, or that they could elect a leader who would be empowered to decide how much the group as a whole should take (contribute) and how much of the total each member should receive (pay). The subjects had to express their preferences before learning what the group total was and before knowing how much money, if any, they were to receive or keep for the task.

After the questionnaire was completed, the experimenter announced the total amount of money that the group either requested or returned. He then allowed each subject to examine the coin that was to be flipped, an Eisenhower dollar. The coin was then tossed, the result observed, and the payments (if any) were made. Subjects were then debriefed and thanked for their participation.

<u>Dependent Variables</u>

The major dependent variables were the amount of money each subject decided to either request or to return and subjects' preferences whether to elect a leader who would control the entire group's choices should the identical experiment be run again.

Results

One question was used to check that subjects did indeed perceive that requesting (keeping) a lot was a riskier option than requesting (keeping) a little. The question read, "Is asking for a lot/keeping a lot more or less risky than asking for a little/keeping a little?" Subjects marked "1" for less risky and "7" for more risky. The mean response to this item was ($\underline{M}$=6.00) much closer to the correct end of the scale than to the midpoint, indicating that subjects were aware of the risk properties of their options. A 2 (Task Type) X 2 (Communication) Analysis of Variance (ANOVA) of the responses to this item failed to reveal any significant differences.

<u>Subjects' choices</u>. In the analysis of subjects' monetary decisions, the amount that subjects requested in the take-some situation was treated as equivalent to the amount that subjects kept in the give-some situation. A 2 (Task Type) X 2 (Communication) ANOVA, with the individual subject as the unit of analysis, was performed on these amounts. The three resulting Fs

were all approximately one or less, indicating that the average amount of the subjects' decisions did not significantly fluctuate as a function of the two variables. The raw data and means associated with the analysis are provided in Table 1.

However, it is obvious from Table 1 that the mean amounts do not tell the entire story and that the data do support two of the hypothesized effects of communication. First, only one of the responses in the communication condition is other than a "4" or an "8", whereas 9 of the 40 choices in the no-communication condition were suboptimal. Furthermore, in 9 of the 10 communication groups, the decisions were perfectly coordinated. This was true in only one of the no-discussion groups.

The consequence of these differences may be summarized by noting that with respect to the environmental uncertainty, group responses of either \$16 or \$32 were optimal and any other response represented an inferior group decision. Nine of the 10 group decisions were optimal by this criterion in the communication condition, whereas only 2 of the 10 were optimal in the no-communication condition ($\chi^2(1) = 12.09$, $p<.001$). Put slightly differently, the expected group payoff for the communication groups is \$15.35, in contrast to \$11.80 for the no-communication groups where the maximum expected payoff is $16. Communication clearly enhances performance although it does not influence risk propensity.

The framing of the decision as a give-some or take-some task had no observable effect at all. We will focus more closely on this finding in the discussion.

Leader Vote. Subjects were informed that they might be contacted at a later date by the experimenter and asked to participate in the experiment again. Given this possibility, subjects were asked to choose how the experiment should be run at this later date. Subjects were given two choices: They could choose to have the experiment run in the same manner, with each subject making his or her own decision regarding how much to request or return, or they could choose to elect a group leader who would make the choices for all of the members.

A 2 (Task Type) X 2 (Communication) ANOVA was performed on these binary data. The analysis revealed a significant communication effect, $F(1,79) = 19.61$, $p<.001$, indicating that a leader was preferred more by a higher proportion of subjects who were denied the opportunity to discuss the task (.68) than by subjects who were permitted a discussion (.23). Contrary to our predictions, however, there was no task effect ($F<1$). The proportions associated with this analysis are provided in Table 2.

Discussion

There are two issues from this experiment that need to be discussed. Why did we find no effects whatsoever for the framing manipulation, and what is the significance of the communication effects? To begin with the framing effect, we immediately acknowledge the perils of interpreting negative results. Having done this, we can attempt to evaluate several reasons why we found no framing effects in this experiment. First, the impressive framing effects that Kahneman and Tversky (1984) describe, perhaps, simply do not characterize social decision making. A similar experiment performed by Rutte, Wilke, and Messick (1985) also failed to find framing effects with individual decisions, although those authors did find that subjects in a take-some task showed a stronger preference for a leader than subjects in a give-some task. One possibility may be that, in a group decision making task of the sort used here, framing effects are not found because the other social sources of uncertainty confuse or distract the subjects.

A second possibility is that the framing effects characterize subjects' choices in hypothetical decision making tasks but do not, or do so to a lesser extent, in real tasks. The subjects in this study had in their possession or saw cash with which they were to be, and were in fact, paid. On the other hand, the situations described by Kahneman and Tversky (1984) were all hypothetical choice situations in which no money changed hands. On the face of it, this may appear to be an improbable interpretation. However, in this experiment, after the data were collected, but before the experimenter flipped the coin and announced the group total, we gave our subjects a hypothetical group decision making task that was identical in structure to the one they had just participated in. The task was either framed as a take-some task (for the subjects in the take-some condition) or a give-some task. For this hypothetical task, which involved larger amounts of money than our NSF budget permits us to use, we did find a significant framing effect, even though it was in the direction opposite to the predictions. Subjects in the take-some version took more hypothetical money than subjects in the give-some version kept.

The most likely interpretation of the failure of framing effect, we believe, is simply that we did not succeed in getting the give-some subjects to view the $8 that we gave them at the beginning of the experiment as their own money. Several subjects made comments to the effect that whatever happened to them, they would not be worse off than they were when they came to the experiment. Such comments imply that subjects are setting their reference values at the pre-experiment levels and are not really incorporating the $8 windfall into their current wealth. Doing this makes hedonic sense, of course, since it allows the subject to code all possible experimental outcomes as equal to or better than what they had before. They cannot lose. If this interpretation is correct, it will take some experimental ingenuity to show framing effects for real payoffs in laboratory situations in which experiments cannot in fact make subjects pay them money.

Turning now to the communication effects, we found that communication allowed the groups to deal effectively with both the environmental uncertainty as well as the social uncertainty. All but one of the 40 group members made either a $4 or $8 decision, and they coordinated their responses so that all members of the same group made the same choice. The communication must have instilled a high level of trust in the seven groups that agreed to request (return) $4 per member, because a single person who decides to go for $8 reduces the expected payoff to the others by exactly half. We can infer a high level of trust, as well as a high level of risk aversion, among the subjects, but what is even more clear is the high level of trustworthiness among these groups. Of the 28 subjects who agreed to request (return) $4, all but one did so. Ninety-six percent did as they agreed even though their choices were anonymous and the others could not learn the identity of the defector.

The fact that most of the subjects chose $4 or fewer in both communication conditions, 27 of 40 in the communication condition, and 28 of 40 in the no-communication condition, suggests that subjects are risk-averse with regard to environmental uncertainty, but are less concerned with or perhaps less clear about the implications of the social uncertainty. Yet in the no-communication condition, 17 of the 28 subjects who made a risk-averse choice of $4 or less had their expected payoffs halved because one or more others in their group requested (kept) enough above $4 to take the group total above (below) $16.

Communication seems to aid performance by clarifying what the correct choices are, by allowing the group members to coordinate their decisions, and by creating a sense of interpersonal trust. However, communication does not appear to have influenced the level of risk aversion although it is not altogether clear exactly how to compare the level of riskiness manifested by the uncoordinated subjects in the no-communication condition to that of the subjects in the communication condition where decisions were jointly agreed upon. The fact that there is no great level difference between the conditions may reflect the fact that two opposing tendencies are established in the communications condition. First, the risk of having one group member spoil things for everyone may be made apparent to all, a fact that should lead subjects to favor going for the $8 option; but this risk may be countered by the explicit agreements that the risk-averse groups made to go for $4. These agreements were not enforceable, but they were bound with mutual trust.

References

Dawes, R.M., McTavish, J., & Shaklee, H. (1977). Behavior, communication, and assumptions about other people's behavior in a commons dilemma situation. Journal of Personality and Social Psychology, 35, 1-11.

Kahneman, D., & Tversky, A. (1979). Prospect theory: An analysis of decision under risk. Econometrica, 47, 263-291.

Kahneman, D., & Tversky, A. (1984). Choices, values, and frames. American Psychologist, 39, 341-350.

Messick, D.M. (1984). Solving social dilemmas: Individual and collective approaches. Representative Research in Social Psychology, 14, 72-87.

Messick, D.M., Brewer, M.B. (1983). Solving social dilemmas: A review. In L. Wheeler & P. Shaver (Eds.), Review of Personality and Social Psychology (Vo. 4, pp. 11-44). Beverly Hills, CA: Sage.

Roby, T.B. (1968). Small group performance. Chicago: Rand McNally & Co.

Rutte, C.G., Wilke, H.A.M., & Messick, D.M. (1985). The effects of framing social dilemmas as give-some or take-some games. Unpublished manuscript.

Samuelson, C.D. & Messick, D.M. (1986). Alternative structural solutions to resource dilemmas. Organizational Behavior and Human Decision Processes, 37, 000-000.

Schelling, T.C. (1960). The strategy of conflict. Cambridge, MA: Harvard University Press.

Thurow, L. (1980). The zero-sum society. New York: Penguin.

Table 1

Subjects' Decisions as a Function of Framing and Communication

	Communication		No Communication		Mean
	Group		Group		
	1	4 4 4 4	1	7 4 4 8	
	2	8 8 8 8	2	2 6 4 4	
Take-some	3	4 4 4 4	3	3 4 8 4	
	4	8 8 8 8	4	8 4 2 4	
	5	4 4 4 4	5	4 4 4 4	
		(5.60)		(4.60)	(5.10)
	1	4 4 4 4	1	4 4 8 4	
	2	8 8 8 8	2	8 4 4 8	
Give-some	3	4 4 4 4	3	4 4 2 4	
	4	4 4 4 4	4	4 5 5 8	
	5	4 4 7 4	5	5 4 4 4	
		(4.95)		(4.85)	(4.90)
Mean		(5.28)		(4.73)	(5.00)

Table 2.

Proportion of Subjects in Favor of a Leader as a Function of Framing and Communication

	Communication	No Communication	Total
Take-some	4/20 (.20)	13/20 (.65)	17/40 (.43)
Give-some	5/20 (.25)	14/20 (.70)	19/40 (.48)
Total	9/40 (.23)	27/40 (.68)	36/80 (.45)

Part Fifteen
Aspects of Distributive Justice

On the behavioral approach to distributive justice
- A theoretical and experimental investigation -

Werner Güth
University of Cologne
Staatswissenschaftliches Seminar
Herbert-Lewin-Str. 2

D - 5000 Köln 41

According to the behavioral theory of distributive justice bargaining situations are exchange relations as usual market relations. Its main axiom is that the same proportion between individual rewards and investments must hold for all bargaining parties. For a selection of experiments it will be shown how the behavioral theory of distributive justice provides straightforward explanations of results, which contradict game theoretic predictions, simply by using other investment or reward standards than those suggested by normative decision theory. Our theoretical considerations concentrate on the problem how to decide between competing investment and/or reward standards. Our main hypothesis is that people rely on the same hierarchy of standards which is derived by the strictness of their prerequisites. Compared to a basic standard a superior standard requires a more subtle description of individual characteristics.

I. The basic rule of distributive justice

Psychologically a bargaining problem cannot be solved by abstracting from its social context including previous experiences and behavioral expectations of all participants. Main feature of the behavioral theory of distributive justice (Homans, 1961) is that bargaining problems are viewed as exchange relations like usual market transactions. Those exchanges by which an individual contributes to the group's success are called his investments. His rewards are the exchanges according to which he participates in what can be distributed. Mostly it is implicitly assumed that investments as well as rewards of the participating parties i can be expressed by nonnegative numbers I_i and x_i, respectively.

The central idea of the behavioral theory of distributive justice is the equity principle. According to the equity principle the relation of investments and rewards for all individuals should be equal (Homans, 1961, Walster, Berscheid, and Walster, 1973, Walster, Walster, and Berscheid, 1978, and Mikula, 198o).

Assume that there is a commonly accepted way to measure investments I_i and rewards x_i. For the reward vector $x=(x_1,\dots,x_n)$ of all n participating parties i=1,...,n with $I_i > 0$ it is postulated that

$$\text{(I.1)} \qquad x_k/I_k = x_j/I_j \quad \text{for } k,j = 1,\dots,n$$

Equation (I.1) will be called the basic rule of distributive justice. It says that men are all alike in holding the notion of proportionality between investments and rewards (Homans, 1961). It is the relative share of a player's investment which determines his relative share of rewards.

The basic rule of distributive justice can be rewritten as

$$\text{(I.2)} \qquad (x_i-I_i)/I_i = (x_j-I_j)/I_j \quad \text{for } i,j = 1,\dots,n$$

In economic terms x_i-I_i can be called subject i's profit from participating in social interaction. Consequently, equation (I.2) can be described as the requirement that social interaction should be equally profitable. This shows that the behavioral theory also can be regarded as an economic concept.

When justifying the basic rule of distributive justice social psychologists usually do not refer to market forces. One mainly argues that confirming the basic rule will be rewarded by other group members whereas any offence against this basic norm leads to punishments by other group members (Austin and Hatfield, 1980). According to Homans (1961) it is dangerous to deviate from the basic rule (I.1) of distributive justice. In all our social relations (e.g. clubs, markets, neighbourhoods) we have experienced that investments were rewarded proportionally. Investments constitute therefore definite expectations which rewards one can reasonably hope to receive. The more to our disadvantage rule (I.1) fails of realization the more likely we are to become angry and to react accordingly. To illustrate this Homans (1961) refers to a biological experiment. Pigeons, used to be rewarded after accomplishing a certain task, displaid strong anger or frustration when their investment was not rewarded.

In the same way men will react when their expectations about a fair result are not met. They will punish or avoid further exchanges with persons who are responsible for not attaining just or fair exchanges. There is a lot of evidence from experiments with human beings to support this belief. In 2-person ultimatum bargaining games which were conducted anonymously Güth et al. (1983) and Güth and Tietz (1985 and 1986) first asked player 1 how much money a_1 of a given positive amount c to be distributed he demands for himself. Player 2 then can only accept player 1's demand a_1 which yields $c-a_1$ for himself or choose conflict in which case both players receive nothing. Demands a_1 with rather low shares $(c-a_1)/c$ for player 2 were usually refused even when player 2's absolute loss $c-a_1$ was rather high (e.g. more than DM 5.-).

The main problem in applying the behavioral theory of distributive justice is to determine for every bargaining situation what constitutes an investment and how to measure rewards. In many bargaining situations it will be rather obvious what should be considered as an investment or a reward. But there can be situations where people differ in their ideas what legitimately constitutes investments and rewards (see Homans, 1961, p. 246). This indicates that the behavioral theory of distributive justice is still incomplete in the sense that it does not specify how to measure investments and rewards in all possible situations.

In many abstract bargaining games like dividing a dollar-games one can obviously assume investments to be equal and rewards to be measured by monetary payoffs. Later we will review some experimental results which will illustrate that in more complex situations there are competing standards to measure rewards and investments. Some a priori counterintuitive results might become understandable by considering other investment or reward standards than those suggested by game theory. To qualify for an investment or reward standard a variable must be generally observable and measurable in the sense that there are information conditions and that there exist measurement techniques which allow any party to specify the individual values of this variable for all participants. Without this one cannot control whether the basic rule (I.1) of distributive justice is justified. The information conditions and measurement requirements of a standard are called its prerequisites.

It is an obvious idea to apply the behavioral theory of distributive justice to bargaining games. Bartos (1978) translates the general rule (I.1) of distributive justice to 2-person bargaining games where he assumes that in abstract bargaining games with side payments all players have the same investments and that rewards are given by monetary payoffs. Bartos concludes that the 50:50-split is the fair solution according to the behavioral theory of distributive justice. His experimental results support this hypothesis. Selten's equity principle also relies on the basic rule (I.1) of distributive justice (Selten, 1978). Selten distinguishes a standard of distribution to measure rewards and a standard of comparison to measure investments or contributions. He doubts that the basic rule of distributive justice is generally applicable since it might be impossible to find always a reasonable investment or reward standard. Contrary to Selten it will be assumed here that men are guided by the basic rule (I.1) even if there is no unambiguous way to measure investments and/or rewards. In such situations different patterns of distribution behavior might be classified and explained by different standards to measure investments and/or rewards.

Often bargaining is not concerned with splitting "rewards" but with sharing costs. Individual investments or contributions are in such situations related to questions like: How much of the total costs has been caused by individual i? To have a specific example of a cost sharing problem in mind consider a condominion with flats differing in size and occupancy. How should the costs of common water usage be assigned to the different units? How should one share duties like cleaning the house, gardening etc. if this has to be done by the tenants themselves? In practice we can find various standards according to which these costs are allocated (e.g. equal treatment of apartments, square meters, or persons). If there is no legal regulation, the standard will often depend on whether the differences in size and occupancy are considerable or not.

II. Experimental evidence of investment and reward standards

In the following we briefly review experimental results indicating the use of different investment and/or reward standards. Not all relevant investigations can be considered here. In most bargaining experiments investment and reward standards are of decisive importance (for surveys on experimental economics see Selten, 1979, and Roth, 1985).

a) Reward and cost allocation experiments

In so-called reward allocation experiments at least two subjects have to perform some kind of work (e.g. writing addresses on envelopes etc.). Mostly there is an exact way to measure how much each subject contributed to the total task. Knowing these individual investments subjects have to allocate the rewards among them. We will concentrate on experiments where a certain subject (the player) is asked to distribute the rewards among all workers (Leventhal-Michaels, 1969, Mikula, 1972, Mikula-Uray, 1973, Mikula, 1977). In spite of the social aspects subjects face a 1-person decision problem. Knowing the inputs of all workers the player has to decide what he demands for himself and how much he is going to leave for his anonymous coworkers. Observe that it is always dominant to demand all rewards for oneself. Thus the experiments also reveal to which extent distribution behavior is determined by investment standards and by strategic considerations. If the dominant strategy is not used, this indicates that the subjects are guided by considerations of distributive justice.

Experimental observations strongly support the basic rule (I.1) of distributive justice. Subjects nearly never ask for more than their fair share according to rule (I.1). If the work is not too long and cumbersome <u>and</u> if the rewards are rather low, they even deviate from (I.1) to their own disadvantage if this causes a more egalitarian distribution of rewards. The latter observation indicates that there are two competing investment or contribution standards governing the allocation of rewards. If work or rewards are not very important, people tend to treat everybody equal. We will say that they rely on the personal investment standard which is defined by the equality

$$(\text{II.1}) \qquad I_i = I_j \quad \text{for } i,j = 1,\ldots,n$$

If both, work and rewards, are of significant importance, the actual investment I_i of player i is no longer independent of the work inputs, but determined by the individual efforts for fulfilling the common task. We will call this the observable work standard. Whereas the personal standard has no prerequisites, i.e. is generally applicable, the observable work standard can only be used if there is a clear way to measure individual efforts. One will have to rely on the personal standard if individual work inputs cannot be easily observed or quantified.

In an experiment (Güth, 1984), designed to test altruism, two subjects with equal rewards had to complete a given amount of work (12 tables with complicated multiplication problems). One of the two subjects (the player) had a considerable comparative advantage in accomplishing this work (he could use a calculator). The player was asked to distribute the total work (the 12 multiplication tables) among the two subjects. Since the player had to allocate work instead of rewards among two individuals with different productivity, we call this a labor allocation experiment. Denote by m the number of work units (multiplication tables) which the player allocates to himself. 12-m is therefore the number of work units which he assigns to his anonymous partner.

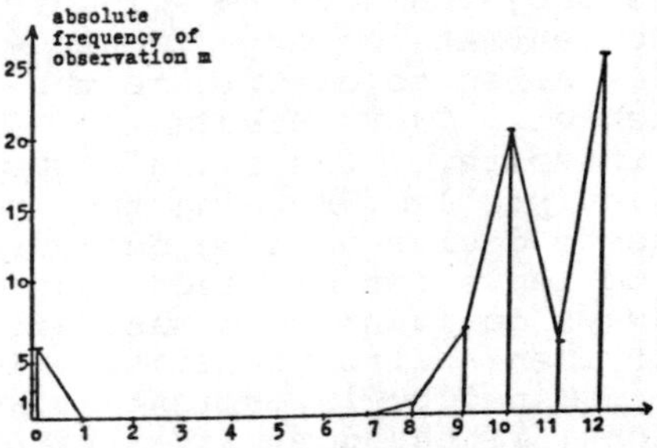

Figure II.1: Observed frequency of labor allocations m in labor allocation experiments (Güth, 1984)

In Figure II.1 we have illustrated the results of 62 labor allocation experiments. Except for the egoistic players with m = 0 most players allocated to themselves considerably more work than to their disadvantaged partner. It is a surprising result that no subject had chosen m = 6, i.e. an equal division of work. This shows that the number of work units was not considered as a justified cost standard. The subjects with $0 < m < 12$, who were not completely egoistic or altruistic, seemingly relied on a more sophisticated notion of effort to measure the individual costs x_i. From the answers to an additional questionaire one can conclude that most subjects with $0 < m < 12$ tried to balance the expected working time for both partners. Thus their behavior can be explained as an attempt to be in line with the basic rule (I.1) of distributive justice.

b) Utility as a reward standard

Many game theoretic solution concepts fail to predict actual decision behavior. A main reason is that positive linear transformations of utilities do not change the game and therefore the optimal behavior whereas people rely on non-transformable reward standards to measure and compare their success. This was clearly demonstrated by the experimental results of Nydegger and Owen (1974) who asked two players to divide an even number of chips which could be cashed after the experiment. The exchange rate for player 1 was double as high as for player 2 what was known to both players. Considering chips as rewards the game is symmetric whereas it is asymmetric if money serves as reward standard. Nyegger and Owen performed 10 experiments with free face to face-communication and no side payments. In all 10 experiment chips were allocated in such a way that both players received the sam monetary reward. There is no doubt in such situations that the personal standard is the appropriate investment standard. What was not a priori clear is whether chips or money will serve as reward standard. The impressive result of Nydegger and Owen suggests that money is a dominant reward standard when there is complete information about monetary rewards and free face to face-communication. Unfortunately, monetary payoffs in the experiments were too low to make sure that subjects are mainly motivated by monetary incentives.

The conjecture that information about monetary rewards is very important for distribution behavior is clearly demonstrated by the illuminating experiments of Roth and Malouf (1979 and 1982), Roth, Malouf, and Murnighan (1981), Roth and Murnighan (1982), Roth and Schoumaker (1983). The experiments were games with complete information in the game theoretic sense although information about monetary rewards was varied. The results show clearly that information about monetary rewards is of crucial importance for the resulting payoff distribution although game theory usually neglects this kind of information.

In the basic experiment of Roth and Malouf (1979) two anonymous subjects bargained over the probability p according to which player 1 would receive a positive monetary prize P_1. With the residual probability 1-p player 2 would get his positive monetary prize P_2. The player, who does not win, receives only zero. Both players i = 1 and i = 2 knew always their own prize P_i and that both prizes are positive. If no agreement was reached, both parties received their conflict payoffs of zero. By setting the von Neumann-Morgenstern utilities $u_i = 0$ for receiving nothing and $u_i = 1$ for getting P_i with certainty, the set U of feasible utility vectors $u = (u_1, u_2)$ can be normalized to

$$\text{(II.2)} \qquad U = \left\{ u \in \mathbb{R}^2_{\geq 0} \mid u_1 + u_2 = 1 \right\} \cup \left\{ (0,0) \right\}$$

It is important to observe that this set is completely known to both players independently what player i knows about the prize P_j (>0) of his opponent j. Thus the game is a bargaining game with complete information, independent on the information about the opponent's prize.

Since U is known to both players, independently whether they know the opponent's prize or not, and, furthermore, symmetric, all unique game theoretic solution concepts select p = o.5 as the solution, i.e. both players will receive their respective prize with the same probability regardless whether the prizes P_1 and P_2 are equal or not. Contrary to game theoretic concepts the experimental results of Roth and Malouf (1979) reveal that information about the opponent's prize has a strong and distinct effect on bargaining behavior. If both parties know both prizes, there is a considerably stronger tendency to balance expected monetary rewards instead of winning probabilities than in the case where both parties know only their own prize.

According to the behavioral theory of distributive justice the experimental results of Roth and Malouf show that expected monetary payoffs dominate winning probabilities as a reward standard. But since expected monetary payoffs can only be equilibrated if both prizes are known, the dominant reward standard cannot be used if this prerequisite is not given (Mikula, 1977, discusses the prerequisites of some basic standards). This interpretation is supported by another study (Roth and Murnighan, 1982) showing that the shift toward equal expected monetary rewards is mainly caused by the fact that the player with the smaller prize is informed about both prizes. This also can be well explained by the behavioral theory of distributive justice. If expected monetary payoffs are the dominant reward standard, a deviation from equal monetary rewards will arise the anger of the unfavored party and imply a high risk of conflict according to the behavioral theory of distributive justice.

Although the Roth et al.-experiments confirm the result of Nydegger and Owen that individual monetary payoff is a superior reward standard, the impressive uniformity in the results observed by Nydegger and Owen has not been reproduced. Roth and Malouf (1982) attribute the absence of variance in the results of Nydegger and Owen solely to the face-to-face bargaining procedure which exerts considerable social pressure. But it might be that also the more significant monetary incentives and/or the expected instead of deterministic payoffs are responsible for the variance in final agreements.

It seems justified to say that the behavioral theory of distributive justice offers an intuitively convincing and straightforward explanation for the experimental results of Roth and Malouf contradicting the most fundamental game theoretic axioms. In our view this explanation is more convincing than the approach of Roth and Schoumaker (1983). They try to explain the experimental observations of Roth and Malouf by different subjective beliefs or expectations in the situations of knowing or not knowing the opponent's prize.

What Roth (1985) calls the focal point phenomenon is in our view just the problem of deciding between two reward standards differing in their prerequisites. One can only wonder why Roth and his coauthors do not even consider the explanation offered by the behavioral theory of distributive justice (the first version of this paper, finished in 1983, was strongly influenced by discussions with Alvin E. Roth). Probably the main reason is that this would mean to finally give up the illusion that people can meet the requirements of normative decision theory.

c) Bargaining experiments with weighted majority games

In a weighted majority game $G = (w_1, \ldots, w_n; m)$ with players $i = 1, \ldots, n (\geq 2)$ resources of players i can be measured by weights $w_i (>0)$. A coalition C of players i is winning if the sum of weights w_i for all i in C exceeds the majority level $m (>0)$. Any winning coalition can freely distribute a given positive amout M of money among its members. Given a weighted majority game G it is by no means clear how to perform bargaining experiments basing on such a situation. This is due to a general deficiency of cooperative game theory which does not specify the individual strategic possibilities and the process of strategic interaction. Bargaining can proceed anonymously or face to face, also communication can be more or less unrestricted. Here we will not go into details and simply refer to the literature where the experimental procedure is documented. Furthermore, only few experimental results will be considered (for a more general survey see Crott, 1979).

In a weighted majority game G rewards are clearly given by the monetary payoff x_i which a player i finally receives. How to measure investments is less obvious. On one side resources as measured by w_i are important contributions since they determine together with m whether a given coalition C is winning or not. But should differences in weights matter even when they are strategically inessential? Consider, for instance, two players i and j with $w_i \neq w_j$ and

$$\text{(II.3)} \qquad w_i + \sum_{l \in C} w_l > m$$

if and only if

$$\text{(II.4)} \qquad w_j + \sum_{l \in C} w_l > m$$

for all coalitions C containing neither i nor j. Clearly, both players enjoy exactly the same strategic power in spite of their different weights. This indicates that one might also neglect inessential differences in weights and assign equal investments. In such a case the personal investment standard will be applied when determining the rewards of i and j.

Now the result which the basic rule of distributive justice implies is very different if one applies the personal standard or the weight standard to measure investments. In the first case all players in a coalition will receive the same monetary rewards. In the latter case rewards will be allocated in proportion to weights, i.e. the relation x_i to w_i is the same for all players i in the coalition. Interesting enough the theory of Komorita and Chertkoff (1973) predicts that players allocate rewards halfway between these two solutions. Since Komorita and Chertkoff were inspired by experimental observations, their study provides strong evidence that the basic rule of distributive justice is the main driving force even if the standards, necessary for its applicability, are ambiguous.

In our view a hypothesis predicting a result halfway between two competing solution points is no satisfactory concept of human decision behavior. One would need to explain why people consider both principles in exactly the way that the solution is halfway between the two distinct predictions. Following our way of reasoning one would have to clarify why subjects allocate half of M by using the the personal standard and the other half of M by using the weight standard to measure individual investments. Furthermore, the empirical evidence for the halfway solution of Komorita and Chertkoff can be a pure consequence of aggregation underlying average decision results (see, for instance, Table 6 and 7 of Komorita and Chertkoff, 1973).

d) Presentation effects in view of the behavioral theory of distributive justice

As already indicated by the experiments reviewed above one often will face competing investment or reward standards when trying to aim at fair bargaining results according to the basic rule of distributive justice. Since subjects have to select one of many possible standards, the way in which the experiment is presented to them may be of crucial importance. Specifically some so-called presentation effects (Pruitt, 1967 and 1970, Selten-Berg, 1970) might be explained by the effects which presentation has for the likelihood of competing standards to be actually used when applying rule (I.1). In oligopoly experiments with sellers as players Selten and Berg (1970) have defined payoffs by the sums of capital stock and profit. Keeping this sum constant for each player by increasing capital stock and decreasing profit by the same amount does not change the monetary payoff of any player. Nevertheless the experimental results of Selten and Berg reveal a strong influence of such changes on market results. Since in market games profit is generally a more reasonable reward standard, a just distribution of total profits will aim more at equal profits than at equal payoffs including capital stocks (see Selten-Berg, 1970). For decomposed prisoner dilemma-games(Pruitt,1967 and 1970) the crucial point seems to be how presentation affects the way how subjects view their decision problem. In view of the behaviora theory of distributive justice one would have to argue that it depends on the presentation whether a certain standard is considered as appropriate or not.

III. Some theoretical considerations about competing investment and reward standards

The experiments reported above have already illuminated how distributive behavior is guided by relying on certain investment and reward standards. Especially, different behavioral attitudes might be explained by the fact that different individuals base their decisions on different standards since they do not view social decision problems in the same way. Nevertheless the behavioral theory of distributive justice still requires a lot of ad hoc-interpretations when being applied to specific bargaining situations. In the following we will try to investigate certain aspects of the behavioral theory of distributive justice more thoroughly. Most of all we will try to explore how people decide when there are competing investment or reward standards.

When deciding which of two competing standards should be applied, people seem to rely on hierarchies between possible standards. Usually one of the two standards reflects a more primitive view of the individual contribution or reward structure. This standard is called the basic standard. Compared to the basic standard the superior standard requires more prerequisites in the sense of more sophisticated techniques of measuring and more subtle information about individual characteristics. The basic standard typically serves as an a priori-hypothesis. To annul this a priori-hypothesis the following two conditions seem to be necessary: First of all the prerequisites of the superior standard have to be fulfilled. Secondly, the results implied by using the superior standard have to differ significantly from those of the basic standard.

To have a specific situation in mind think about two sellers of a homogeneous product who are maximizing their joint profits. Assume, furthermore, that both sellers have identical cost functions except for their different production capacities. Whereas the personal investment standard requires no essential prerequisites, production capacities can only be used as investments if they are easy to quantify not only by the seller himself but also by his competitor. In case this is possible, the basic personal standard will nevertheless be used according to our hypothesis if the difference in production capacities is of minor importance.

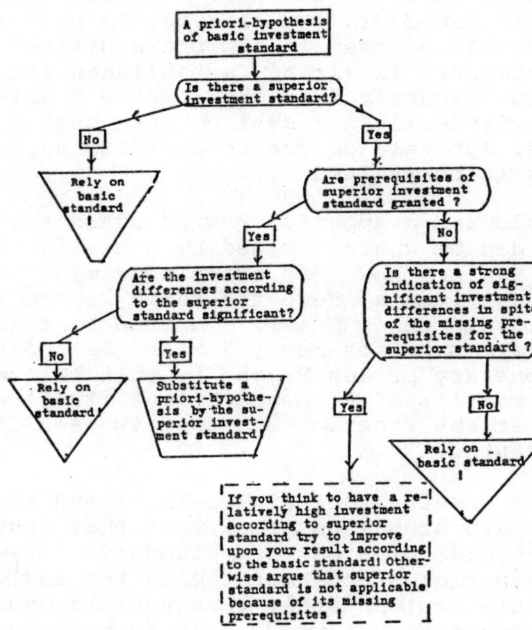

Figure III.1: Intellectual process to decide between a basic and a superior investment standard

The flow chart diagram of Figure III.1 suggests how a bargainer might analyse a distribution conflict with a basic and a superior investment standard. Since a bargainer will try to anticipate what would happen in case of bargaining about competing standards, this reflects, of course, also aspects of a typical bargaining process. The intellectual process has already been interpreted except for the part following the answer "No" to the question "Are prerequisites of superior investment standard granted?". Here one has to specify what will happen if in spite of the missing prerequisites for the superior standard there is nevertheless a strong indication of significant investment differences according to the superior standard. In the example above one can, for instance, imagine that it is commonly accepted that one of the two sellers has a much greater capacity although production capacities cannot be specified unambiguously. We believe that in such situations bargaining talent is especially useful and necessary. A party which is better off with the basic standard will refuse the superior standard by argueing that it does not provide a sound basis for an agreement ("We will fight for ever about our 'investments'"). A party preferring the superior standard will stress the obvious difference in investments and the "injustice" implied by the basic standard ("You know very well that I deserve considerably more than you do").

If in repeated bargaining situations the superior standard has been used in the past, we will say that the superior standard is the a priori-hypothesis for historical reasons. In such situations the superior standard will be used if its prerequisites are granted. If the superior standard is already established its results do not have to differ significantly from the results implied by the basic standard. Behavioristically our past choices must not prejudice our present decisions. But they do create definite expectations which need good reasons to be revised.

When facing a basic and a superior reward standard, the internal decision process can be characterized by a similar flow chart diagram. To have again a specific example in mind, consider the Roth and Malouf-experiments. Here the basic reward is obviously the probability to win one's prize. Compared to this expected monetary payoffs are superior rewards with the additional prerequisite that monetary prizes P_1 and P_2 must be common knowledge. The experimental results of Roth and Malouf (1979) strongly support our hypothesis that the superior standard is used if its prerequisites are granted.

It is important to observe that Figure III.1 and the corresponding hypothesis for reward standards preassumes that most individuals rely on the same hierarchies between standards. It must be commonly accepted that a superior standard reflects the individual characteristics more appropriately than a basic one. Consider, for instance, that monetary rewards have to be allocated among workers. Working time as investment standard will be clearly dominated by individual production amounts and production amounts by individual profitability if the prerequisites of the superior standard are granted. Deviating from a commonly accepted hierarchy of standards involves a high risk of conflict and is likely to result in social isolation. Thus, if a hierarchy of standards is once commonly accepted, it becomes selfstabilizing as the basic rule (I.1) of distributive justice itself.

Assume that individual characteristics are described by a vector c in some space C. A standard could be defined as a projection from C to some lower dimensional space C'. Thus when comparing individual contributions or rewards we do not rely on the full description $c \in C$ but on the projection $c'(c) \in C'$ which neglects some aspects of c. To have something specific in mind think about a condominion with several families. To allocate the costs of total water usage one will just consider the number of family members, the size of the apartment and maybe some variables closely related to water usage although the family characteristics contain many more variables.

A hierarchy of standards can be described as an ordinal order of standards in the sense that a superior standard represents the individual characteristics more appropriately than a basic one. Of course, to become a standard a variable has to be generally observable and measurable. Since a superior standard relies on a more detailed description of the individual characteristics, its prerequisites are stronger than the ones of a basic standard. Figure III.2 illustrates this way to generate a hierarchy of investment standards.

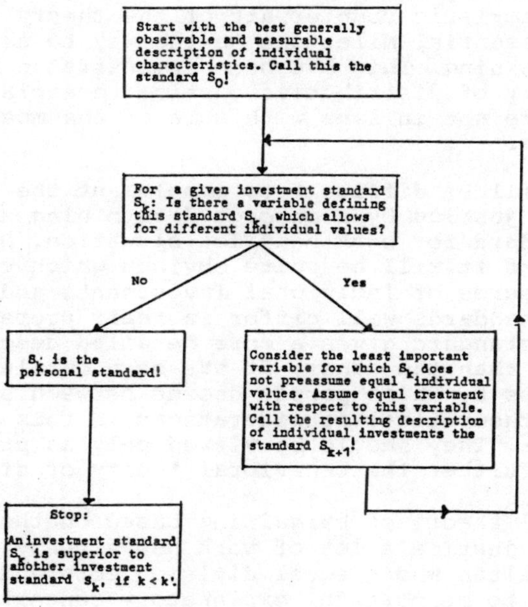

<u>Figure III.2:</u> Generating a hierarchy among possible investment standards.

A similar diagram could be given for reward standards. One comes from a superior to a more basic standard by abstracting from certain aspects of the individual characteristics which on the other side requires less information and reduces the measurement requirements. The construction procedure for hierarchies as described by Figure II hinges, of course, on the assumption that it is always clear which component of the vector describing individual characteristics is the least important one. In many situations the relative importance of the different components describing individual characteristics will be obvious. But there might be situations where this becomes a decisive problem for determining the hierarchy of standards and thereby for applying the behavioral theory of distributive justice. Figure III.2 provides therefore only a basis but not a general method to determine the superior of two competing standards.

As far as the previously reported experiments do not support our theoretical considerations, they are still purely speculative. But it has already been indicated in some instances how one might provide the necessary evidence by additional experiments. Often this will require only minor changes of the scenario in experiments where subjects had already to decide on which of two competing investment or reward standards they want to rely.

Final remarks

The normative theory of individual decision behavior in social conflicts with legitimacy of egoism is the theory of strategic games. The behavioral theory of distributive justice has been considered here as a behavioristic counterpart of the theory of games. In our view it is an essential milestone on the way to develop a behaviorist concept of bargaining. This has been demonstrated by using the behavioral theory of distributive justice to explain many experimenta results which are not in line with some of the most fundamental game theoretic axioms.

Of course, it will be difficult to supplement the behavioral theory of distributive justice by a concept determining a unique investment and reward standard for each conflict situation. But in many social decision problems it will be quite obvious which variables are appropriate measures of individual investments and rewards. Usually two competing standards will differ in their prerequisites in the sense that one standard gives a more detailed description of individu characteristics than the other. It has been outlined how one might model the process by which people decide between such competing standards. Our theoretical considerations in this context are still very speculative. They should be viewed only as preliminary attempts how to develop further the behavioral theory of distributive justice.

For a behavioral theory of bargaining based on the behavioral theory of distributive justice a lot of work has already been done, especially by Selten whose equal division core and its related concepts proved to be powerful explanatory concepts (Selten, 1972 and 1985, Selten and Kritschker, 1983). But observe that the equal division core uses the idea of distributive justice only in a negative way. The objections have to be fair, but not the payoff vectors in the equal division core (see Güth, 1985, for a more detailed discussion). Furthermore, there are many experimental decision data which can help to inspire intuition about the most promising lines of research in this field.

References:

Austin,W.- Hatfield,E., Equity-Theorie, Macht und soziale Gerechtigkeit, in: Gerechtigkeit und soziale Interaktion, G.Miluka (ed.),Wien 1980,25-68.

Bartos,O.J., Negotiation and justice, Contributions to Experimental Economics, Vol.7 (1978),103-126.

Crott,Helmut, Soziale Interaktion und Gruppenprozesse, Stuttgart 1979.

Güth,Werner, Egoismus und Altruismus- Eine spieltheoretische und experimentelle Analyse, in: Normengeleitetes Verhalten in den Sozialwissenschaften (ed.by H.Todt), Schriften des Vereins für Socialpolitik, N.F.141 (1984),35-58.

——— The behavioral theory of distributive justice and experimentally observed payoff distributions, Working Paper, 1985.

Güth,Werner- Schmittberger,Rolf- Schwarze,Bernd, An experimental study of ultimatum bargaining, Journal of Economic Behavior and Organizations, Vol.3 (1982), 367-388.

Güth,Werner- Tietz,Reinhard, Strategic power versus distributive justice - An experimental analysis of ultimatum bargaining-, Economic Psychology (edrs. H.Brandstätter and E.Kirchler),Linz 1985,129-137.

——— Auctioning ultimatum bargaining positions - How to decide if rational decisions are unacceptable? -, forthcoming in a Proceedings Volume, 1986.

Homans,G.C., Social behavior: Its elementary forms, London 1961.

Komorita, S.S.- Chertkoff,J.M., A bargaining theory of coalition formation, Psychological Review, Vol.80 (1973),149-162.

Leventhal,G.S.- Michaels,J.W.. Extending the equity model: Perception of inputs and allocation of reward as a function of duration and quantity of performance, Journal of Personality and Psychology, Vol.12 (1969), 303-309.

Mikula,Gerold, Gewinnaufteilungsverhalten in Dyaden bei variiertem Leistungsverhältnis, Zeitschrift für Sozialpsychologie, 1972,126-133.

——— Considerations of justice in allocation situations, Berichte aus dem Institut für Psychologie der Universität Graz, A-8010 Graz, 1977.

——— Einleitung: Thematische Schwerpunkte der psychologischen Gerechtigkeitsforschung, in: Gerechtigkeit und soziale Interaktion- Experimentelle und theoretische Beiträge aus der psychologischen Forschung, ed.by G.Mikula, Bern 1980,13-24.

Mikula,Gerold- Uray, H., Die Vernachlässigung individueller Leistungen bei der Lohnaufteilung in Sozialsituationen, Zeitschrift für Sozialpsychologie, 1973,136-144.

Nydegger,R.V.- Owen,G., Two-person bargaining: An experimental test of the Nash axioms, International Journal of Game Theory, Vol.3 (1974),239-249.

Pruitt,D.G., Motivation processes in the decomposed prisoner's dilemma game, Journal of Personality and Social Psychology, Vol.14 (1970),227-238.

——— Reward structure and cooperation: The decomposed prisoner's dilemma game, Journal of Personality and Social Psychology, Vol.7 (1967),21-27.

Roth,A.E., Laboratory experimentation in economics, Advances in Economic Theory (ed.by T.Bewley), Cambridge, Mass., 1985.

Roth,A.E.- Malouf,W.M.K., Game- theoretic models and the role of information in bargaining, Psychological Review, Vol.86 (1979),574-594.

——— Scale changes and shared information in bargaining: An experimental study, Mathematical Social Sciences, Vol.3 (1982),157-177.

Roth,A.E.- Malouf,W.M.K.- Murnighan,J.K., Sociological versus strategic factors in bargaining, Journal of Economic Behavior and Organization , Vol.2 (1981),153-177.

Roth,A.E.- Murnighan,J.K., The role of information in bargaining: An experimental study, Econometrica, Vol.50 (1982), 1123-1142.

Roth,A.E.- Schoumaker,F., Expectations and reputations in bargaining: An experimental study, American Economic Review, 1983.

Selten,Reinhard, Equal share analysis of characteristic function experiments, Contribution to Experimental Economics, Vol.3 (1972),Tübingen,130-165.

——— The equity principle in economic behavior, Decision Theory and Social Ethics (eds. W.Gottinger, W.Leinfellner), Dordrecht,1978,289-303.

——— Experimentelle Wirtschaftsforschung, Vortrag N 287 (1979), Rheinisch-Westfälische Akademie der Wissenschaften, Westdeutscher Verlag.

——— Equity and coalition bargaining in experimental 3-person games, Discussion Paper Nr.154 (1985), Institut für Gesellschafts- und Wirtschaftswissenschaften, Universität Bonn.

Selten,Reinhard- Berg,K.C., Drei experimentelle Oligopolserien mit kontinuierlichem Zeitablauf, Contributions to Experimental Economics, Vol.2 (1970),162-221.

Selten,Reinhard- Kritschker,W., Comparison of two theories for characteristic function experiments, Aspiration Levels in Bargaining and Economic Decision Making (ed. R.Tietz), Heidelberg 1983,259-264.

Walster,E.- Berscheid,E.- Walster,G.W., New directions in equity research, Journal of Personality and Social Psychology, Vol.25 (1973), 151-176.

Walster,E.- Walster,G.W.- Berscheid,E., Equity: Theory and research, Boston 1978.

ATTITUDES TOWARDS THE DUTCH SOCIAL SECURITY SYSTEM

Jan Schoormans(1) and Jasper von Grumbkow(2)

(1) Tilburg University,
Department of Economic Psychology, P.O. Box 90153,
5000 LE Tilburg, The Netherlands
(2) Open University, The Netherlands

Abstract: the purpose of this study (N=229) is to develop a scale to measure the Perceived Justice with regard to the System of Social Security.
Four factors underlying Perceived Justice with regard to Social Security emerge; justice of the ideology of the System, justice of the used procedures, justice of the level of premiums and justice of the level of benefits. It turns out that the ideology of the system and the level of the premiums are evaluated as (almost) just; the level of benefits and the used procedures are evaluated as (almost) injust.
The four scales of perceived justice are correlated with a number of attitudinal and income related items for two groups: actives and non-actives. There are differences in correlations between the two groups. This indicates that the justice is perceived in a different perspective by members of the two different groups.

1. Introduction

A slowly increasing part of the gross national product of western countries is absorbed by their Social Security system. Every year a larger percentage of every earned Dutch guilder is used by the Dutch government for the maintenance of the Social Security System. With a high number of non-actives (unemployed people, old age pensioners, disabled) the critique gets stronger that this system costs too much. Politicians warn that the society will disintegrate into two parts: a part that consist of active people with a paid job and a part that consists of a large group of non-actives dependable on the system for their income and without much opportunities to better their positions, Köbben & Godschalk [1].
The Social Security System is a transfer system: the actives supply the system with the money necessary for the maintenance of the standard of living of the non-actives. Eckhoff [2] states that people make judgments with regard to the fairness of ongoing transfers. Both actives and non-actives will make these judgments. In this study we will investigate these judgments and especially the attitudes of both groups in terms of justice and injustice. We think that the perceived (in)justice of the Social Security System will be related to three levels of analysis. First, the perceived justice of the ideology of the system. Second, the perceived justice of the procedures of the system.

Third, the perceived justice of the distributive functions of the system.

2. Ideology of the Social Security System

Several benefit funds are part of the Dutch Social Security System. These funds are feeded by the so-called general provisions and by the so-called social insurances.
The provisions-part is based on the idea that every Dutch inhabitant should be taken care for no matter what he or she contributes to the Dutch society. These provisions supply everybody who has insufficient means of living with a kind of minimum income.
The insurance-part of the Social Security System is based upon the idea that certain (groups of) people have earned a right on a fixed income level by the contribution they made to the society in general. According to this idea the general provisons supply money to old-age pensioners (everybody older than 65 years). Furthermore, it is based on the idea that certain people have earned a right by working a certain period of time and by paying unemployment-premiums.
The Social Security System has other objectives beside providing income, such as the objective that the allocations have to be used to equalize income differences, and the objective to spread the costs of the system in relation to the existing income differences. People can regard these objectives as more or less justified. The perceived justice and injustice of the Sociale Security System will be dependent upon the perceived (in)justice of the different objectives of the system.

3. Procedures of the Social Security System

Leventhal [3] presents six procedural rules people use to evaluate the justice of procedures present in allocation decisions.

1. The ethicality rule: procedures have to match with moral and ethical principles. People may find some of the used procedures like the ones regarding the collection of information, ethically unacceptable. Also, the absence of certain procedures can be perceived as ethically unacceptable.
2. The consistency rule: procedures should be used consistent over people and consistent over time. Perceived lack of consistency can be led to perceived unjustice.
3. The bias suppression rule: people who use and control the procedures should not have any benefit from the allocation process itself.
4. The accuracy rule: information that is needed for decisions should be as reliable as possible. The perception that incorrect or insufficient information is used can lead to feelings of injustice.
5. The correctability rule: people should have the opportunity to modify decisions. The absence (of the transparancy) of the appeal procedures can lead to feelings of injustice.

6. The representativeness rule: the background of the civil servants who decide on the allocations and of the ones who are decided upon should not differ too much. If they belong to different social classes the members of the lower class can feel that they are misunderstood and discriminated.

Procedures used with regard to the non-actives are more inclined to lead to feelings of injustice, because they are related to e.g. the gathering of private information. Besides, the non-actives are subjected to more procedures than the actives are. Generally, insight in the procedures is low. It is difficult to know how decisions are made and/or how to appeal against decisions.

Differences between expected and received benefits can be attributed to all kinds of perceptions of the way the procedures are used and can be related to deviations of the afore mentioned rules of Leventhal, and lead to perceived injustice.

4. Distribution aspects of the Social Security System

The perceived justice and injustice of the Social Security System will be mainly determined by the evaluations of the financial inputs and outcomes of the system. We think that the following factors may influence the perceived distributive justice:

1. The level and character of the inputs one has to make,
2. The level and character of the outcomes one receives,
3. The relation between the own inputs and the own outcomes,
4. The relation between the own inputs and the own outcomes and the inputs and outcomes of comparable others.

We feel that the financial inputs and outcomes are more important for the development of feelings of justice than the non-financial inputs and outcomes. Furthermore, we feel that not only the inputs and outcomes themselves or their relationship are important for this development, but also the effect of these on other behavioral domains. It can happen that certain effects of inputs and/or outcomes are unwanted, e.g. one can expect that a high level of unemploment-benefits leads to a lower work motivation or a lower activity level on the labour-market, and therefore perceive high levels of benefits injust.

5. The study

The central aim of our study is to develop a scale to measure the perceived justice and injustice of the Social Security System according to the afore mentioned three levels of analysis. First, we will study the internal structure of the scale. Second, the external validity of the scale will be checked by correlating the scale scores with some variables (see the method part of this study). Third, the scale scores and the correlations of the actives will be compared with those of the non-actives.

5.1 Method

From the Dutch telefone directories (edition 1985) 500 names with adresses were drawn randomly. In the beginning of January

1986 primers indicating the goal of the study and ensurances regarding the subjects anonimity were sent out. A week later the primers were followed by the questionnaire. Ten days after sending the questionnaire a reminder was sent out. A total of 211 people responded of which 207 questionnaires could be used (41.4%). Within this group there were only 26 non-actives. Non-actives are those respondents who are receiving some kind of social security benefit (In our study we deleted the old-age pensioners). Because of this low number, we decided to try to find a extra number of non-actives via the Employment Bureau. There we handed out questionnaires with the request to return them by mail (we added a return-envelop). From the 80 extra subjects we approached in this way, we received another 22 questionnaires; 20 of them came from non-actives.

5.2 Characteristics of the respondents

The respondents are 192 men and 37 women varying in age between 17 and 89 years. Their mean age is 43.6 years (s.d 15.2). Their educational level ranges from secondary school (12%) to post-graduate education, 60% has post secondary school. Most of the subjects (70%) are living with a partner. Their income level ranges from 400 to 7500 Dutch quilders a month. The mean monthly net income is 2363 (s.d. 1090). 144 respondents have paid work, 30 have old age pension, 46 have some kind of a social benefit. The others have different sources of income.

5.3 The questionnaire

We made up a questionnaire based on the three levels of perceived (in)justice of the Social Security System: the ideological, procedural and distributive level. Furthermore, we compiled a number of questions to measure:

a. the present knowledge of the system,
b. general attitudes towards the system and its functioning,
c. the perceived number of people in one's reference group receiving some kind of benefit,
d. social demographics: age, sex, education, and income level,
e. the amount of income one feels one should receive, the amount of premiums one pays and the amount one feels one should pay.

6. Results and discussion

6.1 Justice-scale

The 5-point Likert format were factor analysed (principal component analyses with varimax rotation). Although the data are of an ordinal character we did not choose to use a princals solution. (This solution proved to be quite similar to the factor analysis, but does not give rotated factor solutions). On the basis of the curve of the eigenvalues we decided to choose a four factor solution, although we expected a 3 factor solution on the basis of our theoretical notions. This four factor solution accounts for 56% of the variance, see table 1.

Table 1:
Factor analytic results (varimax rotation) showing the factor loadings, eigenvalues and variances for the 4 factors of the perceived injustice Scale (factor loading above. 60 underlined to show which items load highest on each factor).

ITEM	FACTOR 1 BENEFITS	FACTOR 2 PREMIUMS	FACTOR 3 PROCEDURES	FACTOR 4 IDEOLOGY
Premiums are equally spread	.11	-.14	-.09	.65
Equalization of income	.20	-.21	.01	.60
Take care for each other	-.02	.00	-.09	.64
Not considering contributions	.08	-.06	-.11	.67
Using tax money for system	.11	.13	-.13	.65
Insight in procedures	-.04	.06	.65	-.17
Decisions difficult to change	-.04	.16	.67	.06
Low insight in decisions	.08	.02	.84	-.09
Impossible to enhance benefit	-.00	.29	.68	-.16
Difficult appael-procedures	-.03	.03	.79	-.13
Level of unemployment benefit	.12	.76	.04	-.08
Level of provision	-.00	.80	.14	-.10
Level of disability benefit	.05	.82	.02	.02
Level of old-age pension	.19	.67	.12	.03
Level of unemployment premium	.78	.22	-.10	.09
Level of old-age premium	.85	.07	.05	.10
Level of disability premium	.89	.03	-.02	.05
Level of taxes for system	.75	.09	.03	.24
Loosing benefit	.04	.45	.12	-.09
EIGENVALUE	3.78	3.43	1.95	1.50
VARIANCE (56.1%)	19.9%	18.0%	10.3%	7.9%

The factors that emerge are clearly interpretable. The expected distributive justice factor is splitted in two parts: an outcome part and an input part. The outcome part (factor 2) has to do with (in)justice with respect to the benefits non-actives receive; the input part (factor 1) has to do with the perceived justice of the level of the premiums one has to pay. Factor 3 concerns procedural justice, and factor 4 concerns the perceived (in)justice with respect to the objectives of the Social Security System.

We feel that the factors found are not totally uncorrelated as was assumed by using the varimax rotation. Therefore we did not want to use factor scores in our analysis. Instead of that we used sum scores. We calculated 4 scales on the basis of sum scores, using items that had a high loading on the respective factors. The internal consistencies of these scales and the intercorrelation between the scales are presented in table 2.

From table 2 comes forward that the 4 scales are only partly correlated with each other. The idea of a more-dimensional perception of justice with regard to the Social Security System seems confirmed.

Table 2:
Correlations between the four Injustice Scales and the internal consistencies (N actives = 118, N non-actives = 44).

	Premiums	Procedures	Ideology
Benefits Act	.33**	.24*	-.08
(=.79) N Act	.34*	.26	-.27
Premiums Act		-.08	.36**
(=.85) N-Act		.22	.02
Procedures Act			-.31**
(=.79) N-Act			-.41**
Ideology (=.67)			

*) $p < .05$ **) $p < .01$

The Ideology Scale measuring the perceived justice of this ideology is negatively correlated with the Procedures Scale: those who regard the ideology of the system more just, regard the used procedures as more unjust. That the system is based on solidarity and trust seems to interfere with the daily practice of the system: severe controlling procedures, based on the idea that people cannot be trusted.
The Ideology Scale is not correlated with the financial scales with exception of the Premium Scale, which correlates positively with the Ideology Scale for the actives. The actives who regard the levels of the premiums as more just, regard the ideology of the system also as more just. The actives, who have to pay the greater part of the premiums probably judge the scale that measures the perceived justice of the levels of the premiums, (the amount of money they have to pay) with the justice of the ideology of the system in mind. Paying is justified if it serves the right goal.

The Benefit Scale, measuring the perceived justice of the levels of the benefits, is positively correlated with the Premium Scale, for both groups. When the levels of the benefits are seen as more just, the levels of the premiums are also seen as more just. The levels of the premiums and that of the benefits are strongly connected in the practice of Social Security System. High levels of benefits demand high levels of premiums. The found correlation is in line with this daily practice.

Only for the actives we find a positive correlation between the Procedure- and Benefits Scale. We don't have a direct explanation for this effect.

To compare the absolute sores on the 4 scales we have given the mean scores in figure 1.

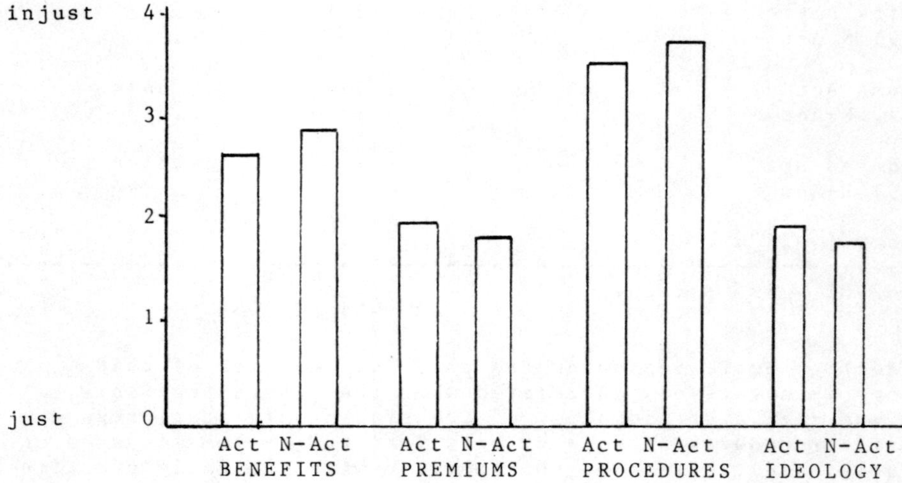

FIGURE 1. Mean scores for the four formed scales, separate for the actives (N=118) and for the Non-actives (N=44). The lower the score the more just the scale.

From figure 1 we can conclude that people perceive the underlying ideas of the Social Security System as (more a less) just. The ideology of the system receives a broad support. The non-actives evaluate the ideology of of the system more just than the actives do (t= -2.15; df= 182, p< .035). The non-actives depend heavily on the system for their financial situation. We think that this dependency leads to this higher score on the perceived justice of the objectives of the system. In an earlier study Becker & Vink [4] found that 50% of a group of non-actives feel that the procedures used in the System are too severe and/ or too private. Here we find that both actives and non-actives regard these procedures as unjust. This means that the ideas and purposes of the system are supported, but that the way these ideas are transformed into practical rules is not supported.

The levels of the benefits are seen as more unjust than just. The non-actives perceive these levels even more unjust than the actives do, (T= 2.41; df= 178; p< .018) The non-actives depend strongly on the benefits. Their evaluation of the justice of the level of the benefits will be influenced by the perception of their own financial situation. This income situation is often perceived as insufficient, see Poppenk [5]; Shortinghuis, Sprangers & Van Raay [6] and less satisfactory Schoormans & Von Grumbkow [7]. The levels of the premiums are perceived as more just than injust. Both groups do not differ with respect to this variable.

6.2. External validity of the justice-scale.

The 4 scales are related to different external variables to check their external validity, see tables 3 and 4.

Table 3: The correlations (2-tailed) between the 4 justice-scales (higher score more unjust) and 5 attitudinal questions with regard to the social security system. The attitudinal questions are agree - disagree questions; low score = agree, higher score = disagree. (Act N=117, N-Act N=44).

		BENEFITS	PREMIUMS	PROCEDURES	IDEOLOGY
1. The system is just	Act	.13	.06	.00	.05
	N-Act	.45*	.28	-.03	-.11
		diff*			
2. The system gives everybody a reasonable existence	Act	.22*	-.05	.08	-.08
	N-Act	.50**	.15	.23	-.24
3. The system works negative	Act	-.20*	-.10	-.14	-.13
	N-Act	-.42*	-.25	-.30*	-.12
4. People profit from the system	Act	.09	-.10	.08	-.17*
	N-Act	.16	-.05	.11	-.35*
5. The system calls for misuse	Act	.11	-.13	.14	-.19*
	N-Act	-.10	.15	.02	-.31*

* p<.05, ** p<.01

Table 4: The correlation (2-tailed) between the 4 justice-scales (higer score more unjust) and 5 validating question, all questions count low score - low, high score - high (Act N=118, N-Act N=44).

		BENEFITS	PREMIUMS	PROCEDURES	IDEOLOGY
1. Net-income	Act	-.38**	-.19	.08	.14
	N-Act	-.25	-.43*	.06	.08
2. Difference between own and "wanted" income	Act	.23	-.20*	.01	-.12
	N-Act	.27	.09	.01	.06
3. Difference between paid and "wanted" premiums	Act	.04	.37**	.06	.28*
	N-Act	.17	.06	.09	.28
4. Number of people in reference group with benefits	Act	.23*	.17	-.11	.08
	N-Act	-.05	.23	.00	-.01
5. Perceived knowledge of the system	Act	.09	-.16	.13	.07
	N-Act	-.01	.48**	.10	.08
			diff*		

* p <.05, ** p<.01

Here again we find that the 4 scales are relatively independent: each correlates with different validating questions.

- The Benefit Scale correlates significantly with some attitudinal statements and with the own-income situation and the reference group situation in case of the actives:

The more one perceives the benefits as just, the more one agrees with the item that the system provides everybody with a reasonable existence; a relation that could be expected. Only for the group non-actives this Benefits Scale correlates with the statement, that the system is just. The more they regard the system as just, the more they perceive the levels of the benefits as just. The overall justice of the system is probably strongly influenced by the levels of the benefits in case of the non-actives. This is a indication that the level of the benefits is a very important aspect of the system for the non-actives. For the actives the Benefit Scale correlates with the own income situation. Actives perceive the levels of the benefits more unjust when they themselves have a lower income. People evaluate incomes in respect to other incomes. A smaller difference between the own income and the income of the non-actives leads to a negative evaluation of the last one. When the actives have more friends with benefits they also regard the level of the benefit less just. This is probably caused by the indirect experiences the actives have with a lot friends with low benefits.

- The Premium Scale correlates with income related questions for the actives and with a scale measuring perceives knowledge of the system for the non-actives. The more the actives feel underpaid and the more they feel that they pay to much premiums the less just they evaluate the level of the premiums. This correlation can be expected. The non-actives feel that the level of premiums is less just when they have a lower income. This income is directly related to the premium level and this correlation can also be expected.

When the non-actives perceive the level of the premiums as more unjust they also feel that they have a high perceived knowledge of the system.

- The Procedures Scale correlates only with one attitudinal item, and only for the non-actives. When the non-actives feel that the system works negatively they perceived the procedures as more unjust. This relation is in the expected direction.

- The Ideology Scale correlates with items measuring perceived misuse of the system. The more both groups feel that the system leads to misuse and is misused the less they perceive the ideology of the system as just.

7. Conclusions

In developing a scale to measure the Perceived Justice with regard to the Dutch Social Security System, we found that we should four use different dimension of the system: inputs (level of premiums), outputs (level of benefits), procedures and ideology.

The formed scales of the 4 dimensions appear to be only partly correlated.

The ideology of the system and the inputs are regarded as just

or almost just. The procedures of the system and the outcomes of the system are perceived as relatively unjust.
The different dimensions correlate different with a number of validation questions. The found correlations are rather easy to understand. It is interesting that we found a number of significant diffences between these correlations for the group of actives and the group non-actives. This gives some indications that these two groups have a different perspective with regard to the justice of Social Security.
Further research will be necessary to make clear to what degree the different groups that can be distinquished within the Social Security System have different perspectives about the justice of the system.

References

[1] Köbben, A.J.F., and J.J. Godschalk (1985). Een tweedeling van de samenleving? (A society split-apart?). Den Haag: OSA.

[2] Eckhoff, T. (1974). Justice; Its determinants in social interaction. Rotterdam: Rotterdam University Press.

[3] Leventhal, G.S. (1980). What should be done with equity theory? New approaches to the study of fairness in social relationships. In: K.J. Gergen, M.S. Greenberg and R.U. Willes (Eds): Social Exchange: advances in theory and research. New York, Prenum Press.

[4] Becker, J.W., and R. Vink (1984). Werklozen, Arbeidsongeschikten en werkenden vergeleken (unemployed, work-disabled and employed compared). Rijswijk, S.C.P. Stukwerk no. 18.

[5] Poppenk, R.W. (1985). Armoede mag je het niet noemen (You can't call it poverty) Amsterdam: Gemeentelijke dienst voor Bejaardenverzorging.

[6] Schortinghuis-Sprangers, R.A., and W.F. van Raay (1985). Rond komen of tekort komen (make ends meet or be short) Rotterdam: Erasmus Universiteit.

[7] Schoormans, J., and J. von Grumbkow (1985). The perception of employed and unemployed of their economic position: some empirical results. In: H. Brandstatter and E. Kirchler (Eds): Economic psychology. Linz, Tranner.

Part Sixteen
Social Security and Income Inequality

MEMORY AND ANTICIPATION PROCESSES AND THEIR SIGNIFICANCE FOR SOCIAL SECURITY AND INCOME INEQUALITY

B.M.S. van Praag

Econometric Institute, Erasmus University Rotterdam,
P.O. Box 1738, 3000 DR Rotterdam, The Netherlands

J. van Weeren

Ministry of Social Affairs and Employment, The Hague,
The Netherlands

1. INTRODUCTION

In the study of human behavior it is common place that most of our behavior is explained to a considerable extent by our past experiences. For instance, in consumer demand theory frequently consumption lags, or a permanent income concept (Friedman [1]) are taken as a point of departure. Intuition and introspection tells us that our behavior may also depend on the future as anticipated. A well-known example in economics is the theory of rational expectations.

At a more refined level we may split up human behavior into two stages. The first stage involves the formation of individual value judgments, and the second stage consists of the actions performed by the individual. For instance, in a consumer context it implies at the first stage the formation of a preference function and derived from it at the second stage the action of purchasing commodities by utility maximization. The logical course is now that past, present and future conditions are co-determinants of our value judgments and that only as a consequence of

---

This research has been made possible by financial support of the Ministry of Social Affairs and Employment, The Hague. The data set has been made available by the Central Bureau of Statistics, Voorburg. For both supports we like to express our gratitude. The paper has been partly prepared at the Center for Research in Public Economics of Leyden University and partly while the first author was a fellow at the Netherlands Institute for the Advanced Study of Humanities and Social Sciences (N.I.A.S.) at Wassenaar.

changes in value judgments we act. Since the question whether we act on preference changes is also influenced by feasibility conditions and transaction costs, it may frequently be that we take no action to change our present situation, although it is no longer optimal according to our present value judgments, when we had to start now from scratch.
It follows that we may get a better insight in the impact of the past and future on the individual's value judgments by studying these value judgments directly than by studying the effects on actions, derived from value judgments, but filtered by the existence of transaction costs and feasibility conditions.

In economic literature the accent has been on the study of actions rather than on the study of value judgments. Think on the inclusion of lags and leads in models to explain purchase behavior of the consumer or production and investment of the firm. The preference for studying the actions instead of the value judgments on which the actions have been based is clearly motivated by the relative simplicity to observe actions (like purchases, etc.) and the relative difficulty to observe value judgments.

In this paper we shall study the direct influence of past, present and anticipated conditions on an individual's value judgment. The subject matter of that judgment is after-tax household income and it will be evaluated in terms of "good", "sufficient", "bad" income. The answer on the question which income level an individual associates with an evaluation "good income", say c_{good}, is an individual value judgment. It will vary among individuals depending on personal factors like family size fs, present income y_0, past income y_{-1}, y_{-2}, ..., expected income y_1, y_2, ... and on the judgments of members of one's reference group. We concentrate in this paper on the time effects. We shall study the functional relationship c_{good} (fs,..., y_{-1}, y_0, y_1,...) and similarly for $c_i(.)$ where i stands for "sufficient", "bad", or other labels. On one hand it is a problem of positive science, akin to the habit formation literature (see e.g. Pollak [2]) and also related to psychophysical studies by Helson [3] and others. On the other hand it is relevant on a normative level for socio-economic policy. Consider for instance the question how people from a higher income level should step downwards to a lower social assistance level when becoming jobless. The pain associa-

ted with the downwards adaptation depends on the relation between past income and the evaluation of the present income level and the income development anticipated for the future.
In a similar way the relationship we like to study is useful when studying income growth patterns over time and the impact of price-inflation on the evaluation of present incomes and present income inequality.

At this point it should be stressed that the influence of past and future on present judgments cannot be assumed to be uniform, irrespective of the subject-matter. This is evident if we think on judgments on religion compared to fashion. Nevertheless, it seems that the method we use with respect to income judgments may be utilized more generally with respect to judgments on other subjects.

Except of the literature at large that deals with habit formation and rational expectations there is one recent paper, viz. that by Van de Stadt et al. [4] that has to be mentioned, as it is based on partly the same dataset and deals partly with the same problem we are studying. However, the differences between the latter paper and ours are six fold. First, our paper does not use a cardinal utility framework. Second, our paper deals with the influence of past <u>and</u> future, while the former considers only the past. Third, this article does not deal with reference group effects. Fourth, we admit for an age-dependent weight pattern. Fifth, we do not need panel data in our approach and sixth, a major part of this paper deals in a novel way with two consequences of our estimation results.

The order of this paper will be the following. In Section 2 we describe the data, develop the model and present the estimation results. In Section 3 we apply our results to the derivation of an adaptation path to a social assistance level. In Section 4 we consider the impact of inflation on income judgments. Section 5 concludes with some discussion on the results.

2. MODEL, DATA AND RESULTS

The data are responses to a battery of questions, called the Income

Evaluation Question (IEQ), where verbal income evaluation levels are supplied to respondents (who are assumed to represent their households) and the responses are after-tax income amounts, associated with these levels. The IEQ runs as follows:

> "Please try to indicate what you consider to be an appropriate amount for each of the following cases? Under my (our) conditions I would call a net income for my household per week/month/year* of
>
> about ... 25.... very bad
> about ... 35.... bad
> about ... 45.... insufficient
> about ... 70.... sufficient
> about .. 120.... good
> about .. 160.... very good
>
> * Underline the reference period chosen".

Typical answers per week of a British respondent in a 1979 survey are filled out (see Van Praag, Hagenaars, Van Weeren [5]).
We shall denote the amounts, answered by respondents j by $\{c_i(j)\}_{i=1}^{6}$. As usual when dealing with incomes it is preferable to consider income ratios or logarithms. We consider from now on $\{\ln c_i(j)\}_{i=1}^{6}$ as our variables of interest.
This kind of data has been extensively analyzed in different contexts in a.o. Van Praag [6], Van Praag, Kapteyn [7], Van Praag et al. [5], Van Praag [8], [9] and Danziger et al. [10].
In these studies it has been found that the variables $\{c_i(j)\}_{i=1}^{6}$ or their logarithmic average over i, say μ_j, is rather well explained by two variables, viz., family size fs and current income y_0.

A typical regression result for c_4 is:

$$(2.1)\qquad \ln c_4 = \underset{(0.22)}{2.98} + \underset{(0.02)}{0.09} \ln fs + \underset{(0.02)}{0.69} \ln y_0 \qquad \bar{R}^2 = 0.68,\ N = 644$$

(Comparable results have been found for c_1, c_2, c_3, c_5 and c_6.)
The value of the (adjusted) $\bar{R}^2$ and the standard deviations in brackets show that the statistical quality of this regression is very good. It is

also indirect evidence for the hypothesis that the stimulus "a sufficient income" conveys a similar feeling of well-being to the respondents. For, if respondents would have strongly different connotations, it would be a matter of mere luck to find a statistically valid relationship like (2.1). The regression coefficients themselves are plausible.

The empirical result (2.1) may be used to derive family-equivalence scales.

If family size increases one needs more to reach a level i. There is a strong dependency on own income or, as we called it before, preference drift. The specific income level c_4^* for which own income is evaluated by level 4 is found by solving (2.1) for $\ln c_4 = \ln y_0$ yielding

$$\ln c_4^* = \frac{2.98 + 0.09 \ln fs}{1 - 0.69}$$

from which we find an elasticity of c_4^* with respect to family size of $9/31 \approx 29\%$. We refer to the quoted references for a detailed treatment.

Now we turn to the specific subject of this paper. We may hypothesize a relationship

$$\ln c_i = \beta_{0i} + \beta_{1i} \ln fs + \beta_{2i} \left(\sum_{t=-\infty}^{+\infty} w_t \ln y_t \right) \quad (i = 1, \ldots, 6), \tag{2.2}$$

where $\{w_t\}_{t=-\infty}^{+\infty}$ are weights adding up to one. The weighted sum may be denoted by $\overline{\ln y}$. The weight distribution describes the relative importance the respondent assigns to past incomes and to anticipated incomes in the future.

If we try to estimate (2.2) the researcher faces two problems, one of a practical nature and one of a conceptual nature as well. The first problem is that we need an income profile $\{y_t\}$ per household. Ideally, this requires a panel data set of considerable length. The second conceptual problem deals with the measurement of anticipated incomes. Suppose we knew the realized income a year ahead, say, y_1, for a specific household, then that level will in general differ from the anticipated income

level $\tilde{y}_1$, as expected by that household at time 0. It follows that there is no other direct way to assess future income anticipations than to ask for them explicitly. It stands to reason that those personal estimates would involve a considerable measurement error.
Our approach to both problems is the following:

a. use all past and present incomes we know.
b. replace unknown incomes, either in the past, or anticipated, by best guesses.

Our "best guess" is an average earnings profile $\hat{y}$ depending on age of the head of the household (= respondent) (AGE), four dummy variables E_1, E_2, E_3, E_4 to characterize five types of education of the respondent and a dummy variable B to differentiate between one- and two-breadwinner households. Hence all unknown incomes are replaced by

$$(2.3) \qquad \ln \tilde{y}_j(t) = \ln \hat{y}(AGE_j(t),\ E_j,\ B_j)$$

where $AGE_j(t)$ is the age of j in year t.

Our data consist of the 1981 wave of an oral interview panel of moderate size, organised by the Dutch Central Bureau of Statistics. We estimated the household-earnings profile as

$$(2.4) \qquad \ln \hat{y}_j = \underset{(1.63)}{-1.80} + \underset{(0.87)}{6.68} \ln AGE_j - \underset{(0.12)}{0.88}(\ln AGE_j)^2 - \underset{(0.07)}{0.66}\, E_{1j} +$$

$$- \underset{(0.07)}{0.48}\, E_{2j} - \underset{(0.07)}{0.36}\, E_{3j} - \underset{(0.08)}{0.16}\, E_{4j} + \underset{(0.03)}{0.33}\, B_j \qquad \bar{R}^2 = 0.41,\ N = 645$$

where the first education level (university) is the reference level[1]. A final specification issue is the measure of t itself and the weight distribution w_t. It lies at hand to set the birth data at t = 0 and to describe the weight distribution by a continuous density function. We tried the gamma- and lognormal density. Discrete weights w_t are calculated as slices of unit width from a continuous density mass, i.e. $w_t = \int_{t-\frac{1}{2}}^{t+\frac{1}{2}} f(\tau)d\tau$. However, the gamma- and lognormal specifications did

did not yield sensible results. The second choice, slightly less obvious is to set birth at $t = -\infty$ and $t = 0$ at present. In that case we looked again for tractable densities on $(-\infty, \infty)$, and the first choice is then the normal density $f(t) = n(t; \mu_\tau, \sigma_\tau)$. Due to its symmetry $\mu_\tau = 0$ implies an equal weight of 0.5 on past and future which is rather implausible. If $\mu_\tau < 0$, more weight is assigned to the past than to the future and we call the individual past-oriented. If $\mu_\tau > 0$ we call him future-oriented. The consequence of this normal specification is clearly that the mode of the density will not be situated at $t = 0$, except by coincidence. Another feature is that the weights do not decline geometrically. Actually, both features do not strike us as counterintuitive. A second specification somewhat more in line with tradition would be to specify the density as composed by two geometric densities, one forward looking and one backward looking. This would involve four parameters, viz. the two slope parameters, the location of the common mode and a ratio parameter specifying the ratio between the total weights assigned to the past and to the future respectively. The gain would be an asymmetric density, but the loss would be imposition of a geometric slope, and an infinitely high modus. The latter point may be repaired by truncation of both geometric densities but this would involve even more parameters and a discontinuity in the density at the modus, which is rather implausible. A third specification might be an asymmetric unimodal tractable continuous density function on $(-\infty, \infty)$, but - a remarkable fact as such - the statistical literature does not supply us with such a density function.

Summarizing, although we are aware that the choice of the normal density is debatable, we chose the normal density for the above reasons, and because of the fact that it did yield sensible and significant results, as we shall see. There is no hard theoretical basis to defend such a choice nor to reject it.

The parameter μ_τ will be called the time focus. The parameter σ_τ describes the width of the density. If σ_τ tends to zero the individual lives by the day. We call σ_τ the time span of the individual.

It seems plausible, although never suggested in economic literature, that the memory and anticipation process varies over individuals. The principal determinant is clearly the age of the individual. So we make the weight parameters (μ_τ, σ_τ) dependent on AGE and we specify

$$(2.5) \quad \mu_\tau = \alpha_0 + \alpha_1 \text{ AGE} + \alpha_2 \text{ AGE}^2$$

$$\sigma_\tau = \gamma_0 + \gamma_1 \text{ AGE} + \gamma_2 \text{ AGE}^2.$$

Equation (2.2) has been simultaneously estimated for six levels yielding 18 β's to be estimated[2)]. Moreover the six parameters α_0, α_1, α_2 and γ_0, γ_1, γ_2 have been estimated, making the estimation procedure non-linear (see Marquardt [11]). The infinite sum in (2.2) was truncated, which is admitted as the tails of w_t tend to zero. In practice we restricted t to the interval [-4,4].

The resulting estimates are presented in Table 1, where the standard-deviations are calculated by means of the inverse of the information matrix. The β'-values in the second to sixth line have to be added to those in the first line, as joint estimation has been done by interaction variables $D_i$ln fs and $D_i$ln y, with D_i dummies. It is seen that all coefficients are significant. The family size elasticity β_1 is decreasing systematically, indicating that family size becomes less important at higher levels of well-being. Similarly the preference drift increases, reflecting that there is more consensus between income classes about low levels of well-being than about high levels of well-being. As relevant log-incomes are far away from the vertical c-axis the estimated relationship may be seen as a valid approximation in the relevant range only. All results with respect to β are virtually identical to those found in earlier versions of the type (2.1).

Most interesting in the present context is the marked influence of age. It follows that the weight distribution over time depends on the age of the individual.

Estimation results for six levels over 1981

	β_0 and dummies	β_1 and dummies	β_2 and dummies	α_0	α_1	α_2	γ_0	γ_1	γ_2
level 1	3.79 (0.15)	0.11 (0.01)	0.56 (0.02)	-4.5736 (0.3242)	0.2039 (0.0134)	-0.002068 (0.000140)	3.7730 (0.2944)	-0.1450 (0.0130)	0.001428 (0.000130)
level 2	-0.40 (0.22)	-0.01 (0.01)	0.05 (0.02)						
level 3	-0.72 (0.22)	-0.02 (0.02)	0.10 (0.02)						
level 4	-0.94 (0.22)	-0.03 (0.02)	0.14 (0.02)						
level 5	-1.23 (0.22)	-0.06 (0.02)	0.19 (0.02)						
level 6	-1.42 (0.22)	-0.08 (0.02)	0.23 (0.02)				$\bar{R}^2 = 0.75$ $N = 598^*$		

Table 2

Values of μ_τ, σ_τ, W_p, W_0, W_f for various ages

Age	μ_τ	σ_τ	W_p	W_0	W_f
20	-1.32280	1.44420	0.71557	0.18098	0.10345
30	-0.31780	0.70820	0.39848	0.47742	0.12409
40	0.27360	0.25780	0.00135	0.80874	0.18992
50	0.45140	0.09300	0.00000	0.69937	0.30063
60	0.21560	0.21380	0.00041	0.90787	0.09172
70	-0.43380	0.62020	0.45750	0.47642	0.06608

Consider Table 2. It is seen that μ_τ first increases with age making a person from past-oriented future-oriented while at the age of about 65 people start to become past-oriented again. The time span narrows in a similar way when approaching midlife and then widens again. Defining the weight on the past by $W_p = N(-\frac{1}{2};\ \mu_\tau,\ \sigma_\tau)$, $W_o = N(\frac{1}{2};\ \mu_\tau,\ \sigma_\tau) - N(-\frac{1}{2};\ \mu_\tau,\ \sigma_\tau)$ and $W_f = 1 - N(\frac{1}{2};\ \mu_\tau,\ \sigma_\tau)$ as the as the weight on the future, those aggregate weights are tabulated in Table 2 as well. When we consider the densities on the past and on the future separately and calculate the respective median values we find for the age of 20 that about 50% of the weight on the past is concentrated between now and 1.6 years ago, while the weight on the future lies for 50% between now and 0.6 years ahead. Similar calculations may be done for the other ages. We notice that the weight density on the past we estimate seems to be much more condensed than what is usually assumed.

Finally we sketch the different densities in Figure 1 for individuals of age 30, age 50 and age 70 respectively.

Figure 1.

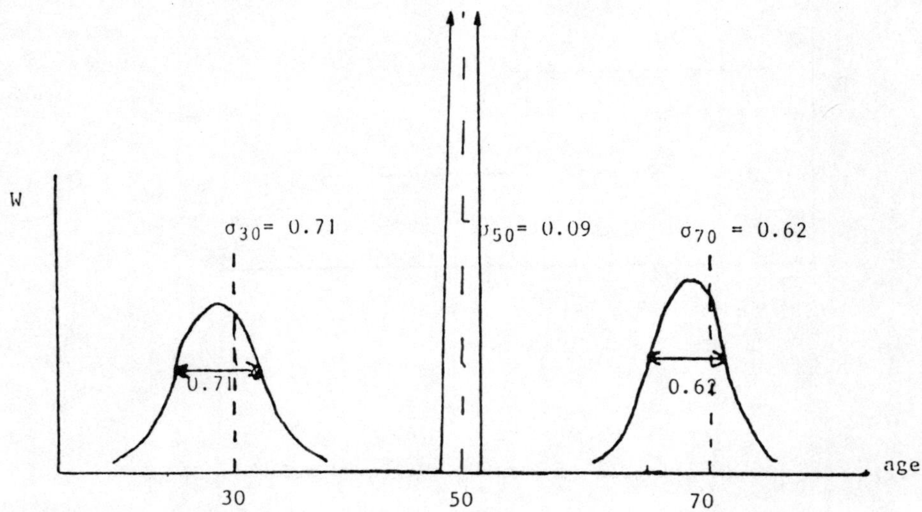

Figure 1. Time-discounting density functions for various ages

The results sketched here have to do with what psychologists call <u>time perception</u>. The behaviour of σ_τ may be interpreted as describing the perceived velocity of time. It is seen that the days are long for young and old persons and rather short for people in midlife. With respect to μ_τ young and old people are past-oriented, while people in midlife are future-oriented. This may be explained by the fact that old people have not much future left, while young people do not have enough fantasy, fed by experience, to have a clear idea about their future.

3. ADAPTATION PATTERNS FOR SOCIAL SECURITY

In this section we apply the previous findings to the question what should be the desirable smoothing or adaptation pattern, if someone looses his job and has to apply for social assistance.

Let us consider a simple income profile, where income is constant over the past and the present, say y_p (= y_0) and y_F in the future. It is sketched in Figure 2. Then

Figure 2

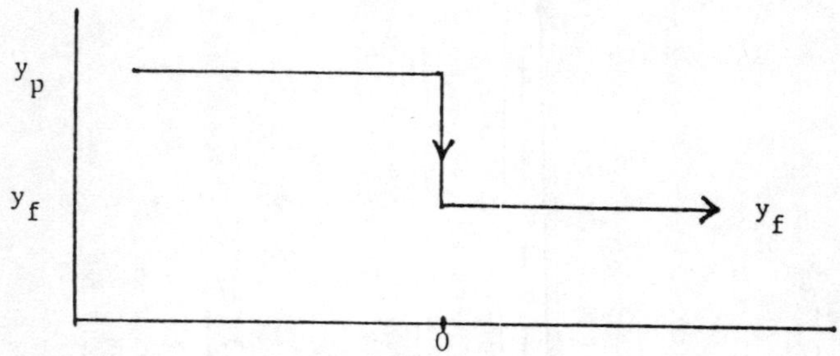

Figure 2. A downwards fall in income

$$(3.1) \quad c_{i,0} = \beta_{0,i} + \beta_1 \ln fs + \beta_2 (W_p + W_0) \ln y_p + \beta_2 W_f \ln y_F$$

where we assume for convenience $\beta_{1i} = \beta_1$ and $\beta_{2i} = \beta_2$ for all levels i, the coefficients set equal at their average value over i = 1,...,6 (see however the next footnote). From (3.1) it is obvious that if $y_F < y_p$ the judgment of what presents an income level, labeled by i, will decrease. Judgments adapt, foreshadowing the anticipated fall in income. A similar upward trend in present judgment is caused by an anticipated income increase.

Apart from its relevance as a psychological phenomenon this is a relevant issue for the politics of social security. Consider the situation where somebody previously had an income y_0 and has to apply for social security benefits or social assistance, due to becoming jobless. Let the ultimate benefit level, fixed by politicians, be y_{min}. As i or $\beta_{0,i}$ in the simplified context represents an ordinal utility scale, it is possible to calculate $\beta_{0,min}$ which corresponds to a stationary income y_{min}. The corresponding utility level is called the minimum utility level. It is found by solving

$$(3.2) \quad \ln y_{min} = \beta_{0,min} + \beta_1 \ln fs + \beta_2 \ln y_{min}$$

with respect to $\beta_{0,min}$ yielding

$$\beta_{0,min} = (1-\beta_2) \ln y_{min} - \beta_1 \ln fs$$ [3)]

Consider now a falling income pattern tending to y_{min}. Then a person asked which income level c_{min} he associates with the minimum welfare level will answer

$$\ln c_{min} = \beta_{0,min} + \beta_1 \ln fs + \beta_2(\Sigma\, w_t \ln y_t) >$$
$$> \beta_{0,min} + \beta_1 \ln fs + \beta_2 \ln y_{min}.$$

Or in words, if one referring himself to higher incomes than y_{min} is asked to tell the income level corresponding to the minimum utility level, he will mention an amount c_{min}, larger than the social benefit y_{min} which is the long-term amount corresponding to minimum utility level. If he is offered an income $y_{min} < c_{min}$, he will temporarily plunge as a result below the minimum welfare level; only after having had y_{min} for a long period he will feel that $c_{min} = y_{min}$ for him. In order to avoid the temporary drop below the minimum utility level we need an adaptation pattern. Ideally this would be of the type $(y_{-1}, y_0, c_{min}^{(1)}, c_{min}^{(2)}, \ldots)$ such that

$$\text{(3.3)} \qquad \ln y_t = \beta_{0,min} + \beta_1 \ln fs + \beta_2\Big(\sum_{\tau=-\infty}^{\infty} w_\tau \ln y_{\tau+t}\Big) \qquad (t = 1, 2, \ldots)$$

where $y_t = c_{min}^{(t)}$ if the individual is on social benefits.

This is a linear difference equation in $\ln y_t$ with constant coefficients and of infinite order. The system can be solved by iterative approximation. Its stationary solution is $\ln y_{min}$. However, this ideal adaptation pattern is not so ideal in at least one respect. It would be an individual pattern, fitted to individual income histories. For administrative reasons a simple and general pattern is needed. We suggest

$$\text{(3.4)} \qquad \ln \hat{c}_{min}^{(t+1)} = \beta_{0,min} + \beta_1 \ln fs + \beta_2\Big(\hat{c}_{min}^{(t)} \Sigma_{\tau=-\infty}^{0} w_\tau + \hat{c}_{min}^{(t+1)} \Sigma_{\tau=1}^{\infty} w_\tau\Big)$$

which may be rewritten as

$$(3.5) \qquad \ln \hat{c}_{min}^{(t+1)} = \beta_{0,min} + \beta_1 \ln fs + \beta_2 (W_p + W_0) \ln \hat{c}_{min}^{(t)} + \\ + \beta_2 W_f \ln \hat{c}_{min}^{(t+1)}$$

This pattern overestimates the ideal pattern as $\hat{c}_{min}^{(t+1)}$ overestimates future incomes and, it underestimates the ideal pattern as $\hat{c}_{min}^{(t)}$ underestimates the incomes in the past, corresponding to minimum utility.

The solution of (3.5), a first-order difference equation, equals

$$(3.6) \qquad \ln \hat{c}_{min}^{(t)} = \ln y_{min} + (\ln y_0 - \ln y_{min})\lambda^t \qquad t = 1,\ldots,\infty$$

where $\lambda = \beta_2(W_p + W_o)/(1 - \beta_2 W_f)$.
It is easy to see that $0 \leq \lambda \leq \beta_2$ with $\lambda=0$ for $W_F=1$ and $\lambda=\beta_2$ for $W_f=0$. We see that $\hat{c}_{min}^{(t)}$ tends to y_{min}. It is obvious that any more refined pattern taking into account, e.g., not only the present income level y_0 but also past or future income levels, may be constructed in a similar way.

A few patterns of type (3.6) are tabulated in Table 3, differentiated with respect to ages and with respect to the relative fall y_o/y_{min} to be imposed. For a fall of 20% at age 30 we see that in the first year a fall of 7.6% of y_{min} is needed, in the next year another 5% and that the fifth-year level is only 2% above the final level y_{min}. For practical purposes it is undesirable to allow for age-dependency or an infinite adaptation pattern. Table 5 suggests that a 3 year period following the pattern corresponding to an age of 30 seems rather reasonable, that is, for a fall by 20% say from 120 to 100, we get first year 112, next year 108, then 105, then 100.

Table 3.

Adaptation profiles from y_0 to y_{min} for various values y_0/y_{min} and various age classes

y_0/y_{min}	age	t=1	t=2	t=3	t=4	t=5
1.1	20	1.064	1.041	1.027	1.017	1.011
	30	1.063	1.040	1.026	1.016	1.011
	40	1.060	1.036	1.022	1.013	1.008
	50	1.055	1.030	1.017	1.009	1.005
	60	1.060	1.036	1.022	1.013	1.008
	70	1.063	1.040	1.026	1.016	1.010
1.2	20	1.126	1.081	1.052	1.034	1.021
	30	1.124	1.078	1.050	1.032	1.020
	40	1.117	1.071	1.043	1.026	1.016
	50	1.107	1.059	1.033	1.018	1.010
	60	1.118	1.071	1.043	1.026	1.016
	70	1.124	1.078	1.050	1.032	1.020
1.5	20	1.302	1.188	1.119	1.076	1.049
	30	1.298	1.182	1.114	1.072	1.045
	40	1.281	1.164	1.097	1.058	1.035
	50	1.255	1.136	1.074	1.041	1.023
	60	1.281	1.164	1.097	1.058	1.035
	70	1.298	1.182	1.114	1.072	1.045

4. THE IMPACT OF GROWTH AND INFLATION

The attention on and awareness of income inequality in society seems to be inversely related to the prosperity of society. In prosperous societies that are well established on a real income growth track it seems that there is more tolerance for income inequality than in contracting economies, where real incomes tend to fall. In this section we shall employ our findings to discuss this phenomenon. Let us assume that all incomes vary over time according to the relation

(4.1) $$\ln y_t(\text{AGE};\delta) = \ln y_0 + (F(\text{AGE} + t) - F(\text{AGE})) + \delta t.$$

The second term at the right-hand side stands for the relative differences between incomes of individuals of different ages according to the general earnings profile. Added to this individual age-dependent development is a general exponential trend, where δ stands for the net effect of nominal growth minus price inflation, that is, δ is the general growth rate of real incomes. The rate δ is the general expectation in society on the growth rate.

Let us now substitute (4.1) into (2.2) where we take for convenience again $\beta_{1i} = \beta_1$ and $\beta_{2i} = \beta_2$. We get

(4.2) $$\ln c_i = \beta_{0i} + \beta_1 \ln fs + \beta_2 \ln y_0 + + \beta_2 \Sigma_{t=-\infty}^{+\infty} w_t[F(\text{AGE} + t) - F(\text{AGE})) + \delta t]$$

which we may write as

(4.3) $$\ln c_i = \beta_{0i} + \beta_1 \ln fs + B_2 \ln y_0 + B_2 g(\text{AGE}) + \beta_2 \delta \mu_\tau(\text{AGE})$$

where $g(\text{AGE}) = \sum_{t=-\infty}^{\infty} w_t[F(\text{AGE}) + t) - F(\text{AGE})]$, and $= \mu_T(\text{AGE}) = \sum_{t=-\infty}^{+\infty} w_t(\text{AGE})t$ [4)]

Let us now look which income level, say $y_0^{(i)}$, is evaluated by i, if the individual gets it, given that he is AGE years old and that real income grows at rate δ. We have to solve (4.3) for the condition $\ln c_i = \ln y_0$ yielding

(4.4) $$\ln y_0^{(i)}(\text{AGE};\delta) = \frac{\beta_{0i} + \beta_1 g(\text{AGE}) + \beta_2 \delta \mu_\tau(\text{AGE})}{1 - \beta_2}$$

It follows that the growth rate δ influences the amount $y_0^{(i)}$. We may write

(4.5) $$\ln y_0^{(i)}(\text{AGE};\delta) = \ln y_0^{(i)}(\text{AGE};0) + \frac{\beta_2}{1 - B_2} \delta \mu_\tau(\text{AGE}).$$

It follows that the income $y_0^{(i)}(AGE;0)$ that is evaluated by i under zero growth has to be multiplied by an equivalence scale $\exp\{\frac{\beta_2}{1-\beta_2}\delta\mu_\tau(AGE)\}$ to be evaluated by the same label i under growth δ. We call $y_0^{(i)}(AGE;\delta)$ the utility-equivalent of $y_0^{(i)}(AGE;0)$ under growth δ. Given that μ_τ depends on AGE (see Table 2) and is first negative, then positive and then negative again, it follows that the δ-equivalence scale for $\delta > 0$ is smaller than one for young and old people and larger than one for people in midlife. If we assume that utility increases with income, it implies that young and old people derive more utility from a given income level y_0 under positive growth than under zero growth, and that people in midlife derive less utility from a given income level y_0 under positive growth than under zero growth. For $\delta < 0$ the inverse relation holds. From (4.5) we see that the δ-equivalence scale does not depend on i. Obviously this is caused by our simplification that β_{1i} and β_{2i} are constant in i. If we had not done that, we would have found a utility-specific equivalence scale, but the theory and model would not change qualitively.

Now we come to the main point of the section. If we may calculate for each individual income $y_0(AGE;0)$ the utility equivalent $y_0(AGE;\delta)$ according to (4.5), we may also calculate the <u>utility-equivalent income distribution</u> $(\tilde{y};\delta)$ under δ growth that corresponds to a specific income distribution $(y_1, \ldots, y_N;0) = (y;0)$ under zero growth. It implies that we apply to each individual n his age-specific equivalence scale, yielding

$$(4.6)\qquad (\tilde{y}_1, \ldots, \tilde{y}_N;\delta) = (y_1 \exp(\beta_2\delta\mu_\tau(AGE_1)/(1-\beta_2)), \ldots,$$

$$\ldots, y_N \exp(\beta_2\delta\mu_\tau(AGE_N)/(1-\beta_2)).$$

Let us now consider the income inequality of both distributions as measured by the variance of log-incomes. We define

$$(4.7)\qquad \sigma^2(\delta) = \mathrm{var}(\ln y + \beta_2\delta\mu_\tau(AGE)/(1-\beta_2)) = \mathrm{var}(\ln \tilde{y}).$$

If $\mu(AGE)$ was a constant, it is evident that the variance of log-incomes would not depend on δ as any log-income is increased by the same constant. However this constancy of $\mu(AGE)$ is empirically shown to be an incorrect assumption.

Given the fact of a strong relationship between income and μ_τ through age, where people in midlife have the highest income and simultaneously $\mu_\tau > 0$, we see that, if $\delta > 0$, the high incomes of those in midlife are mostly multiplied by factors greater than one, while the low incomes in the beginning and the end of life are multiplied by a factor smaller than one. So it is likely that for $\delta > 0$ the utility-equivalent income distribution $(\tilde{y};\delta)$ will be more dispersed than $(y;0)$, that is, $\sigma^2(\delta) > \sigma^2(0)$ for $\delta > 0$. In plain terms, it would say that income inequality is more tolerable, the higher the real growth rate δ in society. Inversely, in a contracting economy with $\delta < 0$ it follows that $\sigma^2(\delta) < \sigma^2(0)$, or in words, in a contracting economy income inequality becomes less tolerable, the higher the contraction rate. In Table 4 we have taken the net income distribution in our sample (1981) of 600 households, roughly representative for the Dutch income distribution as our $(y;0)$ and we have calculated by means of (4.6) its utility-equivalent income distribution $(\tilde{y};\delta)$ for selected positive and negative values of δ. The corresponding $\sigma^2(\delta)$ are presented in Table 4.

Table 4

The log-variance of utility-equivalent income distributions for various values of δ (sample 1981)

δ	$\sigma^2(\delta)$
-30%	.164
-20%	.155
-10%	.156
- 5%	.161
0%	.169
5%	.179
10%	.192
20%	.227
30%	.272

Indeed Table 4 exhibits the phenomenon we suspected. However, we stress that this phenomenon depends wholly on the empirical relation between income and age at one hand and the behavior of μ_τ as a function of age at the other hand. Although this empirical relation seems to be rather regular, it is not something of a law. Actually if δ tends to very large absolute values, say -30% or +30% the correction term gets a dominating influence and especially for very small negative values we see that the utility-equivalent income inequality is increasing again. In order to get a taste for the differences we give some comparable figures in Table 5 for the real net income distribution in a few European countries in 1979 (see Van Weeren, Van Praag [12]).

Table 5

Inequality of after-tax income in Europe (1979)

Belgium	0.263
Denmark	0.331
France	0.326
West-Germany	0.229
Great-Britain	0.189
Italy	0.303
The Netherlands	0.182

Source: Van Weeren, Van Praag [12].

5. CONCLUSION

In this paper we estimated the effect of past and present incomes and the anticipated future income flow on present opinions with respect to what is a good income, a sufficient income and so on.
The opinions, reflected by responses on attitude questions, vary over respondents. We find a marked influence, which may be described by means of a density function over the time-axis where the present is situated at t=0. As such the findings shed light on the memory and anticipation process. Those processes appear to be significantly age-dependent. It should be kept in mind that this time-discounting process may also be

norm-specific, that is, that it is different for opinions on different aspects of life. Actually Table 1, where we find slightly different parameter values for different levels of welfare is already witness to that phenomenon.

In this paper we applied our finding on two issues in socio-economic policy. The first is the construction of an adaptation profile for individuals who have to adapt themselves to a social assistance level from a higher previous income. The second problem we consider is how perceived income and welfare inequality compare between a growing or contracting economy and an economy with constant incomes.

The most traditional field of application, viz. that of individual savings behavior might be another possibility to use the estimates found. The fluctuating value of the ratio $w_F/(w_p + w_0)$ which is lowest in early youth and after the age of 70 would indicate a variable savings propensity over life with a top in midlife.
Finally, it is noted that the empirical material, that hitherto has been mainly used in a cardinalistic utility context (see e.g. Kapteyn, Wansbeek [13], Van Praag [6], Van Praag, Kapteyn [7], Van Praag et al. [14] and Van Praag et al. [5]), is used here in a completely ordinal context.
A first introduction on an ordinal approach to the results of the IEQ is presented in Van Praag [8], [9].

FOOTNOTES

1) Due to the strong positive correlation between ages and education levels of husband and spouse we do not include the characteristics of the spouse as well. The information on unearned income and/or other income earners (children) is not very reliable.

2) Although there may be correlation between disturbances, we do not have to correct for that as it is a situation of seemingly unrelated regressions.

3) It is possible to estimate $\beta_{0,i}$, $\beta_{1,i}$ and $\beta_{2,i}$ as monotonous functions in i and to solve the equation $\ln y_{min} = \beta_{0,i} + \beta_{1,i} \ln fs + \beta_{2,i} \ln y_{min}$ with respect to i. As it raises a number of minor technical points, we ignore it in this context, to continue the main line.

4) Actually we approximate the expectation of the continuous variable t by a discrete sum.

REFERENCES

[1] Friedman, M. (1957), A Theory of the Consumption Function, Princeton University Press.

[2] Pollak, R.A. (1976), "Interdependent Preferences", American Economic Review 66, pp. 309-320.

[3] Helson, H. (1964), Adaptation-Level Theory: An Experimental and Systematic Approach to Behaviour, Harper, New York.

[4] Van de Stadt, H., A. Kapteyn and S. van de Geer (1985), "The Relativity of Utility: Evidence from Panel Data", Review of Economics and Statistics, Vol. LXVII, No. 2, pp. 179-187.

[5] Van Praag, B.M.S., A.J.M. Hagenaars and H. van Weeren (1982), "Poverty in Europe", The Review of Income and Wealth 28, pp. 345-359.

[6] Van Praag, B.M.S. (1971), "The Welfare Function of Income in Belgium: an Empirical Investigation", European Economic Review 2, pp. 337-369.

[7] Van Praag, B.M.S. and A. Kapteyn (1973), "Further Evidence on the Individual Welfare Function of Income: an Empirical Investigation in The Netherlands", European Economic Review 4, pp. 33-62.

[8] Van Praag, B.M.S. (1985a), "Household Cost Functions and Equivalence Scales. An Alternative Approach", Report 84.04, Center for Research in Public Economics, Leyden University.

[9] Van Praag, B.M.S. (1985b), "Linking Economics with Psychology: an Economist's View", Journal of Economic Psychology 6, pp. 289-311.

[10] Danziger,S., J. van der Gaag, M.K. Taussig and E. Smolensky (1984), "The Direct Measurement of Welfare Levels: How much does it cost to make ends meet?", The Review of Economics and Statistics, pp. 500-505.

[11] Marquardt, D.W. (1963), "An Algorithm for Least Squares Estimation of Nonlinear Parameters", Journal of the Society for Industrial and Applied Mathematics 11, pp. 431-441.

[12] Van Weeren, H. and B.M.S. van Praag (1984), "The Inequality of Actual Incomes and Earning Capacities between Households in Europe", European Economic Review 24, pp. 239-256.

[13] Kapteyn, A. and T.J. Wansbeek (1982), "Empirical Evidence on Preference Formation", Journal of Economic Psychology 2, pp. 137-154.

[14] Van Praag, B.M.S., T. Goedhart and A. Kapteyn (1980), "The Poverty Line. A Pilot Survey in Europe", The Review of Economics and Statistics, vol. 62, pp. 461-465.

THE INDIVIDUAL EVALUATION OF THE DUTCH SOCIAL SECURITY SYSTEM;

Results of an Initial Investigation

Theo Poiesz
Jopy Sol (student)

Department of Economic Psychology
Tilburg University
Box 90153, 5000 LE
Tilburg, the Netherlands

Paper submitted to the XIth Annual Colloquium
of the International Association for Research
in Economic Psychology
Haifa, Israel, July 1986

Abstract

In this paper, an attempt is made to form a theoretical psychological basis of the evaluation of the Dutch Social Security System. It was expected that next to income and system dependence the following psychological variables would be relevant for the explanation of system affect: income evaluation, judged system fairness, perceived system complexity, perceived system fraud, and political orientation. Results of an empirical study showed that of these psychological variables only income evaluation and judged system fairness were significantly related to system evaluation. Possible reasons for the absence of some relationships are discussed and future research possibilities are discussed.

The economic growth in the Dutch post World War 2 era was partly utilized to set up one of the most elaborate social security systems in the world. Each step in the economic development was accompanied by an extension of material and immaterial social security measures.
The recession in the seventies and early eighties affected the system in two ways. First, its relative claim on the national resources increased by a reduction of the national income; second, as a result of the recession, more people were entitled to financial help from the system. The consequence of both effects was that, by 1982, about one third of the national income was spent on social security, which amounted to about fifty percent of the collective expenditures. These high percentages prompted questions on the efficiency of the system and on the necessity of some of its components.

One other aspect warranted a closer look at the system. Over the years, the system has been expanding in response to the presumed needs and political interests of the moment - it did not grow in accordance with a prespecified plan. The result, at present, is a very complex sytem consisting of myriads of laws, procedures, rules, exceptions, exceptions to exceptions, and a variety of decisions based upon regional, local and personal judgments. It is likely that, to the individual civilian, the system makes the impression of being utterly complex and intransparant. If so, it might very well lead to misperceptions, expectations of random judgment of individual cases, feelings of victimization, and possibly inadequate or even fraudulent behavior.

Studies on the effects of the Social Security System have been primarily economic and sociological in nature, while some of the negative consequences just described are basically psychological. As far as known, no psychological research has been done to assess how civilians experience the system, both perceptually and evaluatively. In the literature, no distinct theoretical framework is known to be available. Yet, some psychological effects may be anticipated on theoretical grounds next to, of course, effects of socioeconomic and -demographic circumstances. We may expect, for example, that some of the psychological effects that are observed in relation to income also pertain to the personal consequences of the Social Security System. More specifically, when the individual comparison of inputs to and outcomes from the system is the focus of interest, we may refer to the equity theory (e.g. Adams, 1965), and to the notion of subjective justice (Schoormans & Von Grumbkow, 1986) . As comparisons tend to be made in reference to relevant others, also the social comparison concept (Rijsman, 1980) may be included in a theoretical framework. Comparisons are subject to perceptions of structures and procedures applied, and to norms and values held collectively or individually. Thus subjective norms regarding labor, income distribution, responsibility, and individual rights and duties could have an influence on the evaluation of the Social Security System. This, in turn, might be expressed in actual economic behavior.

The primay purpose of the present paper is to explore what types of variables are relevant for the explanation of the evaluation of the Social Security System. For this we will attempt to make a preliminary inventory of the presumed most central explanatory variables. Specifically, we will attempt to identify variables with some psychological significance and if so, which variables seem theoretically worthy of a closer look. Thus, this paper primarily addresses the question of conceptualization and not the question of empirical validation, even though we will refer to some empirical data for the selection of relevant variables. In short, the study is set up to provide results that may be translated into specific hypotheses to be tested in later studies.

In the following we will first try to identify global types of explanatory variables as they relate to the evaluation of the system. Second, we will discuss the results of an empirical investigation that includes the operationalizations of these variables. This study part of a major government sponsored sociological-psychological project at the Tilburg University on the distributive aspects of the Dutch Social Security System. Finally, a conceptual model will be presented as it is suggested by the obtained results.
Provisionally, it is presumed that the evaluation of the system is dependent upon the following financial/economic, perceptual, evaluative, and normative variables.

-Personal financial/economic utility

It may be expected that the trade-off of perceived financial contributions to and perceived benefits from the system has an influence on the evaluation of the system. The more benefits/income a person receives from the system the more positive will be his/her evaluation; if no or only a limited amount of benefits is received and, yet, financial contributions to the system have to be made, the evaluation will be relatively unfavorable.

-Perceived complexity

It is a generally known fact that the Social Security System is very costly. At the same time, the system seems so complex that it is very hard for non-experts to assess the way it is organized and operating. In general, it is expected that the knowledge of the organization and the operation of the system is very limited, and that people will judge the system as highly complex.
For an individual person, the combination of cost and complexity will lead him/her to a negative evaluation of the system.

-Perceived equity/fairness

It may be that the critical aspect of the system is not the size of the absolute financial impact but rather the relative impact - judged in relation to the perceived impact of the system on others. This presumption calls for the inclusion of variables dealing with the perceived fairness of the system. It is expected that the evaluation of the system becomes more positive with the perceived fairness of the system.

-Income evaluation

A positive income evaluation may be expected to parallel a positive evaluation of the system. However, the relationship between dissatisfaction and system evaluation is not easy to predict. Persons dissatisfied with their income, may be unwilling to contribute to a system designed to financially help others, which may be expressed in an unfavorable system evaluation. On the other hand, it is often the person with a dissatisfactorily low income that receives more benefits from the system, which might be expressed in a more positive system evaluation.

-Norms

There are at least two normative aspects of the Social Security System that should be included, the solidarity aspect and the perceived fraud aspect.
1. The solidarity aspect:
It may be expected that individual citizens will differ with respect to subjective norms regarding the financial assistance of needy others. Persons less inclined to endorse a collective security system will evaluate such a system less positively than persons more guided by a solidarity principle.
2. Perceived system fraud:
Even though it is virtually impossible to judge them on their validity, rumors circulate as to the illegal use of the system. There is no fool-proof government check on personal financial situations and activities, which, in principle, heightens the probability that some requests for social benefits may be out of order.

Combining the various hypotheses and expectations, the following conceptual scheme may be presented. This scheme also shows the expected interrelationships among the variables. See Figure 1.

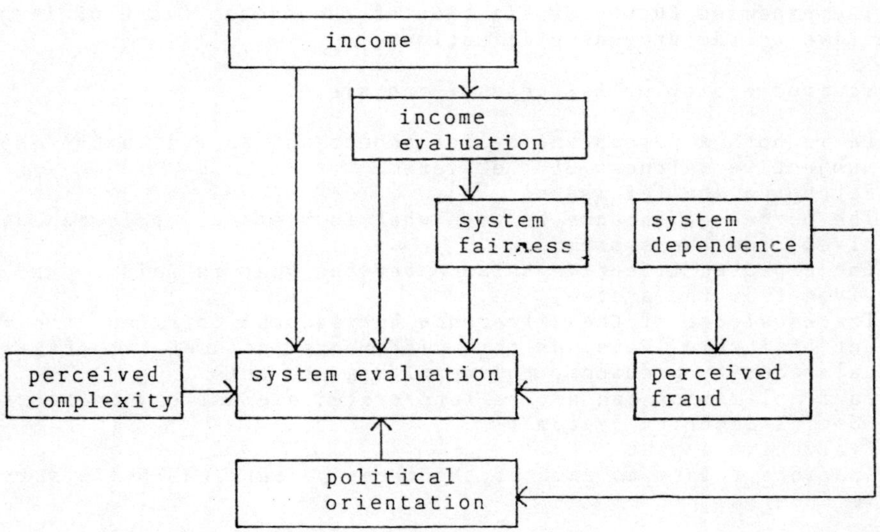

FIGURE 1: Conceptual scheme of the determinants of system evaluation

In the following we will report on a study in which these types of variables have been operationalized and investigated. The results of the study should shed light on their respective relevance for the explanation of system evaluation and on their mutual relationships.

THE STUDY

400 names and addresses were randomly selected from the Dutch telephone directories. Questionnaires with instructions and a stamped return envelope were sent out to the 400 addresses. A card was included with which, by separate mail to guarantee anonymity, a summary of the results could be requested. Nineteen questionnaires could not be delivered (wrong address, addressee moved or deceased). The total response after three weeks was 133 questionnaires or 35 percent response. Considering the content of the questionnaire (income-related, personal), this figure is neither unexpectedly nor unacceptably low, considering the purposes of the study. It is evident, however, that the sample can not be taken as representative for the Dutch population. Also, some bias because of self-selection may not be ruled out.

Operationalizations:
For most of the general variables various operationalizations were employed. These are listed below.

-Personal financial/economic utility

1. On the basis of personal indications of income components, respondents were rather crudely classified as either presently fully dependent, semi-dependent or non-dependent from the system;
2. The self-reported present utilization of the system;
3. The expected future utilization of the system (more or less relative to the present utilization).

-Perceived equity or fairness of the system

There is both a perceptual/belief aspect and an evaluative aspect to subjective fairness of the system.
A. Perceptual/belief aspect
1. The perceived balance between what is presently paid to and received from the system;
2. The expected life-time balance between what is paid to and received from the system;
3. The knowledge of the difference between the total and the net amount of income (note: as this difference includes both taxes and social security premiums, the results as to this operationalization can not be interpreted exclusively in terms of the Social Security System);
B. Evaluative aspect
Evaluations relate to each of the three perceptions/beliefs listed above under A.

-Perceived knowledge and complexity

Here, we may make a distinction between the organization or structure of the system and the procedures applied within the system.
1. The self-reported knowledge of the organization of the system;
2. The perceived complexity of the organization;
3. The self-reported knowledge of the rules and regulations of the

system;
4. The perceived complexity of these rules and regulations.

-Income evaluation

1. The evaluation of income, income according to own definition;
2. Same, but income defined as the regular net monthly income (labeled here 'primary income);
3. Same, but income defined as total income, including income components provided by the Social Security System.

-Norms: solidarity and perceived fraud

1. Solidarity is hard to operationalize due to the high probability of socially desirable answers. Therefore, solidarity is very freely associated with ideology and translated into political orientation: a left wing orientation is taken as relatively solidarity based, whereas a right wing orientation is taken to reflect an emphasis on individual responsibility.
2. Perceived fraud: A distinction has to be made between general income-supplementing benefits such as rent-subsidies or child allowances, and income-replacing benefits, such as old age pensions and allowances for the unemployed.
Questions were asked on the estimated fraud with regard to both general income-supplements and income-replacements. Estimates were to be expressed in both impressions of the incidence of fraude (very much - very little) and in the percentage of people unjustly receiving financial assistance.

In the questionnaire, items were separated if the concerning answers could be expected to have a biasing influence upon one another.

RESULTS

For a description of the sample in terms of a number of socio-economic and demographic variables, we refer the reader to the Appendix. In general, it seems that the sample does not show a bias in a particular direction. If it does, it is because of the instructions provided. For example, the main breadwinner was requested to complete the questionnaire. As might be expected, this request resulted in a higher number of male participants. The respondents were spread more or less proportionally over the various categories of the other variables, relative to the structure of the Dutch society.

1. DESCRIPTIVE RESULTS

First, we will present the general descriptive results per operationalization. The description will be limited to indications of central tendency and spread.

The Social Security System is evaluated quite positively. The average score is 5.65 on a 7-point scale, 7 being most positive (standard deviation, s.d. = 1.37). The distribution of the evaluation scores is negatively skewed: the majority of the evaluations is found in the more positive region of the axis.

-Personal financial/economic utility

On the basis of their indications of types of income components, individual respondents were categorized as either fully-, semi-, or non-dependent from the Social Security System. The fully dependent are about one fifth of the total sample - about 20 percent. About 63 percent of the sample is semi-dependent, and about 17 percent is non-dependent.
On an 8-point scale, respondents could indicate their perceived present utilization of the system.(8 = very much usage; 1 = no usage at all). The average score was 2.89 (s.d. = 2.41). It must be noted that the 'calculated' system utilization does not overlap completely with the self-reported utilization: several persons that, according to their income-components, could be classified as fully system dependent, reported to be not so; more than forty percent of those labeled 'semi-dependent' perceived themselves to be non-dependent; and about half of those actually non-dependent reported to be somewhat dependent. There are several possible explanations for this remarkable lack of complete overlap, one of them being a difference between the interpretation of the word 'utilization'. Another possible reason is that, by habituation, some of the system provided benefits have become such self-evident income supplements that the source of the money is not explicitly identified any more, and the money is automatically assimilated in the household budget.
The expected future usage of the system is stated in terms of more or less relative to the present situation. On the 7-point scale (1 = much more; 7 = much less), respondents score, on the average, 3.45 (s.d. = 1.21), which means something between the same as now and a little bit more.

-Perceived equity/fairness

The questionnaire contained a 5-point scale on which respondents could indicate whether they received more (1) or less (5) than they contributed to the system. The mean score was 3.65 (s.d. = 1.32). That is, on the average, respondents indicated to contribute a little more to the system than they received. When asked how fair respondents experienced this balance to be, they responded with an average of 3.81 (s.d. = 1.65) on a 7-point scale, 7 being 'very unfair'. The average score lies at about the midpoint of the scale, being 'neither fair nor unfair'.
The same two questions were asked for the balance between the life-time contributions to and benefits from the system. No different result pattern appeared. For the life-time balance the average scores were, respectively, 3.65 (s.d. = 1.10) and 3.92 (s.d. = 1.66).
About 14 percent of the respondents indicated to know the exact difference between income before and after taxes (including social security premiums). About 65 percent indicated to know the approximate difference, and about 20 percent reported to barely know or not know the amount of the difference. On an 8-point fairness scale (8 = very unfair), the average score was 4.23 (s.d. = 1.64). Again, we must note, however, that this difference applies to both taxes and premiums.
Of the respondents who are fully dependent upon the system (as compared to the persons being non- or semi-dependent) there are more persons indicating that the amount of contributions to the system is just right ($X^2 = 7.14$, df = 2, $p < .03$).

-Perceived knowledge and complexity

On a 7-point scale respondents could report their estimated knowledge of the organization of the system. They responded with an average of 3.14 (s.d. = 1.77), meaning 'rather little knowledge' (7 = very much). The perceived complexity of the system's organization was rather high, as is reflected in the average score of 5.66 on the 7-point scale (7 = highly complex; s.d. = 1.36). There is a highly similar pattern for self-reported knowledge and perceived complexity of the system's rules and regulations. On identical scales, the respective means are 3.12 (s.d. = 1.73) and 5.51 (s.d. = 1.42). This suggests that respondents may not make a distinction between the organization and the applied procedures. The various knowledge and perceived complexity distributions are all somewhat skewed: very few respondents report to be very knowledgeable with regard to the system. For each of the four variables reported here, no significant differences were found between fully-, semi-, and non-dependent respondents (resp. X^2 = .28, df = 2; X^2 = 7.20, df = 4; X^2 = 2.98, df = 2; and X^2 = 2.63, df = 4).

-Income evaluation

The average income evaluation is little more than neutral, a finding consistent with results from earlier studies (Poiesz & Von Grümbkow, 1983, 1982). This applies to all operationalizations of income included in the study. For a correct interpretation of this outcome, it is necessary to report to what extent the difference between the operationalizations produced different income amounts and evaluations. In general, we may expect results showing that the amount of total income (including all income components) would be highest, followed by income own definition, and that the primary income amount (regular net monthly income) would be lowest. About four out of ten respondents provided equal amounts for each type of income. About the same relative number of respondents provided no different amount for primary income and income own definition but a higher amount for total income. Only one out of ten produced the expected result. Six percent showed an inconsistent order for the amounts of the respective income operationalizations.
On the basis of these aggregate data we may provisionally conclude that, apparently, income supplements provided by the Social Security System, tend to be psychologically ignored when a specification of an income amount is asked for. This is also reflected in the (lack of) difference between the evaluations of the various income amounts: 4.51, 4.43, and 4.58, for income own definition, primary and total income respectively. (The F-value for evaluation differences is less than 1.0). The differences are nonsignificant, even though the modes of the income amounts do differ: 2000-2250 guilders for income own definition and primary income, and 2500-2750 guilders for total income.

-Norms: solidarity and perceived fraud

Respondents' average score is in the middle of the left-right political dimension. No skewness is observed, so that in this sample, right and left seem to be in balance.
The average perceived incidence of fraud, as scored on a 7-point

scale for both income-replacements and income supplements (general provisions) is, respectively, 4.24 and 3.12 (1 = very little fraud).
The presumed percentage of persons misusing the systems benefits is 6-10 percent (mode) for income replacements and 1-5 percent (mode) for income supplements. No external norms can be applied to these figures.

2. THE EVALUATION OF THE SOCIAL SECURITY SYSTEM

With the help of the variables just reviewed it is possible to be more specific as to the basis of the evaluation of the system. Here we will present an overview of the variables as they did and did not show the expected relationship with system evaluation. We must note that variations with regard to this latter variable are primarily in the positive region of the evaluation axis. Because of the observed skewness only nonmetric techniques will be applied to the analysis of relationships involving the system affect.

-Personal financial/economic utility

Of the operationalizations employed only externally determined system dependence (full-, semi-, and non-dependence) showed a significant relationship with system affect ($X^2 = 12.00$, df = 2, $p < .05$). Compared to those either full- or non-dependent, the semi-dependent judge the system more often to be good rather than very good. The self-reported present utilization and the expected future utilization were not significantly related to evaluation (resp. $X^2 = 1.82$, df = 2, and $X^2 = .66$, df = 1). The same is true for the estimated probability of future system usage. Having an income replacement from the system (e.g. because of unemployment) is not reflected in a more positive or negative system evaluation. The expected present and life time balance between contributions and benefits did not show a significant relationship with system affect (resp. $X^2 = 2.59$, df = 4; $X^2 = 1.75$, df = 2)

-Perceived equity/fairness

No relationship was found between the judged relative contribution to/from the system and system evaluation ($X^2 = 2.59$, df = 4). That is, respondents indicating that they have to contribute more to the system than they receive do not regard the system in a more negative sense than respondents with a reported lower relative contribution. The reverse is neither true.
The relationship is also nonsignificant if the balance between life time contributions and benefits is considered ($X^2 = 1.75$, df = 2). However, the subjective evaluation of the balance in terms of perceived fairness does make a difference. Perceived fairness is positively related to system affect ($X^2 = 6.92$, df = 2, $p < .05$). This latter observation only applies to the present situation. The perceived fairness of the expected life time balance does not show a significant relationship with system evaluation ($X^2 = 7.05$, df = 4). The judged fairness of the difference between gross and net income is also positively related to system affect ($X^2 = 7.25$, df = 2, $p < .05$).

-Income evaluation

As expected, income evaluation is positively associated with system evaluation. This applies to all three income evaluation items considered: the evaluation of income own definition, of the primary (net monthly) income and of the total income (after explicit consideration of all income components).
For the three items, the respective association measures are: X^2 = 18.47, df = 4, $p < .01$; X^2 = 18.26, df = 4, $p <$ 01; and X^2 = 19.49, df = 4, $p < .01$.

-Perceived complexity

All four operationalizations were not significantly related to system evaluation. Self-reported knowledge of the organization and system affect: X^2 = 1.27, df = 2; for perceived complexity of the organization: X^2 = 5.05, df = 2; for self-reported knowledge of the rules and regulations: X^2 = 0.34, df = 2; and for perceived complexity of these rules and regulations: X^2 = 8.64, df = 4.

-Norms: solidarity and perceived fraud

As indicated before, solidarity was operationalized as political orientation. This variable is not found to be related to system evaluation (X^2 = 3.30, df = 2).The same applies to the four variables presumed to cover perceived fraud. The various association measures are X^2 = 0.60, df = 2; X^2 = 3.20, df = 4; X^2 = 4.77, df = 2; and X^2 = 0.38, df = 2. Neither one of these X^2-values approaches significance.

-Variable interrelationships

Figure 1 suggests several relationships to exist between some of the variables just discussed apart from the relationships they did or did not have with system evaluation. Here we will briefly, that is, without elaborate statistical detail, present the main conclusions as to these interrelationships.
As expected, considered over all operationalizations simultaneously, income is positively related to income evaluation. Correlations range form .43 to .48 (all significant at the 1% level). Income is also positively related to system dependence: the higher the income, the less dependence - a self-evident result.
Income evaluation is positively related to perceived fairness of the difference between gross and net income (correlations range from .33 to .43), of the present balance between contributions and benefits (correlations range from .31 to .34), and between life time balance between contributions and benefits (correlations between .24 and .29 - all correlations significant at the 1% level).
Income is negatively related to present system dependence for all the variables considered.
System dependence is not related to perceived system fraud and neither to political orientation.

DISCUSSION AND CONCLUSION

Several provisional conclusions may be drawn from the outcomes of the present study.

First, in the present study it was found out that very few respondents judge the system in a negative sense and that overall system evaluations are concentrated in the positive area of the evaluation scale.
Second, there are several indications that the Social Security System is not a psychologically clearly identified entity. Rather, many respondents indicated not to know the system and to experience it as being complex. Also, personal contributions to and benefits received from the system are not assessed correctly by a number of respondents.
Third, if a distinction is made between variables that do and do not have a significant relationship with system affect, the former appear to be more closely tied to the subjective experience of direct personal consequences of the system. More specifically, the results suggest that the perceived fairness of the personal system effects is one of the most dominant explanatory variables of system affect.
Four, the present personal system effects are more closely related to system affect than expected future effects. In essence, this is not a surprising outcome with the concrete present having more psychological significance than an abstract future. However, one of the positive side effects of the system could be the reduction of subjective uncertainty with regard to the future. The data suggest that this latter effect may not be psychologically relevant.

The results are remarkable to the extent that quite a few expected significant relationships were not observed.
- Income is only related to system evaluation if respondents are confronted with all the income components that are provided to them by the system. In other cases - that is, for regular net monthly income and for income own definition, no relationship with system evaluation is found.
- Judged fairness of the sytem is related to system evaluation only if it is operationalized in terms of the present effect of the system. The expected life time balance between benefits and contributions does not show a significant relationship with evaluation.
- It was expected that system dependence differences would be reflected in evaluation differences. This turns out to be only so if system dependence is determined objectively for the respondent (on the basis of his/her income components) and not subjectively by the respondent - perceived utilization of the system's benefits. It may be that respondents are reluctant to present themselves as receiving benefits from the system. Or, which is more likely, respondents do not view some of the income components as system provided.
- Perceived fraud is in no way related to system evaluation. This is a surprising outcome as fraud is held to be one of the system's problems. Also, of the twelve possible relationships between the three operationalizations of system dependence and the four fraud items, only one was significant, which almost reaches chance level. An outcome showing that those having only benefits from the system perceive less fraud relative to those only paying to the system would have been more in line with expectations.
- System knowledge and perceived system complexity do not affect system evaluation. Respondents with relatively more knowledge of the system's organization and operation do not feel more positively or negatively with regard to the system than those with

very limited system knowledge.
- Finally, political orientation, taken here as a crude operationalization of solidarity, is neither related to system affect nor to system dependence - two unexpected results.

The obtained results force us to drastically reduce the conceptual model of system affect to a more limited model, containing three (direct) determinants only: income evaluation, system dependence, and judged system fairness. We exclude the variables system knowledge, perceived complexity, political orientation, and perceived fraud. See Figure 2 for the adapted model.

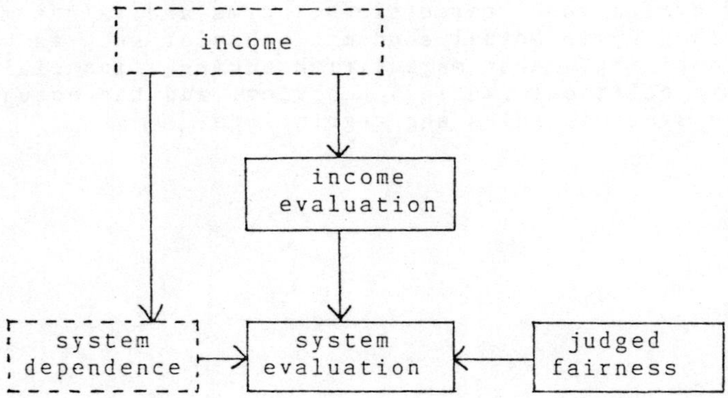

FIGURE 2: Conceptual scheme of the determinants of system evaluation (adapted)

Income does play a secundary role only. There is no direct effect on system evaluation. System dependence is to be taken as an objectively ascertained and not a subjective variable (therefore, the two dotted boxes).

There are several possible reasons for the absence of expected relationships. The first possible reason is that there are no relationships. Second, the variables may have been operationalized incorrectly. Third, the main dependent variable, system evaluation, may have been a too global and thereby insensitive measure to allow for enough variance to make analyses meaningful. Because of this third possible reason an attempt is made to provide an inventory of the various aspects of system evaluation as they may be related to the independent variables considered here.
A suggestion provided by the results is that the direct personal functions of the system need to be elaborated upon when considering system evaluation. These functions will differ with individual perceptions of the system: as a source of happiness, of economic well-being, of socio-economic approval or acceptance, of financial security or as a source of income guaranteeing subsistence only. These perceptions may be expressed in evaluations ranging from very/too generous to very/too restrictive. Personal functions may also refer to presumed

societal effects of the system: it may be instrumental in guarding the political and social stability. Corresponding evaluations pertain to, for example, the lack of clarity of system operation, the amount of government control over the system, and the degree of random judgment presumed within the system. These perceptions may be reflected in evaluations as to the system's cost, rigidity, prejudice, and political bias.

The combinations of perceptions and evaluations may affect behavior in a variety of ways. First, the system may have an effect on an individual's feelings of financial/economic (in)dependence, on the acceptance of personal responsibility to work for income, the individual work ethic, the acceptance or approval of system fraud. Second, the system may affect the way an individual thinks other persons in society feel about (in)dependence, responsibility, work ethic, and system fraud. The various types of evaluations, perceptions, norms and values may be hypothesized to show up in actual economic behavior such as work motivation, job mobility, labor market risk taking, financial planning, economic political (voting) behavior, and the actual acceptance of the system's rules and regulations.

REFERENCES

Adams, J.S. Inequity in Social Exchange. In: L. Berkowitz, Advances in Experimental Social Psychology, Vol 2. Academic Press, 1965.

Poiesz, T. & J. Von Grumbkow. On the reliability and validity of the Individual Welfare Function of Income (WFI). Proceedings 7th Annual Colloquium of the International Association for Research in Economic Psychology, Edinburgh, 1982.

Poiesz, T. & J. Von Grumbkow. Psychological correlates of the evaluation of income-levels and -changes. Proceedings 8th Annual Colloquium of the International Association for Research in Economic Psychology, Bologna, 1983.

Rijsman, J. Sociale Vergelijking: een Theoretische Analyse. In: Rijsman, J. & J. Wilke, Sociale Vergelijking: Theorie en Onderzoek. Deventer, Van Loghum Slaterus, 1980.

Schoormans, J. & J. Von Grumbkow. Attitudes Towards Social Security; Ideology, Procedural Justice and Distributive Justice. (These Proceedings).

APPENDIX: The sample

Sex: male 79%; female 16%; no response: 7%.

Age: No persons younger than 21 years of age participated. For eachh age category (21-30, 31-40, etc. up to 65+ inclusive) the percentage was between 15 and 20, except for the 31-40 age category, which had a percentage of 30.

Marital status: 75% was married or living together; 9% was single, 15% widowed or divorced.

Education: If a crude distinction over educational levels is made, we find for the lower levels 41%, for the intermediate level 51%, and 8% universisty level.

Main source of income:

- employee salary : 64%
- professional (independent): 1%
- pension (gov't and other) : 14%
- social security benefit : 15%
- other : 6%

(Of those employed)
Government employee: yes 24%; no 76%

Breadwinner: yes 96%; no 4%

Part Seventeen
Economic Man: Who He Is, What He Knows

PASSIONS WITHIN REASON: The Strategic Role of the Emotions

Robert H. Frank

Cornell University

Introduction and Summary

Seemingly Irrational Behavior

The bloody feud between the Hatfields and McCoys began more than a century ago. It took place along the remote, mountainous border between Kentucky and West Virginia, and lasted more than 35 years. To this day, no one is sure how it actually started. But once under way, its pattern was one of alternating attacks, each a retaliation for the one preceding, and thus also the provocation for the one to follow.

On New Year's night of 1888, the Hatfields attempted to end the feud by killing the remaining members of the main branch of the McCoy family. Led by James Vance, their strategy was to set fire to the McCoy farmhouse, then shoot the McCoys as they fled from the burning building. Young Alifair McCoy was the first cut down as she emerged from the kitchen door.

> Upon hearing that Alifair had been shot, Sarah McCoy, her mother, rushed to the back door...and continued toward her dying daughter. Vance bounded toward her and struck her with the butt of his rifle. For a moment she lay on the cold ground, stunned, groaning, and crying. Finally, she raised herself on her hands and knees and tried to crawl to Alifair....she pleaded with the attackers, 'For God's sake let me go to my girl.' Then, realizing the situation, she cried, 'Oh, she's dead. For the love of God, let me go to her.' Sarah put out her hand until she could almost touch the feet of Alifair. Running down the doorsill, where Alifair had fallen, was blood from the girl's wounds. Johnse [Hatfield], who was standing against the outside wall of the kitchen, took his revolver and crushed Sarah's skull with it. She dropped to the ground and lay motionless.... (Rice, 1982, pp. 62, 63)

Although Alifair and her brother Calvin were killed, and their mother and several others in the family seriously injured, the Hatfield attack fell short. Randolph McCoy, Alifair's father, was among those who escaped.

In nineteenth century rural Kentucky and West Virginia, few citizens had faith in the power of law to resolve their disputes. So we are not surprised that the main priority of Randolph and the other McCoys in the ensuing years was to kill as many of the remaining Hatfields as they could. Before hostilities finally ended, several more members of both families lost their lives.

Where the force of law is weak, cycles of attack and revenge are familiar. They pervade life in the Middle East today and have been recorded throughout human history. Probably very few of us have not personally experienced the impulse to seek revenge. And yet the costs of acting on this impulse are often ruinous. The McCoys, or the Hatfields, could have ended the violence at any moment by not retaliating for the most recent attack. At each juncture, it was clear that to retaliate would produce still another round of bloodshed. Yet for almost four decades they persisted.

What prompts such behavior? Surely not a clear-headed assessment of self interest. If a rational action is one that serves the actor's purposes, it is manifestly irrational to retaliate in the face of such devastating costs.

The self-destructive pursuit of vengeance is not the only way we ignore our narrow, selfish interests. We trudge through snowstorms to cast our ballots, even when we are certain our votes will make no difference. We leave tips for waitresses at restaurants in distant cities we will never visit again. We make anonymous contributions to private charities. We often refrain from cheating even when we are sure we would not be caught. We sometimes walk away from profitable transactions whose terms we believe to be "unfair." We endure endless red tape merely to get a $10 refund on a defective product. And so on.

Behavior of this sort poses a fundamental challenge to those who believe that people generally act rationally. Philosophers, behavioral biologists, economists, and others have invested much effort trying to account for it. Their explanations generally call attention to some ancillary gain implicit in the seemingly irrational action. Biologists, for example, tell us that someone may give up her life to save several of her immediate relatives, thereby increasing the survival rate of genes like the ones she carries. Or, economists will explain that it makes sense for the Internal Revenue Service to spend $10,000 to prosecute someone who owes $100 in taxes, because it thereby encourages broader compliance with the tax laws. (It is often said that the explanations of economists are either obvious, like this one, or else wrong.)

Much of the time, however, there appear to be no such ancillary gains. The British stubbornly defend the Falklands, even though they have little remaining empire against which to deter future aggression. For much less than they spent in that conflict, they could have given each Falklander a Scottish castle and a generous pension for life.

Many actions, purposely taken with full knowledge of their consequences, *are* irrational. If people did not perform them, they would be better off and they know it. As will become clear, however, these same actions are often part of a larger pattern that is anything but irrational. The apparent contradiction arises not because of any hidden gains from the actions themselves, but because we face important problems that simply cannot be solved by rational action. The common feature of these problems is that they require us to make prior commitments to behave in ways that may later prove contrary to our interests.

The Commitment Problem

Thomas Schelling (1960) provides a vivid illustration of this class of problems. He describes a kidnapper who suddenly gets cold feet. He wants to set his victim free, but is afraid he will go to the police. In return for his freedom, the victim gladly promises not to do so. The problem, however, is that both realize it will no longer be in his interest to keep this promise once he is free. And so the kidnapper reluctantly concludes he must kill his victim.

Schelling (1960, pp. 43, 44) suggests the following way out of the dilemma: "If the victim has committed an act whose disclosure could lead to blackmail, he may confess it; if not, he might commit one in the presence of his captor, to create a bond that will ensure his silence." (Perhaps the victim could allow the kidnapper to photograph him in the process of some unspeakably degrading act.) The blackmailable act serves here as a "commitment device," something that provides the victim with a credible incentive to keep his promise. Keeping the promise will still be unpleasant for him once he is freed; but clearly less so than not being able to make a credible promise in the first place.

In everyday economic and social interaction, we repeatedly encounter dilemmas like the one confronting Schelling's kidnapper and victim. My thesis in this book is that specific, widely recognized elements of our tastes act as commitment devices that help resolve these dilemmas.

Consider a person who threatens to retaliate against anyone who harms him. For his threat to deter, others must believe he will carry it out. But if others know that the costs of retaliation are prohibitive, they will realize the threat is empty. Unless, of course, they believe they are dealing with someone who simply *likes* to retaliate. Such a person may strike back even when it is not in his interests to do so. But if he is known in advance to have that preference, he is not likely to be tested by aggression in the first place.

Similarly, a person who is known to "dislike" an unfair bargain can credibly threaten to walk away from one, even when it is in his narrow interests to accept it. By virtue of being known to have this preference, he becomes a more effective negotiator.

Consider, too, the person who "feels bad" when he cheats. These feelings can accomplish for him what a rational assessment of self-interest cannot-- namely, they can cause him to behave honestly even when he *knows* he could get away with cheating. And if others realize he feels this way, they will seek him as a partner in ventures that require trust.

Being known to have certain tastes enables us to make commitments that would otherwise not be credible. The clear irony here is that this ability, which springs from a *failure* to pursue self-interest, confers genuine advantages. Granted, following through on these commitments will always involve avoidable losses-- not cheating when there is a chance to, retaliating at great cost even after the damage is done, and so on. The problem, however, is that being unable to make credible commitments will in general be even more costly.

Tastes as Commitments

It is no longer controversial to say that we come into the world equipped with nervous systems that predispose us to behave in particular ways. Brain circuits that exist before birth cause a person with low levels of sugar in his bloodstream to feel hungry, and it is that feeling, not any rational meditation about goals, that prompts him to eat. Conscious thoughts may intervene, of course, as when the dieter restrains himself from eating.

But even these "conscious" interventions are themselves merely expressions of the basic motivational pattern: The dieter envisions the social consequences of being overweight, and the anxiety summoned by these images battles the competing feelings of hunger.

In addition to inborn tastes, habits, too, are an important component of motivation. So far as we know, people are not born with a taste for drinking coffee in the morning. But people who regularly do so will develop a powerful taste for it. And they will will experience real difficulty if they attempt to abandon their habit.

Innate behavior patterns and the capacity to form habits are adaptive in a broad sense. Yet a person's behavior should not be viewed as having sprung from a rational, case-by-case assesment of his interests. Rational analysis can, as noted, trigger feelings that affect behavior. It may even guide our choice of which habits to adopt. In this picture, however, the rational assessment is only one of many forces competing for the attention of the feelings that govern behavior directly.

I will say here that a person's tastes "commit" him to act in certain ways. A person who has not eaten for several days is "committed" to eat; someone who has not slept for several days is "committed" to sleep. Such commitments are not to be thought irrational just because we might be able to show in a particular case that it is not in a hungry person's interest to eat.

Within broad limits, psychological commitments of this sort are neither strictly binding nor irrevocable. They are merely incentives to behave in a particular way. The person who feels hungry and doesn't eat must endure continued hunger. The unjustly injured party who doesn't seek revenge must go on feeling outraged. A behavioral predisposition, in economic terms, is thus much like a tax on not behaving in a particular way.

Our concern here will be with the role of such tastes as conscience, anger, vengeance, envy, and even love. My claim is that these tastes often predispose us to behave in ways that are contrary to our narrow interests, and that being thus predisposed is an advantage. For it to be an advantage, others must have some way of discovering we have these tastes. But how do people know that a person's tastes commit him to behave honestly in the face of a golden opportunity to cheat? Or that a person will seek revenge, even when it is too late to undo the injury he has suffered? Or that a person really will walk away from an unfair bargain, even when he would do better by accepting it? Much of the evidence I will later discuss concerns the subtle clues by which we infer such behavioral predispositions in others.

Clues to Behavioral Predispositions

One fall day, some fifteen years ago, black activist Ron Dellums was the speaker at a large rally on the University of California campus in Berkeley. Polls suggested he would soon become the Berkeley-North Oakland district's first radical Congressman. Crowds were easily galvanized in those days, and this one was in especially high spirits. But at least one young man was not moved by Dellums's speech. He sat still as a stone on the steps of Sproul Plaza, lost to some drug, his face and eyes empty of expression.

Presently a large Irish Setter appeared, sniffing his way through the crowd. He moved directly to the young man sitting on the steps and circled him once. He paused, lifted his leg, and, with no apparent malice, soaked the young man's back. He then set off again into the crowd. The boy didn't stir.

Now, the Irish Setter is not a particularly intelligent breed. Yet this one had no difficulty locating the one person in that crowd who would not retaliate for being used as a fire hydrant. Facial expressions and other aspects of demeanor apparently provide clues to behavior that even dogs can interpret. And although none of us had ever witnessed such a scene before, no one was really surprised when the boy did nothing. Before anything even happened, it was somehow *obvious* that he was just going to go right on sitting there.

Without doubt, however, the boy's behavior was unusual. Most of us would have responded angrily, some of us even violently. Yet we already know that no real advantage inheres in this "normal" response. After all, once the boy's shirt was soaked, it was already too late to undo the damage. And since he was unlikely ever to encounter that particular dog again, there was little point in trying to teach the dog a lesson.

Our young man's problem was not that he failed to respond angrily, but that he failed to communicate to the dog that he was predisposed to do so. The vacant expression on his face was somehow all the information the dog needed to know he was a safe target. Merely by wearing "normal" expressions, the rest of us were spared.

A burgeoning literature describes how we draw inferences about people's feelings from subtle behavioral clues. Posture, the rate of respiration, the pitch and timbre of the voice, perspiration, facial muscle tone and expression, movement of the eyes, and a host of other signals guide us in this task. We quickly surmise, for example, that someone with clenched jaws and a purple face is enraged, even when we do not know what, exactly, may have triggered his anger. And we apparently know, even if we cannot articulate, how a forced smile differs from one that is heartfelt.

At least partly on the basis of such clues, we form judgements about the emotional makeup of the people with whom we deal. Some people we feel we can trust, but of others we remain ever wary. Some we feel can be taken advantage of, others we know instinctively not to provoke.

Being able to make such judgments accurately has always been an obvious advantage. But it is often no less an advantage that others be able to make similar assesments about our own propensities. A blush may reveal a lie and cause great embarrassment at the moment. But in circumstances that require trust, there can be great advantage in being known to be a blusher.

The Problem of Mimicry

If there are genuine advantages in being vengeful or trustworthy and being perceived as such, there are even greater advantages in appearing to have, but not actually having, these qualities. A liar who appears trustworthy will have better opportunities to cheat than one who glances about furtively, sweats profusely, speaks in a quavering voice, and has difficulty making eye contact. Critics often warn against being taken in by Ronald Reagan's comforting facade, that beneath its veneer he is no more to be trusted than Richard Nixon. He is an actor, they say, and it is his job to persuade us he feels things he doesn't. (We must assume these critics never saw "Bedtime for Bonzo.")

I have no reason to question Ronald Reagan's honesty. We do know, however, that there are people who can lie convincingly. Adolf Hitler was apparently such a person. In a September,1938, meeting, Hitler promised British Prime Minister Neville Chamberlain that he would not go to war if the borders of Czechoslovakia were redrawn to meet his demands. Following that meeting, Chamberlain wrote in a letter to his sister: "... in spite of the hardness and ruthlessness I thought I saw in his face, I got the impression that here was a man who could be relied upon when he gave his word..." (Ekman, pp. 15-16).

Clues to behavioral predispositions are obviously not perfect. Even with the aid of all of their sophisticated machinery, experienced professional polygraph experts cannot be sure when someone is lying. Some emotions are more difficult to simulate than others. Someone who feigns outrage is apparently easier to catch than someone who pretends to feel joyful. But no matter what the emotion, we can almost never be certain.

Indeed, the forces at work are such that it will always be possible for at least *some* people to succeed at deception. In a world in which no one cheated, no one would be on the lookout against being deceived. And a climate thus lacking in vigilance would obviously create profitable opportunities for cheaters. So there will inevitably be a niche for at least some of them.

Useful lessons about the nature of this problem are contained in the similar instances of mimicry that abound in nature. There are butterflies, such as the monarch, whose strategy for defending themselves against predators is to have developed a foul taste. This taste would be useless unless predators had some way of telling which butterflies to avoid. Thus the monarch has developed a conspicuous pattern of wing markings that its predators have learned to interpret for this purpose.

This has created a profitable opportunity for mutant butterflies, such as the viceroy, who bear similar wing markings but lack the bad taste that normally accompanies them. Merely by looking like the unpalatable monarchs, viceroys have escaped predation without having had to expend the bodily resources needed to produce the objectionable taste itself.

In such instances, it is clear that if mimics could *perfectly* simulate the wing marking with neither cost nor delay, the entire edifice would collapse: The comparatively efficient mimics would eventually overwhelm the others, and the predators' original reason for avoiding that particular marking would thereby vanish. So in cases where mimics coexist alongside the genuine article for extended periods, we may infer that perfect mimicry either takes time or entails substantial costs. The fact that the bearer of the genuine trait has the first move in this game will often prove a decisive advantage.

Similar considerations apply in the case of those who mimic emotional traits. If the signals we use for detecting these traits had no value, we would have long since ceased to rely on them. And yet, by their very nature, they cannot be perfect. For if they were, it would never pay anyone to cheat, and so no one would spend the effort required to scrutinize them. In which case, again, it *would* pay people to cheat.

The inevitable result is an uneasy balance between people who really possess these traits and others who merely seem to. Those who are adept at reading the relevant signals will be more successful than others. There is also a payoff to those who are able to send effective signals about their own behavioral predispositions. And, sad to say, the biggest payoff may go to those who are skillful at pretending to have feelings they really lack.

This outcome is at once in harmony with the view that self-interest underlies all action and with the opposing view that people often transcend their selfish tendencies. The key to resolving the tension between these views is to understand that the ruthless pursuit of self-interest is often incompatible with its attainment. As Zen masters have known intuitively for thousands of years, the best outcome is sometimes possible only when people abandon the chase. Here, we will see that self-interest often requires commitments to behave in ways that will later prove deeply contrary to our interests.

Much of the time, the practical means for accomplishing these commitments will be tastes that have observable symptoms. I will later survey persuasive evidence that at least some of these tastes are inborn. But even if they were transmitted only by cultural indoctrination, they would serve equally well. What is necessary in either case is that people who have these tastes be observably different, on the average, from those who lack them.

Moral philosophers have invested great effort trying to show that honesty is the best policy. Yet none has argued persuasively that a person will do better by not cheating when it is certain he will not be caught. The reason is simply that he will *not* do better. There is a perfectly coherent reason, however, why a rational, selfish agent might choose to have a conscience. And once possessed of a conscience, it will be his *emotions,* not any rational calculation, that prevents him from cheating. Except for that fact, he could never be genuinely trustworthy.

The logic of the commitment problem thus suggests that the locus of moral behavior lies not in rational analysis but in the emotions. This view is consistent with an extensive body of empirical evidence reviewed by Kagan (1984). As he summarizes his interpretation of that evidence (p. xiv):

> Construction of a persuasive rational basis for behaving morally has been the problem on which most moral philosophers have stubbed their toes. I believe they will continue to do so until they recognize what

> Chinese philosophers have known for a long time: namely, feeling, not logic, sustains the superego.

The emotions may indeed sustain the superego. But as the nature of the commitment problem will make clear, it is the logic of self-interest that ultimately sustains these emotions.

The Importance of Tastes

Tastes have important consequences for action. The standard model of rational choice posits certain tastes and constraints, and then calculates what actions will best further those tastes. This model is widely used by economists and other social scientists, game theorists, military strategists, philosophers, and others. Its results influence decisions that affect all of us. In its standard form, it assumes purely self-interested tastes; namely, for present and future consumption goods of various sorts, leisure, and so on. Envy, guilt, rage, honor, and the like typically play no role.

The inclusion of these tastes, and others that help solve commitment problems, substantially alters the predictions of standard models. We will see that it may pay people to feel envious, because feeling that way makes them better bargainers. But people who feel envious will accept different jobs, earn different salaries, spend them in different ways, save different amounts, and vote for different laws than predicted by standard models.

Feelings of envy are also closely linked to feelings about fairness. And without taking feelings about fairness into account, we cannot hope to predict what prices stores will charge, what wages workers will demand, how long business executives will resist a strike, what taxes governments will levy, how fast military budgets will grow, or whether a union leader will be reelected.

The presence of conscience also alters the predictions of standard models. These models predict clearly that when interactions between people are not repeated, people will cheat if they can get away with it. Yet evidence consistently shows that most people do not cheat under these circumstances. Standard models also suggest that the owner of a small business will not contribute to the lobbying efforts of the Small Business Administration. Like one man's vote, his own contribution will seem too small a part of the total to make any difference. Yet many small businesses do pay dues to the Small Business Administration, and many people do vote. Charitable institutions also exist on a far grander scale than would ever be predicted by standard models.

There is nothing mystical about the emotions that drive these behaviors. On the contrary, they are an obvious part of most people's psychological makeup. What I hope to show here is that their presence is in perfect harmony with the underlying requirements of a coherent theory of rational behavior.

The standard version of the rational choice model has proven its usefulness for understanding and predicting human behavior. But it remains seriously incomplete. Most analysts regard "irrational" behavior motivated by the emotions as lying beyond the scope of the model. But it is neither necessary nor productive to adopt this view. With careful attention to the things people care about, we can greatly enrich our understanding of why we behave as we do.

ECONOMIC MEASUREMENT, PUBLIC POLICY, AND HUMAN COGNITION: AN ANALYTICAL FRAMEWORK

Loretta Graziano, California State University

Abstract

Economic measurement generates single numbers which symbolically represent complex phenomena: inflation rates, unemployment rates, deficit totals. These bits of information are often the focus of public policy discourse. Public opinion on such policy issues results from the human cognitive processing of information inputs. That is, economic measurement is the raw material from which individuals build internal representations of external events. Individual cognitions of policy problems are subject to all the limitations of human cognition demonstrated by laboratory research. Thus, the science of human information processing provides a tool for identifying systematic weaknesses in widely-shared cognitions of policy problems.

To operationalize this tool, four cognitive limitations or "pitfalls" of human information processing are synthesized from the literature in neurophysiology and cognitive psychology. These cognitive behaviors are then used to distinguish, for a variety of economic phenomena, the subset of available data that individuals are most likely to perceive, and the meaning such perceptual cues are likely to evoke for the individual. In conclusion, the scope of this cognitive approach to policy analysis is extended from the "decoding" of public affairs information to the "encoding" process. The public's preference for information inputs that have already been encoded into familiar symbols and structures by social institutions such as press, politics and professions, is evaluated.

ECONOMIC MEASUREMENT, PUBLIC POLICY, AND HUMAN COGNITION: AN ANALYTICAL FRAMEWORK

Policy discourse is often provoked by a piece of information: the latest unemployment rate, the latest reading scores, the lastest toxic waste analysis. The discipline of economics in particular focuses on generating a single numerical symbol to represent a complex phenomenon: unemployment, inflation, the deficit. However, information is only significant in the context of human perception and inference, which build internal cognitions from external events. The nature of human information processing has been illuminated by a vast accumulation of research in neurophysiology and cognitive psychology. Such work demonstrates that the faculties which render human cognition powerful also dispose it to systematic error. Thus we would expect such error to be manifest in the cognitions of public affairs that individuals build from economic measurements. From this perspective, public opinion on economic policy issues reflects the limitations of human faculties for building internal representations from external data.

Are inappropriate cognitions at the core of economic policy problems that resist protracted attempts at solution?

Can the democratic process endure a consistent discrepancy between external events and individual cognitions of them?

Human cognition is a key variable in the policy making process. Because it has advanced from philosophical to scientific inquiry, it should be regarded as an essential tool for economic policy analysis.

This paper develops an analytical framework to examine the role of human information processing in public affairs. The framework serves as a guide to identifying probable weaknesses in the cognitions of societal (particularly economic) phenomena that are widely-held by the public. Four limitations or "pitfalls" of human information processing are synthesized from the empirical findings of the cognitive sciences. Each cognitive behavior is clarified with intuitive examples from daily experience, since our information processing apparatus operates without conscious awareness. [1] Then, the impact of each limitation on widely-shared cognitions of economic events. Specifically, insights are generated into 1.) which subset of the available data is most likely to be incorporated into individual cognitions of external events; and 2.) what meaning those perceptual cues are likely to evoke in the context of previously-stored associations.

Although the focus here is on the shortcomings of human cognition, these faculties must also be understood as the source of human intelligence. The human mind's power is rooted in its efficiency--the ability to extract meaning from the infinite array of sensory stimulation provided by the environment. The parsimony of mental activity renders it vastly more powerful than the intuitive model of human thought: a camera and a computer. If the mind registered environmental detail like a camera, rather than limiting its scope to the most important cues, our interpretive "computer" would quickly be overloaded, making even the simplest task impossible. Indeed, when children do not learn from the aimless explorations of infancy to purposively focus their senses, they are labelled learning disabled, hyperactive, even autistic. Similarly, the mind-as-computer model fails because programmed logic can only perform repetitive tasks, while the mind faces new combinations of stimuli each day. With each passing decade of research in artificial intelligence, the task of programming computers to imitate human processing of novel cue patterns seems more arduous.

Human cognition thus achieves power from its ability to selectively perceive sensory cues, and to find meaningful associations for novel stimuli. Indiviual cognitions of economic affairs are not the same as the camera's and the computer's picture of the economy. By understanding the mechanics of human cognition, policy analysts can understand how public opinion is built from economic measurement.

Four basic cognitive behaviors can be distilled from the literature on human information processing:

1. The mind relies on <u>symbols</u> or representative cue patterns stored in memory to identify perceptual stimuli.
2. The mind imposes <u>structures</u> or organizational frameworks on perceptual experience to facilitate the matching of incoming and stored patterns.
3. The mind's <u>search</u> of the perceptual environment is <u>motivated</u> by expectations retrieved spontaneously from memory when provoked by contextual cues.
4. The mind <u>resists revision</u> of neurally-stored patterns, and strives to adjust rather than replace them in the presence of new or conflicting information.

This analysis focuses on the limitations or "pitfalls" inherent in each of these. [2]

Reification of Symbol

The human mind experiences the external environment as stimulation of the perceptual organs, and electrical activation of corresponding neurons in the brain. A cluster of stimuli perceived simultaneously (eg. the word "CAT"), causes an electrical charge to travel a pathway between the neurons representing each perceptual cue. The perceiver associates this pathway, among the infinite possible circuits through the mind's jungle of neurons, with the presence of that particular cluster of stimuli. As in any jungle, slashing a new path is extremely difficult. Each time that path is travelled passage becomes easier, until finally the path becomes a trail which travellers will even detour to follow rather than carving a new path. In the same way, each electrical activation of a neural pathway builds up a chemical bridge between connecting neurons, making that circuit more easily triggered in the future. In this way, frequently-encountered configurations of perceptual cues are "consolidated," or stored, in "long term memory." Bridges are only built between the most recurrent cues rather than the unique variations of each individual encounter with the stimulus. Therefore stored neural patterns are by nature representative or "symbolic."

Stored patterns increase the efficiency of cognition for two reasons: 1.) Familiar patterns occupy only one slot in our limited buffer or "short term memory," while an unfamiliar configuration of stimuli would take up several slots. For example, laboratory subjects have difficulty remembering more than about seven random letters, but they can also remember seven random words though each comprises many letters.

2.) Once meaning is inferred from a familiar cluster of perceptual cues, the mind tends to move on to the next stimulus rather than inspect all the associated details.

For example, studies find only three cues necessary to recognize the capital letter "A": the two points where the horizontal meets the verticals, and the point where the two verticals meet.

Thus recognition is possible whether the "A" is eroded on a buried ruin, done in calligraphy on a diploma, or composed of dancing girls on a stage.

Reification of symbol describes the mind's tendency to see patterns in the environment that correspond to the ones stored in long term memory, and to ignore differences between the two. This cognitive behavior was first described by linguists, who observed that once a word is learned to label a phenomenon, future perception is altered. One becomes more likely to perceive the environmental details he has a label for, and less likely to perceive details that conflict with, or bear no relation to his stock of stored symbols. Because the matching of internal with external patterns is highly automatic, we experience ourselves not as substituting familiar symbols for the more irregular cues in the environment, but as registering exactly what is there. [3]

Familiar symbols are often used to communicate public affairs information, thus disposing individuals toward perceiving one subset of data about the issue, and ignoring others. For example, the Department of Labor's unemployment rate is a widely-shared symbolic representation of the employment situation. Though this statistic only represents incidences of unemployment that conform to a restrictive definition, it tends to substitute in public cognitions for the overall situation. Individuals are thus less inclined to perceive and interpret the data that are left out of or conflict with this symbolic construct, such as information about "discouraged" workers, involuntary part-timers, and employment in the unreported or "underground" sector. This behavior is well-illustrated outside our own society, where a different set of stored associations for employment-related cues are taken for granted. In developing nations, for example, unemployment is regarded is an urban problem, and stark indications of perpetual underemployment in rural areas escape public notice. Alternatively, in Marxist systems, unemployment is considered a disease of ("sick") capitalist societies, and individual incidences of joblessness and widespread underemployment are not conceived as part of a nationwide phenomenon.

Designing a symbol is thus an effective way to enhance perception of existing information. "Social safety net" points attention toward ongoing aspects of welfare programs rather than the aspects that are cut. Seizing the appropriate label for a phenomenon can catalyze action: once the term "farm parity" was attached to data representing rural-urban income disparity, nothing less than "100% parity" would do. New symbols are sometimes introduced to mitigate the retrieval of old associations: "depression" was coined to avoid the emotional overtones of the earlier "panic"; it quickly developed associations of its own, so now "recession" substitutes for mild depression. Consensus on national goals is often achieved by crafting symbols such as "Great Society" or "New Deal," which everyone can imbue with their own meaning. In developing countries, national objectives are often expressed as a particular percentage growth rate, a uni-dimensional symbol that can stand in for more controversial information about the methods and trade-offs along the way. [4]

Is it dishonest to symbolically represent a mouthwash or breakfast cereal as "healthy," or cigarettes as merely "hazardous" to the health? In each case, the consumer could easily adjust this piece of information with an abundance of additional data about the product. But, cognizant of our symbol-reifying tendencies, we create public institutions to monitor the truthfulness of the ultimate cognition that commercial messages evoke, rather than the ostensible message. This holds the communicator responsible for anticipating the meaning inferred by the public. In some cases we go on to shift the task of symbol-building from buyer and seller to the public sector: for gas mileage and interest rates, regulation creates consistent symbols so the consumer need not inspect each enterprise's method of calculation (the "EPA" mileage ratings and truth-in-lending codes); and then actively addresses the consumer's tendency to overlook some information (the obligatory warning "your mileage may differ," and the requirement that borrowers sign a statement declaring that they have been informed of interest obligations calculated according to the prescribed method).

Symbols can satisfy the desire for action, and obscure the limitations of that action, when solutions to a problem are still unknown. For example, investors took great losses from unexpected high inflation in the 70's, and now perceive a great need for any information indicating a resurgence of inflation. Their vigilance is concentrated on the symbolic measure of the money supply (M1, M2, etc.), responding to its movements with frenzied buying and selling. Factions furiously disagree on whether salvation lies in large or small increases in this symbol, but they remain unanimous in their cognitive drive to replace the millions of economic decisions behind inflationary pressure, and the thousands of alternative details about the money supply, with attention to a uni-dimensional symbol.

President Reagan demonstrated an intuition for the public's symbol-reifying behavior when he hailed the rise of full employment from 4% to 6 or 8% unemployment. This would appear to be bad news, because "full employment" is the level of unemployment economists expected to persist at the end of a recession. But Reagan understood the public's stored meaning for this familiar symbol--everything below this rate "doesn't count" (an artifact of the theory that cyclical unemployment is susceptible to policy instruments like aggregate demand management, while structural unemployment is not). Therefore, conceptually raising full employment to 8% automatically knocks 4% off the perceived level of unemployment. [5] Because "structural unemployment" is not a familiar symbol, related data play a limited role in public cognitions, though by the President's own accounting it represents more than half of total unemployment.

Reification of Structure

Before the mind can recognize a familiar symbol or pattern in a cluster of perceptual cues, it must first carve up the amorphous flood of external stimuli into discrete clusters. Cognitive activity is constantly classifying and dichotomizing in order to extract meaning from an environment which is subtle and complex. Structuring reduces the details of external phenomena to the essential properties necessary to relate or distinguish the perceptual data. Two physiological traits underlie this cognitive behavior. First, information in long term memory is accessible because it is stored in relational networks. Projecting these same relations onto external stimuli is the same as thinking about the papers on your desk in terms of which file you are going to put them in. Second, stimuli are structured because the sensory organs only register <u>changes</u> in a stimulus rather than its absolute level. The contrast between an old and new level of a sensory cue is the information that renders it cognitively meaningful. One experiences this when noticing that a white wall has yellowed only after lifting a painting, or becoming aware of an annoying background noise only when the noise stops.

Cognitive structuring explains why it is easier to remember a telephone number with a pattern in it, and why we see the rainbow as distinct colors though light is a continuum of frequencies. Continuums, threshholds, and bipolar oppositions are familiar cognitive structures. They impose meaning on a mass of unfamiliar cues by focusing the mind on essential relationships among groups of cues. A continuum simplifies complex external phenomena, such as a student's retention of a lesson, or a consumer's satisfaction with a toothpaste, into shades of a single property. A threshhold focuses meaning on a particular point or level in a series of data, so that we think of people as "over 18," "nearing 65," "'still' 30," though we certainly know that people age an equal amount each day. A bipolar opposition derives meaning from the difference between two symbolic extremes—national defense are either "strong" or "weak," and economists are either "Keynsian" or "monetarist."

Individuals are not aware that their interpretation of a perceptual cue is influenced by its position in a structure. The mind perceives categories and dichotomies as being an objective part of the external phenomenon. As a result, once the mind has imposed a cognitive structure on a set of stimuli, it has difficulty perceiving alternative structures or organizations of the data. Thus, our faculty for carving up perceptual phenomena and concentrating on relationships both expands but distorts our information processing capacity. Reification of structure describes the tendency to overemphasize differences in the information we have categorized; to overlook information that doesn't fit the superimposed structure; to perceive categorical distinctions as real phenomena rather than as interpretive devices; and to ignore alternative relational structures in a mass of stimuli. We are cognitively disposed to underrepresent the features of an external event lying far from a threshhold point, between bipolar opposites, or unrelated to the property of a continuum.

Reification of structure has a dignified heritage, dating from Aristole's assertion that knowing the categories of existence is knowledge itself. The idea that categories are merely a heurism for grasping reality was introduced by eighteenth-century philosophers such as Immanuel Kant, and demonstrated inter-culturally by anthropologists such as Claude Levi-Strauss. The natural sciences have not only cautioned the observer's role in structuring his own perception of the universe (eg. Heisenberg's paradox), but have cosmically quantified it (eg. Einstein's theory of relativity). Nevertheless, in order to function on a daily basis, we sustain the impression that the breakdown of perceptual stimuli is inherent in the nature of things.

Structure is often reified in our understanding of social reality. Our mania for structuring nations as "communist" or "free" overlooks most of the world--the socialist democracies and the free market dictatorships; and it limits our leaders to two foreign policy alternatives: "soft" or "tough" on communism. We seek many qualities in a political candidate, but we focus primarily on the qualities that conform to a continuum ranging from liberal Democrat to conservative Republican. Investors often focus on the range of yields for alternative investments, and cognitively underweigh cues representing their range of risk, liquidity, transactions cost, and tax consequences. Our cognitive reliance on the "poverty line" as a discrete threshhold of family income has left our social service programs without a policy approach to the "working poor." Because the mind cannot solve simultaneous equations, familiar frameworks are relied on for sorting and interpreting the details of the environment.

Cognitive threshholds explain why "double digit" inflation and unemployment provoke more interest than do rates just below this level. These economic phenomena generally succumb to a bi-polar representation, resulting in the conviction that inflation can only be cured by increasing unemployment, and that more inflation automatically reduces unemployment. Unemployment is commonly represented by carving up workers demographically, inclining us to perceive joblessness as the product of age, sex, race and geographic region. Alternate breakdowns of the unemployment scene are rarely discussed, or even acknowledged, although alternative dichotomies might produce alternative insights into the problem. For example, the unemployed could be categorized by hardship indicators rather than demographic indicators, such as number of weeks out of work, or availability of alternative sources of family income. Solution-oriented indicators are also possible, such as a classification scheme based on skill level, or on training requirements. Other cultures, again, provide an alternative to the cognitions we take for granted: the Swedes use a single structure to classify data on job seekers and job openings; and the Canadians collect periodic information on workers displaced by plant closings to monitor when and how they re-enter the workforce.

The news media exist by structuring the amorphous reality of public affairs into discrete, familiar events. As a result, ongoing turbulence or oppression in a foreign country is more likely to be mass-communicated once it can be represented as "X number killed"--the critical threshhold depending on their prominence or the drama accompanying their demise. It is less cognitively demanding to perceive yet another occurrence of the familiar symbol, "political violence," and embellish it with stored associations, than to interpret the unstructured, complex interplay of social forces which caused the unrest. Similarly, the ongoing story of the budget deficit is structured as a bottom-line number on a tally sheet, as neat but arbitrary threshholds such as $100 billion and $1 trillion, as welfare cheats and corporate tax-dodgers. This simple structure stands in for the reality of millions of little spending and taxing decisions, each responding to a maze of pressures and interests, some of them our own! In the media's shorthand depiction of events, enduring social problems are a simple tug-of-war: worker vs. manager, landlord vs. tenant, consumer vs. investor. Bi-lateral oppositions convey the idea that people are unemployed because they were layed off; that people are homeless because they were evicted; that inflation is caused by price increases. [6] Complex causes and alternative solutions get left out of the cognitive fabric.

Motivation of Search

We have seen that meaning occurs when the mind is able to match a cue pattern activated by the sensory organs with a cue pattern stored in memory. Cognition would not be very efficient if the mind had to search its entire bank of stored representations to come up with an appropriate match for each stimulus. Instead, retrieval (that is, electrical activation) of appropriate stored patterns is guided by clues inherent in the preceding stimulus. Each cluster of incoming cue supplies contextual information which activates a stored pattern for the next cue. As a result, an expected match is generated before the senses actually register the external stimulus. In fact, expectations (electrically-activated neural trails) guide the senses to search for corresponding patterns; that is, expectations motivate search.

Because environmental data vary infinitely, a "match" is never exact. We are constantly making an instantaneous choice between accepting an imperfectly-matched stored meaning and moving on to the next cue, or allocating more cognitive attention to finding a better match for the present one. The decision is part probabilistic (is the oncoming vehicle on a dark night more likely to be a motorcycle or a car with one light broken?); and part cost-maximizing (how does the cost of re-examining the cues compare to the cost of assuming it's a motorcycle and being wrong?).

The presence of expectations is experienced when encountering a typographical error--perceptual data that mismatches the pattern triggered by intital reading of the sentence. (For example: "The tree is very bug.") To decide whether you misunderstood the sentance or have found a misprint, you re-examine the perceptual cues, and search your memory for alternative patterns that explain them more successfully. You are aware of the shift in gears, from automatic to conscious pattern-matching ("passive" to "active synthesizing"), because the latter requires much more cognitive effort.

Fortunately, expectations are often correct, thanks to the significant amount of overlap and repetition in environmental stimuli. Because passive synthesizing requires less time and effort than active, it frees us to process more and know more about our environment. However, by biasing us in favor of existing knowledge, it can also distort or retard learning of new information. When confronted with a novel perceptual environment, we are more likely to extract data that match expectations that an alternative set of equally, or perhaps more significant data. And when confronted with a discrepancy between a cue pattern in memory and a cue pattern in the senses, we are more likely to accept the stored pattern than the perceived one. As a result, our internal cognitions of external reality may respresent some things incorrectly, and leave out other things entirely. Expectations do evolve in compelling situations, but unexpected information remains less likely to be perceived, and less likely to be interpreted when perceived.

The motivation of search is important to our cognitions of social reality. For example, Americans expect variety in individual capabilities, and we mete out praise and blame by perceiving links between broad events and individual actions. In Japan, a high level of homogeneity is expected, and information linking outcomes to individual as opposed to group efforts is rarely perceived. Similarly, Americans measure the intelligence of their children, and this data plays a key role in teachers' perceptions of children. By definition, some of the tested children must fall way below "average." We maintain widely-shared cue patterns to identify a child as "retarded", and indeed succeed at finding many children to fit this expectation. In China, the symbolic construct, "retarded," does not exist, and a child generating the same information would merely elicit the cognition that he needs more help from his comrades than he has been getting.

Since the Great Depression, Americans expect their chief executive to have a strong impact on individual welfare. As a result, people find information linking their household ups and downs to presidential decisions. Indeed, presidents and presidential candidates strive to generate such expectations, seeking to motivate voter perception of a particular subset of information about their present lot in life. More likely, one's individual circumstances (the value of one's home, the prosperity of one's employer) are as heavily affected by local and global forces outside the President's control, but in our cognitions he is not replaced with the mayor or the Prime Minister of Japan. On the other hand, a large volume of information about the Federal Reserve Chairman's impact on individual welfare is not explained by past expectations, and may provoke new ones.

Widely-held expectations provide perceptual consensus of a problem and so facilitate action. Cognitions of how big a Federal deficit is "too big" depend on which subset of information is perceived: the total deficit compared to past year totals? to other countries? to local government budgetary surpluses? to military spending or to welfare spending? as a percent of GNP or of total spending? resulting interest in future year budgets? Until public expectations converge on, and ignore, the same cluster of external cues, deficit-cutting action may be delayed. A lack of widely-shared expectations may obscure not only solutions, but entire problems. For example, most people perceive the headlining symbolic indicators of the economy while ignoring direct sensory information such as the daily sight of empty downtown storefronts. [7] Everyone grumbles about the state of the roads they drive, but most people ignored their sensory input until they saw a few bridges collapse on the nightly news and heard a few legislators invoke the "infrastructure issue." Once these cues evoked perceptual search for the information, and carved a cognitive niche to organize it when found, the infrastructure suddenly seemed to be crumbling. But, to the extent individuals rely on press and politics to generate expectations, this cognition will fade when the infrastructure issue is no longer "hot," with hardly a girder reinforced.

The American expectation of creeping "world communism" serves to organize the wealth of perceptual data on revolutionary activity in the Third World. We are motivated to search for and find the subset of information about Eastern bloc arming of anti-government forces, and about the restraints such revolutions impose on our multinationals. Our cognitive representations of three quarters of the world omit the more voluminous but unexpected data about these rebellions: the ubiquitous corruption and human rights violations of the regimes they oppose; their aspirations for economic sovreignty, not Soviet alliance; their acceptance of Soviet assistance as a last resort after sanction by the US, and being charged cash by less-ideological Europeans; and the meaninglessness of the symbol "free market economy" in a subsistence or barter economy, where the nation's entire GNP is less than each of the multinationals it is trucking with.

Resistance to Revision

Repeated exposure to unexpected data eventually provokes attention and recognition. New stored patterns may emerge when old ones prove inadequate, but the process is not analogous to finding a bug in a computer program and fixing it. The mind may be aware of the bug for a long time without doing anything about it, and when it does, new commands are added to the "program" without removing the faulty ones.

The mind has difficulty discarding old information, even when new information is discovered to be more appropriate. This is because neural pathways are so highly interconnected, with newer ones layered on old, that eliminating a cue pattern stored in long term memory would involve rerouting an enormous number of circuits. (You have experienced the associative layering of stored knowledge if you have eliminated an otherwise-acceptable baby name because you can't think of it without bringing a certain person to mind.) So new patterns are added by storing them alongside old ones, not replacing them. The old meaning is preserved but the new one supplements and adjusts. The future presence of the problem with stimulus will activate the old pattern, which in turn activates the new one, and together they infuse meaning. The resulting vision of the world is equivalent to putting eyeglasses on top of your contact lenses when you need a new prescription.

This cognitive behavior is efficient but problematic, because we tend to experience the adjusted cognition as less real or less correct than the old familiar one. [8] Expectations that emerge effortlessly seem more valid than the adjusting pattern invoked with a bit of cognitive effort. Everyone who has driven on the left-hand side of the road has had this experience. You prepare by rehearsing your movements--how you will look over your right shoulder instead of your left when leaving the curb, and check on the left before making a right hand turn. But despite the effort to activate the circuits you "know" are correct, it feels wrong when you try to carry it out. And you probably respond to the perception of an oncoming car on a country road by swerving the wrong way. A similar experience would be driving a car with unfamiliar gear shift positions or typing on a different keyboard: you know you're giving your hands the right instructions, but it "feels" wrong. Because resolving a discrepancy between stored and sensory patterns is cognitively laborious, and the result is unrewarding, we tend to make less than full use of new information when we do perceive it.

Formally-trained experts have a greater number of stored patterns to explain environmental data than do non-specialists. And they have consolidated these patterns systematically, as an integrated body of knowledge, or "paradigm" (such as "Newtonian" physics, "Freudian" psychology, "Keynsian" economics); whereas non-specialist learning is more individual and experiential. Nevertheless, professional interpretive frameworks are equally resistant to revision, and because the public relied on experts to process of new information, their cognitive limitations are introduced into widely-shared representations of reality. The implications of rigid expert paradigms has its classic case in the natural sciences, where "discoveries" (eg. X-rays, oxygen) often come from old data. Science history shows that because old paradigms resist revision, better explanations of discrepant data rarely emerge before the ascendence of a new generation trained <u>after</u> the discovery of the unexpected data. [9] In the policy process, such "paradigm shift" must succeed twice in order to correct widely-shared cognitions of external events: first within the profession, and then among the public.

The symbol "gross national product" has long resisted revision, both in public cognitions and as the core of the modern paradigm for economic management. The symbol is widely-acknowledged as a poor respresentation of external reality, because it overlooks environmental quality, social justice, and security from violence, illness, and unemployment. Nevertheless, no other widely-used symbol has emerged to represent both material output and "quality of life." Instead, we continue to rely on "GNP," but along with this symbol we evoke the expectation of its limitations. Sometimes GNP information is systematically adjusted, but adjustments generally play a supporting rather than a primary role in the cognitions built from the information. Similarly, the symbolic "household" has long provided a convenient way to structure data for economic analysis and social policy. Though the preponderance of single person, single parent, and two-career households is often noted, they are cognitively just exceptions to a policy framework still rooted in the vanishing traditional household.

The same is true for the Dow Jones Industrial Average--everyone knows that the thirty firms it tracks are not representative of the entire economy. Many broader indexes have become available, but these are generally used to adjust rather than replace the perception inferred from the Dow. Inflation-adjusted data suffer the same problem. Everyone knows that cognitions built on nominal dollars are false when inflation is high, but data reported in nominal dollars seem "more real." We tend to build our perceptions of value by adjusting nominal dollar data with a vague sense of its limitations, rather than basing perceptions on the mathematically-adjusted data now widely-available. Inconsistent evidence is not enough to prevent the mind from retrieving old meanings for perceptual cues.

DISCUSSION

The policy process is driven not by information, but by the internal representations that our cognitive apparatus builds from information. A cognitive perspective highlights the role of stored patterns in perception and interpretation of the social world. In the examples presented, stored associations often restricted the focus of public consideration to a small slice of available information, and sustained public acceptance of ineffective, ill-fitting interpretations of the information. The result: the nature of a problem poorly understood; solutions off-target; new evidence provided by policy failures or new developments obscured, while faulty analyses endure; and an absence of insight into the cycle. The label "cognitive impasse" might be applied to the policy quagmires associated with widely-shared inappropriate cognitions of underlying events. The proposed model of cognitive behavior would predict this condition whenever old problems undergo substantial change, because corresponding symbols and structures are likely to be static; and whenever new problems arise, because familiar patterns fail to recognize and interpret essential data. Cognitive impasse explains the persistent imposition of stored patterns such as "cyclical unemployment" and "average household income" onto the perceptual cues rising from a city of silent factories.

Although cognitions are the joint product of external data and human information processing, this study has focused exclusively on the latter. External data have been assumed to exist objectively and independently. However, in the foregoing examples of public affairs data, the reader may have noted a distinct correspondence between the nature of the data and our cognitive preference for familiar symbols and structures. Some consideration of how the flow of societal events is transformed into sensory inputs is essential for a cognitive approach to policy analysis.

Direct sensory experience is of course one source of input into public cognitions: the length of the line at the unemployment office provides the observer with some information on the employment problem. However, because public affairs are by definition beyond the scope of individual experience, individuals must rely heavily on information communicated by others. Theorists describe communication as the selection of message cues by encoders for the purpose of transmitting meaning to decoders. [10] For example, a newspaper account of the latest unemployment rate represents sensory input encoded by news editors who narrate the data, government agents who collect the data, and economists who design procedures for collecting the data.

In our society, institutions such as press, politics and professions design and disseminate an abundance of messages which supplement direct sensory experience of public affairs. The availability of information already structured and symbolized by these encoders means that individual cognitions of public affairs need not draw on raw detail. To the extent that such institutionally-encoded messages are mass-communicated, they must be in the form of symbols and structures that are convenient to transmit and decode. In the context of the human information processing weaknesses described above, this raises a flood of important questions for further research. Let us briefly reconsider the central themes of perceptual selection and inference in the context of mass communication of public affairs information:

** Do mass-communicated messages provide many alternative subsets of information about external events? Or do the various encoders converge on particular subsets of detail while overlooking others? Is information that fits widely-shared symbols and structures more likely to be mass-communicated? Is information discrepant with or unrelated to widely-held expectations less likely to be encoded?

** Are preponderant symbols and structures chosen by decoders--an expression "consumer sovereignty" in a free marketplace of ideas? Or by encoders? Are encoders' choices motivated by the objectives of their respective institutions? Or simply by the objective of communicating--that is, surviving, where competition for audience is intense, and the resource cost of designing and disseminating messages is high? Does accommodating decoders' cognitive needs in fact enhance a message's "marketability"--ie. do decoders indeed reject mass-communicated messages that are not cognitively convenient, and embrace messages encoded in familiar symbols and structures?

** Does the easy availability of symbolic public affairs information reinforce decoders' inclination to neglect perceptual data that is unstructured or unrelated to stored patterns? Does the ubiquity of such information reinforce decoders' inclination to accept internal cognitions built from shorthand symbols and unidimensional structures as external reality?

** Does the encoding institution become part of the stored association evoked by a communicated message? For example, do decoders tend to regard messages encoded by the news media as comprehensive? Government messages as equitable? Professional messages as rigorous? How is decoder behavior affected by the symbolic attributes of the encoder: if the press is perceived as comprehensive, are individuals less inclined to supplement news messages with data from other sources? If government represents justice, are decoders less inclined to seek out the data needed to evaluate the equity of government-encoded information? If professions represent precision, are decoders inclined to ignore the residual uncertainty of expert-encoded data? When the "encoder is the message," does this result from encoders' efforts to supply that meaning, or decoders' tendency to demand it—that is, decoders' preference for cognitively-convenient information that shifts the burden of search, justice, and risk onto encoders specialized in the respective information-processing task?

Answers to these questions would lead the policy analyst to the root of cognitive impasse, and so perhaps to a solution.

NOTES

1. The automaticity of adult cognition often leads to the erroneous assumption that it is inborn. Forgotten is the laborious childhood work of building the "data base" and the "programs" to interpret the world. For a full description of this process, see Piaget, Jean, The Child's Construction of Reality (New York: Basic Books, 1954), or Hamlyn, D.W., Experience and the Growth of Understanding (Boston: Routledge and Kegan Paul, 1978).
2. The research supporting these behaviors is available in any major text on cognitive psychology; see, for example, Anderson, John, Cognitive Psychology and its Implications (San Francisco: W.H. Freeman and Co., 1980) or Lindsay, Peter, and Norman, Donald, Human Information Processing (New York: Academic Press, 1972).
3. A field of study called "General Semantics" aims at creating awareness of this abstraction process in everyday life. It professes, "the word is not the thing; the map is not the territory"; and encourages the habit of referring back to the raw data behind the abstract symbols that make up our understanding of external reality. For an excellent application, see Magee, John, The General Semantics of Wall Street (Springfield, Mass.: By the Author, 1973).
4. An in-depth analysis of this phenomenon is available in the work of Murray Edelman: The Symbolic Uses of Politics (Urbana, Ill.: University of Illinois Press, 1964); Politics as Symbolic Action (New York: Academic Press, 1971); and Political Language: Words That Succeed and

Policies That Fail (New York: Academic Press, 1977).

5. The reader might expect the public to alter its meaning of full employment, from "not important" to "important," as a result of its doubling. The improbability of this outcome is explained by the fourth cognitive limitation, below: stored patterns resist revision.
6. Television reporting of inflation during a period in the late '70's consisted almost exclusively of official statements, and breakdowns of price increases by expenditure category, according to a Media Institute study; Bethel, Thomas TV Evening News Covers Inflation: 1978-79 (Washington, DC: Media Institute, 1980).
7. The popularity of Megatrends {Naisbitt, John, (New York: Warner Books, 1982)}, which systematically presents data such as this, may reflect an unmet demand for organizing principles to cognitively interpret unexplained sensory information.
8. Is ignoring the cognition built from new information a rational response to the finding, in so many research designs and disciplines, that individuals misuse new information (for example, non-Bayesian decision making studies in economics, functional fixation studies in accounting, "anchoring and adjustment" studies in social psychology)? More likely, this literature is itself explained by the underlying physiological process-- that neural circuits can be expanded but not rerouted. Major works on systematic weaknesses in adjusting for new data include: Simon, Herbert, "Theories of Decision Making in Economics and Behavioral Science," American Economic Review, (June 1959): 223-83); Ashton, Robert, Human Information Processing in Accounting (Sarasota, Florida: American Accounting Association, 1982); and Nisbett, Richard, and Ross,

Lee Human Inference: Strategies and Shortcomings of Social Judgement (Englewood Cliffs, NJ: Prentice Hall, 1980), an excellent synthesis of the original Tversky and Kahneman studies).

9. Thomas Kuhn's famous "paradigm shift," in The Structure of Scientific Revolutions (Chicago: University of Chicago Press, 1962).

10. A full treatment of this topic is provided by Cherry, Colin, On Human Communication (Cambridge, Mass.: MIT Press, 1980).

Choice in a Modern Economy: New Concepts of Democracy and Bureaucracy.

John Raven
Consultant on Psychological Aspects of Economic Development
30 Great King St.,
Edinburgh EH3 6QH,
Scotland.
(031) 556 2912

Overview

In this paper I will argue that the way society works has changed out of all recognition over the past 40 years. This applies with particular force to the economic marketplace. We now live in what is essentially a managed world economy. There are very few sectors of the economy to which anything approaching classical market theory applies. To run our modern managed economy effectively we need new forms of democracy and bureaucracy. In other words, if economic theory is to develop, we need to pay more attention to the politico-bureaucratic context in which economic behaviour takes place. Different societies have made differential progress toward doing things in new ways. However, these new assumptions and understandings tend to be implicit and culturally specific rather than explicit. Psychologists have a crucial role to play in developing the institutions, understandings, and tools which are needed to run modern managed economies effectively. One particular way in which a small team of psychologists and sociologists might do this would be to spend some time in each others' countries with a view to surfacing the otherwise embedded understandings which have been mentioned.

Modern Economies are Essentially *Managed* Economies

As I have shown elsewhere[1], spending of some 75% of GNP is, in all EEC countries, in some sense, under government "control". The precise figure is arguable, as is the meaning of the word "control": in what sense, for example, does government control the spending of transfer payments? But the statement is true enough to signal a fundamental, and largely unnoticed, change in society.

I have also shown that there are good reasons why we have created these managed national economies, and argued that it is for similar reasons that we are now, through the efforts of such bodies as the EEC and the Brandt Commission, moving toward the public management of the world economy. This is because what we do has a crucial effect on our neighbours on the other side of the world, and what they do critically affects us. Obvious examples of these international consequences include the effects many pollutents (including radioactive dust), the effects of political instability fueled by stark contrasts between the rich and the poor, underpricing of exports by failing to charge sufficient to provide health, welfare, housing, pollution-control, and soil conservation services when setting prices on international markets (a failure which influences us both directly [through loss of markets] and indirectly [for example through acid rain and emigration], international transmission of plague and disease, and the unsustainable exploitation of soils, forests, water, food, fish, energy, and minerals.

The effective management of these social, economic, physical and biological processes is dependent on the systematic collection and use of information - especially information on the consequences of alternative policies and on the implications of changes in policy in one area (such as small farms policy) for policy in other areas (such as the kinds of illness the health services must cope with). Difficult though this may be, it is important to note that, *pace* Smith and Hayek, there is no way in which the invisible hand of the marketplace could respond to such connections. We have achieved our present prosperity precisely because of the doings of wise men, not the marketplace, and what we now need to do is to develop more effective management tools.

Some Failings of the Economic Marketplace

The economic marketplace has so many failings[2] that the trend toward its regulation and replacement will continue. It is useful to list some of these deficiencies here in order to set a context for what is to follow.

Although among the most widely touted benefits of the economic marketplace are its ability to offer customers choice, its ability to provide feedback to producers, and its ability to stimulate innovation and efficiency, Adam Smith himself noted that those who do not have the money needed to transform undisputed needs into market demands are debarred from contributing to this process. In fact most of the needs of very many people in the modern world - and many of the needs of most people - cannot be transformed into market demands. This is especially true of those who live in less developed countries.

It is not, however, only lack of economic power which prevents people contributing to this process. People often lack the ability to exercise economic power even when they possess it. Thus many unemployed people who are charged extremely high rents for seriously substandard accommodation find that they can neither move nor complain: if they complain they are accused of serious crimes and summarily evicted. Likewise, many old people cannot employ home helps, not because they cannot afford them, but because they do not know how to set about finding them and are worried about who might turn up if they advertise. Equally, many people do not avail themselves of the market in consumer goods because they are in no position to inform themselves of the relative merits of the alternatives which are available or because they lack the time, the knowledge of the alternatives available, the knowledge of geography, and the transportation required to visit relevant outlets.

Even more serious is the fact that most of the provisions on which the quality of our lives is most dependent can best be purchased collectively: clean water and safe sewage disposal; freedom from theft and violence against the person; education of the type which will benefit the whole community (as distinct from that kind which will only confer a competitive advantage on those who can purchase it); pollution control; communication and transportation networks; the elimination of those kinds of oppression and poverty which make the world unsafe for all; freedom from the need to comply with the whims of authority; beautiful, liveable, social and physical environments; research and development; conservation of non-replaceable resources and replacement of others; and planning for continued economic and social development itself.

The result of these two processes is that most of us are debarred from commenting on most of the provisions, policies and activities which most crucially affect the quality of our lives.

Next there is the problem that the pursuit of private interest is often detrimental to the common good. As Keynes noted, capitalists', in their pursuit of private profit, are inclined to neglect their own long term interests, never mind those of society as a whole. The commons dilemma is well known: the more sheep and cattle are put out to graze on a common the worse off everyone becomes. But it does not make economic sense for any one person, acting individually, to graze less cattle.

Even when producers and suppliers wish to act in the common interest, they often find themselves forced to do things they know to be wrong. Small grocers cannot afford not to water the milk and put sand in the sugar. Large food manufacturers cannot afford not to use sub-standard meat and put padding and poisonous preservatives in the food. Drug companies cannot afford not to recover their development costs by marketing deformity-causing drugs in countries which do not have legislation to ban them. Farmers cannot afford not to use dangerous pesticides and horticultural techniques which destroy the land, and to exploit labour.

Not only does classical economics not handle these problems well, the images conjured up by terms like "customer", "price", "labour" and "employer" are commonly inappropriate. Thus, most of us now work, directly or indirectly, for the public service: we are either employed in the public sector, or our products (from books to aeroplanes) are purchased by the public sector. If we ourselves are not employed in either of these ways, our customers are.

Likewise, most customers are not individuals who can make their views felt by voting with their pennies. They are corporate customers purchasing on behalf of thousands, if not millions, of people who have great difficulty making their voices heard. These corporate customers purchase on behalf of hospitals, health services, school boards, airlines, telephone companies, governments, and, as with defence systems, international alliances of countries.

Prices are often treated as if they still bear some meaningful relationship to the costs of production. But it follows from our earlier observation that some three quarters of GNP is, at least in some sense, under government control is that, on average, some three quarters of the price of any good or service is made up of taxes. The direct "labour" content is therefore relatively insignificant. Internationally, prices are primarily determined, not by the productivity of national labour forces, but by what governments and trans-national companies do to control rates of exchange and structures of taxation. As an example of the former we may take the fact that the £:US$ rate of exchange has fluctuated between approximately 3$ to the £ to 1$ to the £ over the past 5 years. As a result the price of the same British car in the US has varied between $5,000 and $15,000. Compared with such upheavals, marginal international differences in the productivity of labour pale into insignificance. The way in which countries raise taxes also have a dramatic effect. Those which raise much of their revenue from VAT, and relatively little from income tax, produce cheap exports whilst imposing heavy taxes on imports. (We may note in passing that the success of such devices as duty-free ports is entirely dependent on the degree to which they make it possible for producers to avoid contributing to the costs of local public provision whilst allowing their employees to continue to enjoy those provisions). Then again, the apparent costs of goods and services are mainly dependent on conventions which determine which costs are included in the calculation: the costs of dealing with pollution, of rejuvenating our soils and forests, of taking legal action against shoplifters from supermarkets (instead of performing the same function by means of the corner store counter) can all be excluded by adopting appropriate accounting conventions. These costs are fairly obvious, but others include the costs of monitoring the activities of drug companies - both at home and in other countries (where they are not noted for voluntarily conforming to policies which are elsewhere imposed on them by governments which are better able to afford to collect relevant information and impose appropriate monitoring), the costs of policing legislation designed to ensure "fair" trading, the costs of treating disease and deformity caused by inhumane production processes, the costs of monitoring cross-subsidisation of product lines, and the costs of raising taxation (including health service charges).

The overall effect of the changes which have been described may be indicated by saying that, whereas money may once have provided - at least for those who could pay - a mechanism through which people could vote with their pennies to influence the direction in which things moved, money is now best viewed as a tool which is used to orchestrate the achievement of goals established through the public, information-based, politico-bureaucratic process. In short: the functions of money have been overturned.

There is, of course, nothing wrong with that. There is nothing sacrosanct about money: it is merely a tool to be used to organise economic activity and we can change it or alter its design and functions to suit our purposes. But we do need to be aware of this fact and willing to capitalise upon it so as to transform money into a tool which is better adapted to our purposes.

There are, in fact, good reasons for making further changes:

Firstly, the distribution of wage and salary differentials is by no means equitable: some people are highly paid for contributing very little to society; others are poorly paid for contributing a great deal. Disproportionate reward seems to be more dependent on such things as the coercive power of the closed shop (as in law and medicine) or being in a position to manipulate the financial system itself (as in banking and stockbroking).

Secondly, the way we calculate costs does not take due account of replacement costs - as in forests, food and energy. (In the case of food, the prices we pay do not cover the costs of rehabilitating workers who are often employed on dehumanising terms, the costs of political and military intervention to restabilise political systems, or the costs of re-stabilising, de-salinating, and rejuvenating soils and rivers - whether destroyed by over-cropping and erosion or fertilisers). They do not take account of the costs of dealing with pollution (as in nuclear energy and plastics and steel production). They do not take account of the true costs of transportation (such as the costs of planning and policing highways, dealing with death and injury, dealing with lead poisoning, or dealing with such things as the effects of acid rain caused by failure to control the composition of exhaust gases). They do not take account of externalised costs (such as the costs which open supermarkets place on society by way of police activity, legal and judicial processes, and the supervision and maintenance of prisoners).

Thirdly, the way we provide for mandatory non public service pensions generates huge notional paper profits which enable pension companies to make promises which they can never fulfil in real terms[3]. They make for concentration in the ownership of land, property and businesses in the hands of the pension companies, and control over the activities of the businesses so owned by distant finance managers who have little interest in, and are in no position to make informed judgments about, the innovative activities which are required for continued development. They create a demand for high rates of profit in place of an interest in what the business is doing or its employees. They deprive citizens of the right to influence what is done with their money.

But perhaps the most important reason for making further changes is so all pervasive that it tends to be overlooked. We have moved from a world situation in which it could be assumed that resources were unlimited, in which one person's gain did not have to be at someone else's expense, to a situation in which that is no longer true. We can no longer even assume that the environment can absorb the by-products of our way of life. Development, if it is to occur, must now take account of the world-wide, long term, ecological balance. This represents a basic challenge to our value system - which has for thousands of years been based on the *feasibility* of unlimited growth. And one of our most pressing problems is the *infeasibility* of that assumption is least apparent in the United States of America - which is the main sources of he culture which perpetuates the outmoded value-system worldwide.

If the thought of making further changes in the nature, role, and function of money and the marketplace makes the reader uncomfortable, he may find consolation in the fact that it was the gunboats which we sent to India and China, and not the rationality of Adam Smith's marketplace, which led those countries to trade with us on, at best, a very inequitable basis and, in the case of China, enabled us to force upon them opium which did untold social harm. If we modified our monetary system we would not be replacing a system of self-evident merit by a bad system. We would be trying to make a bad system better.

Some Problems with Public Provision

So far, I have argued that the quality of our lives is primarily dependent on what public servants do by way of providing water, sewage disposal, drainage, health services, pensions, social security, housing, education, research and development, transportation networks, beautiful, liveable, environments, freedom from crime and vandalism, managing the trade balance and international competitiveness, monitoring and regulating the doings of national and transnational companies, stimulating a concern with innovation and efficiency, and managing wider social, political and economic forces which affect, or emanate from, the other side of the world. Put another way, I have argued that the quality of our lives - our wealth - what other people would be - are - prepared to pay high financial - and other - prices to move here to get - is primarily determined by the doings of our public servants. If we wish to increase our wealth it is to the way in which we manage the public sector that we must attend.

But, while our public servants, by giving us control over forces which were previously beyond the control of men, have contributed more than anyone else to economic development, there are problems.

Let me discuss a couple of examples.

In the course of some research which we conducted between 1959 and 1963 we showed that high-rise family housing:

. was unacceptable to the tenants - and for good reason: it imposed a sedentary way of life on them (because they felt that any noise they made would disturb their neighbours); they were unable from their kitchens to supervise children at play outside; the lifts often went wrong or were vandalised; they were isolated because they found it difficult to get to know their neighbours (because they never saw - let alone met - them on neutral territory), and they were unable to alter their houses in order to adapt them to their own particular needs (something which - as the growth of DIY has since demonstrated - many owners of two-storey housing spend a considerable amount of time doing).

. was more costly to build than equivalent two-story housing

. was more costly to maintain than two story housing

. accommodated less people per acre than two story housing - which could, if properly developed, also provide greatly desired garages, gardens, and access to public open spaces at the same density.

Despite this high quality research - which reached the pernickety standards demanded in civil service research units - no action was taken[5]. Building high rise family housing continued into the 80s. The disaster is now recognised for what it is and these expensive tall blocks are being demolished.

The most important lesson to be learnt from this example is not that the policies in force were misguided. It is that we need to evolve structures which will make it possible to ensure that action is taken on the basis of good information.

This does not conclude the lesson, however. Research conducted at the same time showed that not only did people want very different types of housing, the creation of vast single-class suburbs - many as large as whole towns - made it very difficult for young people who aspired to other ways of life to make contact with like-minded people or gain sufficient insight into the values and way of life of a range of other people to make meaningful choices. Finally, bureaucratic rules made it difficult for tenants to establish the community support networks which are associated with "unplanned" working class communities. This forced many people to lead isolated lives of demeaning dependence on welfare agencies and tranquilisers.

These further observations illustrate that not only do we need some (social-research based) means of ensuring that public servants attend to the needs of their clients and try to invent better ways of meeting those needs, they also illustrate the importance of (a) legitimising the notion that choice is required in public provision, (b) providing the public with the (social research based) information they need to make meaningful decisions, (c) providing public servants with the (social research based) tools they need to administer that choice, and (d) (in part through social research) evaluating and improving each of the choices so as to better meet the needs of those concerned.

Why have public housing at all? First, because it was necessary to build housing - and whole new towns - on an unprecedented scale. Second, because those for whom it was intended had, in the past, been badly catered for, and mercilessly exploited, by builders, landowners and landlords. Third, because, although those concerned had a clear *need* for housing, they often lacked the resources which would have been required to transform that need into an economic *demand*. Fourth, because, even when they had the necessary cash and assured income in the future, they often did not have the collateral information and power needed to ensure that they were not exploited. And, fifth, because the knock-on effect of a large number of street people or impoverished families who lived in poor and insanitary housing (both immediately in terms of disease and crime and, in the longer term, through the community's inability to make use of the considerable talents which undernourished and alienated youth could otherwise develop) would be so great. (It may be noted that these needs still exist among our vast army of poorly paid and unemployed people, and, in particular, among the single unemployed.)

There is another lesson to be learnt from this case. Public servants were, and remain, remarkably blind to issues which involve linkages between Departmental responsibilities. One of these has to do with the linkages between housing policy and economic development. To accumulate the "points" required to demonstrate "housing need", one had both to have children and to have lived in the same locality for many years. If one moved from one local authority to another, one lost one's entitlement. This markedly restricted geographical mobility. Survey results showed that 84% of public housing tenants in England were unwilling to move under any circumstances.

Smith and Hayek have, of course, argued that it is precisely this inability to appreciate connections, relationships and cumulative consequences which is the strongest argument for leaving such decisions to the invisible hand of the marketplace. Unfortunately, it was precisely the failings of the marketplace which led men to try to manage these processes. What is more, with the aid of Information Technology, we are now in a much better position to study and identify relevant relationships and consequences. The true conclusion to be drawn is that we need to establish policy research, evaluation, and development units whose brief it is to examine such issues, and then to find some way of ensuring that public servants take account of the results.

Another, and in many ways more disturbing, set of examples of the failure of public servants to act on information and consider the needs of their clients comes from education. Education was one of the first sectors of the economy to be socialised. This was for two main reasons: firstly, because education is intended to benefit everyone and not just those who pass through the system, and, secondly, because the poor are in no position to pay for the education of their children. This is not only unfair on the children concerned, society will be deprived of their talents.

Good though the reasons for socialising education are, research we have conducted since 1965[6] shows that some two thirds of the money spent on secondary education is wasted so far as the development of human resources is concerned. Secondary schools do little to foster the qualities which most parents, teachers, employers and ex-pupils think they are there to foster and which other research confirms that it is, indeed, most important for them to foster. The qualities which are required include initiative, the ability to work with others, and the ability to understand and influence society. There are many reasons why schools tend to neglect these goals which interested readers can trace through our publications. The point to be made here is that the public servants concerned have not only failed to monitor and attend to the needs and reactions of the clients of the educational system, they have also failed to act on the information which <u>was</u> available. As if this were not serious enough, they have also failed to note that there are a wide variety of pupils within the educational system who have very different motives to tap and talents to develop and offer to society. Schools have made very little attempt to tap these motives or identify and develop these talents.

So here we have evidence - which has been available for 20 years - of another vast misuse of public money, further evidence of the need to provide variety in public provision, and further evidence of the need to hold public servants accountable against different criteria. It is important to note that the problem could not be solved by "returning" the activity to the market place. This is because (a) if our society is to develop, many attitudes and skills - which it is the responsibility of the educational system to identify and foster - need to be widely shared in society and not just possessed by an elite, (b) societey needs a wide variety of people who possess different combinations of specialist information the need for which cannot become clear until after the event and which one is therefore unlikely to purchase as an individual, (c) many people are in no position to pay for themselves or their children, and (d) the main benefits are not going to be derived by people *as individuals* but by them as members of a society which has developed *as a whole*. Everyone is going to benefit (even those who have no children), so everyone should pay. People would be most likely to pay as individuals for those "educational" programmes which were most likely to lead to credentials which would in turn buy entry to protected occupations. But these credentials would neither testify to development of important competencies nor lead those who provided the courses to focus on fostering such competencies. What is more, those who could pay and expect to recover the costs from increased personal income would be those who used the educational system most ruthlessly to promote their own advancement. Yet such are not the sort of people whom we should be appointing to senior management positions in our society. The people we need are those who are most committed to orchestrating communal action for the common good[7].

One could multiply examples of the deficiencies of public provision - in health, welfare, defence, and the management of agribusiness and international trade. At a more micro level, the inability of public servants to act in the public interest are well documented in Chapman's book *Your Disobedient Servant. In concluding this section it seems appropriate, however, to return to, and underline, the need to do more to examine the linkages between one area of policy and another. The policies enacted tend to be domain specific. Thus, the way we provide for social security makes for the subjection of large numbers of people to a demeaning and dehumanising way of life which kills initiative and enterprise. The way we provide health care separates it from agricultural policy, housing policy, and environmental policy - including job design and transportation policy: for example, we spend a lot of time treating diseases which can be attributed to agricultural policy. Some are caused by overconsumption of milk and beef products and others by pesticides or hormones. But both the production and the use of pesticides are encouraged by agricultural policy. We spend a lot of time treating depression caused by neighbourhoods which breed isolation[4]. We treat the symptoms of stress caused by the way we organise work. And we treat accidents and lead poisoning caused by motor vehicles. The need for cars in turn derives in part from the way we finance housing (for this deters people from moving their homes closer to work) and the way we organise job allocation (for this does not make it easy for people to find work near their home). The way we allocate position and status creates a "demand" for expensive "education" which in reality confers few benefits on those concerned other than a passport to a protected occupation.*

It is the growing awareness of these deficiencies which has led many to embrace privatisation. (Evidence for this assertion comes from our own quality of life surveys[8] which show that people are dissatisfied with their washing machines and cars. They are more dissatisfied with the quality of the environments in which they live. They are still more dissatisfied with social, welfare, health and educational provision. But they are *most* dissatisfied with their relationships with public servants and politicians).

In spite of all this evidence of public servants' failure to act on the available evidence and in the public interest, it is important to avoid drawing the conclusion that public servants are the villans of the piece. The problems stem from widely held beliefs about the role and duties of public servants, the criteria against which their performance is judged, and the institutional framework - the structures of local and national bureaucracy and democracy - which have been adopted in an attempt to oversee their work.

The Way Forward

Privatisation is, in reality, no solution to these problems: one either creates vast private monopolies in place of public monopolies, or else one creates private organisations which are dependent for their continued existence on the patronage of one or more public servants or public service Departments. It also transpires that the reduced operating costs which it is hoped that privatisation will achieve are often only gained at the the expense of the weakest members of the community: they get paid less and are deprived of their welfare and pension rights. Indeed, special legislation had been introduced to enable the firms concerned to evade pension and social security requirements. Alternatively, or additionally, the costs of monitoring and policing the activities of vast organisations (like telephones and transport) may be externalised. Nor does breaking up large organisations necessarily make the provision cheaper, more efficient, or more responsive to customer needs: witness the law, old people's homes, and small private landlords. To exercise economic power effectively one needs many other powers.

I would suggest that, in place of this fashion for privatisation, based as it is on an unwillingness to examine the reality to which it refers, what is needed are:

New expectations of the public service and the way it should operate.

New criteria against which to judge the performance of individual public servants - criteria which include "initiating the collection of, and considering, relevant information".

New tools which make it possible to evaluate the behaviour of public servants against these criteria.

Means of generating better information on the consequences of alternative decisions and feeding that information into public debate.

New tools to provide and evaluate choice in public provision. The problem is not only to provide choice but also to ensure the clients who are making choices fully understand the consequences of the alternatives. (The consequences to be documented are not only short term and personal but also longer term and societal).

New tools to hold senior public servants accountable for making their sections hum: for creating climates characterised by dedication, initiative, sensitivity to clients' needs, and a concern to invent better ways of meeting those needs.

If I am right, psychologists could play a major role helping to articulate and develop these concepts, institutional structures, and tools.

Many readers will say that I am wrong, that democracy, and staff- and performance-appraisal systems within the public service, are designed to do precisely these things. My question is whether they work - and my tentative answer, based on the evidence presented above, is that they do not. My submission is that the level of public activity is now so great that our traditional concepts of bureaucracy and democracy are inadequate. Because of the role which it has now come to play in modern society, government is grossly overloaded and in no position to make good decisions. Our expectations of our public servants are no longer appropriate. My conclusion is, therefore, that we need to develop new forms of democracy, bureaucracy and citizenship - and new expectations of, and tools and procedures to supervise, our public servants[9].

Let me return to education to illustrate what I have in mind. The available information suggests that individual teachers (public servants) need to be held accountable for studying each of their pupils' talents and finding ways of helping them to develop them. To find out whether teachers are achieving this goal we need new, research-based, appraisal instruments. But, it is also true that if teachers are to monitor their performance and take the initiative needed to find better ways of meeting their clients' needs, they must devote a great deal of time and energy to risky, frustrating, innovative activity. In fact they need more than time for, as we have seen, their job descriptions need to change so that they are expected to take initiative and be inventors. They need a structure which encourages contact with teachers in other classrooms and schools and which provides support for them when things go wrong, as they surely will. And even that does not bring us to the end of the changes which are needed - because what teachers can do in their classrooms is mainly determined by forces from outside. Teachers therefore need to be encouraged to band together to gain control over some of the wider social forces which otherwise prevent them doing their jobs - even when narrowly defined - effectively. Beyond that, they need some means of getting credit for their accomplishments.

In the last paragraph we saw that, as a society, we need new expectations of teachers, new tools to enable teachers to take stock of their students' needs, their own performance, and the performance of the schools in which they work, and for staff and organisational appraisal. What now needs to be said is that, if this information is to be used effectively, it will be necessary to have some public supervisory structure which does not depend on a long chain of authority to a distant elected representative who is necessarily ignorant of the work of a particular teacher and the issues in his or her school - and who, in any case, has many other things to do. Teachers therefore need to be accountable to some local group. Since what it is appropriate for one teacher to do must necessarily depend on what other teachers, locally and nationally, are doing, any one teacher, and his or her supervisory group, must be part of some network of monitoring groups. The same conclusion emerges from the fact that supervisory groups which are too heterogeneous (like Parent-Teacher Associations) will not work. Parents must be able to find a group which has congenial values. To do this they must know what is available.

So now we have the task of working out how such a network of supervisory or monitoring groups ought to operate. It is important to note that "the information needed to make the system function" includes taking what is "known" on one register - in the way in which many teachers know a great deal about what is wrong with the educational system and about the limitations of their colleagues - and making it known on another - more explicit - register which makes it useable. One way in which this can be done is by adopting the strategies of the "illuminative" evaluator[10], but other possibilities include the development of formal tools designed to surface such information. Examples of such tools include classroom, school, organisation, and community climate survey instruments. Such instruments would enable monitoring groups of the kind we have described to look at what is going on, decide whether they like the look of what they see, and, if appropriate, decide to change it. (Howard[11] describes a system of educational monitoring and improvement based on both the structures and climate surveys described here).

The evolution of new ways of thinking about monitoring structures, the understandings of the public service, and the development of the necessary stocktaking and information-gathering tools are all tasks for psychologists.

We are now in a position to draw two other points out of this discussion.

First, if the kind of innovation in the social process envisaged above is to come about, there is a need for an unprecedented public debate about the goals of society, the state of that society, and what is to be done about it. This debate cannot take place without the assistance of the media, and those who take part in that debate need some mechanism through which they can make their views known. As Toffler has pointed out, modern information technology makes it easy for people to vote from their living rooms. But the value of feedback of this sort is not only dependent on the dissemination of information, it is also dependent on psychologists developing sets of survey questions which yield more meaningful results than those obtained from opinion polls. If meaningful conclusions are to be drawn from such data, it will also be necessary for those concerned to develop understandings of democracy which do not suggest that majority decisions should be binding on all, but which instead emphasise that some means must be found to enable people with different priorities to get equitable treatment, geared to their priorities, from the public service.

Second, the time required for many members of the population to engage in the kind of participative - as distinct from representative - democratic process which is required to oversee the public sector activities which dominate our society will be considerable. It is therefore important to note that such civic activity contributes to the efficiency of our society and the quality of life of all. In other words it is <u>wealth-creating</u> activity. It therefore merits financial reward. (It is not inappropriate at this point to emphasise that the costs of providing the economic marketplace are enormous: two thirds of the cost of the average article goes on distribution and marketing. Yet this work, unlike the chore of supervising the public sector, tends to be viewed as contributing to wealth creation.)

In the course of this paper we have seen that a substantial investment in policy monitoring, development and research units is required. What now needs to be added is that those units must be concerned with studying the long term personal and social consequences of the alternatives. The results must then be fed back into to a vital public debate[12]. And some means must be found to give effect to the results of that debate.

Implications for Psychologists

My objective in this article has been to show that modern society needs new concepts of democracy, the public service, the role of the public servant, wealth, wealth-creation, work, and citizenship. Psychologists have a major role to play in helping society to evolve these new concepts and the structures which are required to implement them. To run a modern, managed, economy effectively, we also need new tools for staff and policy appraisal, to administer and evaluate choice within the public sector, and to create innovative climates in which problems can be addressed and new solutions sought. Psychologists have a crucial role to play in developing these alternatives to the economic marketplace.

Yet, although, in a sense, new, what has been said in this article represents little more than a crystalisation and formalisation of moves which are already afoot. Indeed, as noted above, different societies have made differential progress in addressing these problems, but the new understandings they have evolved are embedded in cultural assumptions and thoughtways. My impression is that Japan has moved further than others toward finding ways of conducting informed public debates and studying and acting on information - especially, as it happens, about the workings of politico-economic systems on the other side of the globe. Norway has moved further toward finding ways of monitoring the workings of private corporations and harnessing them to the public good. It has also moved further toward the development of satisfactory resource accounting procedures. It would therefore be desirable to establish a small team of psychologists and sociologists who would each spend some time in each others' countries, not familiarising themselves with the research literature, but attempting to get a feel for the embedded assumptions about priorities and ways of doing things which are made in those cultures. The contrasts between the assumptions made in different countries should force the differences to the attention of those concerned. The aim would be to produce a book entitled "The Economy of the 21st Century" or, more arrogantly, but perhaps more appropriately, "The New Wealth of Nations". I would greatly welcome contact with other psychologists seriously interested in contributing to this exercise.

NOTES

[1] Raven, 1975, 1977

[2] Robertson (1985) provides an excellent discussion of some of these and further examples will be found in Ekins (1986).

[3] Bellini, 1981

[4] We urgently need to find ways of involving more people in the community-support networks which could better cater for our pension, welfare, child-care, education, economic development, environmental quality, crime prevention, and health needs - and do so in which a way as to avoid implying that such activity is not "real work" which merits financial reward. For a fuller discussion see Robertson 1985 and Ferguson, 1980

[5] Raven, 1967

[6] See Raven, 1977 for a summary.

[7] See Raven, 1984, Hope 1985

[8] Raven 1980

[9] Some of these ideas are elaborated in Raven, 1984, but the network of monitoring groups is a more recent addition which echoes Ferguson, 1980.

[10] See Hamilton (1977), Eisner (1985), Raven (1985).

[11] Howard, 1982

[12] The role and management of such research units, and the relationships to be established between policy makers and researchers, is discussed in Raven, 1975 and 1985

Bryan Dockrell, who kindly commented on the first draft of this chapter, has suggested that the failure of the retail cooperative movement in the UK - which was designed to give consumers *more* power than they would have had as "mere consumers" - would repay study.

REFERENCES

Bellini, J. (1980). Rule Britannia: A Progress Report for Domesday 1986. London: Jonathen Cape

Eisner, E.W. (1985). The Art of Educational Evaluation. Lewes: The Falmer Press.

Ekins, P (ed) (1986). The Living Economy: A New Economics in the Making. London: Routledge and Kegan Paul.

Ferguson, M. (1980). The Aquarian Conspiracy: Personal and Social Transformation in the 1980s. London: Paladin.

Hamilton, D. (Ed.) (1977) Beyond the Numbers Game. London: MacMillan Education.

Hope, K. (1985). As Others See Us: Schooling and Social Mobility in Scotland and the United States. New York: Cambridge University Press.

Howard, E. (1982). Involving Students in School Climate Improvement. New Designs for Youth Development. Tucson: Assocations for Youth Development Inc.

Howard, E. (1982). Successful Practices for Making the Curriculum More Flexible. Denver: Colorado Department of Education.

Howard, E. (1982), Instrument to Assess the Educational Quality of Your School. Denver: Colorado Department of Education.

Raven, J. (1967). Sociological Evidence on Housing, I: Space in the Home and II: The Home in its Setting. Architectural Review, 142 p68f and 143 p236-239

Raven, J. (1975). Social Research in Modern Society: I: The Role of Social Research. II: The Institutional Structures and Management Styles Required to Execute Policy-Relevant Social Research. Administration, 23, p.225-246 and 247-268

Raven, J. (1977). Education, Values and Society: The Objectives of Education and the Nature and Development of Competence. London: H K Lewis. New York: The Psychological Corporation.

Raven, J. (1977). Government Policy and Social Psychologists. Bull. Br. Psychol. Soc. 30, p.33-39

Raven, J. (1980). Parents, Teachers and Children. Edinburgh: The Scottish Council for Research in Education.

Raven, J. (1984). Economic Policy in Modern Society. London: The Tawney Society.

Raven J. (1984). The Role of the Psychologist in Formulating, Administering and Evaluating Policies Associated with Economic and Social Development in Western Society. J.Econ.Psychol. 5 1-16.

Raven, J. (1984). Competence in Modern Society: Its Identification, Development and Release. London: H.K.Lewis.

Raven, J. (1984). Some Limitations of the *Standards*. Evaluation and Program Planning 7 p363 - 370

Raven, J. (1985). The Institutional Framework Required for, and Process of, Educational Evaluation: Some Lessons from Three Case Studies. in Searle, B. (ed) Evaluation in World Bank Education Projects: Lessons from Three Case Studies. Washington, DC: The World Bank, Education and Training Dept. Report EDT5 p141-170.

Robertson, J. (1985) Future Work: Jobs, Self-Employment and Leisure after the

Industrial Age. Aldershot: Gower/Maurice Temple Smith.
Toffler, A. (1980). The Third Wave New York: Bantam Books.

SUBJECT INDEX

NAMES INDEX